History and the Law

Focusing on everyday legal experiences, from those of magistrates, novelists and political philosophers, to those of maidservants, poor and pauper men and women, down-at-heel attorneys and middling-sort wives in their coverture, *History and the Law* reveals how people thought about, used, manipulated and resisted the law between the eighteenth and the twentieth centuries. Supported by clear, engaging examples taken from the historical record, and from the writing of historians including Laurence Sterne, William Godwin and E. P. Thompson, who each had troubled love affairs with the law, Carolyn Steedman puts the emphasis on English poor laws, copyright law and laws regarding women. Evocatively written and highly original, *History and the Law* accounts for historians' strange ambivalent love affair with the law and with legal records that appear to promise access to so many lives in the past.

Carolyn Steedman is Emeritus Professor of History at the University of Warwick. Her previous books include *Landscape for a Good Woman* (1986), *Dust* (2001), *Master and Servant* (Cambridge, 2007), *Labours Lost* (Cambridge, 2009), *An Everyday Life of the English Working Class* (Cambridge, 2013) and *Poetry for Historians* (2018).

History and the Law

A Love Story

Carolyn Steedman

University of Warwick

CAMBRIDGE
UNIVERSITY PRESS

CAMBRIDGE
UNIVERSITY PRESS

University Printing House, Cambridge CB2 8BS, United Kingdom

One Liberty Plaza, 20th Floor, New York, NY 10006, USA

477 Williamstown Road, Port Melbourne, VIC 3207, Australia

314–321, 3rd Floor, Plot 3, Splendor Forum, Jasola District Centre, New Delhi – 110025, India

79 Anson Road, #06-04/06, Singapore 079906

Cambridge University Press is part of the University of Cambridge.

It furthers the University's mission by disseminating knowledge in the pursuit of education, learning, and research at the highest international levels of excellence.

www.cambridge.org
Information on this title: www.cambridge.org/9781108486057
DOI: 10.1017/9781108623506

First published 2020

Printed in the United Kingdom by TJ International Ltd, Padstow Cornwall

A catalogue record for this publication is available from the British Library.

Library of Congress Cataloging-in-Publication Data
Names: Steedman, Carolyn, author.
Title: History and the law / Carolyn Steedman.
Description: New York : Cambridge University Press, 2020. | Includes bibliographical references and index.
Identifiers: LCCN 2019044094 | ISBN 9781108486057 (hardback) | ISBN 9781108736985 (ebook)
Subjects: LCSH: Law--Great Britain--History. | Law--History.
Classification: LCC KD532 .S74 2020 | DDC 349.42--dc23
LC record available at https://lccn.loc.gov/2019044094

ISBN 978-1-108-48605-7 Hardback
ISBN 978-1-108-73698-5 Paperback

This is the kind of law
history loves, which contains
its own demise.

> Stephen Dunn, 'History', *The New Yorker*, 10 March 2008.

If you have mind to have Law you shall have enough...

> Judges Notebooks of the First Earl of Mansfield, *c.* 1742–1785.

Contents

Acknowledgements

I am very grateful to Stephen Dunn for his interest in this project and for permission to use his poem 'History' as the book's beginning. I am particularly grateful to archivists Gwyneth Endersby, Dot Salmon and Gail Falkingham at the North Yorkshire Country Record Office, Northallerton, for all their help with North Riding of Yorkshire quarter sessions records. I am in debt to Tina Lupton, Mark Philp and Wilf Prest for reading a draft manuscript of this book: their comments and suggestions make it a better thing than it was in the beginning. I also owe a very great deal to the acute commentary of two anonymous readers for Cambridge University Press.

Abbreviations

ASSI	Assize Court
BM	British Museum
BMNL	British Museum Newspaper Library
ECCO	Eighteenth-Century Collections Online
EED	Ernest Edward Dodd
EPT	Edward Palmer Thompson
HMSO	His/Her Majesty's Stationery Office
H&R	'History and Romance'
KB	King's Bench
NA	Nottinghamshire Archives
PRO	The Public Record Office
QS	Quarter Sessions
SCH	Somerset Heritage Centre
TNA	The National Archives
TSCA	The Stationers Company Archive
WCRO	Warwickshire County Record Office
WMRC	University of Warwick Modern Record Centre
WO	War Office

A Beginning: 'History', by Stephen Dunn

It's like this, the king marries
a commoner, and the populace cheers.
She doesn't even know how to curtsy,
but he loves her manners in bed.
Why doesn't the king do what his father did,
the king's mother wonders—
those peasant girls brought in
through that secret entrance, that's how
a kingdom works best. But marriage!
The king's mother won't come out
of her room, and a strange democracy
radiates throughout the land,
which causes widespread dreaming,
a general hopefulness. This is,
of course, how people get hurt,
how history gets its ziggy shape.
The king locks his wife in the tower
because she's begun to ride
her horse far into the woods.
How unqueenly to come back
to the castle like that,
so sweaty and flushed. The only answer,
his mother decides, is stricter rules—
no whispering in the corridors,
no gaiety in the fields.
The king announces his wife is very tired
and has decided to lie down,
and issues an edict that all things yours
are once again his.
This is the kind of law
history loves, which contains
its own demise. The villagers conspire

for years, waiting for the right time,
which never arrives. There's only
that one person, not exactly brave,
but too unhappy to be reasonable,
who crosses the moat, scales the walls.

Stephen Dunn, 'History', *The New Yorker,* 10 March 2008, in
What Goes On, W. W. Norton, New York, 2013, p. 172.

1 Its Ziggy Shape

Here's none of your strait lines here – but all taste – zig-zag – crinkum-crankum – in and out–

George Colman and David Garrick, *The Clandestine Marriage: As It Is Acted at the Theatre-Royal in Drury-Lane*, A. Leathley and eight others, Dublin, 1766, p. 29.

This is,
of course, how people get hurt,
how history gets its ziggy shape

Stephen Dunn, 'History', *What Goes On*, W. W. Norton, New York, 2013, p. 172.

History and the Law is about people's relationships with, to and under the law in the past, and modern historians' understanding of the law as experienced by those people. With some zig-zaggery into the seventeenth and twentieth centuries, the eighteenth to the nineteenth century is this book's time frame. The ziggy shape is history's shape, not history as 'the past' but history as stories that get told about the past. 'The law' here is English law – *The Laws of England* – with its common law system of precedent as opposed to written code; the common law's regime of adversarial procedure as opposed to the inquisitorial (or 'truth-finding') systems of Continental Europe. It is English law, with its overlapping circles of never-quite-binaries: common law/ statute law, criminal law/civil law, high law/low law, public law/private law, law/equity… all of it but the very last 'the common law' in one way or another and designated incomprehensible by many commentators. It is an adversarial legal system of fairly recent origin: now-familiar lawyer-dominated procedures came into being over the century from about 1750.[1] This is one of the reasons for some historians (*not* legal historians) having trouble with this law. Assured by great authorities,

---

[1] John H. Langbein, *The Origins of Adversary Criminal Trial*, Oxford University Press, Oxford, 2003.

1

like Sir William Blackstone in his *Commentaries on the Laws of England*, that we are looking at an immemorial system, pertaining time out of mind, we have not known until very recently that, writing in the 1760s, Blackstone was in fact describing a system in the making.

Historical accounts of this law are contradictory. It has been said that from the mid-seventeenth century onwards, ideas about people's relationship to the law became a 'nationalist ideology … that was absorbed into the mainstream identity of modern England'. It is also said that in the later eighteenth century this view of the common law as the prime expression of English identity declined, although it was sometimes still employed by radicals who, for political and rhetorical purposes, 'took common-law doctrine at face value, and turned it back to its masters'.[2]

But far from the connection between law and Englishness being severed, the nineteenth century provided new historical lessons for law students and children in schools about the indissoluble connection between the liberties and freedoms of 'being English' and being subject to its legal regime.[3] These ideas and connections are still expressed, in popular and professional circles, by conservatives and radicals. 'The common law is perhaps the single most distinctive feature of the condition of Englishness', says *Standpoint* magazine. 'Together with our language, it is at the heart of what makes us different from the nations of continental Europe'.[4] A former barrister concludes her harrowing 2018 collection of modern law stories (stories of ordinary people in relationship with the law) with an expression of pride in having served courts and a criminal justice system 'considered among the fairest in the world'.[5]

---

[2] Robert Colls, *Identity of England*, Oxford University Press, Oxford, 2002, pp. 13, 23, 27, 31.

[3] Gordon Batho, 'The History of the Teaching of Civics and Citizenship in English Schools', *The Curriculum Journal*, 1:1 (1990), pp. 91–100; David Sugarman, 'Legal History, the Common Law and "Englishness"', Karl Modeer (ed.), *Legal History in Comparative Perspective*, Institute for Legal History, Stockholm, 2002, pp. 213–27; John Hudson, *F. W. Maitland and the Englishness of English Law: Selden Society Lecture Delivered in the Old Hall of Lincoln's Inn July 5th 2006*, Selden Society Lecture; 2006, Selden Society, London, 2007; F. W. Maitland (with Sir Frederick Pollock), *History of English Law before the Time of Edward I*, Cambridge University Press, Cambridge, 1895.

[4] Jonathan Gaisman, 'Will the Genius of the Common Law Survive?', *Standpoint*, February 2018. The journal describes its mission as a celebration of western civilisation: 'its arts and its values – in particular democracy, debate and freedom of speech – at a time when they are under threat'. www.standpointmag.co.uk/features-february-2018-jonathan-gaisman-will-the-genius-of-the-common-law-survive. Accessed 3 July 2018.

[5] Sarah Langford, *In Your Defence: Stories of Life and Law*, Doubleday, London, 2018, pp. 268–70.

Legal historians continue to discuss the very great puzzle of the 'the great litigation decline' from the seventeenth to the eighteenth century. In the Tudor and Stuart periods, all sorts and degrees of people appear to have had 'first-hand knowledge of legal processes and concepts'.[6] Social historians agree that this kind of law experience led to a sense of community (local and national) and high expectations of good governance.[7] Personal experience of litigation gained in the sixteenth and seventeenth centuries may have empowered some participants because such experience created expectations that government was bounded by law and might be held to account if it failed to act accordingly.[8] Legal historians agree that this kind of law experience deteriorated among eighteenth-century people; it appears they were far less willing to 'go to law' – to defend their reputation, their local social and political standing, their property interests – than their ancestors had been.[9] Perhaps new forms of association in the new century, new kinds of self-disciplined social subjects, and newly available knowledge of the law spread by the print industry can account for a decline in litigation. There were newer and cheaper ways now of settling family, community and employment disputes. These explanations for a decrease in litigation centre on lay-people; but attorneys too experienced rising legal costs, and – as we shall see – may have developed less litigation-centred ways of doing business.[10]

Nevertheless, decline or not, and as shall be discussed, E. P. Thompson found the law 'everywhere' he looked in the English eighteenth century: 'the ruled – if they could find a purse and a lawyer – would actually fight for their rights by means of law … When it ceased to be possible to

---

[6] David Lemmings (ed.), 'Introduction', *The British and Their Laws in the Eighteenth Century*, Boydell Press, Woodbridge, 2005, p. 8.

[7] Steve Hindle, *The State and Social Change in Early Modern England*, Macmillan, Basingstoke, 2000, pp. 236–7; James Sharpe, 'The People and the Law', *Popular Culture in Seventeenth-Century England*, Barry Reay (ed.), Routledge, London, 1988, pp. 224–70.

[8] Christopher Brooks, 'Litigation, Participation and Agency', *British and Their Laws*, David Lemmings (ed.), pp. 155–81.

[9] Wilfrid Prest, 'The Experience of Litigation in Eighteenth-Century England', *British and Their Laws*, pp. 133–54; W. A. Champion, 'Recourse to the Law and the Meaning of the Great Litigation Decline, 1650–1750: Some Clues from the Shrewsbury Local Courts', *Communities and Courts in Britain, 1150–1900*, Christopher Brooks and Michael Lobban (eds.), Hambledon, London, 1997, pp. 179–98.

[10] David Lemmings, *Law and Government in England during the Long Eighteenth Century: From Consent to Command*, Palgrave Macmillan, Basingstoke, 2015, pp. 56–80. See Chapter 3 for attorneys doing business outside the courts.

continue the fight at law, men still felt a sense of legal wrong: the propertied had obtained their power by illegitimate means...'[11]

For the main part, *History and the Law* is concerned with the men and women who did not have even these small means to 'go to law'; they were brought before it, interpellated by it, not as voluntary litigants but as required by law to produce an account of themselves in bastardy or settlement examinations before local magistrates. The fiscal-administrative state expanded dramatically during the second half of the eighteenth century; poor law legislation and taxation law wove a legal web around many lives. This kind of everyday encounter with the law probably increased during the course of the century.

There are magistrates, high court judges, and a lord chief justice here; and poets, and novelists, and political philosophers, but many more maidservants, and poor and pauper men and women, and down-at-heel, low attorneys, and middling-sort wives in their coverture – all of them thinking, talking, manipulating, resisting the law, for the purposes of their everyday life. The law those people knew has shaped (some) modern historians' love affair with the law itself. And not only historians. Writing about his 2014 novel *The Children Act*, Ian McEwan said that most stories, maybe all stories, are to be found in the operation of the family division of the UK high courts. He could have said: not just the family division, but all British courts of law from the seventeenth century onwards.[12] He did not say that – maybe – he is half in love with the law, seduced by its authority as a way of thinking and telling; its glamorous, enticing opacity. In the novel he quotes many high court judgments, real and half-invented, for the elegance of their legal reasoning, the bewitching cleverness of their thought.[13]

It takes one to know one – to know McEwan's love for the law: I too suffer from the law-envy which is so close to love: the desire to *understand* the law, to speak its language, to be able to tell its stories. Romantic attachment grows from wanting to please; from paying close, admiring attention; from earnestly struggling to know and

---

[11] E. P. Thompson, *Whigs and Hunters: The Origins of the Black Act* (1975), Penguin, Harmondsworth, 1977, p. 261; Daniel H. Cole, '"An Unqualified Human Good". E. P. Thompson and the Rule of Law', *Journal of Law and Society*, 28:2 (2001), pp. 177–203.

[12] Ian McEwan, 'The Law versus Religious Belief', *Guardian*, 5 September 2014; Ian McEwan, *The Children Act*, Faber, London, 2014.

[13] In modern Britain, these may be read on a daily basis by any member of the public who has elected to receive by email 'Courts and Tribunals Judiciary All Judgments' from www.judiciary.uk/judgments/.

understand the desired object: giving it everything you've got, and showing it. For the writing of my three books before last, I kept a glossary of eighteenth-century legal terms permanently book-marked on my computer and *Jacob's Law Dictionary* to (virtual) hand. But I was never sure that I'd properly understood, or was worthy of understanding, should it ever come. In *The Needle's Eye* (1972) Margaret Drabble has her heroine's mind skitter and slide over the pages of (the fictional) *Everyman's Lawyer, Law for the Layman:* 'she had tried to educate herself gently... It had been a horrible experience, made worse by the fact that she seemed to understand so little of what she read... The details and refinements of the explanation remained totally obscure, and it was only by an immense effort of will that one could understand the main drift'.[14] If you're going to write something out of your attempts, and to add to the gloomy sense of your own incapacity, there is a nervous apprehension of your legal readers, who will find your use of law vocabulary so odd, so very off-key. To have these anxieties is not unreasonable: we shall see William Godwin suffering the condescension of lawyer-reviewers of his novel *Things As They Are* (1794); they thought the law story he told in it risible at best and wrong at worst.[15] I thought at first that my own difficulties with the law ('she had to convict herself, as she struggled, of real stupidity'[16]) were to do with not having Latin, like Rose in *The Needle's Eye*. But understanding legal terms and language is not to do with translating vocabulary. Joseph Woolley, the Nottinghamshire stocking maker (c. 1769–1840) whose diaries provide several of the law stories told in this book, did not have Latin either and probably could not have provided a definition of *mittimus* to satisfy a lawyer. But he used the word with ease and confidence, in his writing and down the alehouse, because it was embedded in his life and conversation.[17]

Some late eighteenth-century opinion was that Joseph Woolley couldn't possibly have understood the law that threads through his diaries. In *Pig's Meat*, Thomas Spence reproduced an address to a provincial radical society's inaugural meeting to excoriate 'A criminal code of law sanguine and inefficacious; – a civil code so voluminous

---

[14] Margaret Drabble, *The Needle's Eye* (1972), Penguin, Harmondsworth, 1973, pp. 143–6.
[15] Below, pp. 181–5.
[16] Drabble, *Needle's Eye*, p. 143.
[17] Carolyn Steedman, *An Everyday Life of the English Working Class: Work, Self and Sociability in Early Nineteenth-Century England*, Cambridge University Press, Cambridge, 2013.

and mysterious as to puzzle the best understandings; by which means, justice is denied to the poor, on account of the expence attending the obtaining of it'.[18] (In *Pig's Meat*, Spence often reproduced claims that *no one* understood English law, not even the lawyers.) But Joseph Woolley *did* understand, or understood enough for the purposes of his everyday life and writing. His friends and neighbours, often at a sharper end of the law exercised by the local magistrate than he, also appear to have understood the law well enough. I wanted to understand as much as did the average maidservant seeking her settlement in a justice's parlour. I wanted to understand and use law's obfuscating language with the ease of Joseph Woolley and his friends and neighbours, all talking law in the bar of the Coach and Horses in Clifton, c. 1805.

I shall claim good taste for this book (none of your straight lines here). How could I not with a book that concerns the eighteenth century and its forthright discrimination of the properties (aesthetic and otherwise) of history and the law? In the English eighteenth century, history writing was discussed as much for its form and compositional qualities as it was for its content. There was discussion of law writing too, although much more of the tedium and exhaustion of those who had to read law's graceless prose. In the early 1740s, an eighteen-year-old Oxford graduate enrolled at the Middle Temple to study law. Young William Blackstone had spent the previous three years with his Muse, reading and writing poetry. Now he had to bid her farewell, enter 'wrangling courts and stubborn law, / To smoke, and crowds, and cities draw: / There selfish faction

---

18   'THE DERBY ADDRESS. At a Meeting of the Society for Political Information, held at the Talbot Inn, in Derby, July 16th, 1792, the following Address, declaratory of their Principles, &c. was unanimously agreed to, and ordered to be printed: To the Friends of Free Enquiry, and the General Good', *Pigs' Meat; Or, Lessons for the Swinish Multitude. Published in Weekly Penny Numbers, Collected by the Poor Man's Advocate (An Old Veteran in the Cause of Freedom) in the Course of His Reading for More Than Twenty Years. Intended to Promote Among the Labouring Part of Mankind Proper Ideas of Their Situation, of Their Importance, and of Their Rights. And to Convince Them That Their Forlorn Condition Has Not Been Entirely Overlooked and Forgotten, Nor Their Just Cause Unpleaded, Neither by Their Maker Nor by the Best and Most Enlightened of Men in All Ages ... The Third Edition*, printed for T. Spence, at the Hive of Liberty, London, 1795, pp. 230–5; 233. Spence published penny numbers between 1793 and 1795, later reprinting them in three volumes. Malcolm Chase, Alastair Bonnett, Keith Armstrong et al., *Thomas Spence: The Poor Man's Revolutionary*, Breviary Stuff, London, 2014; Jon Mee, *Print, Publicity, and Popular Radicalism in the 1790s: The Laurel of Liberty*, Cambridge University Press, Cambridge, 2016.

rules the day, / And pride and avarice throng the way'.[19] The worst of
it will be law's language; its 'sounds uncouth and accents dry, / That
grate the soul of harmony'. Blackstone anticipated by a century Charles
Dickens' agonised chronicles of law learning. As a young man, Dickens
worked as a law clerk (he inhabited a much lower position in the legal
hierarchy than Blackstone ever did), later enumerating the articled and
salaried clerks, and 'the middle-aged copying clerk[s] ... always shabby
and often drunk' with whom as a boy he had laboured in dusty, airless
rooms.[20] In 1833, one of the last wrote to the *Legal Observer* about the
wastelands of his working life, the arid copying of law's narratives, day
after day, into eternity.[21] All boys in training for the law were advised to
practice almost incessant copying, of text they did not understand – that
was beyond understanding.[22]

In the 1740s, later in his 'Farewell to his Muse', and then even later
in life as Sir William Blackstone, author of *Commentaries of the Laws
of England* (1766–1769), the former poet will find another, new Law-
Muse holding a 'sacred page', 'Where mix'd yet uniform, appears / The
wisdom of a thousand years. / ... Clear, deep, and regularly true', which
is indeed the message of all four books of the *Commentaries*. So too, in
the poem and in the *Commentaries*, he will discern the 'mighty Alfred's
piercing soul' pervading and regulating 'one harmonious rule of right'.
The middle-aged Blackstone will fashion a new Muse in the shape of
Alfred the Great, founder of English law.[23]

After 1765, when the first book of the *Commentaries* appeared, readers frequently remarked on the simplicity, ease and clarity with which

[19] William Blackstone, 'The Lawyer's Farewell to His Muse', Robert Dodsley (ed.),
A Collection of Poems in Six Volumes: By Several Hands, R. and J. Dodsley, London,
1758, Vol. 4, pp. 224–8; David Kader and Michael Stanford (eds.), *Poetry of the Law:
From Chaucer to the Present*, University of Iowa Press, Iowa City, 2010, pp. 36–39;
xiii–xiv; Wilfrid Prest, *William Blackstone: Law and Letters in the Eighteenth Century*,
Oxford University Press, Oxford, 2008, pp. 40–60.
[20] Thomas Alexander Fyfe, *Charles Dickens and the Law*, Chapman and Hall, London,
William Hodge, Edinburgh, 1910, pp. 38–40.
[21] 'Hardships of Lawyers' Clerks', *Legal Observer, or Journal of Jurisprudence*, 8: 225
(1834), pp. 412–13. This correspondent called himself 'a copying clerk'. Also John
Taylor, *Autobiography of a Lancashire Lawyer, Being the Life and Recollections of John
Taylor, Attorney-at-Law ... edited by James Clegg*, Bolton, 1888, p. 23, for the 'little
office comfort ... [and] much drudgery in doing a copy clerk's work'.
[22] Jacob Phillips, *A Letter from a Grandfather to His Grandson, an Articled Clerk: Pointing
Out the Right Course of His Studies and Conduct*, George Wilson, London, 1818; Alfred
Cecil Buckland, *Letters to an Attorney's Clerk, Directions for His Studies and General
Conduct*, for the author, London, 1824; Francis Hobler, *Familiar Exercises between an
Attorney and His Articled Clerk*, J. F. Dove, London, 1831.
[23] William Blackstone, *Commentaries on the Laws of England. Book I: Of the Rights of
Persons* (1765), Oxford University Press, Oxford, 2016, pp. 50–5.

Blackstone had made harmonious the common law's dingy and discordant history.[24] Blackstone had not yet done his work when young Edmund Burke complained that 'the law has been confined, and drawn up into a narrow and inglorious study... our jurisprudence presented to liberal and well-educated minds, even in the best authors, hardly anything but barbarous terms, ill explained, a coarse, but not a plain expression, an indigested method, and a species of reasoning the very refuse of the schools... '[25] But even after the *Commentaries*, law's 'sordid scribe' – its problem of writing – will always have to be circumnavigated in order to see 'how parts with parts unite... / See countless wheels distinctly tend / By various laws to one great end'. Some ordinary readers, however, remained as baffled and perplexed as modern historians: on the very next page of Dodsley's *Collection* in which Blackstone's 'Farewell' appears, a woman poet *just can't see* the harmony. She praises her brother's efforts in *actually reading* Coke upon Littleton; but he has had to work a dark and rugged mine to find gold; force each dark page of the law to 'unfold its haggard brow'.[26]

William Blackstone did not fall in love with the law (at least not in his 'Farewell'), but some modern writers, including historians, have done so. It's a complicated, ambivalent kind of love; it is unreciprocated, which in some post-Romantic philosophies is the reason for going on hopelessly... loving. Law will never love the historian back. One reason for its indifference may originate (in propositions later to be discussed) in the eighteenth-century's endeavour to write the law as if it existed out of time. Legal scholars provided a knowledge of the past 'conceived as "precedent", of a past which was the container of the substantive accumulated wisdom concerning which kinds of governmental and legal decisions were best', says Tim Murphy.[27] Law writers – legal

[24] Blackstone, 'Lawyer's Farewell', p. 38; *Commentaries on the Laws of England. Book I*, General Editor's Introduction, pp. vii–xv; *Commentaries on the Laws of England. Book II: Of the Rights of Things* (1766), Oxford University Press, Oxford, 2016, Simon Stearn, Introduction, p. xxiv.

[25] Edmund Burke, 'Fragment: An Essay towards an History of the Laws of England c. 1757' (1757), T. O. McLoughlin, James T. Boulton, William B. Todd (eds.), *The Writings and Speeches of Edmund Burke, Vol. 1: The Early Writings*, Oxford University Press, Oxford, 1997, pp. 321–31.

[26] 'Miss COOPER – (now Mrs. MADAN) [written] in her Brother's Coke upon Littleton', Dodsley (ed.), *Collection*, pp. 228–9. Valerie Rumbold, 'Madan, Judith (1702–1781)', *Oxford Dictionary of National Biography*, Oxford University Press, 2004. Accessed 12 January 2017.

[27] W. T. Murphy, *The Oldest Social Science? Configurations of Law and Modernity*, Clarendon Press, Oxford, 1997, pp. 77–108; 86–7.

authors – of the seventeenth and eighteenth centuries constructed a past which collapsed temporality into simultaneity; they did not search for origins: 'the past of the common law was the continuing consolidation of a perpetual present which was somehow out of time'. Origins were lost, gone, in some time 'beyond memory'. The lawyers' 'history' was about harmony, not difference, about making the past of the law conform to the present and to the future. It neither needed nor cared about beginnings; it 'could thereby treat on one footing the distance from the present of two or two hundred years'.[28] This was done even by Blackstone in his *Commentaries*, which provided, as we shall see, harmony and timelessness *by means* of a series of history lessons. And this by a writer and a lawyer who advanced the field of Enlightenment historiography, used archival sources with creativity, and was much concerned to adumbrate cause and effect in the making of England's legal system and constitution.[29]

A major part of the project to make Law history-less (that is, without history) was undertaken when 'History' in its modern mode was tentatively finding its way in the world, as a way of thinking and understanding. Writing and history 'were combined to thematize the passage of time as a problem, by conferring specificity on the past'.[30] 'History' proposed the radical disjuncture of then from now; the utter difference of the past from the present. 'History' underscored the importance of making out the beginning of things – of society – so that eighteenth-century historians might restructure an undifferentiated mass (then/ the past/once upon a time) into a thing measured by change, by temporality. But Law did not care for historians. It didn't then, and it doesn't now. Law will never take notice of you, no matter how much you hang around the bike shed after school, hoping for just one look, just one glance sent your way.

The common law's timelessness – absence of time, indifference to history – is discernable in the most practical and mundane activities of the historian's working life. Nothing has dates! It takes a lot of time to find out when a case, stated in 'The All England Law Reports', *actually happened*. This is the compendious, digitised version of the Victorian endeavour (started in 1865) to gather together in one place all decisions of the high courts stretching back to remote medieval times. Cases are

[28] Murphy, *Oldest Social Science*, pp. 89–90.
[29] Wilfrid Prest, 'Blackstone as Historian', *Parergon*, 32:3 (2015), pp. 183–203.
[30] Murphy, *Oldest Social Science*, p. 99.

headed (as was nineteenth-century practice) with the names of plaintiff and defendant (*Wilkins* v. *The Parish of Hardington Obscure*, for example); there is the abbreviated title of the original published volume of reports, and the year, usually noted on the monarchical system (23 Geo. 3 for example, which is 1783). You're lucky to have that, and even luckier to have the short-title (Bur.) for James Burrow, *Decisions of the Court of King's Bench upon Settlement Cases; from the Death of Lord Raymond in March 1732, to June 1776, inclusive … Second Edition …* His Majesty's Law-Printers for E. Brooke, 1786. But when you find him, Reporter Burrow will not tell you when a trial took place or the date of the events about which the trial was concerned. He restricts himself to '*Hilary Term 4 Geo. 3. Rex* v. *Inhabitants of Salford*'. Happy those who, like the Bertram girls in *Mansfield Park* (1814) were forced to get by heart the reigns of the English monarchs! But at least you know the case was heard sometime between January and March 1764, and you can start searching other sources. The blithe disregard for your purposes (happenings are pretty meaningless to a historian unless they have a date and a context by which to interpret them) can make Law the more alluring … and those of us who complain about its opacity and indifference are told to *just get over it*: 'it must be obvious that … [legal] records were created for an entirely different purpose from that of enriching the study of history'.[31]

Then, long ago I learned to love the kind of law story that Stephen Dunn tells in his poem 'History'. It is the story that modern social history tells: of resistance to oppression imposed by law, and, usually as end-stop, the restoration of law and order – oppression – in some new, more resolute form. Then, perhaps, further conspiracy and rebellion. In this kind of history narrative, there is often a plangent, heart-wrenching epilogue referring to 'the experience of defeat'. This was Christopher Hill's 1984 title for a book that described how, after 1660, radical clergy, intellectuals and writers responded to the failure of the English Revolution. Because they *did* respond – reformulated their faith, found new ways of justifying the ways of God to man, took a new view of the social order and wrote about all of this – their reaction was not one of abject surrender to things as they were (or had turned out to be).[32]

---

[31] John Baker, '"Authentic Testimony"? Fact and Law in Legal Records', *Collected Papers on English Legal History*, Cambridge University Press, Cambridge, 2013, Vol. 3, pp. 1513–27.

[32] Christopher Hill, *The Experience of Defeat: Milton and Some Contemporaries*, Faber and Faber, London, 1984. E. P. Thompson also, and more famously, wrenched triumph from defeat at the end of *The Making of the English Working Class* (1963), Penguin, Harmondsworth, 1968, p. 915.

On the website that accompanies Penelope Corfield's *Time and the Shape of History*, Corfield discusses, among all the possible shapes of history, 'the zigzagging revolutionary dialectic of history, as defined by Marx'. Here too is the elegant, ziggy 'Revolutionary Jumps' diagram (along with 'Time Random Walk', 'Time Lines' and 'Time Cycle') to make things plain.[33] It has been said that from the middle years of the eighteenth century, history began to be conceptualised as taking place *through* time, not *in* time, as previously imagined, *not* as events contained within a pre-given time made by, or of, God, but as a thing with time running through it. Now, says Reinhart Koselleck of the later eighteenth century, 'time [was] metaphorically dynamicised into a force of history itself'.[34] But this is not to describe the shape, or dimensions, or structure, or attributes of 'a History', which is a narrated, often a written, thing made out of a past which may indeed be imagined in this way, but which is not the same as History, or a history. Corfield's 'shapes of history' are really the many shapes of *time* with which history gets imagined and told; the book describes the shape of *time*, as it is and has been imagined and written by those who write and tell history (and those who read it too), not the shape of the stories (histories) told about its passage.

And yet 'History is the sum of what happens, in any era in which humans have lived', Corfield says; it 'contains the sum of all human actions, multiplied by the multifarious actors outside and beyond human control'. Really? Everything? Even 'visits home, heartbeats, a first kiss, the jump of an electron from one orbital position to another'?[35] It seems so: when she uses the word *history* without any

---

[33] Penelope J. Corfield, *Time and the Shape of History*, Yale University Press, New Haven, CT and London, 2007. 'History and Time' www.penelopejcorfield.co.uk/time.htm. 'Ziggy' and 'zig-zag' are not terms used in the book, where the shapes of history are given as: Time Cycles (48–56), Time Lines (80–8), Time Ends (113–21), Time Pieces (185–93) and Time Power (224–32). 'Time' is a major area of investigation for modern historians of concepts. Cesare Cuttica, 'What Type of Historian? Conceptual History and the History of Concepts. A Complex Legacy and a Recent Contribution', *History and Theory*, 51:3 (2012), pp. 411–22.

[34] Reinhart Koselleck, *The Practice of Conceptual History: Timing History, Spacing Concepts*, Stanford University Press, Stanford, CA, 2002, p. 165. Also *Futures Past: On the Semantics of Historical Time*, Columbia University Press, New York, 2005. Legal theorists have been interested in these propositions. See Matthew Craven, 'Theorising the Turn to History in International Law', Anne Orford and Florian Hoffmann (eds.), *The Oxford Handbook of the Theory of International Law*, Oxford University Press, Oxford, 2016, pp. 21–37; 27.

[35] Paul A. Roth, 'Narrative Explanations: The Case of History', *History and Theory*, 27:1 (1988), pp. 1–13; 8.

further qualification, it refers 'to the entire past or, as dictionaries specify, the "aggregate of past events in general"'.[36] This is a view in opposition to the idea of history as an imagined and constructed thing, as a thing made out of a *past* that did and does exist because things happened and we have evidence of them. But the past is not history; history is *fashioned*: something made, imagined, told and written, and repeated and known, not necessarily by historians, although they may be the majority of its originators. The conflation of the past and history is particularly obfuscating if you attempt to use it to think about law's (historically ascertained, eighteenth-century) endeavour to collapse the historical past into one long continuous, ever-happening present of the common law.

As far as its story is concerned, Stephen Dunn's poem 'History' has some affinity to the zigzagging narrative of social history (or 'revolutionary jumps') derived from the Marxist philosophy of history. The poem was published a year after Corfield's book.[37] But we are not after provenance and influences on the poet here. It is anyway a commonplace of modern politicians and political journalists that history doesn't run in straight lines, that 'history's zig-zag shape runs through us'.[38] The poem has, at first glance, the form of a fairy tale, but the story is not complicated enough to be one. Classic theory of the fairy tale insists on a hero or heroine, one who leaves home on a journey perhaps, or encounters villainy at home from within the family; sometimes helped, sometimes not, the hero resists, or faces a task; wickedness is exposed and vanquished. The hero comes into the kingdom/marries a princess. The princess, formerly in disguise as a goose girl, may kiss a frog and marry what the frog becomes. The End. This little straight line of a structure is not anywhere near as detailed as the actually existing morphology that the fairy tale proposes, but in any case, Dunn's poem is not one, despite the remote kingdom, the turreted palace, the wicked Queen Mother, the peasants toiling in the fields.[39] And is not one despite the opening line, which is as close to *once upon a time* as

---

[36] Corfield, *Time*, pp. xiii, xiv, xvi, xvii, 7, 18, 80.

[37] In which, as observed, the word *zig-zag* does not occur. The inauguration date of the website, where it is illustrated, is unclear.

[38] Nick Maloutis, 'History's Zig-Zag Shape Runs Through Us', *Business*, 21 November 2016, reporting on Barack Obama's speech to the Stavros Niarchos Foundation Cultural Centre in Athens.

[39] Vladimir Propp, *Morphology of the Folktale* (1928); Joseph Campbell, *Hero with a Thousand Faces* (1948). The distinction between the folktale and fairytale does not delay us here.

modern English gets, except (again) that this is the present tense (*It's like this*), not the past. It takes place in a polity governed by law, albeit of the feudal kind. There is no place for these subjects outside the king's will, his personhood and his laws. The political inscribes the personal; the domestic life of the castle *makes* the subjects of this realm. This is why, when the king marries a commoner, achieves a personal desire, the people cheer in a formulaic kind of way, and a strange, unfamiliar democracy shines like the sun across the fields. The people can now dream of things being in another way because they have already become so. But dynastic and sexual relationships within the palace still dictate common life. The people are punished for the queen's infidelity, and democracy is abrogated: all that was once the king's, and briefly bestowed on the people, is restored to him. He issues an edict to say that all things yours (ours) are once again his. This is indeed the kind of law that social historians love. It sounds like the cycle of revolution and counter-revolution, of resistance and oppression. We love to watch the people *get something*, in sure and fateful knowledge that it will be soon be taken away from them.

Or is it true that history loves the kind of law that can so easily be revoked? The law that, in this case, provided more equal property distribution and widespread hopefulness? Does all law carry within it the seeds of its own revocation? Can Dunn mean (I know that I am not using a technical term with 'mean', and poets, anyway, are not obliged to mean anything) that historians find a grim, told-you-so satisfaction in seeing yet another radical change thwarted and the old despotic ways restored? Or does a ziggy line imply a zaggy one? One that necessarily, at some point, turns another way? Certainly, from the mute, despondent villages, one figure emerges, slips out into the night and, from years of repressed conspiracy, attempts another turn. Assassin-like, he (or she) swims the moat, scales the palace walls. He (or she) does this not because he (or she) is brave, but because he (or she) is far too unhappy to listen to the reason of the order of things.

The narrator pauses once to tell us what's going on here: 'this is . . . / . . . how history gets its ziggy shape'. 'This' – the poet's intervention – comes after we have been told about the widespread dreaming and general hopefulness that followed on the early happiness of the king's marriage and the disapproving retreat of the old guard, the queen mother, to her chamber. The democracy, the hopefulness, together form a false political and social dawn. They cannot last, for they are promulgated by the body and the persona of the ruling elite. And 'this' is also how *people get hurt*. Hurt by change itself? Hurt by a democracy false, because falsely given, and not achieved by the people themselves? 'History is what hurts', Frederic Jameson once said.[40] Naive of interpretation (not to say glib), I found satisfaction in this line by remembering Dr Johnson's supposed refutation of idealist philosophy. Johnson kicked a stone, and ejaculated: *Sir. I refute it thus.*[41] He knew the stone was there because kicking it hurt his foot. We know history is there – that something happened which has been narrativised into history – because the story of it has the power to hurt, as the history Stephen Dunn tells hurts those to whom it happened and the readers of his poem, especially if they are social historians in the Marxist tradition. But Jameson said that the hurt was experience of necessity: all that sets limits to what we want, can want, and to all possibilities of action. Necessity here is not content or stuff; it is 'the inexorable form of events', as perceived and experienced. This hurtful history – history with the capacity to hurt – is not a thing or a force; it can only be apprehended through the effects it has – in causing us pain. And Jameson delivered his aphorism as part of a discussion of the extreme difficulties of the revolutionary (Marxist) tradition when conceived of as being continuous with the critical, theoretical and labour traditions that want to criticise, defend or even just tell it.[42]

McEwan is not the only novelist to structure his plot by the idea of the law or to make his protagonists out of it. Novelists, from the eighteenth to the twentieth centuries, who plot by the law, who inform their readers about the law as it determines their characters and their stories, who play with the idea of the law as the grandest founding narrative of them all will thread their way through this book. But Laurence Sterne (1713–1768) is the most useful of them all for current purposes.

---

[40] Frederic Jameson, *The Political Unconscious: Narrative as a Socially Symbolic Act* (1981), Methuen, London, 1983, p. 102.

[41] This was about the difficulty of challenging a philosophy that appeared self-evidently false but impossible to refute. What Boswell *actually wrote* about the 1763 stone-kicking incident was: 'After we came out of the church, we stood talking for some time together of Bishop Berkeley's ingenious sophistry to prove the non-existence of matter, and that everything in the universe is merely ideal. I observed, that though we are satisfied his doctrine is not true, it is impossible to refute it. I never shall forget the alacrity with which Johnson answered, striking his foot with mighty force against a large stone, till he rebounded from it, "I refute it thus"'. James Boswell, *The Life of Samuel Johnson, LL.D*, Vol. 1 (1791), J. Davis, London, 1820, p. 218.

[42] For the many perorations on Jameson's dictum, see Steven Helmling, 'Failure and the Sublime. Frederic Jameson's Writing in the '80s', *Postmodern Culture*, 10: 3 (2000), pp. 6–35; Alexander R. Galloway, 'History Is What Hurts. On Old Materialism', *Social Text*, 34:2 (2016), pp. 125–41.

In *Tristram Shandy* (1759–1767), the narrator (who may, or may not be, Laurence Sterne, or Tristram Shandy) and other characters comment constantly on the law and on the writing of history. The ziggy shape of the historian's writing comes from *Tristram Shandy* and Tristram Shandy; it comes from Sterne. Well into Volume I, the narrator, who has already named what you have in your hands as a 'history', comments on what he is writing. He thinks of driving on 'his history, as a muleteer drives on his mule, – straight forward; – for instance, from Rome all the way to Loretto, without ever once turning his head either to the right hand or to the left'; such a narrator would be able to tell you, to the hour, 'when he should get to his journey's end'.[43] But 'the thing is impossible'. Any man (let's say, historian) 'of spirit' will 'have fifty deviations from a straight line to make with this or that party as he goes along, which he can no ways avoid'. Not only that, but the historian will have various

> Accounts to reconcile:
> Anecdotes to pick up:
> Inscriptions to make out:
> Stories to weave in:
> Traditions to sift:
> Personages to call upon:
> Panegyrics to paste up at his door;
> Pasquinades at that: –…To sum up; there are archives at every stage to be looked into, and rolls, records, documents, and endless genealogies, which justice ever and anon calls him back to stay the reading of it: – in short, there is no end of it.[44]

Later, he will explain the form of writing he uses to account for the zig-zaggery of his research: 'the machinery of my work is of a species by itself; two contrary motions are introduced into it, and reconciled, which were thought to be at variance with each other. In a word, my work is digressive, and it is progressive too, – and at the same time'.[45] *Lines* – tolerably straight; bendy; angular – preoccupy him as he describes what his characters *do*, their conversation and anecdotes and his writing of them.

---

[43] Laurence Sterne, *The Life and Opinions of Tristram Shandy, Gentleman (1759–67)*, Penguin, Harmondsworth, 1967, pp. 64–5 (Volume I, Chapter 14). He writes of 'a historiographer' driving on his history – 'historiographer' in the eighteenth-century meaning of one who writes history.

[44] For the pasquinade, see below, p. 41.

[45] Sterne, *The Life and Opinions of Tristram Shandy* (1967), Vol. 1, p. 95 (Volume I, Chapter 22).

In the *fourth* (!) volume he says he that he is now 'beginning to get fairly into ... [his] work'. He should now, near the end, be able to get into a 'tolerable straight line'; he has been on a 'vegetable diet, with a few of the cold seeds' in order to *write straight*. He then provides line diagrams of what you've been reading – five of them – none of which are straight, and none of them zigzag either. His lines are all over the place, although they do remain (kind of) lines.[46]

He is a historian in the eighteenth-century manner: one who produces an account of a person, thing, or event – a narrative collection of facts and observations about it or them – that culminates in the object before the reader's eyes: the book in her or his hand. 'Did anyone ever read such a book as Locke's essay?' he exclaims in the second volume: 'I will tell you in three words what it is. It is a history. – A history! of who? what? where? when? Don't hurry yourself. – It is history-book ... of what passes in a man's own mind'.[47] 'History writing is a semi-serious theme throughout *Tristram Shandy*', says Nicolas Visser, though 'Sterne is not one to observe the sort of historical chronological ordering of a Scott or a Tolstoy or other authors of more properly historical novels'. 'Properly historical' is a term devised *after* Scott and Tolstoy had written. In the mid-eighteenth century, there was a 'customary association of "novel" with "history" (*The History of Tom Jones*, etc.)', and with this in mind, Tristram/the narrator/Sterne 'comments famously on the difficulties of shaping narrative history'.[48] Commentary on the law and legal thinking in *Tristram Shandy* is of a different kind: history emerges as the wavering juddering line of its telling, whilst law is its content, its *stuff*. In one account, the casuistry, the eternal argument of cases between his protagonists, as they *tell it another way* a thousand times, shows the world to be 'a collection of cases, some of which we encounter in the course of our existence, knowing all the while that others are nonetheless also possible ... beyond this mere possibility is a whole infinity of its possibilities, of which only casuistry, understood as the never-ending study of cases, can allow itself to conceive'. It is the 'the dream of literature – to consider the possibility of everything', just as the formality of legal argument allows 'lawyers to imagine possibilities, to play with hypotheses, that go way beyond the boundaries of social acceptability, artistic rules,

---

[46] Sterne, *The Life and Opinions of Tristram Shandy* (1967), p. 173 (Volume III, Chapter 30) pp. 453–4 (Vol. VI, Chapter 40).

[47] Sterne, *The Life and Opinions of Tristram Shandy* (1967), pp. 106–7 (Volume II, Chapter 2).

[48] Nicholas Visser, '*Tristram Shandy* and the Straight Line of History', *Textual Practice*, 12:3 (1998), pp. 489–502.

or economic necessity'. Thus, in *Tristram Shandy* 'law is the real world of imagination. Of this world, literature can only offer an approximation. And *Tristram Shandy* is the closest that literature can get'.[49]

In the everyday world of *Tristram Shandy*, there is law talk among friends – 'I see plainly, Sir, by your looks, (or as the case happened) my father would say,–' and detailed account of the ecclesiastical courts (for which reason we shall shortly adumbrate) where 'the Letter of the Law ... sits ... invulnerable, fortified with CASES and REPORTS [these last words were set in law gothic, or blackletter] so strongly on all sides'. The sermon Sergeant Trim reads in Volume II, and during which Dr Slop falls asleep, was the sermon Sterne himself, Church of England clergyman, had preached at the opening of York assizes in 1750.[50] There is denigration of lawyers, as in 'a coalition of the gown, from all the bars of it, driving a damned dirty, vexatious cause before them, with all their might and main, the wrong way'; a detestable character 'seems to have been taken from some Lawyer'.[51] There is much about the law of women and of *coverture* (which we shall come to, by and by).

Biographers discuss Sterne's attraction to the law, his reading in an eclectic collection of continental and English jurists – Grotius and Pufendorf, Coke and Selden.[52] There was an ecclesiastical lawyer in his wider family and he was highly conscious of the power and influence that those who served the consistory courts were able to acquire. It is not very likely that Sterne considered the common law as a profession, says Ian Campbell Ross, for the expense of training for it would have been prohibitive. But his later life, like his writings, show him to have had 'an unmistakable penchant for the law'.[53] But the legal cases and legal scenes in *Tristram Shandy* are written in relationship to the ecclesiastical courts, not the common law courts like quarter sessions. An assize court (assizes were held in the localities by the perambulatory judges

---

[49] Laurent de Sutter, 'Legal Shandeism: The Law in Laurence Sterne's *Tristram Shandy*', *Law and Literature*, 23: 2 (2011), pp. 224–40.

[50] For discussion of the juridical meaning of the assize sermon in the seventeenth century: Hugh Adlington, 'Restoration, Religion, and Law: Assize Sermons 1660–1685', Peter McCullough, Hugh Adlington, Emma Rhatigan (eds.), *The Oxford Handbook of the Early Modern Sermon*, Oxford University Press, Oxford, 2011, pp. 423–41. Also William Gibson, 'Sermons', Jeremy Gregory (ed.), *The Oxford History of Anglicanism: Volume II, Establishment and Empire, 1662–1829*, Oxford University Press, Oxford, 2017, pp. 270–88.

[51] Sterne, *The Life and Opinions of Tristram Shandy*, p. 78 (Vol 1, Chapter 19); pp. 146, 149 (Vol II Chapter 17); pp. 207–8 (Vol III Chapter 18); Ian Campbell Ross, *Laurence Sterne: A Life*, Oxford University Press, Oxford, 2001, p. 135.

[52] Ross, *Laurence Sterne*, p. 149.

[53] Ross, *Laurence Sterne*, p. 44.

of the high courts) figures once in *Tristram Shandy*, when Sterne reproduces one he preached at the opening of the York assizes in 1750, but is
overshadowed by the ecclesiastical courts of North Yorkshire in which
he served as prebendary and judge.[54] There is much more of ecclesiastical law and lawyers in *Tristram Shandy* than there is of magistrates and
their sittings in quarter sessions or in their own justicing room (on my
reading, there are no magistrates' sessions in *Tristram Shandy*).

However, from the early twentieth century onwards, Sterne's biographers have assured us that he was appointed to the commission of the
peace (became a magistrate) in the year of his marriage, 1741, when he
had just obtained the living of Sutton-on-the-Forest, North Yorkshire.[55]
After 1965, biographers were able to quote one of Sterne's former servants on his memories of his master at Quarter Sessions (QS). Their
source was now an interview with Richard Greenwood, undertaken in
1807 by the antiquarian Joseph Hunter, the transcript of which had been
deposited in the British Museum in the 1860s.[56] 'Sterne was a Justice
of peace' old Greenwood told Hunter; '& would often espouse a cause

---

[54] Wilbur L. Cross, *The Life and Times of Laurence Sterne*, Macmillan, New York, 1909,
pp. 57–86; Arthur H. Cash, *Laurence Sterne: The Early and Middle Years*, Routledge,
London, 1992, pp. 128–43, 247–55. For the work of the ecclesiastical courts in
the first half of the eighteenth century, particularly those of the Diocese of York,
J. A. Sharpe, '"Such Disagreement betwyxt Neighbours". Litigation and Human
Relations in Early Modern England', J. A. Bossy (ed.), *Disputes and Settlements: Law
and Human Relations in the West*, Cambridge University Press, Cambridge, 1983,
pp. 167–87; Diane Carlile, '"A Comon and Sottish Drunkard You Have Been".
Prosecutions for Drunkenness in the York Courts c. 1660–1725', *York Historian*, 16
(1999), pp. 32–44; Fay Bound Alberti, '"An Angry and Malicious Mind"? Narratives
of Slander at the Courts of York, c. 1660–c. 1760', *History Workshop Journal*, 56
(2003), pp. 59–77; Joanne Bailey, 'All He Wanted Was To Kill Her That He Might
Marry The Girl. Broken Marriages and Cohabitation in the Long Eighteenth
Century', *Cohabitation and Non-marital Births in England and Wales, 1600–2012*,
Rebecca Probert (ed.), Palgrave Macmillan, Basingstoke, 2014, pp. 51–64, 219–21.

[55] The self-proclaimed 'first "Life"' of Sterne that has been put before the world' did
not mention the circumstance: Percy Fitzgerald, *The Life of Laurence Sterne, in
Two Volumes*, Chapman and Hall, London, 1864, Vol. I, pp. vii, 147–78 (this is a
Shandean footnote; these are the pages where it *would be mentioned*, were it a circum-
stance). Cash, *Laurence Sterne*, does not mention the North Riding Commission of
the Peace. Neither is Sterne's being appointed to it noted in *The Florida Edition of the
Works of Laurence Sterne. Vol. VII. The Letters, Part I: 1739–1764*, Melvyn New and
Peter de Voogd (eds.), University Press of Florida, Gainesville, FL, 2009. Margaret
R. B. Shaw, *Laurence Sterne: The Making of a Humorist, 1713–1762*, The Richards
Press, London, 1957, p. 69 asserts that it *was so*, with nary a footnote. Ross, *Laurence
Sterne*, pp. 99–100, for the most recent assertion that he was a justice of the peace;
first asserted in Cross, *Life and Times*, pp. 55–6.

[56] James M. Kuist, 'New Light on Sterne: An Old Man's Recollections of the Young
Vicar', *PMLA*, 80: 5 (1965), pp. 549–53; British Library, BL Add. MS 2446,
'Collectanea Hunteriana, Vol: XII Being Memoirs connected with the literary his-
tory of Great Britain', ff. 26–7.

which be was [sure] of bringing thro' at the Quarter Sessions, he could talk down the Lawyer so – this he delighted in'. But it is impossible to find Sterne in the Quarter Sessions records of the North Riding of Yorkshire. He makes one brief appearance as part of a panel convened to discuss an enclosure in 1749, as a 'clerk' – a clergyman – along with several 'gentlemen', not as a magistrate; but his presence at Quarter Sessions is nowhere to be found in the North Riding QS Minutes and Orders books, from 1740 to 1768.[57] Neither is he to be found in the York City Quarter Sessions records for the same period. He could conceivably have been appointed to the commission of the peace for the town, and he certainly spent much time in York. (He is unlikely to turn up anywhere across the whole Riding in the 1760s, after the rip-roaring success of *Tristram Shandy* and prolonged absences from Yorkshire.) Consistent recording of magistrates present at a QS meeting did not become common in the North Riding records until the late eighteenth century; the names of many magistrates lie concealed under the formula 'present others, their Fellows…Justices assigned to keep the peace'.[58] Geography, terrain and weather in the North Riding may have made Sterne's attendance at Thirsk for Quarter Sessions (Thirsk became the predominant quarter sessions town in the 1730s) extremely difficult or impossible; several North Riding magistrates made but one appearance at Quarter Sessions in twenty years.[59] But in the 1740s and 1750s, the triannual court of quarter sessions rotated (not regularly) between Easingwold, Guisborough, Northallerton, Richmond, very occasionally Scarborough, and Thirsk. Easingwold is but six miles from Sutton-on-the-Forest. York, which Sterne visited regularly, was eight miles away, although the York road may have been better than the one to Easingwold. Or Greenwood may have got it wrong and confused Sterne's activities as a prebendary in North Newbald, and as judge in several North Yorkshire ecclesiastical courts, with his being a magistrate. No magistrate's notebook or diary of sittings at Sterne's own house survives – if he ever kept one (if he ever *were* a magistrate). It was unusual

[57] North Yorkshire Record Office, North Riding Quarter Sessions Records, QSM 2/21, Quarter Sessions Minutes and Order Book, 1716–1749 for Sterne's one appearance; QDO(S) Justices Sacrament certificates and oaths (1740–1741); QJO Justices Qualification oaths (1745–1779); QSM 2/22 North Riding Quarter Sessions Minute and Order Books (1740–1741, 1745–1749, 1750–1763), for the records in which he isn't to be found.

[58] This from York City Archives Y/ORD/5/2/1 (17), Quarter Sessions Minute Books, 1740–1749.

[59] James Cockburn, 'The North Riding Justices, 1690–1750: A Study in Local Administration', *Yorkshire Archeological Journal*, 41:3 (1965), pp. 481–515.

for a magistrate sitting alone to preserve his own notes (they were not required to do so until the nineteenth century), but much knowledge of the operation of everyday law in the long eighteenth century comes from the few dozen who did.[60] In the vast archive that preserved the everyday administrative and legal business of the court of quarter sessions (the Quarter Sessions Bundles [QSB]) Sterne's signature is not under 'taken and acknowledged' (recognizances); no depositions were 'sworn before' him; he did not sign to examinations 'sworn at [some place] aforesaid'; he never wrote next to another justice's signature 'given under our hands and seals' in a bastardy or settlement examination document or on removal or maintenance orders; his name is not among the magistrates signing that someone 'was this day committed' to the House of Correction; he never was one of the ministers of the Church of England affirming that someone had taken the sacrament.[61] He never signed to 'seen and allowed this bill' or that 'this work appears necessary to be done' to an estimate for repairing a bridge.[62] The biographical trail back from now to Laurence Sterne as justice of the peace grows cold at the publication of Wilbur Cross's *Life and Times of Laurence Sterne*, in 1909, where there is the bare assertion that he was one, with no footnotes or references to help.[63]

[60] Carolyn Steedman, *Labours Lost: Domestic Service and the Making of Modern England*, Cambridge University Press, Cambridge, 2009, pp. 181–3; Gregory J. Durston, *Fields, Fens and Felonies: Crime and Justice in Eighteenth-Century East Anglia*, Waterside Press, Hook, 2016, pp. 19–20.

[61] Those seeking to hold any public office, or civil or military position by appointment of the Crown or who received pay from the Crown, were required to make an oath of loyalty to the Crown and Church of England. They attended church and received communion; they were given a sacrament certificate signed by the Church of England minister and churchwarden of the parish. This they took to a court of Quarter Sessions, where they made an oath of loyalty to the Crown and also affirmed that they did not believe in transubstantiation.

[62] North Yorkshire County Record Office, QSB 1741, 1742, 1743, 1744, 1745, 1749, 1762. These dates because Sterne married and gained a living and was supposedly appointed to the commission of the peace in 1741; because of the unreliable witness Greenwood who worked for Sterne for three years, quitting his service at Michaelmas 1745; 1749 because Sterne is mentioned in QS minutes in 1749; and 1762 because ... see below.

[63] Cross, *The Life and Times*, p. 55. Cross *must have* read Joseph Hunter's manuscript account of talking to Sterne's former servant, available in the British Museum Reading Room from 1861, even though there's no reference in his bibliography. The acquisition 'about ten years ago' was noted in 'Notes and News', *The Academy*, 101 (11 April 1874), pp. 395–8. Or maybe someone told him about it. See above, page 18, note 56. None of the semi-autobiographical accounts of Sterne which appeared between 1775 and 1806, which Kuist refers to in his article on Greenwood and Hunter, mention Sterne's being a magistrate. Kuist, 'New Light on Sterne', p. 552, Note 19.

Sterne as a North Riding magistrate is not so much the wavering diagrammatic lines, or the black blank page (to signify Parson Yorick's death) of *Tristram Shandy*, as a hole in the page on the other side of which is – nothing. But even when you've given up, there are 'archives ... to be looked into'.[64] Enough may be enough, of 'rolls, records, documents, and endless genealogies'; enough of all this 'buttoning and unbuttoning'.[65] But then Sterne liked a buttonhole: 'There is something lively in the very idea of 'em', he said.[66] Something goes through a buttonhole, to the other side, where there is some*thing*. In The National Archives there is one brief note of 'Laurence Sterne of Coxwold' (the living of Coxwold was presented to Sterne in 1760) among fiats for North Riding Justices of the Peace, for May 1762. He is among 28 other clerics whose names might be now inserted on the commission of the peace for the North Riding – for the first time, according to these records. The magistracy was an appointment of the Crown; if Sterne *were* appointed to the Commission of the Peace in 1741, he really ought to be listed in the records of Lord Chancellor's Office for that year.[67] But he appears only in the list for 1762 – nowhere else – across all the records for the North and East Ridings held by the central government for the years 1740–1770. And he isn't among those names for 1769 or 1770 listed to be removed, 'they being dead'. (Sterne died in 1768.) He is either *still* a North Riding magistrate, was never one in the first place, or a remarkably inactive one. It looks as if he never swore his oath in 1762 or indeed that the North Riding Clerk of the Peace never received his

---

[64] It is possible that Sterne was appointed to the East Riding Commission of the Peace. Sutton-on-the-Forest, North Riding, where Sterne lived in the 1740s and 1750s, was closer to the East Riding than it was to Thirsk. But searches in The National Archives, in the Crown Office's Fiats for Justices of the Peace, suggest that this wasn't the case. TNA, C234/42, Chancery and Lord Chancellor's Office: Crown Office: Fiats for Justices of the Peace. Yorkshire (East Riding), 1706–1923.

[65] As Lord Byron wrote in his journal for 7 December 1813. *The Works of Lord Byron: Letters and Journals*, Rowland E. Prothero (ed.), John Murray, London, 1898, Volume 2.

[66] *Tristram Shandy*, Book IV, Chapter 15.

[67] TNA, C234/43, Chancery and Lord Chancellor's Office: Crown Office: Fiats for Justices of the Peace. Yorkshire (North Riding), 1706–1923. This ancient system of appointment has recently changed: 'Prior to October 2013, the Lord Chancellor appointed magistrates. Under the Crime and Courts Act 2013, and from 1 October 2013, the statutory power to appoint magistrates transferred to the Lord Chief Justice, who delegates the function to the Senior Presiding Judge for England and Wales'. www.judiciary.uk/about-the-judiciary/who-are-the-judiciary/judicial-roles/magistrates/.

dedimus, or if he did, no oath was administered to Laurence Sterne.[68] And anyway, Sterne spent the entirety of 1762 (and 1763, and half of 1764) in France, in pursuit of better health, among other things. He does not mention the North Riding Commission of the Peace in his letters home – or letters anywhere.[69] The law in *Tristram Shandy*, being mainly of the ecclesiastical kind, attests to these absences, including Sterne's absence from the North (and East) Riding magistracy.[70]

Which was not the case with the magistrate-novelist Henry Fielding. The law Fielding knew as magistrate and that he administered as justice of the peace infuses *Tom Jones* (1749); it has been said that Fielding-the-magistrate *writes* the novel, that it is a novel *about* law.[71] Fielding's later *Amelia* (1751–1752) is book-ended by two magistrates, one ignorant and corrupt, one knowledgeable and judicious.[72] But Sterne's law content

---

[68] A dedimus is a kind of writ, issued in this case by the Crown Office, giving a commission for a local luminary or the county Clerk of the Peace, to administer an oath of office to a justice of the peace. TNA, C231/10, Chancery and Lord Chancellor's Office: Crown Office: Docket Books, 1721–1746; C231/11, Chancery and Lord Chancellor's Office: Crown Office: Docket Books, 1746–1763; C202/142/2, 3; C202/149/2; C202/152/1, Chancery: Petty Bag Office: Writ Files, return of writs; C193/44, Chancery and Lord Chancellor's Office: Crown Office: Miscellaneous Books, 1738–1746; C193/45, Chancery and Lord Chancellor's Office: Crown Office: Miscellaneous Books, 1746–1783. This last contains 'An account of dedimusses to swear the justices of the peace taken out of the crown office'. See Richard Burn, *The Justice of the Peace, and Parish Officer*, 3 vols, A. Millar, London, 1762, Volume 2, pp. 318–19, for 'The Justice of the Peace His Oath of Office'. See also L. K. J. Glassey and Norma Landau, 'The Commission of the Peace in the Eighteenth Century. A New Source', *Bulletin of the Institute of Historical Research*, 45 (1972), pp. 247–65. North Yorkshire Record Office, QDO(S) Justices Sacrament certificates and oaths (1740–1741); QJO Justices Qualification oaths (1745–1779).

[69] *Florida Edition of the Works of Laurence Sterne. Vol. VII. The Letters, Part I: 1739–1764*, pp. 224–387.

[70] Perhaps the insistence of biographers that Sterne was a magistrate, comes from a footnote in a pamphlet of 1758, in which a 'Mr Sterne' is listed among 'the Justices present' at a meeting. *An Answer to a Letter Addressed to the Dean of York, in the Name of Dr Topham*, for the author, York, 1758, p. 17. Sterne was much involved in this affair of ecclesiastical governance and preferment – it was largely *about* him–; he was at the meeting described, but he was not there as a justice of the peace. Ross, *Laurence Sterne*, pp. 183–96, has an account of the affair.

[71] Henry Fielding, *Tom Jones* (1749), ed. and intro. R. P. C. Mutter, Penguin, London, 1966, p. xxvi; Claude Rawson (ed.), *Henry Fielding (1707–1754): Novelist, Playwright, Journalist, Magistrate – A Double Anniversary Tribute*, Associated Universities Press, Cranbery, NJ, 2008, pp. 233–72; Lance Bertelsen, *Henry Fielding at Work: Magistrate, Businessman, Writer*, Palgrave, New York, 2000; K. G. Simpson, *Henry Fielding: Justice Observed*, Vision, London, 1985.

[72] Henry Fielding, *Amelia: In Four Volumes*, A. Millar, London, 1751–1752.

is different from Fielding's: the law stories in *Tristram Shandy* are not about the fornications and adulteries and the slanderings and betrayals that Sterne *could have* heard in a 1740s consistory court as well as in his (chimerical) justice's parlour.[73] In the ecclesiastical courts, he had access to the same, desperate stories of everyday life and sexual relations that Fielding had in his justice's parlour. But the poor laws, and the law concerning bastard children which shape so much of *Tom Jones*, are not the kind of law story Sterne tells. His stories are not about the poor living, loving and labouring in a rural village but about the genteel inhabitants of Shandy Hall and, to be sure, their servants who, it must be remarked, never once have cause to even think about the law of settlement. The gentlemen, their body servants, and Mrs Shandy upstairs in her closet reading over her marriage settlement (we shall come to Mrs Shandy, by-and-by) are inscribed by equity, the Court of Chancery, and some very grand and abstract legal theory, much of it derived from the operations of the ecclesiastical courts of Yorkshire.[74] It was these courts – spiritual courts – that gave Sterne the opportunity to indulge what Ross calls his 'weakness for the law'.[75] There are, it seems, many different ways in which a historian can love the law, and the beloved object has many faces. But still law will sit, unmoved by the historian's ardour, 'invulnerable, fortified with CASES and REPORTS' all around'.

★★★

Do you really need to be told that a historian – this historian, any historian, E. P. Thompson, or William Godwin, philosopher and historian – has had trouble interpreting legal documents, understanding legal processes and records, and the law itself? There would be no book if historians' law troubles were not its organising rhetorical strategy,

---

[73] Ross, *Laurence Sterne*, pp. 148–54. For the decline of the church (consistory) courts from the English Revolution onwards, their main line of business (testamentary and probate) before and after it, and their eighteenth-century role, see R. B. Outhwaite, *The Rise and Fall of the English Ecclesiastical Courts, 1500–1860*, Cambridge University Press, Cambridge, 2006, pp. 78–103. Richard Burn, *Ecclesiastical Law ... in two volumes*, H. Woodfall and W. Strahan, London, 1763, is a good guide to their eighteenth-century operation. Also, Alberti, '"An Angry and Malicious Mind"?' for their continued although diminished involvement in questions of sexual impropriety and alleged slander in early eighteenth-century Yorkshire.

[74] Dieter Paul Polloczek, 'Trappings of a Transnational Gaze. Legal and Sentimental Confinement in Sterne's Novels', Dieter Paul Polloczek (ed.), *Literature and Legal Discourse: Equity and Ethics from Sterne to Conrad*, Cambridge University Press, Cambridge, 1999, pp. 20–71.

[75] Ross, *Laurence Sterne*, p. 255.

but that is a cheap answer to the question. A better one points to the recent proliferation of autoethnography. Autoethnography is a type of qualitative research method in which a scholar uses self-reflection and personal experience to explore wider cultural, social and political meanings and understandings. It is deemed to be both a methodology *and* a form of writing, occupying a place somewhere between anthropology and literary studies.[76] The literature on it is enormous; histories of its development and use have been written.[77] All manner of scholars, including legal scholars, write autoethnography.[78] Literary historians use its methods; some see *their* strategies as related to the even more recent rise of 'autofiction' and to the scholarly text that makes a life lived with a particular and much-loved novel its framing device.[79] Historians have not embraced autoethnography as a methodology with the fervour of, say, sociologists, although they have always been willing to write traditional autobiography, usually when retired from the hurly-burly of archival research.[80] In its turn, 'the archive' and experience of it as institution and theory of knowledge have been discussed by many more cultural theorists than practising historians. Recently however, historians of the emotions have made attempts to write about historians' feelings in and about archives – and elsewhere.[81]

---

[76] Carolyn Ellis, Tony E. Adams, and Arthur P. Bochner, 'Autoethnography: An Overview', *Forum Qualitative Sozialforschung/Forum: Qualitative Social Research* [online] 12:1 (2011), no pagination, Web. 31 October 2018.

[77] Barbara Tedlock, 'From Participant Observation to the Observation of Participation: The Emergence of Narrative Ethnography', *Journal of Anthropological Research*, 47 (1991), pp. 69–94; Deborah Reed-Danahay (ed.), *Auto/Ethnography: Rewriting the Self and the Social*, Berg, Oxford and New York, 1997.

[78] David Kennedy, 'Autumn Weekends: An Essay on Law and Everyday Life', Austin Sarat and Thomas R. Kearns (eds.), *Law In Everyday Life*, University of Michigan Press, Ann Arbor, MI, 1995, pp. 191–236; Elaine Campbell, 'Exploring Autoethnography as a Method and Methodology in Legal Education Research', *Asian Journal of Legal Education*, 3:1 (2015), pp. 95–105.

[79] Christina Lupton, *Reading and the Making of Time in the Eighteenth Century*, Johns Hopkins University Press, Baltimore, MD, 2018. Rebecca Mead, *My Life in Middlemarch*, Penguin Random House, London, 2015, speaks for itself. Polly Clark, *Larchfield*, Quercus, London, 2017, is a poet who lives a (fictionalised) life in the story of another one, W. H. Auden. 'Suddenly this kind of "autofiction" – fictionalised autobiography that does away with traditional elements of the novel such as plot and character development – is everywhere'; Alex Clark, 'Drawn from Life: Why Have Novelists Stopped Making Things Up?' *Guardian*, 23 June 2018.

[80] Jeremy D. Popkins, *History, Historians, and Autobiography*, University of Chicago Press, Chicago, IL, 2005; Jaume Aurell, *Theoretical Perspectives on Historians' Autobiographies: From Documentation to Intervention*, Routledge, London, 2016.

[81] Jan Plamper, *The History of Emotions: An Introduction*, Oxford University Press, Oxford, 2015; Stephanie Downes, Sally Holloway, and Sarah Randles (eds.), *Feeling Things: Objects and Emotions through History*, Oxford University Press, Oxford, 2018.

Historians are reticent perhaps, because they worry quite as much as anthropologists about the ethics of autoethnography, about the ever-present danger of elevating one's own experience over others' (in the fragments and records they leave behind) – once lived, once felt, but now no more. Moreover, historians have had more trouble with 'experience' as a category of social being than have other scholars of the social and human sciences.[82] There are profound philosophical and practical barriers to the idea of experiencing 'history', if you conceive of history as 'the past' that is gone and is no more. But you *can* experience the detritus (records; pieces of paper and parchment – two thousand pieces of paper and parchment in the North Riding Quarter Sessions bundles for 1741, 1742, 1743, 1744, 1745, 1749, 1762…; material objects) of the past, so it is a puzzle that historians in general write less about the flotsam that ends up in archives than do social and cultural theorists. The long and short of this peroration is that historians' testimony to their bewildered, frustrated encounters with the law, past and present, may be seen as a form of autoethnography as much as self-indulgence.

William Blackstone personified his first love as Poetry, made the 'Companion of… [his] tender age' into a Muse and the 'Gay queen of Fancy, and of Art'. He did not personify history (not his brief; he had yet no doings with history), but he did something with law in the 1740s. In his poem, in a secret shade sits a 'venerable maid' who, by attributes of mind rather than of person (she's very *old*) becomes justice towards the poem's end. Here, in *History and the Law*, history's love of law *is* personified – as the odd historians who have loved it. It is time to set off on the zigzag path of this love. It passes through many novels and hybrid forms of literature, high and low; through other, humbler forms of writing: letters fictional, real and threatening; instructional literature and literature for children. We shall start with two modern historian's law troubles – expressed *in* letters – letters *about* other, legally threatening letters. We can see E. P. Thompson's difficulties with eighteenth-century English law as the other face of love (exasperation, incomprehension) which also inscribed the relationship between two historians (Thompson and

---

[82] Kenneth Bartlett, *The Experience of History*, Wiley, Malden, MA, 2016, pp. 119–35; Michael Oakeshott, *Experience and Its Modes*, Cambridge University Press, Cambridge, 1986; Joan W. Scott, 'The Evidence of Experience', *Critical Inquiry*, 17:4 (1991), pp. 773–97; Peter Icke, *Frank Ankersmit's Lost Historical Cause: A Journey from Language to Experience*, Routledge, London, 2011; John Tosh (ed.), *Historians on History*, 3rd ed., Routledge, Abingdon, 2018, pp. 285–314.

his elderly research assistant, Edward Dodd). We then move to the letters ('lawyer's letters') purchased by some working and middling-sort people to further their own interests at law and in everyday life. Understanding lawyers' letters as a type of threatening letter makes the law-material Thompson and Dodd worked on in the 1960s and 1970s easier to interpret than it was for them. Chapters 3, 4 and 5 of this book concern women and the law – the law as promulgated by the high courts and as experienced in the everyday lives of women of all sorts, including the writers who created characters and plotted their stories by the idea of law, equity and *coverture*. Chapters 7 and 8 trace the journey of philosopher and novelist William Godwin from hating the law (as a philosopher) to writing about it as a historian in an access of feeling and understanding that was something like love. The end is not a chapter, and not a story: how can history write the law that doesn't happen? Or that hasn't happened yet? Looking backwards from the end, it is possible to read all of it as a comment on the writing of history. History's story *content* may be ziggy, or zigzag (the edict is revoked – the law is repealed – peace turns into war – the revolution fails – everything goes back to the way it was before – new forms of conspiracy and rebellion develop), but history's *form* can't be ziggy, for it is a story; it is some kind of written line of narrative. It is best then, it has been said to me, to read about Edward Thompson's and Edward Dodd's edgy, unequal, uncomprehending relationship with each other and with eighteenth-century law as a kind of index to the love story told in this book. Or as the outer circle of – William Godwin said this – law's endlessness, the way it *never stops*. But you must read as you wish. Of course.

2   Law Troubles: Two Historians and Some Threatening Letters

> To the grave and learned Writers of Histories, my Advice is, that they meddle not with any Point or Secret of any Art or Science, especially with the Laws of this Realm, before they confer with some Learned in that Profession.
>
> *The Reports of Sir Edward Coke Kt. in English, in thirteen parts compleat; (with references to all the ancient and modern books of the law.) Exactly translated and compared with the first and last edition in French … To which are now added the respective pleadings in English. The whole newly revised*, London, 1738, Vol. 3, p. xiii.

Down in the villages of History (in Stephen Dunn's poem), during the long years of mute, resentful conspiracy, did just one person, not exactly brave, but too miserable to think of anything else, borrow a pen from the alehouse keeper and on the back of the King's notice of revocation, write an anonymous, threatening letter to say that: We The People have had enough; *have their number*, them up in the castle – that the day of reckoning will come – that something will be burned – someone killed–? Maybe no one crossed the moat under cover of darkness; maybe some village laundress folds the anonymous letter in among the clean linen, which her friend, working as chambermaid in the royal household, unfolds. That's the only way the Queen Mother will get to see the declamatory written threat that begins: *You ould bich unles you …*

Working on threatening letters (like this invented one) for 'The Crime of Anonymity' (1975), E. P. Thompson had a good deal of trouble with the law, much of it experienced at first hand by his elderly research assistant Mr Dodd.[1] Understanding and misunderstanding eighteenth-century law on anonymous, threatening and malicious communications, dictated the course of research (for both of them) and

---

[1] E. P. Thompson, 'The Crime of Anonymity', Douglas Hay, Peter Linebaugh, John G. Rule, E. P. Thompson, and Cal Winslow (eds.), *Albion's Fatal Tree. Crime and Society in Eighteenth-Century England* (1975), Verso, London, 2011, pp. 255–344;

Thompson's writing up of it. What Thompson published in 1975 has been superseded in many ways, but the 'Crime of Anonymity' remains an important study of threatening letters in their own right, and was the first to discuss an epistolary practice of the poor as a form of legal thinking.[2]

But the law brought both modern historians trouble, in and out of the archive. Edward Ernest Dodd (1887–1981) worked for Thompson from 1964 to 1979, doing much of the legwork for what would become 'The Moral Economy of the English Crowd', 'The Crime of Anonymity', *Whigs and Hunters*, and many chapters of the later *Customs in Common*. In the Preface to the last, Thompson thanked 'the late E. E. Dodd, who undertook many searches for me in the Public Record Office', not mentioning here Dodd's work on the *London Gazette* and its weekly notices offering rewards for information about writers of anonymous threatening letters. Dodd worked on the back-files of this official government 'newspaper' in the British Museum Reading Room and in the Public Record Office (PRO), Chancery Lane (now The National Archives [TNA] at Kew). At the PRO he also called up the Home Office files in which the original letters, forwarded by dismayed magistrates and citizens were deposited, after a transcription had been sent to the *Gazette* printing office. In these files are also anonymous threatening letters which were *not* transcribed and *not* 'gazetted'. Dodd provided Thompson with his own transcriptions or photocopies (xeroxes, in the language and technology of the day) of some of these; Thompson made his own choice of what to discuss in 'The Crime of Anonymity'.

Dodd and Thompson wrote to each other about anonymous letter-writers of eighteenth-century England. They opened the letters of eighteenth-century writers and recipients for a wider view on

257 for Dodd. The correspondence (1964–1979) between E. P. Thompson and E. E. Dodd is deposited in Warwick University's Modern Record Centre. It was used for Thompson's *DNB* entry: John Rule, 'Thompson, Edward Palmer (1924–1993)', *Oxford Dictionary of National Biography*, Oxford, 2004, accessed 17 January 2017. This chapter is a reworking of 'Threatening Letters. E. E. Dodd, E. P. Thompson and the Making of "The Crime of Anonymity"', *History Workshop Journal*, 80:2 (2016), pp. 50–82.

2 For recent accounts of the anonymous, threatening letter, Carl J. Griffin, *The Rural War: Captain Swing and the Politics of Protest*, Manchester University Press, Manchester, 2012; Kevin Binfield, *Writings of the Luddites*, Johns Hopkins University Press, Baltimore and London, 2011; Lowri Ann Rees '"The Wail of Miss Jane". The Rebecca Riots and Jane Walters of Glanmedeni, 1843–1844', *Ceredigion*, 15:3, 2007, pp. 37–68; Robert Lee, *Rural Society and the Anglican Clergy, 1815–1914. Encountering and Managing the Poor*, Boydell Press, Woodbridge, 2006; Stephen Randolph Gibbons, *Captain Rock, Night Errant: The Threatening Letters of Pre-Famine Ireland, 1801–1845*, Four Courts, Dublin, 2004.

eighteenth-century law and society. They wrote letters to each other about letters. It was good fun (maybe only a historian's kind of fun) to work on documents (letters exchanged between two historians) that had eighteenth-century letters as their topic. This is not a claim that eighteenth-century threatening letters were the same kind of written artefacts as the typed letters Edward Dodd put into a Richmond post box in, say, 1971 addressed to Thompson's Worcestershire home. A letter communicating the information that a farmer's barns would be fired in, say, 1795 unless the price of grain be reduced in the neighbourhood, was a one-off statement of threat. No one *replied* to a threatening letter; Thompson and Dodd, on the other hand, conducted a correspondence: an exchange of letters over fifteen years. Reading the two sets of documents (letters) together, focuses attention on the ways in which writers, whether they be angry and hungry eighteenth-century agricultural workers or twentieth-century historians, present themselves to their readers; the *personae* they display; the knowledge they take for granted in the recipient; and how they tailor their requests, demands and instructions to the knowledge, including law-knowledge, they presume the other to possess. Letters are acts of communication that convey more than the words penned or typed on the page. That is their value as historical documents.

The Thompsons and the Dodds had known each other in the 1950s when they lived in Halifax and Bingley, respectively. The preface to Dodd's *Bingley: A Yorkshire Town Over Nine Centuries* (1958) acknowledges the help of 'E. P. Thompson (and Mrs Thompson)'. In retirement from his post as classics master at Bingley Grammar School, Dodd produced a steady stream of local history, published in book form and in the journal the *Bradford Antiquary*. One pre-war publication had been *A History of the Bingley Grammar School, 1529–1929*.[3] But he remained uncertain about his own abilities as a historian; perhaps he felt the diffidence that comes from thinking about the ownership of history and the right to write any but one's own: 'it may be thought that the best historian is not one who has made his home in Bingley

---

[3] E. E. Dodd, *A History of the Bingley Grammar School, 1529–1929*, Percy Lund, Humphries, Bradford, 1930 (for Dodd's call for information, *Times Literary Supplement* 1435, 1 August 1929, p. 607); 'Bingley Enclosures', *Bradford Antiquary*, 7:35, 1950, pp. 293–302; 'Priestthorpe and the Rectory of Bingley', *Bradford Antiquary*, 8:36, 1952, pp. 1–20; *Bingley Parish and Township Records*, Harrison, Bingley, 1953; 'Bingley Chantry Endowments', *Bradford Antiquary*, 8:37 (1954), pp. 91–9; 'Two Bingley Postscripts', *Bradford Antiquary*, 8:39 (1958), pp. 194–6; 'Bingley Volunteers in the Napoleonic War', *Bradford Antiquary*, 8:39 (1958), pp. 209–12; *Bingley: A Yorkshire Town through Nine Centuries*, Harrison, Bingley, 1958; 'Alarm at Elland', *Bradford Antiquary* 12 (1964), pp. 124–30.

for not much more than half his life', he wrote in the preface to his history of the town; 'an "off comed 'un" cannot share the intimate traditions which the Bingley-born man inherits'.[4] He was active, locally and nationally, in Labour and Fabian politics; his wife Isabel was daughter of trade unionist John Hill;[5] he was President of the Bradford Historical Society from 1957 to 1959. A reviewer of his 1940s work on the colonial question thought it would appeal to 'the intellectual element of the left wing', and that is how I have thought of him, reading his books, articles, pamphlets and letters.[6]

The Thompsons and the Dodds could have met each other anywhere in the left-ish landscape of the West Riding, but it is likely to have been in Bingley, where the Dodds lived. Thompson taught Bingley adult education classes in literature from 1949 to 1952; Dodd was probably one of his students. Andy Croft discusses the Bingley classes in his account of Thompson as literature tutor, his moaning about the absence of 'proper' workers from the classroom – full as it was of housewives and retired schoolteachers, not the miners he would really have liked to teach.[7] A letter from Thompson is the first in the correspondence, dated September 1964, written from Halifax where the Thompsons were still – just about – based, to Edward Dodd, now relocated from

[4] Dodd, *Bingley*, p. viii.
[5] Alastair J. Reid, 'Hill, John (1863–1945)', *Oxford Dictionary of National Biography*, Oxford, 2004; accessed 27 February 2016. John Hill died at Bingley in 1945. His daughter Isabel (Isa) was surprised not to find her father in the first volume of *The Dictionary of Labour Biography*; Warwick Modern Records Centre (WMRC) MSS 369/2/76, EED to EPT, 16 August 1974. He *did* appear in volume 3 with acknowledgement to Mrs Dodd for information supplied; but the couple were disappointed with all of them. After a trip from Richmond to Kensington to read the second (his local library wouldn't buy it for them), it appeared to Mr Dodd *to be as lacking in plan and proportion as the first one*. MSS 369/2/78, EED to EPT, 30 October 1974.
[6] 'Some Colonial Questions' (Review of *Four Colonial Questions: How Should Britain Act?*), *Times Literary Supplement*, 2245 (10 February 1945).
[7] Andy Croft, 'Walthamstow, Little Gidding and Middlesborough: Edward Thompson the Literature Tutor', *Beyond the Walls: 50 Years of Adult and Continuing Education at the University of Leeds, 1946–1996*, Richard Taylor (ed.), University of Leeds, Leeds, 1996, pp. 144–56; David Goodway, 'E. P. Thompson and the Making of *The Making of the English Working Class*', idem, pp. 133–43. Also Peter Searby and the Editors, 'Edward Thompson as Teacher: Yorkshire and Warwick', *Protest and Survival: The Historical Experience*, John Rule and Robert Malcolmson (eds.), Merlin, London, 1993, pp. 1–23. I am grateful to Alex Hutton for speculations about the Thompsons and Dodds in West Yorkshire. Alexander Hutton, '"Culture and Society" in Conceptions of the Industrial Revolution in Britain, 1930–1965', PhD thesis, University of Cambridge, 2014, pp. 131–73, 207–310. For Thompson's West Riding years, Clancy Sigal, *Weekend in Dinlock*, Secker and Warburg, London, 1961, pp. 82–3; Carolyn Steedman 'A Weekend with Elektra', *Literature and History*, 6:1 (1997), pp. 17–42.

Bingley to Richmond, London. Perhaps they had recently run into each other in the British Museum Reading Room, or at the PRO. They are both working on legal records. Thompson knows that Mr Dodd (as he is here addressed) is working on Assize records; Thompson has found the notes he provided enormously useful; he reports that he has all the necessary materials for some sort of general article or two on prices, forestalling and popular attitudes to both.[8] He has been working in the British Museum Reading Room and spent his own PRO day on William Blake and the charge of sedition made against him 1803. He enclosed his notes for Mr Dodd's interest.[9]

Two working historians wrote to each other in 1964 and renewed some kind of acquaintance. Their first meeting in, say, 1950, in, say, Thompson's tutorial class had been between a 26-year-old and a man of 63. In 1964 they were aged 40 and 77 respectively. The age-gap goes some way to explain the form of their address. Thompson's first letter was to 'Mr Dodd'; Mr Dodd replied to 'Dear Edward'. A year later he wrote *Dear Professor Thompson That, I take it, is the dignity you have attained in the University of Warwick.*[10] From the Warwick School of History Thompson replied: *NO I am NOT a Professor, and the more I see of them the more determined I become not to become one.*[11] Then, after a two-year gap in the correspondence Mr Dodd became 'Dear Ernest', and after another year had passed Dodd replied to 'Mr Thompson'.[12] *I thought we had got as far as 'Ernest' and 'Edward' terms? I was delighted to see you in the P.R.O. on Monday and sorry we were both in such a rush,* responded Thompson.[13] A formal style of address implied no lapse of friendship, replied Mr Dodd; he grew up with the curious English avoidance of christian names *to the extent that at home my brothers and*

---

[8] In this chapter, all quotations from letters, including those between Thompson and Dodd, are set in italics; I believe this makes for easier reading. It was eighteenth-century practice to set reported speech and quotation in italics: transcriptions of anonymous threatening letters in the *Gazette* were italicised. Speech marks were a later innovation. For eighteenth-century theories of punctuation, Carolyn Steedman, 'Sights Unseen, Cries Unheard. Writing the Eighteenth-century Metropolis', *Representations* 118 (2012), pp. 28–71.

[9] WMRC, MSS 369/1/1, EPT to EED, 16 September 1964. Dates in brackets were inserted by either Dodd, his family, or by WMRC archivists (this by Dodd). There was no need to do this with Dodd's letters for he was meticulous in dating documents; there is a whole file of Thompson's labelled 'undated'.

[10] WMRC MSS 369/2/2, EED to EPT, 10 December 1965.

[11] WMRC MSS 369/1/2, EPT to EED, 20 December 1965.

[12] WMRC MSS 369/1/4, EPT to EED, 13 December 1967; MSS 369/2/3, EED to EPT, 28 October 1968.

[13] WMRC MSS 369/1/5, EPT to EED, 16? October 1968 [misdated].

I called each other by initials, and even now I am generally known by my intimates as E. or E. E.; but if you prefer the contemporary fashion, well and good.[14] From now on he was 'E. E.' to Thompson and Thompson was addressed as 'Edward'. In this chapter I call them EED and EPT: it places them on an equal footing, which I believe both of them (from rather different perspectives) would have appreciated, though here, sometimes, out of respect for his age, EED has been 'Mr Dodd' to me. Like most of us EPT could not really tell the age of older people. *I was amazed to learn from your earlier letter that you claim to be 87 ... I had thought you were a full ten years younger than that,* he wrote in 1974.[15] After discovering EED's age, EPT did not become a different kind of employer, though perhaps more insistent that EED charge for travelling time as well as the hours he put in. He *was* concerned when EED had a fall in January 1973, but appeared to be as blithe about a man in his eighties shimmying up ladders in the PRO – all the hard physical labour of the archive on which Mr Dodd was so eloquent – as he had been three years before.[16]

In the early years of the move to Richmond (Dodds, 1963?) and Leamington Spa/University of Warwick (Thompsons, 1965), Mr Dodd found things for EPT when he was working in the PRO for paying clients, and passed them on, as one interested historian to another. He also had his own research and wanted EPT's advice: *Following a suggestion you once made for possible work of my own I have been going through the HO* [Home Office] *papers for 1824–1829 in the hope of finding a subject. But I have been discouraged by the fact that every pack I asked for was in the hands of the microfilm people ... this seemed to indicate that someone else was working on this period ... I am given occasional small jobs (generally for American ladies!).* Three years later he was still looking for things to do: *I still plod on with bits of work in the P.R.O, mostly unpaid – so you need not hesitate to send along any interesting items to look up, funds or not funds.*[17] A university post and access to research funding enabled EPT

[14] WMRC MSS 369/2/4, EED to EPT, 8 November 1968.
[15] WMRC MSS 369/98/I, ii, EPT to EED, 8 December 1974; MSS 369/1/58, EPT to EED, 11 October 1972.
[16] WMRC MSS 369/2/42, EED to EPT, 16 December 1972; MSS 369/1/65, EPT to EED handwritten note 9 January 1973; MSS 369/2/13, EED to EPT, 4 July 1970.
[17] WMRC MSS 369/2/2, EED to EPT, 10 December 1965; he was also thinking of *writing to Maurice Beresford to see whether he wants any assistance on Deserted Villages.* EED maintained a long-standing interest in this topic; MSS 369/2/2, EED to EPT, 10 December 1965. *I plod on with Deserted Villages when nothing else turns up;* MSS 369/2/19, EED to EPT, 5 December 1971. For Beresford and deserted villages, Christopher Dyer, 'Beresford, Maurice Warwick (1920–2005)', *Oxford Dictionary of National Biography,* 2009, accessed 16 January 2016.

to pay EED as a research assistant. He was a good employer. It was he who first put the relationship on a proper financial footing, writing in 1968 that *this year I do have a budget ... you should charge me the rate for the job ... please do not undercharge.*[18] EED accepted with some alacrity: he would make *the customary charge of 15s an hour.*[19] EPT was punctilious in paying EED, often sending him more than he claimed. *I don't think you charge enough,* he wrote on more than one occasion. He was concerned that EED cost his travel time and bill for it.[20] After Thompson started paying Mr Dodd he asked more directly for things to be done (and done again) and posted off lists of references as instructions rather than suggestions.[21] That it *was* a formal employment relationship (and recognised by both parties as such) is witnessed by EPT's interest in EED's tax status: *ps: Let me know sometime if you get taxed on this. I want to know whether I can claim relief or expences.*[22] The British state had first shown an interest in the employment of a servant's labour and designated it a taxable item in the later eighteenth century. Relief on payment to an assistant undertaking intellectual labour was an extension of eighteenth-century fiscal policy.[23]

In the way of the eighteenth-century service relationship, the employer told much more of his personal life than did the employee, graciously bestowing confidences in an entirely one-way traffic of the self. EPT's letters described family holidays with the children, breaks in Wales with his daughter, a son's illness, visitors *like crocuses* at Wick

[18] WMRC MSS 369/1/5, EPT to EED, 16? October 1968 (misdated as to day).

[19] WMRC MSS 369/2/4, EED to EPT, 8 November 1968. There are no accounts but it is clear that EPT was not the main source of Dodd's post-retirement income.

[20] WMRC MSS 369/1/30, EPT to EED, 25 March 1971; MSS 369/1/39, EPT to EED 7 February 1972; MSS 369/1/40 EPT to EED 15 February 1972; MSS 369/1/67, EPT to EED handwritten note 1 February 1973.

[21] Tim Wales has pointed out to me the difference between Maurice Beresford's acknowledgement of Mr Dodd's work on deserted villages (see footnote 17), and that of Thompson. Beresford outlined Dodd's systematic contribution to the project in The Medieval Settlement Research Group, *Annual Report I*, 1986, p. 11 (available at http://archaeologydataservice.ac.uk/archive); also Beresford, *Deserted Medieval Villages*, London, 1971, p. 71. Dodd evidently contributed voluntary unpaid work, with perhaps reimbursement of out-of-pocket expenses; he was paid by Thompson. Tim Wales thinks that this reinforces the idea that theirs was a contractual relationship.

[22] WMRC MSS 369/1/30 EPT to EED, 25 March 1971; MSS 369/1/62, EPT to EED handwritten note, 13 November 1972, MSS 369/1/84, EPT to EED, 6 December 1973.

[23] Carolyn Steedman, *Labours Lost: Domestic Service and the Making of Modern England*, Cambridge, 2009, pp. 87, 129–65; Carolyn Steedman, 'The Servant's Labour: The Business of Life, England 1760–1820', *Social History*, 29:1 (2004), pp. 1–29. In 1760, William Blackstone adjudged that intellectual work *was* labour; below, p. 110.

Episcopi and the holiday house in Wales, sometimes, it appears to this reader, as an excuse for not having met EED in London as he had intimated he might. There was a long discourse on Having the Builders In just before Christmas 1971 (a nightmare three months as labourer and acting foreman, said EPT). He described his writing life and work routine in a way that EED never did: *Flying between Wales, Worcester, and the Lake District where I must be this week at a Wordsworth Summer School – off in a minute*; creeping downstairs at midnight to write when there were visitors in the house.[24] He kept EED informed about what he was writing and the stage he was at with drafts of articles and books.[25] EED did none of this. It was as late as 1975 that he told EPT that his youngest daughter was *a lecturer, nominally in English, to American troops in Scotland and to the Open University*, and then because he wanted to report that she was deep in the *Making of the English Working Class* and had been thrilled by a lecture Thompson had given (*in Edinburgh?*).[26] Mr Dodd was sharpish, quite often, about EPT's blithe assumption that the whole world was conversant with his: he was pleased to get EPT's postcard in June 1973 – *but its message is a mystery to me – who are Doug and Beattie and should I know them?*[27] When EED wrote about himself he told a sadder tale than EPT's busy one, often recited in relation to his work for an employer.

I enclose notes of my failure wrote Mr Dodd in February 1972, having spent weeks fruitlessly trying to find prosecutions of those who had offended under the Black Act. He spent much time at Thompson's behest on 'The Blacks', and the 'Hampshire Blacks' of *Whigs and Hunters*.[28] Perhaps Kings Bench material might be more rewarding? suggested EPT; *it is difficult to believe that all records of these trials have*

---

[24] WMRC MSS 369/1/35, EPT to EED Worcester Tuesday August? 1971?; 369/1/49, EPT to EED, dated by Dodd as late March 1972.

[25] But only about the historical work. He told Dodd nothing about the political essays, the 'Peculiarities of the English' (1965), the 'Open Letter to Leszek Kolakowski' (1973). I am grateful to Keith McClelland for pointing this out.

[26] WMRC MSS 369/2/85, EED to EPT, 15 April 1975.

[27] WMRC MSS 369/2/53, EED to EPT, 11 June 1973. They were presumably Doug Hay and J. M. Beattie. EPT's card not present. He apologised on this occasion, explaining that *the message about 'Doug' and 'Beattie' got written onto the bottom of the wrong postcard!* MSS 369/1/79, EPT to EED, 13 June 1973.

[28] The Black Act (9 Geo. 1 c. 22) was the 1723 Act of Parliament in response to a series of raids by poachers known as the Blacks. 'Blacks' came from the practice of blacking their faces as disguise when undertaking their depredations. WMRC MSS 369/1/41(1972), EPT to EED, 17 February; MSS 369/2/22, EED to EPT, 19 February 1972.

disappeared completely. He reassured Mr Dodd of the real value of his labours: *here is an example of our co-operative efforts,* he said; he was sympathetic about archives he knew well himself: *You are certainly having a tough time of it* – in KB [Kings Bench] 33.[29] He was generous in praise of hard work: after EED's many days in Surrey Record Office, EPT returned Mr Dodd's notes, not sure that the parchment slips he'd found were the bonds for bail he was after, but [*in*] *any case you are certainly coming up with good material here.* Would he please carry on? – *You don't seem as yet to have located the cases I sent you a note about.*[30] He was aware of the worker's alienation from his labour: *I thought you might like to look at the first draft of the first half only of my Waltham Blacks piece. It may make a bit more sense of all you were doing.*[31] Having read it, EED agreed that it put the cases he had been pursuing into an *intelligible setting.*[32] When EPT sent him an advance copy of *Whigs and Hunters* in 1975, EED replied with self-deprecation: *When I glance over your immense collection of references I realize what a small proportion of the whole undertaking my efforts have been ... the interest of my reading is that all the disconnected ... names now become linked up into one theme – a sort of super-detective story.*[33]

Together and apart, they spent more time working towards *Whigs and Hunters* than they did towards 'The Crime of Anonymity'. For both works, substantial amounts of time were spent (or wasted) in pursuing what legal historians think of as social history's criminal fix. Mesmerized by the criminal law, by the judges making it, the magistrates administering it, the ordinary people becoming felons by breaking it, we have made the same kind of pursuit as EPT, who *longed* to find some writers of anonymous threatening letters *actually prosecuted,* quite as much as he longed for trials of men accused of deer poaching and bark stripping under the Black Act.[34] EPT sent EED haring after trial records in the PRO and Surrey Record Office; he went haring himself in all the country record offices of southern England and the East Midlands.

[29] WMRC MSS 369/1/45, EPT to EED, 7 March 1972; MSS 369/1/46, EPT to EED, 16 March 1972.
[30] WMRC MSS 369/1/53, EPT to EED undated 'Wednesday' (EED, or his daughter, who deposited the correspondence, dated it as 'June/July 1972?').
[31] WMRC MSS 369/1/50, EPT to EED, 26 May 1972.
[32] WMRC MSS 369/2/28 [on reverse], EED to EPT, 21 June 1972.
[33] WMRC MSS 369/2/90, EED to EPT, 5 September 1975.
[34] We were (are?) mesmerized say some, because the 'pre-eminent ... inspirational sources' for social-history research remain 'the classic studies of the "Warwick school"' dating from the 1970s 'which emphasized oppressive features of the administration of justice'. David Lemmings, 'Introduction', *The British and Their Laws in the Eighteenth Century*, Lemmings (ed.), Boydell, Woodbridge, 2005, pp. 3–5.

The making of 'The Crime of Anonymity' can be time-tabled like this: in October 1968 EPT writes about the work EED had done for him on food riots *several years* ago. In November EPT is working on food riots with help of an assistant (not EED) and going over work EED did for him *several years ago.* In January 1969 he writes about plans for a whole book devoted to riots; he mentions material in HO and WO [War Office] at the PRO, and tells EED that he wants anonymous posters, handbills, and letters forwarded to both offices. In May 1969, he first mentions what he calls the *Gazette project*, explaining that *it may seem an unlikely source for the history of the poor but it has recently come to my notice that it is … it became customary … to offer a reward for information leading to the apprehension of the authors of anonymous letters which contained threats to person or to property. In such cases, the letter was often printed in full with the original orthography (in order to aid in the detection of the authors) and if not printed in full, it was fully summarised … All that I have done myself so far is to dip rapidly into odd volumes here and there and flip through …* What he would like from EED is a list of such letters and copies of the more interesting ones, which *clearly have relevance to economic and social protest.* EED can transcribe or xerox, whichever is most convenient. He also asks for notices of rewards offered for information about affrays or crimes *of clear social significance,* especially smuggling or riot; *I can give you an example of how it could be treated taking the first months of the London Gazette, late 1782–early 1783, which I have recently been consulting.*[35] In Thompson's historical imagination, anonymous threatening letters were very closely bound to the idea of popular protest and its legal proscription.

Mr Dodd delivered the goods. In June 1970 EPT reported that *I am now at work on these London Gazette xeroxes and am preparing a paper for a research week which we are having here in early July.* (The paper was delayed; in July one of his children was ill.[36]) He sent his preliminary analysis of the letters to EED.[37] From holiday-time Wales, he writes that when he clears his office at Warwick (he has handed in his notice to the University), he will send EED a string of references which he'd like checked in the PRO. In the meantime, if

[35] WMRC MSS 369/1/10. i., EPT to EED, 21 May 1969.
[36] WMRC MSS 369/1/22, EPT to EED, 19 July 1970. 'Here' was the University of Warwick History School.
[37] WMRC MSS 369/1/19, EPT to EED, 16 June 1970: 'Anonymous Letters and Handbills in Gazette', typescript, 3 pages dated 18 June 1970 by EED, MSS 369/1/20.

EED feels like a change of work, he could go to the British Museum, or to its Newspaper Library at Colindale (BMNL) to see if any of the letters could be traced locally; *the technique would be to limit investigation to the 'rich' years identified in my summary*... that is, 1800–1802, 1766–1768, and 1795–1796.[38] Then in November 1970 EPT's focus appears to shift to riots and rioters, though *I am giving my postponed anonymous letters paper in just over two weeks time, and it would be most helpful if I could locate one or two cases of writers of 'incendiary' letters who were actually brought to trial.*[39] By December 1970 they are both pursuing the prosecution of letter-writers and related riots. In January 1971 EPT mentions a *letter book* – a whole book on the topic. He gives the paper on anonymous letters, which in his account did not go down too well. He is still thinking about riots and anonymous letters written in protest against forestalling, ingrating, and price hiking, though 'The Moral Economy' has already been accepted by *Past & Present*.[40] In July 1971 comes the first mention of *the Blacks*, and by December all work on the letters has stopped. Anonymous threatening letters are not mentioned again until June 1973 when, just back from the United States, EPT reports that he *had a good visit and the Watergate business was fun.* He is writing up eighteen months of EED's (and his own) research, he says: *most of the Blacks is now done bar some checking. The position is that the chapter has now got to be small book length, so that I must contribute something else to the joint book, on 18th century crime. I've decided to work up the anonymous letters into an article. This might require some assistance from you, but I'm not exactly clear what as yet.* Does Mr Dodd fancy swapping the BM for the PRO? There are some *Gazettes* from the 1720s to the 1730s he thinks it worth going through.[41] Then in August he decides that he *will leave the anon. letters on one side for a while*... *and concentrate on tidying up a few outstanding matters regarding the Blacks.* Two pages of instructions accompany this letter.[42]

---

[38] WMRC MSS 369/1/23, EPT to EED, 21 August 1970. Oh, how the heart of anyone who ever worked at Colindale bleeds for Mr Dodd! Colindale involves such a long journey which doesn't leave much of a working day, he writes; research is time consuming and expensive; it costs *so much* to post the full-sheet xeroxes the Newspaper Library provides so he's cut off irrelevant columns. So many issues of provincial papers are missing... MSS 369/2/15, EED to EPT, 20 October 1970 [reverse].

[39] WMRC MSS 369/1/27, EPT to EED, 21 November 1970 (from Lansdowne Crescent, Leamington Spa); EPT no longer had an office at Warwick having left the University at the end of September.

[40] WMRC MSS 369/1/29, EPT to EED, 14 January 1971.

[41] WMRC MSS 369/1/79, EPT to EED, 13 June 1973.

[42] WMRC MSS 369/1/80, EPT to EED, 27 August 1973.

Mr Dodd continues to work on anonymous letters until October 1973, when EPT announces that he has been *very busy writing up my essay on anonymous letters: so you should at least see some of the fruits of that work. My 'Blacks' grew too big for the collective book on crime [Albion's Fatal Tree] ... therefore I am filling the hole left by it in the collective book with the anonymous letters essay ... In the course of working up the anonymous letters a few points have arisen, as they always do. I am enclosing a list of xeroxes required in this connection.*[43] In November 1973 Thompson asks EED to go back to material he collected in 1969: *Since it is one of the only C18 letters which came to prosecution I would like to know about it and the outcome, if possible ...* In December EED pursues the prosecuted in the PRO Assize papers, though there is no word about the letter project all this month, and EPT's attention appears to have turned to enclosure, and rough-music and other forms of popular protest.[44] Both get distracted by other topics: assault on excise officers, Thomas Paine's flight from England... all the way through to July 1975, when EPT announces that 'The Crime of Anonymity' will be out in October.[45] EED read *Whigs and Hunters* but only dipped into *Albion's Fatal Tree*, assuming, he explained, that EPT had less to do with it, there being so many editors.[46]

Once *Whigs and Hunters* and *Albion's Fatal Tree* came out, there was far less for Mr Dodd to do. In August 1976 he reported that he had been keeping himself *busy – or as busy as suits me – with various odds and ends of work*; he had found that his name was on the list of searchers for the India Office Library, which was a wonderful place to work, but it was not much of a job he'd been given; he had *lapsed into the lists for the names of Deserted Villages.*[47] EPT explained that *the fact is I find it difficult to give you exact suggestions and proposals for research when I am not myself closely involved in the research (or writing) myself. When we worked together on the 'Blacks' this was excellent. But just now I am in-between USA and India and find it difficult to settle to any one piece of work ... I agree that it would be difficult to do anything in the India Office Library in such a short time and from such a very general brief.* (He had written earlier to say that in India he might perhaps lecture on eighteenth-century English food riots and their legal dimensions; maybe EED could provide him

43 WMRC MSS 369/1/81, EPT to EED, 18 October 1973.
44 WMRC MSS 369/1/83, EPT to EED, 1 November 1973.
45 WMRC MSS 369/1/102, EPT to EED, 19 July 1975.
46 WMRC MSS 369/2/90, EED to EPT, 5 September 1975.
47 WMRC MSS 369/2/91, EED to EPT, 26 August 1976.

with Indian comparisons...?)[48] In April 1977 EED was still looking for *anything I can usefully do. I shall be glad to have something to keep me busy – even my deserted Villages have deserted me of late.*[49] He did bits and pieces for Thompson, but the pace of work was nothing like that of the Blacks and threatening-letters years. In March 1978 it was too cold to venture out *even if it had been to the Kew PRO, and, to tell the truth I have not yet got broken in to that very magnificent but rather alarming institution with its computers and bleepers* (the PRO had relocated to Kew, close to the Dodds' Richmond home). He mused on his own career as research historian: *I would not deceive myself that after coming to London within reach of the PRO I could have done anything comparable to this and your other recent books. No doubt it was too late anyhow. But had I dreamed that I should have so many years here I might (perhaps!) have made greater efforts to find a subject of my own instead of filling up my time with a lot of bits and pieces.*[50] He was now 91 years old.

Over the years EPT often attempted to talk EED up, imbuing the older man with a sense of purpose and usefulness: a splendid package of xeroxes had arrived in February 1972: *So...fine! And MORE! Dear E. E., you say very kindly 'I find it hard to believe that the information you get is worth this much!' Believe me, it is, abundantly. Please don't forget that if I was to come down and do the same work, I would have train fares amounting to some £5 straight away, and perhaps overnight expenses in London. I think you undercharge. Thank you again! We are really getting somewhere.* Mr Dodd's crumbs of information were *all filling in little white patches of my jigsaw.*[51] *You sound a bit depressed,* wrote EPT in 1974: *I hope this is not the case. It has been a dreary wet summer. You sometimes say that you regret that you haven't got a research project of your own... Well, what about the whole affair in the 1750s about the rights to Richmond Park and Princess Amelia...it would make an excellent article, or even a little book.*[52] He went on to praise an unpublished article EED had completed several years before and shown him, back in 1972. *It is a really good study,* said EPT, *and you must publish it* (forgetting that EED had already tried); *surely there is a good Surrey Local history journal which might be interested?*[53]

[48] WMRC MSS 369/1/110, EPT to EED, 19 October 1976; MSS 369/1/109, EPT to EED, 24 September 1976.
[49] WMRC MSS 369/2/94, EED to EPT, 4 April 1977.
[50] WMRC MSS 369/2/101, EED to EPT, 1 March 1978.
[51] WMRC MSS 369/1/40, EPT to EED, 15 February 1972.
[52] WMRC MSS 369/1/96, EPT to EED, 3 November 1974.
[53] WMRC MSS 369/5/1-2, Art. on Richmond Park by E. E. D: *I once wrote up a short History of the Park, based apart from local tradition, mainly on State Papers, and offered it to History Today, but they didn't want it*; MSS 369/2/26, EED to EPT, 19 March 1972; MSS 369/2/28 [reverse] EED to EPT, 21 June 1972; MSS 369/1/52. EPT to EED, 25 June 1972.

'Little book', 'little bits of a jigsaw', and 'local history journal' were perhaps not much of a comfort to a published historian who had never been
afraid to move beyond the boundaries of history and into new intellectual endeavours, experiencing the feelings that are now seen as an almost
inevitable consequence of old age.[54] In January 1979 a postcard from EPT
ended their correspondence (the correspondence deposited at Warwick):
*I have been down to the PRO myself so please <u>CANCEL</u> that commission. If you
did it, that's fine – I shall still need the copy. But if you didn't, you can leave it
now) Brrrr! Cold!*[55] Edward Ernest Dodd died in 1981.

★★★

Before I knew what I was doing, or what my questions were, I surveyed
the *London Gazette* (now digitised) using the Thompson/Dodd date
boundaries and their search criteria, legible from EPT's preliminary
analysis of June 1970.[56] In 'The Crime of Anonymity' EPT discussed 284
gazetted letters or handbills written between 1750 and 1811. This was
an average of four per year. My count is roughly similar to Thompson's,
though I did not include handbills – varieties perhaps, of the *pasquinade*
that Laurence Sterne did say it was the duty of the historian to consider.[57] I counted letters, addressed and directed to named individuals,
groups, and institutions. If it was found in the street, or impaled on a
burnt stick in a farmer's yard, yet addressed to a person *&c*, then in my
terms, it was a letter. My first search terms (*anonymous* + *threatening*)
were not adequate for digital searching, for I did not yet know about
the multiple legal names for an anonymous threatening letter. I counted

---

[54]   For Dodd's work with the Fabian Colonial Bureau, see E. E. Dodd, 'Reconstruction
in Burma and Malaya', *Four Colonial Questions: How Should Britain Act? Papers
Prepared for the Fabian Colonial Bureau by Col. S. Gore-Browne, Rita Hinden,
C. W Greenridge and E. E. Dodd*, London, 1944; E. E. Dodd, *The New Malaya,
Research Series No. 115*, London, 1946; Julie Pham, 'J. S. Furnivall and Fabianism.
Reinterpreting the "Plural Society" in Burma', *Modern Asian Studies*, 39:2, 2005,
pp. 321–48. For other, earlier political interventions (to which EED brought the
full weight of his historical knowledge – which cannot be said of his work on Burma
and Malaya), Edward Ernest Dodd, '"A Useless Hearing". To the Editor of the
Manchester Guardian', *Manchester Guardian*, 26 July 1922; 'Latin Teaching', *The
Times*, 44471, 5 January 1927.
[55]   WMRC MSS 369/1/4. i, EPT to EED, 13 December 1967; MSS 369/1/120, postcard
from EPT to EED, 23 January 1979.
[56]   WMRC MSS 369/1/20. 'Anonymous Letters and Handbills in Gazette', typescript,
3 pages dated 18 June 1970 by EED.
[57]   See above, p. 15. Pasquinades were satires or lampoons, displayed or delivered in a
public place, not necessarily anonymously.

published *notices* (sometimes three of the same letter), because my focus was on repetition as experienced by readers. When I had the terminology right, I found 623 *Gazette* notices concerning 240 named individuals, groups and institutions that, between 1750 and 1811, received one or more anonymous threatening letter. I began to understand how much legislation, and clerkly, office and departmental practice, local and central, determined their designation.

On average a *Gazette* notice ran for three, not necessarily consecutive, issues. So we are talking about 240 gazetted-letter *recipients* between 1750 and 1811. Writers and recipients were the focus: 240+ writers (singular and plural) and 240 recipients had this experience. Ten of these 240 individuals *&c* received two or more to-be-gazetted letters, but it is the anxiety of the 240 recipients (the majority of them receiving only one letter), their families, their communities, and the reaction of *Gazette* readers as well, that I looked to. Over a half century the *Gazette* published 623 notices concerning the enemy within, fomenting in this way, a particular kind of readerly terror.[58] The *Gazette* was produced three times a week; there were four new notices on average per annum. Terror was made by repetition: 623 over sixty years meant 10 letter-notices a year, enough to make you think that this sort of thing happened every month, all over the county. But '10 letter-notices a year' is as unhelpful as EPT's 'on average 4 per year': what about 1789, when there were 10 notices in the *Gazette* involving three recipients, or 1769, when there was one; or what EPT called the *annus mirabilis* for threatening letters, 1801, when there were 79 notices in the *Gazette*, concerning 35 recipients? There had been 6 in 1799; there would be 14 in 1801, and 23 in 1802. No other year exceeded 1800 for *Gazette* notification of anonymous letters; no other year got near the notification of terror compared with 1800.

We need to take into account the longevity of the printed word, the unequal distribution of the *Gazette* across time and distance, and factors we do not yet know about: how long it was kept, *how* it was read by different constituencies, and its meaning for them as individuals

---

[58] The official history of HMSO suggests a steady circulation for the *Gazette* of between 400 and 600 during the period discussed here. Hugh Barty-King, *Her Majesty's Stationery Office: The Story of the first 200 Years 1786–1986*, London, 1986. But more recently a readership of between 2,500 and 5,000 has been suggested, at least in the early years of the century: Natasha Glaisyer, *The Culture of Commerce in England, 1660–1720*, Woodbridge, 2006, p. 160; H. L. Snyder, 'The Circulation of Newspapers in the Reign of Queen Anne', *The Library* 23, 1969, pp. 206–35. For pre-Revolutionary Atlantic-world circulation http://allthingsliberty.com/2014/02/london-gazette/ and http://founders.archives.gov/.

or groups. In any case, we're talking about *notices* of letters received, inserted in the *Gazette*, not about numbers of threatening letters over a half century. The fluctuations – the years in which there were no notices posted at all – may have something to do with threatening letters in and of themselves, the practice of writing them, their responsiveness to national and local circumstances. But the figures speak most to changing office practice, locally and at the Home Department, local policing considerations ('police' in its broad eighteenth-century sense), government policy and the shaping force of legislation, defining and redefining the *anonymous – threatening – malicious – incendiary – inflammatory* (in any combination of those terms) communications, across sixty years.

Thompson says that 'the *Gazette* was involved only when an official pardon was offered for information leading to a conviction'. He also pointed out that the 'number of letters gazetted gives no constant index to the actual number of letters written'.[59] His categories of analysis (letters expressing 'private' as opposed to 'social' grievance; letters threatening murder, arson, machine breaking, armed rebellion and treason...) served him well.[60] Thompson focused on anonymous letter-writers and the threats they made. He listed categories of recipient in descending order: gentry, manufacturers, tradesmen, millers, office holders (including mayors and magistrates), farmers, clergymen, excise men, and blacklegs. In the first, delayed seminar paper he gave on the topic, he focussed on the letters themselves, though his audience did not appreciate his discussion of epistolarity: *I never succeeded in writing it up properly,* he told EED. It had been *thematically a bit scrappy and critics at the seminar thought that some of the excellent material in the letters might be better used in connection with studies of particular grievances ... rather than as a study on their own.*[61] He followed the advice of the seminar, concentrating on categories of grievance expressed in writing.

Some notices in the *Gazette* described postmarks many miles away from the target's address – their being put into the post office in London and received in Durham, or arriving in London with a Portsmouth postmark. Sometimes, when members of the nobility received a letter, no place was named in the *Gazette:* it was assumed that the Earl of

---

[59] Thompson, 'Crime of Anonymity', pp. 257, 261.

[60] These are most clearly laid out in WMRC MSS 369/1/19, EPT to EED 16 Jun 1970: 'Anonymous Letters and Handbills in Gazette', typescript, 3 pages, dated 18 June 1970 by EED, MSS 369/1/20.

[61] WMRC MSS 369/1/29, EPT to EED, 14 January 1971.

Leicester and Lord Ailesbury *were* their place – their lands and estates – and that the High Sheriff of Cornwall was, in some deep legal and structural sense, the county itself.[62] In the case of the last, in January 1757, John Sawle Esq's correspondents addressed him in his role as chief magistrate of Cornwall: *We the poor this Niborhood do desire you as you are chief at present that you will pertishon His Majesties Grace to hinder the Maltstors that they make no more Malt for this Year for we can live without Drink but not without Bread, for Wee must all Starve if not Timly prevented.*[63] Most recipients were addressed in population centres. In Lancashire, for example, all but one belonged to Manchester; recipients in Northumberland were mostly town or city dwellers. All the North Riding addressees belonged to York. This was not only to do with the location of employers and businesses, but with the internal legal organisation of a county: magistrates and poor law officials were addressed in the population and policing centres where they operated and sometimes lived.

Some counties (and London) experienced the anonymous threatening letter across all Thompson's years of investigation. Watford curate Revd Windham Jones received Hertfordshire's last reported letter in 1800: *SIR, August 20, 1800. I take this opportunity to write these few lines as I think they may be of service to you but take me neither for friend nor foe but it is to inform you that … in a Weeks Time we will serve you as we said in our last letter you do not quit this town or alter your perceeding you may depend upon it that there is a conspiracy against you to take away your Life and I am one who has been of the Gang.*[64] Hertfordshire's first anonymous threatening letter had been reported in the *Gazette* in 1757, informing William Buckley Esq of Oxey near Watford that his Court of Requests

---

[62] *London Gazette*, 8 December 1753, Issue 9327, p. 2; 18 December 1753, Issue 9330, p. 2 ; 22 December 1753, Issue 9331, p. 2; 1 January 1754, Issue 9333, p. 3; 1 January 1754, Issue 9334, p. 2; 5 January 1754, Issue 9335, p. 2: six notices about two letters received by Thomas, Earl of Leicester (only the second gazetted): *we [don't] want French Men, nor Irish men; if Mr Stockdale ant taken down in a Weeks Time we will serve you as we said in our last letter*). *London Gazette,* 6 October 1804, Issue 15743, p. 1256; 9 October 1804, Issue 15744, p. 1271; 13 October 1804, Issue 15745, p. 1285: three notices concerning one untranscribed letter received by Lord Aylesbury at Tottenham Park Wilts.

[63] *London Gazette*, 25 January 1757, Issue 9656, p. 2; 29 January 1757, Issue 9657, p. 2; 1 February 1757, Issue 9658, p. 2: three notices concerning one letter received by John Sawle Esq., High Sheriff of Cornwall. Writers implore him with their tears to do what they demand in regard to the maltsters; if Sawle *lies sleeping* they will burn his house and those of all the county magistrates.

[64] *London Gazette*, 6 September 1800, Issue 15291, p. 1021.

was carried on *in a very base manner.*[65] Lincolnshire experienced its only gazetted threatening letter in 1799 when Mr Butler, Post Master at Market Deeping, was asked to pass on to *Mr. Myers [at] Eddenham near Bourn* the statement that *Sir, H. Hardy is innocent and if you don't let her out of Jail, we will set your House on Fire and all There were two of us concerned and before the Year is out, we will fire him* [the presiding magistrate in Hardy's case] *and his old thatched Buildings and all He is a Rascal You cannot find us out, and we will do his old thatched Place soon Doctor Holland is a Rascal ... Yours &c. Tinker Bob. We will do his old thatched House Bob. I swear. I swear.*[66] Mr Myers and Dr Holland were magistrates; this was the type of letter that EPT classified as attempting 'to influence the course of justice' though he did not quote from or cite this particular one.[67] In Worcestershire the first gazetted incident of a threatening letter received was in 1761, when the Revd Mr Brookes of Over-Arely was told that *If the Lord Lyttelton had sent the Devil among Us, We could not have a worse Enemy than We have of You. For, what Business had [you] To go to Stafford for a Levy, when it was to be a Turnpike Road, but to run the Parishioners to Charges, And if You do not turn up the Office to another Man next Spring, or behave better in it amongst the poor Labourers than You have done, there will come a blue Plumb (that is, I suppose, a Bullet), out of some Hedge; between Arely and Churchill.*[68] The last gazetted letter in the county was in 1773, when events in Carmarthenshire caught up with a gentleman now resident at Boycott near Droitwich: *no Inglish or french man Should Coume into our Cantry to taike our Land fran us We will if You and all the Sirvents ... [do not] go direactly go from Pen-de-rimark Burn Your House Murder You and all the English famely ... and kill Your Cattle*

[65] *London Gazette*, 31 December 1757, Issue 9753, pp. 2–3. For Courts of Request, below, pp. 69–70.

[66] *London Gazette*, 19 November 1799, Issue 15205, p. 1200. Repeat notice 22 February 1800, Issue 15233, p. 187.

[67] WMRC MSS 369/1/20. The accompanying letter (MSS 369/1/22, EPT to EED, 19 July 1970) also thanked him for his last-minute spurt with the *Gazette*. This had occupied Mr Dodd for a full month. MSS 369/1/19 EPT to EED, 16 June 1970: *The finds which you made in this last batch, make me interested in pressing forward enquiry for just a few more years;* maybe, if EED was not weary, he might go up to 1820? If an index got EED to the letters themselves – quickly please – then he would be most interested.

[68] *London Gazette*, 13 January 1761 Issue 10070, p. 2. EPT did not cite this letter. For 'the wicked Lord Lyttelton' and the pious one, his father, referred to in this letter, Christine Gerrard, 'Lyttelton, George, first Baron Lyttelton (1709–1773)', *Oxford Dictionary of National Biography*, Oxford, 2004, accessed 1 February 2016; John Cannon, 'Lyttelton, Thomas, second Baron Lyttelton (1744–1779)', *Oxford Dictionary of National Biography*, Oxford, 2004, accessed 3 March 2016. The writers thought the first baron not so good.

if You Dont all go oute of the Contry in a few days you shall be murdered By god and Your houses sett on fire and Youre Horses all killed by us and a 100 more brave Welch men. Signed by *A Welchman*, it had been left at a 'Dwelling-House at Panderimark'. Forwarded to Worcestershire, it was gazetted (three times) as a Worcestershire incident.[69]

For insertion in the *Gazette*, a letter had to be taken seriously enough by a secretary of state for an official pardon to be offered to an informer. But there is the disposition of different secretaries to take into account: Thompson reported the Duke of Portland several times advising caution in the publicising of terror, being not inclined to 'to give any notoriety to it, by an advertisement in the *Gazette*' ('Crime of Anonymity' 262). Gazetting a letter involved delay (the majority of notices appeared three weeks after it had been received and reported), and money. An insertion cost £3 3s 6d in 1800, says EPT. Also, as he pointed out, recipients might insert their own notices of reward for information in the local press; they might ignore the letter and hope for the best; an unknown number of recipients may have coughed up when money was demanded, or done something of what the writers wanted ('Crime of Anonymity' 261). In my count of 240 named individuals (and groups of people and institutions) receiving one or more such letters between 1750 and 1811, 8 received (in my reading) straightforward demands for money. Perhaps these were subsumed in EPT's category 'clearly blackmail or private grievance'.[70] Under the Theft Act 1968, Section 21, the criminal offence of blackmail consists of making an unwarranted demand with menaces, with a view to making a gain or causing a loss. But 'blackmail' did not mean this in the eighteenth century and the term was not then used in the way Thompson used it in 1975.[71]

***

---

[69] *London Gazette*, 17 August 1773, Issue 11380, p. 2; 21 August 1773, Issue 11381, p. 2; 28 August 1773, Issue 11383, p. 1.

[70] As in WMRC MSS 369/1/19, EPT to EED 16 Jun 1970: 'Anonymous Letters and Handbills in Gazette', typescript, 3 pages, dated 18 June 1970 by EED, MSS 369/1/20.

[71] Richard Burn, *A New Law Dictionary: Intended for General Use, As Well as for Gentlemen of the Profession. By Richard Burn, Ll. D. Late Chancellor of the Diocese of Carlisle. And Continued to the Present Time by John Burn, Esq. His Son, One of His Majesty's Justices of the Peace for the Counties of Westmorland and Cumberland. In Two Volumes*, T. Cadell, London, 1792, 'Blackmail'. But see Anthony E. Simpson, 'The "Blackmail Myth" and the Prosecution of Rape and its Attempt in Eighteenth-Century London: The Creation of a Legal Tradition', *Journal of Criminal Law and Criminology*, 77, 1986, pp. 101–50; Gary Dyer, 'The Arrest of Caleb Williams. Unnatural Crime, Constructive Violence, and Overwhelming Terror in Late Eighteenth-Century England', *Eighteenth-century Life*, 36:3, 2012, pp. 31–56. Also Frank McLynn, *Crime and Punishment in Eighteenth-Century England*, Routledge, London, 1989, p. 141.

Dodd and Thompson discussed their problems with the law and legal documents from different perspectives. EPT designated the research but did only some of it; for the main part he issued instructions to a researcher labouring deep in the dirt of the archive: EED was in the front line of law-trouble. In August 1971 EPT sent EED a long list of instructions to do with Black Act; he typed out details of the law terms (Michaelmas, Trinity, Hilary . . .) which EED had asked for, and without which it is impossible to know *when* anything happened in the law (or at least in the law courts).[72] EED made law-jokes (EPT not at all) – a kind of workplace joke: doing research for Gray's Inn lawyers in 1973 he said they *want translations of a large batch of documents. But they are not apparently in a great hurry. I doubt if lawyers ever are*; he announced finding a proclamation EPT had been searching for with: *I suppose in English law a precedent can be found for anything.*[73] Thompson's own uncertainty about the law sent Mr Dodd on many a wild goose chase. It was his *own* confusion about Assize Circuits, EPT said; he too was unfamiliar with legal documents and *legal jargon*;[74] but – a tentative suggestion – perhaps EED could try King's Bench Crown Rolls on this occasion – ? Also please write to tell him which bundles of KB Precedents he's looked at. He might have a go himself during the Dodds' upcoming holiday. And where *are* these records? At Chancery Lane or the PRO's storage facility at Ashridge?[75] They spent time bemoaning the state of Assize records as many who use them feel compelled to do.[76] *The assize papers are the dirtiest and worst kept I have seen in the P.R.O. – apparently untouched since they came in from the local offices. I am pretty sure they would be impossible to xerox* EED reported in 1969.[77] *I appreciate everything you say about them,*

---

[72] WMRC MSS 369/1/34, EPT to EED, 4 August 1971. EED wondered why he'd asked about the Law Terms in the first place; he had Bond's 'Handy Book', after all. But there were so many problems with dates and moveable feasts when trying to reference documents...This was John James Bond's *Handy-book of Rules and Tables for Verifying Dates with the Christian Era*, Bell and Daldy, London, 1869 (many other editions and imprints). But all the handbooks in the world will not help those who are not lawyers, working on legal records.

[73] WMRC MSS 369/2/56, EED to EPT, 29 August 1973; MSS 369/2/55 [reverse], EED to EPT, 11 August 1973. For law and lawyer jokes, Chapter 3.

[74] WMRC MSS 369/1/7i, EPT to EED, 21 January 1969.

[75] WMRC MSS 369/1/47, EPT to EED, 20 March 1972.

[76] Carolyn Steedman, *Dust*, Manchester University Press, Manchester, 2001, pp. 17–37.

[77] WMRC MSS 369/2/6 [reverse], EED to EPT, 26 January 1969.

replied EPT; but xeroxing was what he wanted: *Indeed, I think that I or Mr Thomas will probably have to do this ourselves.* Was this EPT's own threatening letter? A threat to use a different, more academic and accomplished researcher?[78] Eighteen months later EED reported that he had still not had much success in PRO Assize papers; since the last time he'd worked on ASSI, documents had been cleaned a bit, or dust rubbed in rather than left on the surface; but there were many gaps in the list that EPT had supplied...no Cambridgeshire indictments; he couldn't find any trace of Manchester Assizes for the entire eighteenth century.[79] In 1972, another *pile of the dirtiest imaginable rolls (or packages) poured out, with no sort of distinguishing marks.*[80] Thompson (and perforce Dodd) spent a very long time with ASSI trying to find those prosecuted for riotous and seditious behaviour and for writing threatening letters, much hampered by not understanding (who does?) the legal and clerkly filing system that dictated the location of their deposition in the PRO.[81] Mr Dodd appeared frustrated when EPT moved back to the early eighteenth century for what would become *Whigs and Hunters*, writing in February 1972 that *I confess I find your wealth of suggestions a bit confusing...You give me too much credit for facility in reading these things*: the script was the worst he'd ever encountered; he had to make up stories about the letter-forms in order to decipher it.[82] He wrote about the problem of annotating legal formularies; he simply didn't know enough: *My difficulties apply in greater to KB*, he said; he was not as familiar with King's Bench records as he was with ASSI.[83]

Law trouble was compounded for EED by the archive being a place of work in a way it wasn't for EPT, however many local record offices he visited (and he did visit many during the fourteen years of

---

[78] WMRC MSS 369/1/8, EPT to EED, 30 January 1969. For Malcolm Thomas, Dorothy Thompson (ed.), *The Essential E. P. Thompson*, New Press, New York, 2001, p. 423; 'Crime of Anonymity', p. 257, Note 3; 'Malcolm Thomas (1945–2010)', *Library of the Society of Friends Newsletter*, 7 (2011). Thompson wrote several threatening letters of resignation to the Warwick Registrar this year: Carolyn Steedman, 'Social History Comes to Warwick', Miles Taylor (ed.), *The Utopian Universities*, forthcoming.

[79] WMRC MSS 369/2/14 [reverse], EED to EPT, 24 November 1970.

[80] WMRC MSS 369/2/21, EED to EPT, 16 February 1972.

[81] For a brilliant discussion of this point, by one who does understand, Paul D. Halliday, 'Authority in the Archives', *Critical Analysis of the Law*, 1:1, 2014, pp. 110–42. I am very grateful to Paul Halliday for drawing this article to my attention.

[82] WMRC MSS 369/2/20 [reverse], EED to EPT, 11 February 1972.

[83] WMRC MSS 369/2/25, EED to EPT, 18 March 1972.

their correspondence).[84] Deterioration of Mr Dodd's working conditions during several seasons of discontent added to the difficulties: *There was a blackout at the PRO yesterday (I suppose one ought to sympathise with the miners, but it is difficult when it affects one's own convenience!).* There was enough daylight to write by, but warnings that Monday and Thursday were likely for further cuts.[85] *The PRO was closed 'owing to industrial action',* he wrote in 1974, *which perhaps might be translated as 'non-industrious inaction' (with which it is not so easy to be sympathetic when it involves oneself).*[86] There were eternal problems with reproduction services and he didn't like clogging up storage space in the PRO with documents that EPT might or might not want, and that he might or might not arrive to consult himself.[87] *Things are not too easy in the Round Room* [of the PRO]: *there are now some new assistants who are very willing to oblige but not terribly intelligence* [sic], he reported in July 1974.[88] There was the fiction put about at the Newspaper Library *that their whole stock of pre-war provincial papers was destroyed in the 'blitz'.*[89]

He worried about the mail – *our reformed post office is not yet infallible* – but more about EPT's tendency to put the wrong address on the envelope and his failure during the Warwick/Leamington years to provide him with a home address.[90] EED was told clearly what EPT was after: *anonymous letters which contained threats to person or to property ... Occasionally, you get anonymous letters which appear to have nothing more than personal grievance behind them-threats by servants against employers and so forth. Unless it is clearly a trades dispute or economic grievance, I think there would be little point in transcribing or xeroxing.*[91] But EPT's tendency to veer off into riot and popular disturbance was as

---

84 WMRC MSS 369/1/36, EPT to EED, 1 December 1971; MSS 369/37 ii, EPT to EED, 14 January 1972?; MSS 369/1/39, EPT to EED, 7 February 1972?; MSS 369/1/45. EPT to EED, 7 March 1972.
85 WMRC MSS 369/1/40, EED to EPT, 11 February 1972 (on reverse of MSS 369/2/21) EPT to EED, 15 February 1972.
86 WMRC MSS 369/2/76, EED to EPT, 16 August 1974.
87 WMRC MSS 369/2/73, EED to EPT, 19 July 1974.
88 WMRC MSS 369/2/75., EED to EPT, 30 July 1974.
89 WMRC MSS 369/2/15, EED to EPT, 4 October 1970. What I remember were Colindale Reading Room request slips returned with a mark against 'destroyed by enemy action during the Second World War'.
90 When EPT left Warwick University in September 1970, he finally provided 'Lansdowne Crescent Leamington Spa'.
91 WMRC MSS 369/1/10. i., EPT to EED, 21 May 1969.

much a factor in EED's working routine as confusing instructions or the opaqueness of the law.[92] *'Knowing your affection for riots, [I] supposed that it might be worth a xerox'*, he wrote of a Privy Council file in January 1973. He was concerned to get it right with Thompson's categories of grievance: whether what he'd found was *of any 'social significance' I don't know*.[93] Then a month later from EPT: No more highway robbery please! unless it is of *social significance*; but he was still interested in smuggling; arson; customs and excise; riot; poaching; and destruction of trees, crops and animals.[94]

★★★

Edward Dodd was the primary reader of the letters during the intense period of work on them (1969–1970); he thought about them and their authors. He had gone through the *Gazette* for 1758 (many letters); 1759 (very few) and 1760 (again frequent). Why this variation? he asked. Was winter a factor? Or just…hard times?[95] *I am copying…* *every* *anonymous letter that I find*, he reported in February 1970. Some of them were *mere attempts to extract money; but it is easier to put such* [in] *for copying than to consider what lies beneath them.* He had seen some *from small shopkeepers apparently in desperate need because of the state of trade…and in any case taking them to the xerox counter is quicker than summarizing them.* He generally summarized affrays unless they could be tied to a threatening letter. *My pace gets slower, as you will have observed, the later* [Gazette] *volumes are so enormous'.*[96] Dodd's speculations were used by EPT in the final version of 'The Crime of Anonymity'. *Do you tink* [sic] *it likely that there were many such letters unrecorded in the Gazette?* EED asked. *Could it be that some cases were dealt with locally and never found their way into the Gazette? I was tempted as I ran over the letters to draw highly conjectural conclusions of my own. Some, I imagined, were the work of hardened professionals following a well-established pattern of unheroic robbery, others of pathetically desperate poor men raking up all the swear-words they knew to intimidate a rich man into handing over a little (but this would cover only your minority of 'private' cases). Then I imagined that with the outbreak of a war the number suddenly dropped, as though both these classes were swept into the*

---

92 WMRC MSS 369/2/42, EED to EPT, 14 January 1973.
93 WMRC MSS 369/2/9, EED to EPT, 27 August 1969.
94 WMRC MSS 369/1/12, EPT to EED, 16 September 1969.
95 WMRC MSS 369/2/10, EED to EPT, 23 September 1969.
96 WMRC MSS 369/2/11, EED to EPT, 11 February 1970.

forces; but this embryo-theory seems clearly disproved by your figures for war years...[97] As a result of EED's labours (and EPT's too) in the BM and the PRO, and the bulky packages of photocopies sent from Richmond to Warwickshire and Worcestershire, EPT found that in 1800 only 25 per cent of letters sent to the Home Department were gazetted, and that after 1812 it became usual to publish the fact of a letter rather than a transcription of its contents ('Crime of Anonymity' 263). The 'originals', especially the minority of letters that did appear in the *Gazette*, were often based 'on copies made by gentlemen or parish clerks of the true originals'. Where he was able to compare the two, they were poorly transcribed, he said ('Crime of Anonymity' 309).

Transcription was only a small part of the passage of a letter from the pen of the writer to a notice in the *Gazette*. The story of the letters (what happened to the letters) has the potential to add to our historical understanding of letters as legal artefacts, produced and read in social space. It is a story of letters gone astray, gone missing in the post, ripped up, secreted in the bodice of many a heroine of eighteenth-century fiction and of real life; read by someone not the addressee; stolen letters; the letter you're after (for it will reveal *everything*) but that you can't see for looking at it, lost in plain sight as in Poe's 'Purloined Letter' (1844). For a letter to be a letter, in the realm of literary theory and in real life, it needs to be read by someone – not by the writer, who will do that anyway, and not necessarily by the addressee. This is what happened to one found in Hanley, Staffordshire, in September 1800. At six o'clock on a Monday morning, John Jenkinson (about 12 years) and William James (about 10) were on their way to work at the glass factory when they picked up a sheet of paper. On arrival, and as neither of the boys could read, they gave the paper to apprentice Robert Barton, who could. He passed it on to William Laney, local attorney. Laney wrote a letter of his own, attaching the anonymous one, to Richard Sims of Shelton (possibly a magistrate, though I have not traced him), who in his turn passed it to Earl Gower, Lord Lieutenant of the county. Gower enclosed it – and the attorney's letter – with his own when he wrote to the Home Office a week after the boys had found it. It had passed through at least six pairs of hands in its journey from Hanley and over six miles from there to Trentham, via Shelton, and thence the 160 miles to London. There, one presumes, it was handled again by secretary of

---

[97] WMRC MSS 369/2/4, EED to EPT, 6 August 1970. The 'tink' is a slip of the fingers on the typewriter keys. Mr Dodd typed *all* his letters to EPT, for which I am very grateful, as his handwritten notes are very difficult to read.

state and undersecretaries, but *not* by copying clerks, messenger boys, Gazetteer (editor) or compositors, for this letter was not gazetted (and not noted by EPT). It was headed 'Birmingham' with (as the National Archives cataloguer notes) the impossible date of 17 August 1780 – perhaps a slip of the pen for 1800–? It warned that the poor would rise up if the price of corn (wheat) did not drop to eight shillings a bushel before November; if not, then on 1st November 200,000 poor would gather in St James's Park – go to the Bastille prison – set the poor souls free – then proceed to William Pitt's – tie him to an ass's tail – drag him through the streets until he was dead. Parliament should consider how a man might feed his family, what with 1s 6d for rent, 5s a stone for flour, 1s 6d a pound for butter and cheese. The authors hope their message will spread rapidly through the country, that all finders will copy and distribute it; that *everyone* will rise up on the appointed day.[98]

Dozens of readers, many copies, long journeys... a letter could also be messed about with in a pub. It was really best not to pick one up, unless it were addressed to you, as in the case of one directed to Mr Manning of Wycombe, Bucks, in 1800. Examined by the mayor (magistrate by virtue of his office), Richard Wright, miller, stated that on 6th October he had been drinking at the Queen's Head when at about 8 o'clock in the evening one Thomas Gardiner, horse keeper, came in and reported that when at Mr Manning's earlier on delivering a parcel, he saw a letter in the courtyard. On his way out he noticed that it had been *opened by some person present and read.* He had brought it to the pub. A few minutes after he'd told his story, a Mr Cumings came into the bar, had a look at it, and immediately sat down to make a copy. Then Wright sealed up the letter – with a seal belonging to Lord Carrington's steward. He just happened to have this on him, for it had been left with the watch the steward was having repaired. (Why Wright had it, and not Ball the local watchmaker, also present, I do not know. The mayor and the town clerk knew exactly who all these people were.) Wright had been going to put the sealed letter in the post, but then suddenly thought it better to take it back *to Mr Mannings and threw the same in...* [his] *yard where Gardiner informe'd him he found it. [B]eing asked why he carried it back to Mr Mannings and not delivering it himself, said he feared Mr Manning would have imagined the said Examinant was concerned in writing the said Letter, or causing the same to*

<hr>

[98] TNA HO 42/51/55, Folio(s) 126–128B, 13 September 1800. This can be read as a rent-a-letter job. Or it could be display of a fine politico-historical sensibility in which tropes of cataclysmic historical events are used to interpret current circumstances.

be written.[99] A farrago, thought mayor and town clerk: *Cummins is sus-pected of being the writer of the letter and Wright of throwing the letter into Mr Manning's courtyard.* In that pub, one might note, *everyone* knew about letter writing, the law concerning it, and the postal system, offi-cial or not. The letter was gazetted and noted by EPT for its appeal to a 'moral code of charity, grounded upon the Gospels'.[100]

But other magistrates and officials might not take much notice of a summer season of threatening letters in the locality – after an initial panic and transcription of one of them for submission to the Home Office (by pony express). This is what happened in Bristol in 1791, when Mayor John Harris wrote a second time to say that despite the receipt of further such letters in the city, the magistrates and constables had been very active in their several wards and he now had *the happi-ness to acquaint you that no sort of Disturbance has taken place*; the troops ordered to hold themselves in readiness in Marlborough and Devizes against trouble in Bristol could now be redeployed.[101] The Home Office been alarmed enough to order a movement of troops: *The terms of the anonymous Letter you have transmitted to me, and the mode in which it was conveyed to you are of a nature to create a serious apprehensions* [sic] *of what is therein threatened*, wrote Secretary Henry Dundas the day he received it.[102] Perhaps after that, the letter was read by no one (not EPT, not EED), until a cataloguer perused it prior to digitisation in the 1990s.

A magistrate might be in two minds about what the letter brought to him actually *was*: *I have enclosed a letter for your inspection which was found – late on Friday last – on the Steps of a Dwelling House & Shop*

[99] From John Charsley, Town Clerk of Wycombe, Bucks forwarding the examinations of Thomas Wright, Richard Wright and Matthew Wood concerning an anonymous threatening seditious letter directed to Mr Mannin 23 October 1800: TNA HO 42/52/121, Folio(s) 292A.

[100] Thompson, 'Crime of Anonymity', p. 302; *London Gazette*, 15301, 11 October 1800, p. 11723; 15302, 14 October 1800, p. 1185: *Sir whe have Long Considered the great Evil and hardships of the dreadful times Butt Wee find itt Chifly to loy among Rich farmers and Mealmen inrechin them Selves at the Expence of the Lives and distreses of the poore yo nede not Call out your You men ... on Market Day for thea'r will be no Rioting in Wycombe whe have taken another meathod We think it best to priveatly to dispatch a few of the leding Villins an that veary soon unless an alteration in the nesaseary of Life–, I have you to take Care of your self.*

[101] Four letters and enclosed threatening letters, dated 21st, 22nd, 22nd July, 10th September 1791: TNA HO 42/19/48, Folio 233; HO 42/19/50, Folio 238–39.

[102] The letter enclosed with Harris's first: *(COPY) ... – There is Sir at this present moment upwards of 900 Men mostly all of the same degree as myself working mechanics &c & we shall by Monday next joined by greater number from Birmingham & Taunton – We are all firm & steady ... your life depends on your secersy – adieu much Respected Sir your Hble Servt Bristol 21 July 1791 Mr Harris May of Bristol.*

belonging to one ____ Fallows, wrote Revd Bancroft, from Bolton Le Moors, Lancashire, in 1799. *Whether it be a mere jeu d'esprit for the sake of creating alarm, or it be some mysterious arrangement of some Insurrection plan, you will be better able to distinguish. If it is (as I first believed) unmeaning and harmless, you will excuse the liberty I have taken, if otherwise, I trust I may be instrumental in your hands, to develope their Iniquity.*[103] The Staffordshire clerical magistrate Alexander Bunn Haden of Bilston, on the other hand, had no doubts about the seriousness of what he transmitted to the secretary of state in October 1800.[104] This was not gazetted and not discussed in 'The Crime of Anonymity'. An anonymous letter had been dropped *this morning near the House of Mr Proud of this place. Threatening Letters have been sent to myself and others of this Neighbourhood, which I did not think of consequence sufficient to trouble your Grace with: but the present being a very flagrant one, & conceiving your Grace might think it right to publish it in the Gazette … determined me to trouble your Grace on the occasion.* He enclosed both the original and a copy of the letter *with Explanations by which your Grace will see who the Persons are therein alluded to.* He was a careful magistrate: *The Names written on the back are only signed by Witnesses to identify it in case a Discovery should be made and a prosecution to follow;* for these reasons he requested return of the original. From his annotation we know that recipients were the captain commandant of the Bilston Loyal Association of Infantry, a cornet and a private in the same, a corn dealer at West Bromwich, a miller at Bilston and Mr Proud, *who keeps a House in Bilston for the reception of Lunatics.* The letter addressed *Friend Sam. Proud I am sorry to inform thee thou art an unfinished man … For thee guillotine* [thou shalt be guillotined?] *by the populace, whose applause you lately had but now [lost?] again cursed he who oppress the Poor.* Revd Haden intimated the meaning of what he enclosed: *Provisions are still advancing in price, and the miseries of the Poor consequently increasing in proportion. A Disposition to riot shows itself at times …*

You might be clearer than Revd Bancroft (above) that what was going on was no joke, but still find time to bemoan the letter-writers' spelling and handwriting: in March 1800, Henry Walford, commanding

---

[103] TNA HO 42/47/137, Folio(s) 311–312B. Bancroft had written earlier in April intimating that Mr Fallows was known to be a Jacobin; he could also provide information about a very well organised association of weavers, if required. The letter itself is noted as 'not present'. No reward was mentioned; it was not gazetted; not mentioned in Thompson, 'Crime of Anonymity'.

[104] Letter from Bunn Haden forwarding the original of an anonymous threatening letter 26 October 1800: TNA HO 42/52/108, Folio(s) 265–8.

officer of the Bicester Loyal Volunteers, reported that he had not until recently *apprehended any Probability of Disturbance in this Place but now I am sorry to State to your Grace that on Account of the present high Price of Provisions ... Mischief and Destruction of Property has manifested in a threatening Letter of which I inclose a Copy ... The original is in a bad hand and many Words improperly spelt and not easily legible. Inhabitants* have met several times on the subject and offered a Reward of £100 for the Discovery of the Offenders. The letter is 'not present' in the archive, but it was gazetted (*Here is to all Bieester Gentlemen as calls themselves clever Gentlemen if they don't rise Poor Mens pay as they can live better we will rise and Fight for our Lives better fight. and be killed nor be starved an inch at a time ... if, we don't have more Bread in short time we will have more Blood*), and was discussed in 'The Crime of Anonymity'.[105]

A gazetted letter might be the sole precipitation of a maelstrom of dark threat, insurrection, and religious antagonism. From its one notice in the *Gazette* the letter received by Sir Wilfrid Lawson Bart of Braylon, Cumberland, in March 1799 appears to have been a case of extortion: with a Wigton postmark, it demanded £500.[106] It appeared once, not transcribed but summarized with its warning that if the demand were not immediately met, Lawson's *Buildings should be laid in Ashes in a very short Time*. The *Gazette* notice floated on a sea of unpublished local trouble. A further communication from Cumberland in May revealed that the supposed writer had been apprehended and that he, one George Rook, was about to come to trial. This information came from Humphrey Senhouse, Netherhall, who had received exactly the same letter as Lawson had (his name had not been mentioned in the March *Gazette* notice). Senhouse enclosed another letter received by Joseph Saul, a Quaker and master of a local academy. The letter to Saul, about reforming societies across the county, was from William Rook, brother of the apprehended George. William, said Senhouse, was a failed shopkeeper of Maryport now imprisoned for debt at Liverpool. Senhouse made reference to another threatening letter (also with a Wigton postmark) addressed to Mr Curwen of Workington Hall on 24 January (two months before Lawson and he received theirs) alluding to the secret manufacture of arms, a plan for seizure of all the banks in England, and the intended assassination of the ministry and the royal family. Curwen had been desired to provide £1000 to defray the expenses of manufacturing arms for the purposes

---

[105] TNA HO 42/49/134, Folio(s) 292A–B; *London Gazette*, 15244, 1 April 1800, p. 322; 'Crime of Anonymity', pp. 331–2.

[106] *London Gazette*, 15118, 23 March 1799, p. 278.

of insurrection. Senhouse believed that the January letter, written in the name of the Council Committee of United Englishmen at Workington, was in the same handwriting as those received by him and Lawson; that they had been written by George Rook. Nine other gentlemen in the county were said to have received similar letters indicating *that a Revolution is already effected in the Minds of the Masses of the People, more especially in those of the Peasantry and lower Orders of Men*; that it would be at *the expense of blood*. He advised that cavalry be stationed at Maryport.[107]

And to add to all that might happen to a letter in its passage to a local magistrate or newspaper, to a county town or to London, to the *Gazette*, to many readers along the way, and to the reading historian, two hundred years later – things happened (and continue to happen) to letters in the archive. A letter from JP John Clark, Bulwick Hall, Northants, enclosed copies of an incendiary letter that had been distributed in the parishes of Harringworth and Bulwick in 1800. The letter was gazetted nine days later on 27 December. EPT noted that 'on the envelope, besides the addressee's name, was written "Valentine"'. He enjoyed the letter-writers' dark humour, their dangerous play at the satiric edge of things.[108] But the envelope is not there; just like the letters Clark sent on, it is 'not present'. The Valentine envelope (and the inverse valentine; a proclamation of death, not love) slipped out of the file sometime between 1970 (the last year in which either EED or EPT looked for later eighteenth-century letters in TNA) and the year in which HO 45/55 was digitised.

At the formal level, EED and EPT (unwittingly) reproduced and replicated the chains of transmission characteristic of how letters came to be gazetted in the first place (information transmitted from province to centre, from subordinate to superior; from paid researcher to historian and writer). I don't want to labour this point, as it is so much a consequence of paying someone else to do a lot of your archival research. And, of course, the two processes (how letters got into the *Gazette* and how they got from there into 'The Crime of Anonymity') are not identical – not even very much alike; except that…EPT's insistence that EED only send letters with 'social significance' gives some insight into what EPT *wanted* from eighteenth-century anonymous letter writers and the poor in general: he wanted their own conscious articulation of antagonism towards an inequitable legal system. He was willing to

---

107 TNA HO 42/47/11, Folio(s) 26–31.
108 Letter from John Clark Bulwick Hall, Northants enclosing copies of incendiary letters [not present] distributed in the parishes of Harringworth and Bulwick, 18 December 1800: TNA HO 42/55/55, Folio(s) 125–7; *London Gazette* 15323, 27 December 1800, p. 1455; Thompson, 'Crime of Anonymity', p. 300.

treat threats against people and property as comparable, but only on the basis of the apparent *communal* motives behind the threats. Personal and neighbourly grievance about the inequities of everyday life was far less interesting to him, and he did not ask his research assistant to make legible letters signalling the private, the personal, or the oddly criminal, or even to transcribe them. Those 'personal' grievances were less legible to him, the twentieth-century historian, than they were to many an eighteenth-century magistrate, who knew not how to draw a distinction between our modern categories of 'private' and 'social'.

But whatever it was the historian wanted from eighteenth-century threatening letters and their authors, he described them with an inspired political sensibility – as communications on the vertiginous edge of terror and laughter. He knew their authors *as writers*, with their own understanding of the power of the pen; he knew that hungry, desperate, angry men (and women, I assume, from the historiographical distance of forty years) might yet write a terrifying comedy. Their comedy was in the mode described by Vic Gattrell in his analysis of visual satire in the period: the horror of knowing that what you write is both true (William Godwin's 'Things As They Are') and yet only a picture of the truth, which is *your* truth, not that of gentlemen, farmers and magistrates. The letters acknowledge this in handwriting as do the satires Gattrell discusses in line drawing. Therein lies their terror when read by those who knew nothing – or very little – of those feelings, but whose character and motives are picked apart in writing by a low set of men.[109] I think Thompson's final assessment of the minds that shaped anonymous threatening letters to be the finest piece of writing he ever produced. 'It would now seem', he wrote

> that half the valets of pre-Revolutionary Paris, who followed the nobility servilely through the suave *salons*, were nourishing in their reveries anticipations of the guillotine falling upon the white and powdered necks about them. But, if the guillotine had never been set up, the reveries... would remain unknown. And historians would be able to write of the deference, or even consensus, of the *ancien régime*. The deference of eighteenth-century England may have been something like that, and these letters its reveries.[110]

I also believe he took far too much notice of the 1971 seminar audience which thought that the letters would be better used as an account of particular social grievances, not as a study on their own. Had he

---

[109] Vic Gattrell, *City of Laughter: Sex and Satire in Eighteenth-Century London*, Atlantic, London, 2006.
[110] Thompson, 'Crime of Anonymity', pp. 307–8.

followed his instincts and focussed on the letters, we might have spent the last decades with a history of literacy, of communication, of legal consciousness, – of *mentalité* indeed – much better than the ones we've had. We might now be able to work with *their* own complex understanding of how the law related to their own lives, recognise their elegant abilities in knowing the minds and sensibility of their readers: how they *got* (as in *getting a joke*; as in *having their number*) their readers, and wrote to, for, and at them. There is still time, as Thompson suggested, to get to know better their dreams, their reveries, about things being, not As They Are, but in a different way … *widespread dreaming,/a general hopefulness*. We might also have a foundation of the largest archive of working-class writing in the West, always taking into account the down-at-heel gentlemen, tradesmen desperate for a bill to be paid, under-the-counter attorneys, and organised criminals, who also wrote anonymous threatening letters.

★★★

Edward Dodd's last contribution to the *Bradford Antiquary* in 1964 (long before EPT dreamed up his letter project) had described a 'scrap of paper' found near the bridge at Elland, Halifax, in 1795. Its jacobinical message alarmed the local magistrate and clergyman very much indeed, promising as it did 'a performance' to be announced by the 1790s version of 'telegraph' across the county. Many letters were sent off to Secretary of State Portland describing local panic; the vicar who found the paper knew a man who knew a man who knew a jacobin; magistrate Bushfield thought 'the present situation of this Part of the Country must give serious Alarm to everyone who is a well wisher to the Peace and Prosperity of it'. Dodd described how Portland dealt with consternation in West Riding in three letters, all dated 20 November. In the one sent 'to the energetic Mr Bushfield, he gave what can only be described as a very polite brush-off': Portland suggested that Bushfield pass the whole affair over to Halifax magistrates. EPT read a draft of Dodd's article; in a footnote their differences in reading the scrap of paper was noted: 'Mr E. P. Thompson, who has kindly read the MS of this article, thinks that "there may have been 'rather more fire beneath the smoke' than might be inferred: there is evidence of continuing underground Jacobite organisation in Yorkshire and the story should not be assumed to be merely alarmist".'[111] In his communication with Dodd, Thompson himself presumably put 'fire beneath the smoke' in

---

[111] 'Dodd', 'Alarm'. 'Jacobite' *is* in the published version, not 'Jacobin' or 'jacobin'. Maybe Dodd's or the journal editor's or the compositor's error?

inverted commas, which Dodd reproduced in his footnote. But EED still wrote, *con brio*, the comic turn of the magistrate, the reverend, and the Jacobinical hordes of Elland.

Quiet disagreements between EED and EPT continued throughout their correspondence, and not only in interpretation of threatening letters. In 1972, they had both watched Prime minister Edward Heath on the telly (this was after the settlement of the miners' strike and in the aftermath of Bloody Sunday).[112] EED had mentioned a current context of 'laissez-faire anarchy' (the letter does not survive). *Yes, but...*, replied EPT, *doesn't the beginning of a forward movement often look like this? The thing is that ordinary men and women often have to get moving under some very special sectional impulse: but in the course of moving after this, they bump up against all kinds of other problems and start thinking of politics as a whole. This is what I hope is beginning to happen now... Let's hope so.* Thompson didn't bring this vision to bear on the *mentalité* discussed in 'The Crime of Anonymity' because he insisted so much on the pre-given structuring 'social significance' of letters rather than the 'problems' – often sectional, sometimes personal – they articulated. Neither did the historian's judgement of 'social significance' leave much room to explore those writers' consciousness of the law and the legal structure of their everyday life – which is the topic of the next chapter.

---

[112] Roger Fowler, *Language in the News: Discourse and Ideology in the Press*, Routledge, Abingdon, 1991, p. 240.

3   Letters of the Law: Everyday Uses of the Law at the Turn of the English Nineteenth Century

> Did you go the next morning to an attorney? – Yes, I did. – For what purpose; was it to send the prisoner a lawyer's letter? – Yes … – Did you see the attorney? – No: I saw the clerk.
>
> 'Bridgewater Assizes Rex. On the Prosecution of Eliz. Minson Against R. Bartlett for A Rape', *The Times*, 24 August 1819.

There's not much law around in the villages and hamlets of Stephen Dunn's History. It sounds as bleak and lawless a terrain as the West Yorkshire of *Wuthering Heights*. At one point in the novel, when Heathcliff suggests something very like a forced marriage between the younger Catherine and his son Linton, the servant Nelly Dean cries out, 'Let him dare to force you … There's law in the land, thank God there is! Though we *be* in an out-of-the-way place. I'd inform, if he were my son, and it's felony without benefit of clergy'.[1]

The law of marriage, of women, and the property law inscribing (fictional and real) husbands like Heathcliff will turn out to be important to this book, by and by. It's the only law present up Gimmerton way, where particularly conspicuous in its absence is the Poor Law and the Law of Settlement and Removal, by which many attorneys earned the greater part of their income and which would (were what we're talking about be real) have had a discernable effect on the lives of all the servants and farm labourers who, with Nelly Dean, form the book's Greek chorus.[2] There's a corrupt and high-handed attorney in the picture, but only one resident magistrate in the entire narrative, and that is Mr Linton, resident of Thrushcross Grange and father of the man to

---

[1] Emily Bronte, *Wuthering Heights* (1847), Penguin, Harmondsworth, 1965, p. 305. For an earlier version of this chapter, Carolyn Steedman, 'A Lawyer's Letter: Everyday Uses of the Law in Early Nineteenth-Century England', *History Workshop Journal*, 80:1 (2016), pp. 62–83.

[2] Carolyn Steedman, *Master and Servant: Love and Labour in the English Industrial Age*, Cambridge University Press, Cambridge, 2007, pp. 193–230.

whom the older Catherine makes a disastrous marriage. Let's acknowledge that we're talking about the setting of a novel, not a real place, and that the topography of *Wuthering Heights* may not have been written out of Haworth, West Yorkshire, *at all*; but since the 1920s, its terrain has been obsessively mapped and measured.[3] The village of Gimmerton (just over a mile from The Heights) has an apothecary and a Church of England incumbent, but no attorney, just as no attorney was listed in trade directories of Haworth for the 1830s and 1840s. Attorney Green lives at some distance from Thrushcross Grange (which is itself some six miles from The Heights).[4] Edgar Linton of The Grange lies dying and wishes to change his will; Mr Green is sent for to take instruction and thus prevent Heathcliff from inheriting Thrushcross Grange. But Green has sold out to Heathcliff and delays his journey. Edgar dies before the will can be changed.[5] The attorney appears to live at some (unspecified) distance, for it takes the servants a while to reach his house (Chapter 28), though not as much time as they are required to wait for his return home from some other, also unspecified, business. It is the very old, almost incomprehensible (of speech) Heights servant Joseph who points out these empty legal spaces in the text. He is hardwired into a history of law and society in a way that Nelly is not: he knows who the magistrate is; he knows about Assizes, the travelling circuit of common-law judges (126); he knows what a coroner's inquest is (142); he knows that the doctor and the priest must come running together over the fields when someone dies (84).[6] But not an attorney: there's not one within twenty miles, not in this text.

But law personnel – magistrates and attorneys – were part of the landscape of poor and working people's lives, as when in November 1806 Nottinghamshire magistrate Sir Gervase Clifton of Clifton was visited at his house by one of his poorer neighbours, 'a pauper of the village of Wilford'. William Kirwin was attempting to sort out complicated domestic arrangements within the framework of the law that

---

[3] 'The Reader's Guide to *Wuthering Heights*', www.wuthering-heights.co.uk/, incorporates Charles Percy Sanger's 1926 *Structure of Wuthering Heights*, which explains how Bronte used late eighteenth-century law rather than 1840s' law to show how Heathcliff acquired his extensive property.

[4] For the location of late eighteenth-century attorneys, high and low, see Philip Aylett 'A Profession in the Market Place: The Distribution of Attorneys in England and Wales, 1730–1800', *Law and History Review*, 5:1 (1987), pp. 1–30. Also Pat Hudson, *The Genesis of Industrial Capital: A Study of West Riding Wool Textile Industry c. 1750–1850*, Cambridge University Press, Cambridge, 1986, pp. 211–34.

[5] Charles Percy Sanger, *The Structure of Wuthering Heights*, Hogarth Essays XIX, Hogarth Press, London, 1926.

[6] For the doctor and priest running over the fields in their long black coats, Philip Larkin, 'Days', *The Whitsun Weddings*, Faber and Faber, London, 1964.

governed his family's life. He told the magistrate about his mother-in-law, a widow, currently living in Tollerton. 'She is in a very distressed state', he said; he and his wife wanted her to come and live with them 'so that she may be better taken care of & kept from want'. He had asked the Wilford overseers for permission to take her in but they had refused. The family had tried to help when her husband died: her son (with wife and children) had moved into her cottage on the understanding that 'they would take care of her during her Life & allow her good victuals drinks firing & good cloathing'. Something had evidently gone wrong with that arrangement, but we are not to know what, or how, as the entry in Clifton's notebook breaks off here (as is the case with many items of magisterial business he recorded). But there's enough to see that Kirwin was highly aware of local ratepayers and tensions between parishes in regard to their financial responsibilities under the old poor law: what he proposed would keep his mother-in-law from 'troubling the...parish of Wilford', he said. He told the magistrate that she was financially independent, or at least on marriage she had 'brought a many good with her & such as a beds & other goods'. He knew that a justice of the peace was a point of appeal in the vast, complex edifice of ancient statutory law (poor and settlement law) that dictated the way he and his family lived.

Clifton kept his notebooks between 1771 and 1815, recording some 250 items of magisterial business. Together with his management of the settlement system – and involvement with local overseers' maintenance of their parish poor, unmarried pregnant women naming the father before him at the behest of parish officials, men complaining about parish officers no longer supporting the bastard child they had taken on at marriage to the mother – the poor law business, in its broadest sense, comprised the largest category of law administration in his notebooks.[7] Very early in his magisterial career, in January 1773, the Rempstone Overseer of the poor complained against William Roper, about 'his having behaved himself in a bad and unbecoming manner...on the 19th [when] at night he turned his Wife out of his house and left her to the parish when he was in a parish house – and moreover refused to employ himself in work being appointed thereunto by the Overseers of...Rempstone contrary to Law'. The information about marital

---

[7] Carolyn Steedman, 'At Every Bloody Level: A Magistrate, a Framework Knitter, and the Law', *Law and History Review*, 30:2 (2012), pp. 387–422. Nottinghamshire Archives (NA), Notebooks of Sir Gervase Clifton JP, M8050 (1772–1812), M8051 (1805–1810). Undated entries are referred to by the cataloguer's pagination. For Kirwin, M8050, 17 November 1806.

violence was contained within the complaint about William Roper's infringement of the poor laws. The Ropers were parish poor; they occupied a parish house, work-task was imposed on the husband; their life was entirely bound up in the poor laws: how and where they lived, and their relationship with each other, was inscribed by seventeenth-century statute law. Roper's thoughts on these matters are implied by his refusal to do work-task; William Kirwin appears to have been highly conscious of his status as pauper and attempted make it work for his family, as best he could.[8]

Kirwin and Roper were not in a position to employ an attorney, but they – cheap lawyers and the uses made of them by the working poor (men and women like Joseph and Nelly Dean) between about 1770 and 1830 – are what this chapter is about. Some working people used the law by paying a local attorney to write a letter – to someone who had offended them in some way, or who owed them money or wages. The letters themselves, 'lawyers' letters' as they were called, may have served as one of the models for the anonymous threatening letters of the previous chapter which, for the main part and as far as we can tell, people wrote for themselves.

Three of the following accounts of the lawyers' letter come from Joseph Woolley (c. 1769–1840) framework knitter, or stockingmaker, of Clifton village, Nottinghamshire.[9] Sir Gervase Clifton was his neighbour, his landlord and the local resident magistrate. 'November the 20 [1803]' wrote Woolley, 'mr hopewell sent John holt of Glp ton [Glapton] a Lawyers Letter for a sum of money Seven pound nine shillings and nine pence and they sittled it on the 22 nov'. Mr Hopewell was a farmer, John Holt probably a yeoman framework knitter like Woolley, doing a bit of everything, including carrying and carting. He kept a few cows, as did Woolley's family. He weaves and wavers his way through Woolley's dairies, drinking, fighting, gambling...being the 'fool as he always is when he has had aney bear'.[10] In this letter story, the farmer, rather than the working man, paid for a lawyer's letter; it appears to have been one of the letters calling in debts on behalf of clients which made up a good proportion of provincial attorneys' office business.

---

[8] NA, M8050, 20 January 1773.
[9] Nottinghamshire Archives (NA), Nottingham, DD 311/1–6, Diaries of Joseph Woolley, framework knitter, for 1801, 1803, 1804, 1809, 1813, 1815. These are photocopies made available to researchers. For the originals, of which there are five (the volume for 1809 was deposited in photocopy), DD 1704/1–5. Carolyn Steedman, *An Everyday Life of the English Working Class: Work, Self and Sociability in the Early Nineteenth Century*, Cambridge University Press, Cambridge, 2013.
[10] NA, DD 311/1, 26 December 1801.

For example, the first extant volume of W. F. Wratislaw, Solicitor of Rugby's letter books, which survive for years 1825–1827, shows 159 letters sent out and recorded in the out-letter book. Seventeen of these were 'lawyers' letters' of the type John Holt received, threatening legal action unless something were done by the recipient. To Mr Wilkinson Farmer, Brinkslow, near Coventry, 17 December 1825: 'Sir Unless you call and settle Mr Worth's demand within One week from this time I have his positive Command to force a writ agst you'. On the same day, to Mr Palmer, Maltster, Coleshill: 'I have Extended to you every Indulgence in my power as to Mr Worth's money, and if I don't hear from you by Friday, you must Excuse my arresting you. Yours truly W. F. W'.[11] Seven of the 17 letters were sent on preprinted forms, an office innovation not unique to Mr Wratislaw. The printed letters involved smaller sums of money than those demanded in the handwritten letters, and the addressee was not always 'Mr'. In 1825 the cost of 'writing a letter' – any kind of letter – was 5 shillings; it is not clear whether or not the preprinted demands were cheaper and if there were a scale of charges differentiating between letters written during the ordinary course of managing a client's business and a legally threatening letter. These calculations do not include all the letters in which Wratislaw *asked* for debts to be settled, for himself and others; 'the lawyer's letter' threatened some kind of legal action. The seventeen also involved the metonymic notion that Wratislaw would 'arrest' someone or 'serve a writ' – as if he, personally, were going to do that.

Mr Hopewell from 1803 Nottinghamshire was no more a poor, ordinary user of the law than were the farmers and maltsters of Warwickshire on the receiving end of an attorney's threats. But Joseph Woolley *heard* about the letter Hopewell received, and noted it as of interest; he knew what kind of law was going on here. The second lawyer's-letter story (though the first to be told by Woolley) is much more interesting. Earlier in the year, 'Janeware the 1 [1803] or Some time ther a bout' he recorded that 'Sall Waldram and barker fell out at Langfords [the Coach and Horses public house] and he kicked hir over the Shins and She went to mr tompson for a warrant but his Clark would not Let hir see his mr [master] So She went to see a Lawyer and Got a Lawyers Letter for him and took it to mr Lamberts [where Barker worked] and mrs Lambert sent it over to barkers and when mr Lambert came home he [Barker] and the mr differed about it'.[12] The letter passed from hand to hand, was puzzled

---

[11] Warwickshire County Record Office (WCRO), CR3036/1, Wratislaw, W. F., Solicitors Rugby, firm's letter book 1825–1827, entries for 17 December 1825.

[12] NA, DD 311/1, January 1801.

over by employers, neighbours and friends. Sarah Waldram (probably a stocking seamer) had a lot of trouble with William Barker (and he with her; she gave as good as she got) and a very long and salacious – and indelicate – story about what happened the night he kicked her is told in several episodes throughout Woolley's first volume.[13] He noted on 8 January that 'Sall Waldram and barker make an End of their Law Sute and barker was obliged to hone him Self in a falt and pay all Expences and make hir some recompence into the bargin'. Sarah Waldram's letter – her lawyer's letter – was effective. Before obtaining it she had tried the usual channels, going first to a local magistrate with a warrant in mind, though the magistrate's clerk would not admit her to the house. But 'owning himself to be at fault' sounds like something Barker did before a magistrate, rather than in an alehouse or at home; and Woolley mentioned 'expenses', which magistrates routinely laid on complainants and accused in the justicing room. It *is* the case that Woolley used the language of the law in all of his writing; 'warrant', 'owned himself', 'expences', are the everyday words of his writerly lexis, and such legal formularies were part of Clifton village's common discourse: men in alehouses discussed the niceties of *mittimus*.[14] Nevertheless, it does sound as if at some point during the first week of January 1803, a local magistrate *was* involved in the case. And it would be very useful to know how much Sall Waldram's letter cost her – and how she could possibly have afforded one. Three shillings and fourpence, or three shillings and sixpence, it may have cost her in Birmingham, in the 1790s; it may have cost her five shillings in Rugby in the 1820s, for such a letter.[15] If she were a seamer, then Sall Waldram earned perhaps 6 shillings a week. In May 1803, Woolley was paying his seamer 2s 1d for doing 28 pairs of stockings.

The last of Woolley's lawyer's-letter stories was told in February 1815. The legal process at work is much clearer to see, and reading this account in comparison with the accounts from twelve years before makes it possible to imagine people familiar with a quasi-legal system, indeed to imagine that paying for a lawyer's letter may have been seen *as* a legal procedure. But perhaps that impression comes from Woolley's experience as a writer and his almost-first-hand knowledge of the

---

[13] Steedman, *An Everyday Life*, p. 112.

[14] 'Sept the 29 [1803] thomas hardy was taken before Sir Ger Clifton [Gervase Clifton Bart, the local magistrate]; he wrote his mittermus because he would not marry moll robbins'. NA, DD 311/2. A mittimus is a warrant committing a person to prison.

[15] The Library of Birmingham, Archives and Collections, MS 3069/11/11, Birmingham Attorney's Day Book 1785–1790; WCRO, CR3074/1, Bretherton's Solicitors Rugby, Daybook 1814–1818.

events described, rather than from some sociolegal reality. 'Some time in feb Joseph Cartwright had some of his Hens and is Cock poisoned by Accident' he wrote; 'and he laid it to a person that did [a neighbour's] ... Garden and the man Being Inecent He sent them a Lawyers Letter'. Mr and Mrs Cartwright went straight to Sir Gervase Clifton (Clifton Hall was just up the driveway from the village, practically next door) to get advice. Clifton granted them a warrant and arranged for two other local magistrates and his own attorney William Jamson to be present at the sitting. (The firm of Jamson and Leeson was a pretty big hitter in Nottingham.) Woolley said they were all called in 'to Assist him' when he examined the man, who remains anonymous throughout Woolley's account (and everywhere else, for that matter). 'Cartwright and his whife Swore that they saw him Lan the poisen at 6 o'clock at night and Sir Ger Cummitted him to prisen and he Lay [there] till the Saturday following'. Then, noted Woolley, it 'Come out how the hens where posnd'. Another, different, neighbour had laid ratsbane, spreading arsenic paste on stale bread and butter. The rats hadn't gone for it; it was swept into the dunghill by his wife, where the hens fell on it with clucks of joy. She remembered what she'd done, and the story was conveyed to Sir Gervase. 'The truth Came out', wrote Woolley; the man 'was set at Liberty and it is said that Cartwrights had all the Expences to pay and ... three pounds three shillings [expenses] for the time he lay in prison'. 'I was told this by John Smith', Woolley noted; 'and he says that old Gerves told him [,] so if I set down Lies they were told mee first but it Cost [the] Cartwrights a deal of money and Sarved them Rite for if they Could have transported the man they would'. He thought that the couple had also been attempting to get neighbour Lambert (who employed the gardener) evicted from the tenancy held of Sir Gervase.[16]

Again, a day-labourer employed as a gardener knew how to obtain the services of an attorney and the money to pay for them. He initiated legal proceedings, not by going to the magistrate but by responding to the Cartwrights' accusations with an attorney's letter. Only then did the Cartwrights access the 'official' legal system. Magistrate Clifton was not responding to the lawyer's letter by issuing a warrant or in his decision not to hear the case sitting alone; he was responding to an accusation of livestock poisoning, a serious property offence. But most of the draft lawyer's letters in attorneys' archives were types of dunning letters written by legal men, which appear to have produced some effect without recourse to the formal legal system. This was the case with

[16] NA, DD 311/6, February 1815. Woolley had three friends called Gervas/Gervase. A lot of baby boys in this village were named after the magistrate (and landlord).

the first of Joseph Woolley's letter stories. In the case of the Hens, the Cartwrights, and the Gardener, the lawyer's letter was an overture to the formal, legal procedure that lies at the centre of the story.

So too was it in a case from Somerset in 1819. The interest of Sall Waldram (Nottinghamshire 1803) and Hannah Minson (Somerset 1819) is that they were women of the poorer sort who appear to have been familiar with the process of obtaining a lawyer's letter. The newspapers reported the Somersetshire Summer Assizes in July under the headline 'Bridgewater Assizes Rex. On the Prosecution of Eliz. [Hannah] Minson Against R. Bartlett for A Rape'.[17] 'It would appear', the prosecuting barrister was reported as saying, 'that on the 31st May the prisoner met the prosecutrix about seven in the evening, as she was returning from seeing a female friend part of her way home. He accosted her, asking her if she would take a walk; and after some further conversation, offered her money if she would go with him; she said she would not; he said she must; and laying hold of her, forced her to a hay-stack at some distance, and after ineffectual resistance on her part, completed his purpose'. She was a servant she said in court, out of place, or between jobs, living with her married sister in the village of Hardington Mandeville, about three miles from Yeovil.[18] She described the

---

17 'Somerset Midsummer Assizes', *Taunton Courier and Western Advertiser for Somerset, Wilts, Dorset Devon and Cornwall*, Thursday, 2 September 1819; and 'Bridgewater Assizes Rex. On the Prosecution of Eliz. Minson against R. Bartlett for a Rape', *The Times*, Tuesday, 24 August 1819. The young woman's name was actually Hannah, not Elizabeth, at least according to the magistrate who issued a warrant against the alleged perpetrator, and to the Somerset Assizes felonies file in the National Archives. TNA, ASSI 25/15/16, Somerset. Felonies & Assgs Sumr: 1819, 59th Geo 3rd; ASSI 23/10. Western Circuit Goal Book, Somerset Summer Circuit 1819; also ASSI 21/38, Summer 1819, Crown Minute Book, Somerset. The newspapers named the alleged rapist as R. or Richard, but a 'Matthew Bartlett 25 [years was] Committed by J. Phelips Esquire changed on the Oath of Hannah Minson with having assaulted and Ravished her Warrant dated July 6' (ASSI 25/15/16). In court R. Bartlett was called a labourer, as indeed was Richard Bartlett of Hardington Mandeville, Somerset. The only Matthew Bartlett in the village was a baker; a Robert Bartlett of approximately the same age was a weaver. Somerset Heritage Centre (SHC), D\PC\hard.m/6/3/5, Overseers' Accounts and Rates, 1813–1822, parish of Hardington Mandeville; also D/PC/hard m 6/3/27, Hardington Mandeville Bastardy Orders; also baptism and marriage records, D\P\hard.m/2/1/2; D\P\hard.m/2/1/4; D\P\hard.m/2/1/5. The last were checked for me by Philip Hocking, Researcher, SHC. I am very grateful for his help. The man who assaulted Hannah Minson is most likely to have been Richard Bartlett, not Matthew, even though the latter is the 'official' record of his name.

18 Often described as an out-of-the-way place on the border of West Dorset, Hardington Mandeville was an important centre for sailcloth manufacture. Tom Carter, *Stories of Hardington Mandeville*, Hardington Mandeville, 1994; *Hardington Mandeville Village Design Statement 1999*, Hardington Mandeville Parish Council in partnership with South Somerset District Council, April 1999; House of Commons Papers; Reports of Committees (224), 'A Digest of Parochial Returns made to the Select Committee appointed to inquire into the Education of the Poor', Session 1818. Vol. I. The village reached its peak population of 760 in 1840.

assault in great detail, and with the utmost clarity, reporting how 'I told my brother-in-law as soon as I got home that the prisoner had used me very ill, but I did not tell him the particulars. I told my sister the same: two days afterwards I told my sister all the particulars. I did not know the prisoner exactly: I knew his person, not his name. My brother-in-law... knows the prisoner very well. I told my sister what I have now told the Court'.

Under cross-examination Hannah Minson was asked 'Did you go the next morning to an attorney?' (That would be the morning of 1st June if we use the newspapers' dates; she probably went into Yeovil to find the nearest.) Yes, she had. 'For what purpose'? she was asked; 'was it to send the prisoner a lawyer's letter? – Yes. Had... [he] torn and injured your clothes? Yes. – Did you see the attorney? – No: I saw the clerk. – On what terms did you tell the clerk you would settle the business [pay for it]? – [He] asked me, I said I could not settle the business, but that my brother-in-law if agreeable, would. – You did not perhaps tell the lawyer what you have told here today? – No. – Only to send the prisoner the lawyer's letter? – Yes. – As you did not bear malice, perhaps you did afterwards receive money from the prisoner's wife to make the matter up? – The prisoner's wife came to me and pressed me, and I did. – Upon easy and friendly terms: you took 3£, did you not? – Yes.'

In the Assize papers in TNA, the assault was described as taking place on 18 April; the newspapers reported the 31st of May. When did Hannah Minson set in train the process of compensation? How soon after she'd persuaded the attorney's clerk that her brother-in-law would cough up for a letter, did Richard (or Matthew or Robert) Bartlett's wife come round with the money? Did she visit before Tuesday, 6 July, which is the date on which a warrant was issued for Bartlett's arrest? Bartlett was committed by John Phelips Esquire [JP] 'on the Oath of Hannah Minson with having assaulted and Ravished her'. That would have been five weeks (or eleven weeks, if the assault took place in April), with space for Hannah Minson to decide that £3 wasn't enough, or that she wanted justice for more than some torn and dirtied clothes.[19] The rape taking place on 18 April – on a Sunday – makes more sense of the visiting and walking with her friend than does than Monday, 31 May. Hannah/ Elizabeth's wearing of her Sunday-best was described in court. And it gives Hannah Minson eleven weeks rather than six to decide – or be persuaded – to take the case before a magistrate, to move into the train of the formal legal system. Minson was a poor user of the legal system (and so too was Bartlett a poor man, though he was not

---

[19] The later date also gave more time to determine whether not she was pregnant.

proactive in his use of the law).[20] Minson had choices – she perceived choices – about the law available to her; she knew how to access it; she displayed, we might say, a high level of legal consciousness.[21]

Just after evidence about the £3 had been given, Mr Justice Best interrupted proceedings to point out to the jury that this was a *capital* trial: 'whatever suspicions might be entertained as to the conduct of the prisoner, and he had no doubt he had used the young woman very ill, yet in a case so penal, and under the facts now elicited by the counsel for the prisoner, it would be a departure from the just caution exercised in such cases to permit the cause to proceed further. The prisoner was therefore acquitted'.[22] She *had* received some compensation, and a rape was not worth a man's life – is one way of explaining Best's legal thinking. That she had taken Mrs Bartlett's money on 'easy and friendly terms' perhaps suggests that no one involved in the case thought Bartlett's behaviour utterly heinous.[23]

There may be more lawyer's-letter stories to be found, but there is something useful to be said about everyday legal thinking among early nineteenth-century people, even now, even if a mere four remains the total. *A copy of a letter*, or miraculously, an *actual* letter, sent, received, folded and unfolded as it is shown to neighbours: *What does this mean?* – would be an extraordinary find, though a letter written on behalf of a working-class client like Sall Waldram or Hannah Minson is too much to hope for. But the lawyer's-letter joke suggests what may have been lost.

---

[20] Richard and Robert Bartlett, both young married men with small children, received poor relief for 17 (Richard) and 12 (Robert) separate months between 1813 and 1822. The early spring of 1813 and the winter of 1816–1817 were particularly hard on them and their families. SHC, D\PC\hard.m/6/3/5, Overseers' Accounts and Rates, 1813–1822, parish of Hardington Mandeville.

[21] For Nottinghamshire legal consciousness in this period, Kevin Binfield, *Writings of the Luddites*, Johns Hopkins University Press, Baltimore and London, 2011, pp. 20–32, 47, 65, 133; Steedman, *An Everyday Life*, pp. 122–49.

[22] *Times*, 24 August 1819; *Taunton Courier*, 2 September 1819; TNA, ASSI 21/38, Summer 1819, Crown Minute Book, Somerset; G. F. R. Barker, 'Best, William Draper, first Baron Wynford (1767–1845)', revised. Hugh Mooney, *Oxford Dictionary of National Biography*, Oxford University Press, 2004, accessed 24 February 2017.

[23] We do not know Mr Justice Best's mind; his DNB (Oxford Dictionary of National Biography) entry suggests that he was a person of 'experience' who may have been willing to excuse the sexual peccadilloes of young men. (But a young man of the poorer sort? Probably not.) See Barker, 'Best, William Draper'. Perhaps a lawyer's letter was (or by this time was generally assumed to be) something 'answered' by monetary payment. But a high court judge is not likely to have been cognizant of popular law thinking.

Lawyer's-letter comedy was a variant of the lawyer joke, which had been running, to wearied reception, since the middle of the seventeenth century: jokes about attorneys' avarice, their obfuscating language, their dining upon fat capon and other people's sorrow, and above all, jokes about how they charged you for getting out of bed in the morning. Even a Lord Chief Justice cracked attorney jokes.[24] Very high places indeed were a perfectly acceptable site for denigrating lawyers, well into the twentieth century. On the second reading of the Legal Aid and Advice Bill in 1948, MP Tom Driberg remarked that 'Hazlitt said that the only thing that gave him any respect for the House of Commons was the contempt felt there for lawyers', though *he* would 'never venture to echo such seditious words'.[25]

But more to our purpose here are sincere attorney jokes from the sentimental eighteenth century, in its new exploration of human nature, the kind that William Hutton told in his 1787 book about the Birmingham Court of Requests: 'Two parties in contest, like two bodies in friction, naturally create a warmth' he wrote; 'by the violence of both, aided by the interested, the fire may be blown into a flame…I once hinted at this practice to a very honest attorney of my acquaintance, who replied with a smile, "If it was not for quarrels, we could not make the jack turn the roast meat."'[26] All attorneys, even the virtuous ones, were after one thing, and one thing only: their fee. The Birmingham Court of Requests Commissioners once said to a complainant that he surely could trust the matter in hand to 'an upright attorney'–? The response according to Hutton was '"I am afraid…to employ one, for a person very recently owed me twenty-four pounds; I employed an attorney, who got it, and

---

[24] One from Lord Mansfield, chief justice of the court of King's Bench, 1756–1788, on the theft of silverware by a person thought to be an attorney: 'Mansfield half-whispered to the prosecutor: "Come, come, don't exaggerate matters; if the fellow had been an attorney you may depend upon it, he would have stolen the *bowl* as well as the *ladle!*"' Norman Poser, *Lord Mansfield: Justice in the Age of Reason*, McGill-Queen's University Press, Montreal and Kingston, London and Ithaca, 2013, p. 208.

[25] Commons Sitting of Wednesday 15 December 1948, Parliament 1948–1949, *Hansard* Fifth Series, Volume 459, 1177–352. For legal aid legislation, see below, pp. 226–31. Hazlitt did indeed express this opinion: *Political Essays: With Sketches of Public Characters*, William Hone, London, 1819, pp. 153–4.

[26] Courts of Request were minor equity courts of medieval origin which were revived as small claims courts under eighteenth-century legislation. They disappeared under the County Court Act of 1846. William Hutton, *Courts of Request: Their Nature, Utility, and Powers Described, with a Variety of Cases, Determined in That of Birmingham*, Pearson and Rollason, Birmingham and London, 1787, p. 8; Christopher W. Brooks, *Lawyers, Litigation and English Society since 1450*, Hambledon, London, 1998, pp. 39–45; Margot Finn, *The Character of Credit: Personal Debt in English Culture, 1740–1914*, Cambridge University Press, Cambridge, 2003, pp. 202–5; Great Britain, House of Commons, Courts of Request, Abstract Return of the Courts of Request, Courts of Conscience, and all other Courts in England and Wales, 1840 (619) XLI.555.

very honourably paid it; but it cost me forty guineas!".' [27] Some thought
the Birmingham stories about debt, credit and lawyers that Hutton told
in his book *were* a joke, albeit an instructive one.[28]

In the jest books and magazines there were satiric love letters written in an attorney's voice, so that he spoke the moral denigration of his
kind, as in 'To a lady', written as an 'indenture of love': 'Condescend,
therefore, to bargain, sell, assign, and to farm-let all that fair tenement
of beauty, which is yourself, unto one who cares not what he gives for
the purchase...'.[29] These were very popular in the 1770s, and always
a little bit dirty, especially when they mentioned watercourses, as did
this one. The popular joke books repeated them, well into the nineteenth century.[30] The early nineteenth-century comic stage and novel
put forward the scene in which a lawyer's letter was opened: breakfast
time usually, much consternation ...[31] It is said that the scene (in jest

[27] Hutton, *Courts of Request*, p. 81.
[28] Richard Lovell Edgeworth, *Essays on Professional Education*, J. Johnson, London,
      1809, p. 303, recommended *Courts of Request* as 'a serio-comic book'; useful in the
      education of boys to the law, it would afford ample matter for the study of trials
      and the evaluation of evidence. 'The titles of some of the cases (such as) "the meek
      Husband and bouncing Wife"...the whimsical mixture of good sense, oddity, and
      honesty in this volume, will pay those who take the trouble of looking it over'.
[29] C. Latitat, 'A Lawyer's Love-letter to His Mistress', *The Weekly Magazine, or, Edinburgh
      Amusement*, VI, 1769, p. 402. For denigration of attorneys, *Reflections or Hints founded
      upon Experience and Facts, touching the Law, Lawyers, Officers, Attorneys, and others
      concerned in the Administration of Justice...*, for the author, London, 1759, pp. 28–9;
      Alexander Grant, *The Progress and Practice of a Modern Attorney; exhibiting the Conduct
      of Thousands towards Millions! To which are added, the different Stages of a LawSuit, and
      attendant Costs...Instructions to both Creditors and Debtors...Cases of Individuals who
      have suffered from the Chicane of pettyfogging attornies...*, for the author, London, 1795;
      'Character and Conduct of an Attorney: To the Editor of the Legal Observer', *The Legal
      Observer, or Journal of Jurisprudence*, 8:203 (1833), pp. 72–3; John Lyes, '"A Strong
      Smell of Brimstone": The Solicitors and Attorneys of Bristol, 1740 to 1840', *Bristol
      Branch of the Historical Association*, Bristol, 1999; Michael J. Kirton, 'The Eighteenth-
      Century Country Attorney, Professionalism and Patronage: The Hodgkinsons
      of Southwell', *Transactions of the Thoroton Society of Nottinghamshire*, 115 (2011),
      pp. 119–37. In Samuel Warren's *The Moral, Social and Professional Duties of Attornies
      and Solicitors*, Blackwood, Edinburgh and London, 1848, p. 47, a barrister lectures
      the 13,000–14,000 (his estimate) attorneys of the British Isles on how to be genteel.
      A young barrister in training thinks about how 'we must be civil to these fellows',
      Reithra, 'The Lawyer's Dream', *The Metropolitan Magazine*, 13:51 (1835), pp. 330–6.
[30] *The Wit's Museum: Or an elegant Collection of Bon Mots, Repartees, &c. rational and
      entertaining. Many of which are original...*, William Lane, London, 1789.
[31] Thomas Dibdin, *The Will for the Deed: A Comedy in Three Acts, As Performed at the
      Theatre-royal Covent Garden*, Longman, London, 1805; *Alinda; Or, the Child of
      Mystery: A Novel*, 3 vols., B. & R. Crosby London, 1812, Vol. 3, p. 63; Mary Russell
      Mitford, *Our Village: Sketches of Rural Character and Scenery*, Vol. 5, Whittaker,
      London, 1824, p. 61; John Wight, *More Mornings at Bow Street: A New Collection of
      Humorous and Entertaining Reports*, for the author, London, 1827, p. 46.

book or on the theatrical stage) in which a lawyer's letter is opened is the central motif of a type of international tale, dating from at least the end of the European sixteenth century. English versions of the tale persisted well into the nineteenth century, with two East Midlands versions published.[32]

A summation of developments in the attorney's-letter joke is in George Stephen's *Adventures of an Attorney in Search of Practice* of 1839 (written under the pseudonym Sharpe), which is a wry, self-deprecating, and often darkly hilarious account of the actual lawyer and slavery abolitionist making his way in the legal world.[33] He describes the 'very unpleasant affair' of Simkin & Soft, merchants, who come to him deeply upset by a letter they have received: '"Pray, what is it, gentlemen?" and this plain question, rather abruptly put, surprised them into a plain answer. "An attorney's letter," replied Simkin, in a most lugubrious tone. "It is indeed," hysterically added Soft; "it is an attorney's letter, begging your pardon, Mr. Sharpe." "Well, gentlemen, there is no great harm in that: here is a score of them (pointing to my desk), and you might eat them for any harm they would do you"'.[34] He 'could scarcely forbear laughing out-right at the awful deliberation with which the letter…was submitted to… [his] inspection'. It's from Snappit & Smart; dated 1827, it demands payment for a consignment of cotton goods sent to New York from Manchester: 'until the same is forthwith paid, together with 6s 8d for the costs of this application, we shall proceed against you, without further notice'. So it's the type of legal dunning letter the drafts of which crowd the attorney records. It is not the type of letter purchased by Sall Waldram or the Clifton gardener. But it is interesting that the attorney tells his clients that letters like this are as common as muck and perfectly useless.

Stephen thought that this kind of business for attorneys had increased dramatically in the new century. He said that businessmen now did practically nothing in their working life that didn't require the counsel

---

[32] Herbert Alpert and Gerald Thomas, 'Two Patterns of an International Tale: The Lawyer's Letter Opened', *Fabula: Zeitschrift für Erzählforschung/Journal of Folktale Studies/Revue d'Etudes sur le Conte Populaire*, 42:1–2 (2001), pp. 32–63. One tale shows an interesting intersection of formal and informal law: after the letter-business has done its work, two disputants make up their quarrel, get matey, very drunk and decide on revenge on the lawyers. They are charged with breach of the peace; a magistrate bursts into laughter and dismisses their case. This is called the 'avenging coda'.

[33] George Stephen, *Adventures of an Attorney in Search of Practice*, Saunders and Otley, London, 1839; Leslie Stephen, 'Stephen, Sir George (1794–1879)', rev. Peter Balmford, *Oxford Dictionary of National Biography*, Oxford University Press, 2004, accessed 23 January 2017.

[34] Stephen, *Adventures of an Attorney*, pp. 91–8.

of a solicitor: there was a vast increase in clients using insurance law,
the law of partnership, of bankruptcy, of bills of exchange... The
increase of public companies, of parliamentary business, and the great,
global business of the colonial enterprise all brought attorneys business. And the social world was a better place he thought, than it had
been at the end of the last century: the lower classes possessed more
property now – more work for the attorney.[35] He thought that the profession had become more respectable or that, at least, their lower-class
clients believed them to be so: 'to be an attorney is itself a great step in
life, a sort of gentility of station, in the estimate of the lower ranks of
shopkeepers and mechanics'. But there were still many 'adventurers'
in the game, some with manners that would 'exclude them from our
servants' hall'. Low attorneys had a particular way of proceeding: 'the
secret of their art is to establish a familiar acquaintance with any humble class where the ceremony of special introduction is of small account,
and... "to push it as far as it will go."'[36] They exercised their dark arts
on thoughtless sailors home from sea; – on inferior tradesmen on the
verge of bankruptcy; – and on 'the pigeon, who after plucking, hesitates
between reform and desperation'. All ruined spendthrifts were drifting
towards the low attorney's net.[37] These were low but honest clients. The
dishonest class was less accessible but far more profitable, for thieves
and bilkers setting their affairs in order would pay ready money; where
there was no trust, there were no written bills.[38]

There has been much illuminating work on the varieties of law available to ordinary – and not so ordinary – people in the long, English eighteenth century. Peter King's message from all his work is about working
people's canny searching out of the right sort of magistrate for their purposes, and the legal knowledge they displayed in the justice's parlour.
Women used locally available law in particularly innovative ways.[39] By
this historical work, we have become fixated on the common law, by the

---

[35] Ibid., pp. 192–4.
[36] Ibid., p. 197.
[37] Ibid., p. 198.
[38] Ibid., pp. 198–202.
[39] Peter King, 'The Summary Courts and Social Relations in Eighteenth-Century
England', *Past and Present*, 83 (1984), pp. 125–83; *Crime and the Law in England 1780–
1840: Remaking Justice from the Margins*, Cambridge University Press, Cambridge,
2006, pp. 56–7. Also Christopher Brooks, 'Litigation, Participation and Agency in
Seventeenth- and Eighteenth-Century England', David Lemmings (ed.), *The British
and Their Laws in the Eighteenth Century*, Boydell, Woodbridge, 2005, pp. 155–81;
Drew D. Gray, 'The People's Courts? Summary Justice and Social Relations in the
City of London, c. 1760–1800', *Family & Community History*, 11:1 (2008), pp. 7–15.

judges making it, the magistrates administering it, and the ordinary people whose lives were shaped by it.[40] There were other forms of law available, and eighteenth-century people knew it. They understood equity, for example, in a way that is difficult to understand now, in a sociolegal culture that wedded it to common law a century and a half ago.[41] Susan Staves discusses the 'remarkable plurality of laws' that pertained in the long English eighteenth century, Margot Finn the proliferation of courts of conscience (or Courts of Request, 'Small Debts Courts' like the one William Hutton worked for in Birmingham) in the second half of the eighteenth century.[42] These were summary tribunals serving labourers, artisans and petty producers in the recovery of debts. They aided the small debtor outside the common law system and its much vaunted protection, says Finn, at the same time as she explains equity.[43] Equity is a legal doctrine embodying 'the meliorist principle by which legal rules may be mitigated to ensure the realisation of the spirit or intention of the law'. Equity privileged judicial discretion over precedent, looking 'not only to the legal cause but also to the human person, tempering the strict enforcement of contractual obligation, by taking particular cognisance of the defendant's character and circumstances'.[44] Back in Birmingham, in 1787, William Hutton agreed, saying that 'Law, with its rigid fetters, binds what conscience sets free. Law know no mercy. Equity knows no rigour. If [a] Court [of Conscience] cannot proceed contrary to law ... [it] can proceed without it'.[45] And he added: 'there are cases ... where the Bench

---

40 David Lemmings, 'Introduction', David Lemmings (ed.), *British and Their Laws in the Eighteenth Century*, Boydell, Woodbridge, 2005, pp. 1–26; Brooks, *Lawyers, Litigation*, pp. 188–9.

41 Freeman Oliver Haynes, *Outlines of Equity*, Macmillan, London, 1858; Chaloner William Chute, *Equity under the Judicature Act; or, The Relation of Equity to Common Law*, Butterworth's, London, 1874; Sydney Edward Williams, *Outlines of Equity: A Concise View of the Principles of Modern Equity*, Stevens, London, 1900; Stephen Waddams, 'Equity in English Contract Law: The Impact of the Judicature Acts (1873–75)', *Journal of Legal History*, 33:2 (2012), pp. 185–208.

42 Susan Staves describes 'three radically different coexisting legal systems, each with separate and distinct subsystems': The ecclesiastical court system; the traditional system of customary English law administered throughout the country in manorial courts by lords of the manor; the nationally administered system of common law and equity'; *Married Women's Separate Property in England, 1660–1833*, Harvard University Press, Cambridge, MA and London, 1990, pp. 18, viii.

43 Finn, *The Character of Credit*, p. 202.

44 Finn, *The Character of Credit*, p. 14. Equity as an independent legal procedure has so completely disappeared that I find it difficult to even think about whether or not Judge Best was exercising equity or 'thinking equity' in his acquittal of Richard/Matthew Bartlett in Bridgewater in 1819.

45 Hutton, *Courts of Request*, p. 88.

ought to act against the injured, and even assist the culprit. This step is out of the reach of the law, and can only be obtained by equity. Law knows no attribute but that of justice; equity can introduce mercy'.[46] What does a Commissioner [like Hutton] need?: 'Only two words are necessary...*common sense*'.[47] But common sense masked the partiality of commissioners, their lack of legal knowledge, and the absence of juries.[48] Hutton himself unmasked the 'Commissioners...who attended business without studying it, [and] sometimes forgot to treat the suitors as brethren whom they were bound to assist, but brow-beat them, as little men, in little office are apt'. This was especially the case with the 'particular classes of suitors, besides the quarrelsome, whose faces are repeatedly seen in [the Birmingham] Court, as the huckster, the club members, the milk-maid, the publican, &c. These being often wounded, apply often for a cure'.[49]

Margot Finn tells us that when Parliament legislated for courts of request, great hostility was displayed towards attorneys. In some places, legislation prohibited them from acting as commissioners or forbade their advocacy in them.[50] This was not the case in Birmingham, but William Hutton did not like attorneys very much. He writes about 28 actual or typical attorneys in his book. When he gave them attributes, 15 were described as liking fees, promoting law over equity, showing off their legal knowledge; 2 as liking the sound of their own voice; 2 as friends useful as sources of information; 1 as ignorant of case and client. Only one was described as 'honest', 'wise', 'of my acquaintance'.[51] From the 1750s onwards, all legislation concerning the operation of the law brought in its train disparagement of attorneys. The end of Law Latin and the compulsory use of English by mid-century was predicted not only to encourage 'Bankrupt Tradesmen and broken Shopkeepers, who can read and write a tolerable Book-keeping Hand, set up for special Pleaders...some Persons who have been Servants to Lawyers have crept into the Office of an Attorney...!' (Or so it was said.)[52] In 1795, Alexander Grant fulminated against 'the lowest species of petty-fogging

---

[46] Ibid., p. 106.
[47] Ibid., pp. 373–4.
[48] Brooks, *Lawyers, Litigation*, pp. 43–4
[49] Hutton, *Courts of Request*, pp. 240, 373.
[50] Finn, *The Character of Credit*, p. 205.
[51] Hutton, *Courts of Request*, passim. Hutton has something to say about an attorney every sixteenth page (or so) of his 446-page book.
[52] Anon., *Reflections or Hints founded upon Experience and Facts, touching the Law, Lawyers, Officers, Attorneys, and others concerned in the Administration of Justice*, L. Davis and C. Reymers, London, 1759, pp. 11–14.

tricks' performed by those who were *not actually attorneys*, but by 'the vermin ... who pretend to collect in small debts, by suing for their recovery in ... county and sheriffs' courts, and courts of request. These fellows ingratiate themselves with poor house-keepers in public houses, who recommend them to laundresses, ignorant women who let lodgings, &c to collect their debts'.[53] The attorney's clerk who had abandoned his indentures and gone freelance may have become one of these 'specimens'.[54] A young man without the money to set up on his own after completing his apprenticeship might spend a lifetime as a writing or office clerk and be grateful for a little on the side.

I do not know that I will ever be able to call these men 'lay-attorneys' or 'independent law practitioners' because I do not think I will ever find one. But one young man something like this was to be found in Gosport, Hampshire, in the early 1830s. Henry Pollexfen, who had served five years of his clerkship (and was thus technically an attorney, though he had not been admitted to practice by a judge[55]) was acquitted of sending a letter to a local magistrate 'threatening to shoot, kill, and murder him'.[56] This was during the Hampshire Swing Disturbances

---

[53] Grant, *The Progress and Practice*, p. 26.

[54] Philip Aylett hints at the existence of provincial 'hedge solicitors' in 'A Profession in the Market Place'. Penelope Corfield discusses 'so-called "under-strappers" at law, also known as "hedge-attorneys" or "Wapping attorneys" on the margins of respectability', in 'Eighteenth-century Lawyers and the Advent of the Professional Ethos', *Droit et société en France et Grande Bretagne: Law and Society in France and England*, Philippe Chassaigne and Jean-Philippe Genet (eds.), Publication de la Sorbonne, Paris, 2003, pp. 103–26. She points out their usefulness in poor neighbourhoods.

[55] Joseph Day, *Thoughts on the Necessity and Utility of the Examination directed by several Acts of Parliament, previous to the Admission of Attorneys at law and Solicitors; Together with Some Observations on the Constitution and Regulations of the Society of Clerks to His Majesty's Signet in Scotland, and on several Rules of the Courts of King's Bench and Common Pleas relating to Attorneys; The Whole applying to a bill proposed to be brought into Parliament for the incorporating and better regulation of attorneys at law and solicitors*, for the author, London, 1795, on the difficulties encountered by the high court judges in examining attorneys for entry into the profession. Also Christopher W. Brooks and Michael Lobban, 'Apprenticeship or Academy? The Idea of a Law University, 1830–1860', *Learning the Law: Teaching and the Transmission of English Law, 1150–1900*, Jonathan A. Bush and Alain Wijffels (eds.), Bloomsbury, London, 1999, pp. 353–82; Albert J. Schmidt, 'Lawyer Professionalism in Rural England: Changes in Routine and Rewards in the Early Nineteenth Century', *Lincolnshire History and Archaeology*, 32 (1997), pp. 25–39.

[56] 'Special Commission. Winchester. Thursday Dec. 23', *The Times*, 24 December 1830; 'Special Commission for Hants', *Morning Post*, 25 December 1830; 'Special Commission', *Spectator*, 25 December 1830, p. 6; TNA ASSI 24/18/3. Special Commissions 1830, Recognizance Book, County of Southampton, Callendar of the Prisoners, in the County Goal at Winchester, for Trial at the Special Session ... 18 December 1830; TNA HO 130/1. Hants. Report of Convictions &c under the Special Commission.

of 1830.[57] It was clear to the judge presiding at the Special Assizes trying the rioters that the letter was not in Pollexfen's handwriting; the question of whether he ever wrote an attorney's letter for anyone else is truly imponderable. But Pollexfen's not-letter allows us to imagine that on the fringes of the attorney trade, among office writing clerks, among those who had left their places unqualified, there may have been the odd class-warrior, offering law-letter-writing services to the poor.[58] The great hardship of the law clerk's life was the ceaseless copying he had to do.[59] 'Consider, that the pen of an Attorney and Solicitor, is really scarcely ever out of his hand', advised Samuel Warren in 1848.[60] But the qualified attorney *was* sometimes free of the pen. He travelled to meet clients (later sending a bill 'for attending on you many times'[61]) and to quarter sessions and assizes. He *drafted* the letters for his clerk to write. But the most important thing about the letter (which Pollexfen did not write) was the question of social action and formalised threat, which E. P. Thompson raised in 1975.

In some places, as we have seen, courts intended for poor users in regard to debt proscribed the presence or employment of attorneys. In other places, working men and women sought out attorneys (or maybe, not-actually attorneys) in order to further their own interests. The two places that produced my tiny, unrepresentative cohort of lawyer-letter users, Yeovil district, Somerset, and south Nottinghamshire, had no Court of Requests.[62] But only one of the four cases discussed above involved a debt, and a Court of Requests had no remit with assault and employment cases (unless unpaid wages could be construed a debt). But it may be possible to add the lawyer's-letter system to the 'plurality of law' by which law-users of the poorer sort lived their lives. And it was not that these men

---

[57] Pollexfen is to be found by reading E. P. Thompson, 'The Crime of Anonymity', Douglas Hay, Peter Linebaugh, John G. Rule, E. P. Thompson, and Cal Winslow (eds.), *Albion's Fatal Tree. Crime and Society in Eighteenth-Century England* (1975), Verso, London, 2011, pp. 255–344.

[58] Pollexfen does not appear on any of the published Law Lists in the 1830s and 1840s, though Portsea and Gosport attorneys and clerks who had known him during his clerkship (and who gave evidence at his trial) do: Samuel Hill, *Clarke's New Law List; being a List of the Judges and Officers of the Different Courts of Justice … and a Complete and Accurate List of Certified Attornies, Notaries &c in England and Wales with the London Agents to the Country Attornies*, J. & W. T. Clarke, London, 1816.

[59] Jacob Phillips, *A Letter from a Grandfather to His Grandson, an Articled Clerk: Pointing Out the Right Course of his Studies and Conduct*, George Wilson, London, 1818; Alfred Cecil Buckland, *Letters to an Attorney's Clerk, Directions for his Studies and general Conduct*, Taylor and Hessey, London, 1824; Francis Hobler, *Familiar Exercises Between an Attorney and his Articled Clerk*, J. F. Dove, London, 1831.

[60] Warren, *Moral, Social and Professional Duties*, pp. 65–6.

[61] For example, WCRO, CR 556/1 T. Tidmas of Warwick, office ledger *c.* 1812–1832.

[62] Great Britain, House of Commons, *Courts of request … 1840*.

and women purchased a commodity that they could not have produced themselves. We know that letter writing was a perfectly ordinary and well-understood activity in working-class communities at the end of the eighteenth century.[63] R. A Houston writes in great detail about the changing rhetorical and writerly strategies of peasant petitioners in the British Isles, from the seventeenth to the nineteenth century.[64] There was much experience of the petition and of petitioning across the society, sometimes spoken of (now, rather than then) as the epistolary device of the powerless.[65] Joseph Woolley, the framework knitter, wrote and received letters; he once charged a neighbour 3d for writing one.[66] His friends and neighbours knitted letter-writing into the fabric of their lives: one St Monday at the Coach and Horses, Clifton, a man finds he has not enough money to pay for his evening of strenuous drinking. He borrows a pen from the landlord and 'pretended to rite a Letter to is whife to send him to pound and sent it by Sam hoe and he new verey well that she had not too shillings of is money in the house at the same time and when she had red the Letter she told Sam that they miht keep is Cloths for She would not send him [anything]'.[67] Letter-writing manuals had been telling the middling sort how to write threateningly about unpaid debts for at least half a century. One much reprinted model from the 1780s was: 'From a Tradesman to another Sir I am exceedingly displeased to find your bill for £80 returned...You may remember, Sir, that I gave you your own time, which I always do, in order to prevent disappointment. I must confess that you have used me very ill, and if the bill be not taken up within six days, I shall put it into an attorney's hands. Yours J. Blunt'.[68] But here, in the lawyer's-letter stories told above, the poorer sort purchased law, or legal action, embodied in a letter written by an attorney (or someone calling himself an attorney).

---

[63] Frances Austin, 'Letter Writing in a Cornish Community in the 1790s', *Letter Writing as a Social Practice*, David Barton and Nigel Hall (eds.), John Benjamins, Amsterdam and Philadelphia, 1999, pp. 43–61; Gary Schneider, *The Culture of Epistolarity: Vernacular Letters and Letter Writing in Early Modern England, 1500–1700*, University of Delaware Press, Cranbery, NJ, 2005, p. 13; Susan E. Whyman, *The Pen and the People: English Letter Writers 1660–1800*, Oxford University Press, Oxford, 2009, p. 45.

[64] R. A. Houston, *Peasant Petitions: Social Relations and Economic Life on Landed Estates, 1600–1850*, Palgrave Macmillan, Basingstoke, 2014, pp. 73–108.

[65] Clare Brant, 'The Tribunal of the Public: Eighteenth-Century Letters and the Politics of Vindication', Caroline Bland and Máire Cross (eds.), *Gender and Politics in the Age of Letter Writing, 1750–2000*, Ashgate, Aldershot, 2003, pp. 15–28.

[66] 'the 22 [Sep] for riting a Letter...3d'. NA, DD 311/5.

[67] NA, DD 311/3, 1804.

[68] George Brown, *The New English Letter-writer...Agreeable to the Forms...Executed by the Most Eminent Attorneys*, Hogg, London, 1780 (but not a word about 'lawyers' letters'); James Wallace and Charles Townshend, *Every Man his own Letter-Writer*, J. Cooke, London, 1782; Thomas Chapman, *The New Universal Letter Writer*, T. Sabine, London, 1790.

We could now move to the letters themselves, to understand what kind of legal thinking and action their use embodied. But the lawyer's letter is an absent object; and not only absent, but its absence layered over by many other kinds of writing. Even the formal, over-the-counter letters written by attorneys on behalf of clients pursuing monies owed them exist only as draft notes for the writing clerk to pen the next day, or as part of a draft bill for '6s 8d...the easiest way of raising a pound ever invented'.[69] Surviving office ledgers rarely show the fee for writing a single letter. The proto-letters in attorney archives, notes to someone else for writing a letter, are sometimes lists of tasks completed for the client, with the 'you' (who will be the addressee when the entries are used to compose an actual letter) appearing two lines on after the first line naming the client.[70] Writer and addressee merge; the actual letter-writer is effaced. The notes have the form of little letters to yourself. Modern epistolary theory does not deal with letters to yourself, though perhaps modern legal theory could: these are letters from a lawyer to a client, with the lawyer formally and legally a proxy for the person for whom he acts. And yet a further source for thinking about lawyer's letters is how unlike they were from letters described by historians of the early modern period! At the turn of the nineteenth century, there was no worrying about postal instability, misdirection, slowness, epistolary lag...; no anxiety of reception, for attorneys made sure they got there; no purloined letters, for that would be an additional crime or misdemeanour; no 'what does this letter really mean?' – for that would be a recipient's question about legal language, not about love. No expressions of affect; no worries about how emotion was being textualised. No troubles about the dynamic between physical presence and morality because now the dynamic between the oral and the written was not in flux, as it is said to have been a century before. These are all attributes claimed for the seventeenth-century letter.[71]

Modern epistolary theory deals in the idea of 'correspondence', the network of affect woven by letters exchanged.[72] It is for the main part *dependant as theory* on an extant corpus of letters exchanged over time

---

[69] Grant, *The Progress and Practice*, p. 29. Here Grant satirised the common way of making out an attorney's bill. Six shillings and eightpence was a third of £1.

[70] NA, DDME 3/1–10, Attorneys Day Book regarding day-to-day working for various clients. The firm concerned is presumed to be the predecessor of Messrs Mee & Co [of East Retford?], 1824–1884.

[71] Schneider, *Culture of Epistolarity*, pp. 16–17, 75–108.

[72] Liz Stanley, 'The Epistolarium: On Theorizing Letters and Correspondences', *Auto/Biography*, 12 (2004), pp. 201–35; Margaretta Jolly and Liz Stanley, 'Letters as/not a genre', *Life Writing*, 2:2 (2005), pp. 91–118; Liz Stanley, 'The Epistolary Gift, the Editorial Third-Part, Counter-Epistolary: Rethinking the Epistolarium', *Life Writing*, 8:2 (2011), pp. 135–52.

between any number of writers (as in the case of the Dodd/Thompson correspondence).[73] It does not deal with the one-off statement of threat that was the 'lawyer's letter'. Who ever *replied* to a letter like this sent by an attorney? Not even in the joke books. Historians investigated business letters, with which lawyers' letters appear to be aligned, in the decades following Kitty Locker's 'Sir, This Will Never Do', on model dunning letters.[74] Locker said that dunning letters fell into three categories: the apologetic, the vituperative, and the businesslike. The last, she said, ranged from mild to harsh letters with threat of legal action. We have here been dealing with harsh letters, real and fictional. But in following Locker, historians appear to have been compelled by the idea of the *network*, and the *correspondence*; in the way the capitalist enterprise was spun around the globe by family members' and merchants' letters.[75]

What may well turn out to be most useful in understanding the lawyer's letter as purchased by the poorer sort, and as a social and legal practice, is the threatening letter, as discussed in the last chapter. At the turn of every social crisis, farmers, merchants and landowners were reminded about the laws in force against those who wrote, sent, or delivered letters containing threats against their property or person.[76] During the Swing crisis of 1830, information on the law of threatening

---

[73] Jacques Derrida, *The Post Card: From Socrates to Freud and Beyond*, trans. Alan Bass, University of Chicago Press, Chicago, 1987; Jolly and Stanley, 'Letters as/not a genre'; Stanley, 'The Epistolary Gift', *Life Writing*, 8:2 (2011), pp. 135–52; Sarah Poustie, 'Re-Theorising Letters and "Letterness"', *Olive Schreiner Letters Project Working Papers on Letters, Letterness & Epistolary Networks*, Number 1, Edinburgh, 2010; Esther Milne, *Letters, Postcards, Email: Technologies of Presence*, Routledge, New York, 2010.

[74] Kitty Locker, '"Sir, This Will Never Do": Model Dunning Letters, 1592–1873', *International Journal of Business Communication*, 22:2 (1985), pp. 39–45.

[75] Emma Rothschild, *The Inner Life of Empires: An Eighteenth-Century History*, Princeton University Press, Princeton, NJ, 2011; Toby L. Ditz, 'Formative Ventures: Eighteenth-Century Commercial Letters and the Articulation of Experience', *Epistolary Selves: Letters and Letter-Writers, 1600–1945*, Rebecca Earle (ed.), Ashgate, Aldershot, 1998, pp. 60–78.

[76] William Marriott, *The Country Gentleman's Lawyer; and the Farmer's Complete Law Library…4th ed. To which is added the…acts of Parliament…passed since the publication of the 3rd ed., viz. from 1801 to 1803*, F. C. & J. Rivington, London, 1803; John Thomas Becher, *Observations on the Punishment of Offenders, and the Preservation of the Peace, Occasioned by the Trespasses, Riots, and Felonies Now Prevalent in the County of Nottingham*, S. & J. Ridge, Newark, 1812; T. Williams, *Everyman His Own Lawyer, or, A Complete Law Library: Containing the Laws Affecting in Every Possible Circumstance and Situation in which Persons can be placed in the Ordinary Occurrences of Life, with an explanation of the most frequent Terms of Law…Second Edition*, Shirley, Neeham and Jones, London, 1818; *The London Tradesman, A Familiar Treatise on the Rationale of Trade and Commerce, as Carried on in the Metropolis of the British Empire: By Several Tradesmen*, Simpkin & Marshall, London, 1819. Williams, *Everyman His Own Lawyer*, p. 390, explained the law as it stood at the beginning of the nineteenth century with particular clarity.

letters was delivered in seriocomic form.[77] From the passing of the Black Act (1723) onwards, magistrates were routinely informed about the changing shape of legislation concerning threatening letters and their many varieties: with signature or anonymous? Signed with a fictitious name? Knowingly sent? Sent *and* delivered? Or delivered by someone not the writer?[78] Our understanding of popular literacy and of working-class writing has changed profoundly since Eric Hobsbawm and George Rudé discussed threatening letters in 1963, and Thompson discussed them in 1975. It would be difficult now – sociolinguistics has taught us this – to see what was expressed in a threatening letters as 'the usual luggage of the pre-political poor', or the letters themselves as 'semi-literate, ill-scrawled missives', or to feel a momentary (and somewhat condescending) sentimentality for their 'touching epistolary formalities'.[79] In *Writings of the Luddites* Kevin Binfield noticed how profoundly law shaped the fighting words of Nottinghamshire Luddites. He found discourses of equity and common law in Luddite proclamations, in their posters, poetry, advertisements, and letters. Luddite writers, he says, used juridical forms and language much as they were to be found in magistrates' warrants; their anonymous notices and letters used the language of depositions and writs.[80] He remarks that 'the fact that... [Luddite] legalistic discourse appears to resemble or derive from official forms but also to contradict the official forms... may have caused scholars such as E. P. Thompson to concentrate... on the directly

---

[77] *A Dialogue on Rick-burning, Rioting, &c. between Squire Wilson, Hughes, his Steward, Thomas, the Bailiff, and Harry Brown, a Labourer,* C.J.G. & F. Rivington, London, 1830; Henry Nelson Coleridge, *The Genuine Life of Mr. Francis Swing,* W. Joy, London, 1831.

[78] 9 Geo. 1. c. 22 (Criminal Law Act, 1722; 'The Black Act'); 27 Geo. 2 c.15 (1754, Persons Going Armed and Disguised Act); 30 Geo. 2 c. 24 (1757, Obtaining Money by False Pretences Act); Samuel Glasse, *The Magistrate's Assistant; Or, A Summary of Those Laws, Which Immediately Respect the Conduct of a Justice of the Peace,* for the author Gloucester, 1788; Edward Barry, *The Present Practice of a Justice of the Peace; and a Complete Library of Parish Law: Containing the Substance of All the Statutes and Adjudged Cases,* 4 vols., G. G. and J. Robinson, Oxford and Cambridge, 1790, Volume 3; Thomas Leach, *Cases in Crown Law, Determined by the Twelve Judges; by the Court of King's Bench... from the Fourth Year of George the Second, 1730, to the Fortieth Year of George the Third, 1800,* 4 vols., J. Butterworth, T. Cadell, and W. Davies, London, 1800, Vol. 2; Joseph Chitty, *A Practical Treatise on the Criminal Law,* 4 vols., A. J. Valpy, London, 1816, Vol. 3, pp. 276–8; James Ebenezer Bicheno, *Observations on the Philosophy of Criminal Jurisprudence,* R. Taylor, London, 1819.

[79] Eric Hobsbawm and George Rudé, *Captain Swing,* Lawrence and Wishart, London, 1969, p. 65; E. P. Thompson, 'The Crime of Anonymity', *Albion's Fatal Tree: Crime and Society in Eighteenth-Century England* (1975), Douglas Hay, Peter Linebaugh, John G. Rule, E. P. Thompson, and Cal Winslow (eds.), Verso, London, 2011, pp. 255–344, this quote on p. 299.

[80] Binfield, *Writings of the Luddities,* pp. 65, 71, 133.

threatening letters as more uniquely Luddite...'[81] He calls the letter-writers' usage a 'double treatment of law' by the Nottinghamshire men and women who lived through Ned Ludd's times. We can speculate that there was yet another, alternative law practice available to these people: the epistolary threat that they could purchase from an attorney (or perhaps, his writing or copy clerk, at the side door of the office or in a pub), yet another system of law at work in Luddite writers' minds, as they penned their threatening proclamations and notices: the lawyer's letter; a law that you might pay for and make your own; a warning that you might dictate (in both senses of the word), with the hope of enforcement and making something happen in the world, to your advantage.

In the lawyer's-letter stories discussed here, men and women got *something* by the purchase of a threatening letter from an attorney. Hannah Minson wanted more than the £3 (which, as the equivalent of a current £250, would have helped replenish her Sunday wardrobe), but the price of clothes was a ready index of other forms of recompense. Another of Woolley's sagas of assault and resistance in Clifton, this time, ten years on, between a different Sall and a different Tom, described a rumbustious Friday night in a local bar (not the Coach and Horses this time), after which Tom threw Sall Holt's cap in a hedge and Sall offered to strip and fight him to the ground. Tom went round to her lodgings to complain about the rumours she was spreading about him. Sall was not there; her landlady opened the door. Tom 'spoak not so plesand to old marey as he might have done so she dashed a sliping of yarn in is face and he dashed it in hir face again and gave hir a black Eye with it'. The next morning Sall and Mary 'set of to Nottingham for a warrant...and they thaught to have Got a deal of money out of him...[old] marey...thaught of haveing a new gown out of him but she was disapointed'.[82] The town magistrates dismissed the inconsistent story they told. On this occasion in 1813, Sall did not then go on to buy a lawyer's (threatening) letter, which was one more way to make something happen in the world, the same kind of action as walking three miles into Nottingham to find a sitting magistrate on a Saturday morning.

In the 1830s, attorneys began to name their ordinary office practice of writing lawyer's letters in a new way. The *Legal Observer* reported on the response to a perfectly ordinary attorney's letter ('if you do not immediately discharge the amount...I have my clients' instructions

---

[81] Ibid., p. 28.
[82] NA, DD 311/5, February 1813. Sir Gervase Clifton was evidently absent from Clifton Hall, as he so often was. Nottingham was the closest place to find a sitting magistrate on a Saturday.

to adopt measures, if the matter be not arranged in the course of to-morrow'). The debtor's attorney replied with: '7 & 8 G. 4 ss 8 & 9. for sending a threatening letter, &c Sir, We give you notice, that we intend preferring a bill against you at the next Old Bailey sessions. Your obedient Servants, H. Dod & Son. To John Blachford, Esq, Solicitor'.[83] The law had given attorneys a name for what they had been doing for all manner of client for a century past: writing menacing demands; writing threatening letters; power of a sort, sold and bought.

---

[83] 'Court of King's Bench. Attorney's Letter. – Probable Cause', *Legal Observer, or Journal of Jurisprudence*, 2:29 (14 May 1831), pp. 29–30. The 7 & 8 Geo. IV. c. 39 (Larceny Act 1827) made it a transportable offence to send a letter containing menacing demands. These matters were further discussed in 'Law of Attorneys. Attorney's Letter. – Tender', *Legal Observer, or Journal of Jurisprudence*, 4:95 (11 August 1832), p. 240; and 4:96 (18 August 1832), p. 255.

4 The Worst of It: Blackstone and Women

As... every subject is interested in the preservation of the laws, it is incumbent on every man to be acquainted with those at least, with which he is immediately concerned; least he incur the censure, as well as inconvenience, of living in a society without knowing the obligations which it lays him under. And thus much may suffice for persons of inferior condition, who have neither time nor capacity to enlarge their views beyond that contracted sphere in which they are appointed to move. But those, on whom nature and fortune have bestowed more abilities and greater leisure, cannot be so easily excused.

William Blackstone, *Commentaries on the Laws of England: Book I. Of the Rights of Persons* (1765), Oxford University Press, Oxford, 2016, p. 11.

But what did it signify my having been at Blackstone's lectures – I knew nothing of the matter as a justice – Burn furnished every thing I wanted, and him I left to the management of my clerk. What nonsense to suppose a knowledge of Blackstone... necessary for a justice – when there is scarce a justice that I meet at the quarter-sessions who has ever heard of Blackstone or his lectures – Why lord! if our farmers were to read law before they take out their Dedimus, how should they pay their rents?

Harriet; Or, the Innocent Adultress: In two volumes, R. Baldwin and J. Bew, London, 1779, Vol. 2, p. 34.

While the *Cookeries* of Hannah Glasse out circulate the *Commentaries* of Blackstone, authors will be found, who prefer the compilation of receipts to that of records, as the easier and more profitable talk of the two.

The Caledonian Bee; Or, A Select Collection of Interesting Extracts from Modern Publications: With elegant copperplates, R. Morison, Perth, and Vernor and Hood, London, 1795.

The working people discussed in Chapter 3 understood enough of the law to attempt to access it and to make it work for them, sometimes successfully. Here we turn to men and women – particularly women – of higher degree, and their understanding of the law.[1] In 1926, Percy Sanger expressed no surprise that Emily Bronte knew so much about the law that pertained during the plot-time of *Wuthering Heights* (*c.* 1770–1800) and the 1840s law of its time of composition. 'Novelists sometimes make their plots depend on the law and use legal terms. But they frequently make mistakes and sometimes are absurd', he wrote. But Emily Bronte was not absurd. 'What is remarkable about *Wuthering Heights* is that the ten or twelve legal references are … sufficient to enable us to ascertain the various legal processes by which Heathcliff obtained … [his] property'. Then Sanger pauses, apologises, saying 'I must explain very shortly the law of entails'.[2] There was need to do this in the 1920s; readers would not understand in the way a genteel young woman of the early nineteenth century understood. We – historians – who *have to* understand as much as Emily Bronte did to know what is going on in her text and in West Yorkshire at the turn of the nineteenth century – know far less than they did. Discussing the marriage law that frames much of *Wuthering Heights*, Susan Staves says that 'it is not necessary to be a lawyer to understand [its] … history'; but still…[3]

This chapter considers the law of marriage as promulgated from the highest point of authority in the English legal system, as it affected women – and men. What ordinary people and extraordinary writers on both sides of the Atlantic, from 1770 to the present day, *believed* William Blackstone had said in his *Commentaries on the Laws of England*, about women, and coverture, and the married state, turns out to be as important historically speaking, as what the lawyers, writing their innumerable guides to the law of everyday life, told them he *had* said about the law of women. However, a magistrate consulting one of those handbooks and the poor woman before the bench, listening to his pronouncements about the state of her settlement under the Old Poor Law and imminent removal with her children to the parish of her absconded husband, did not often read (the magistrate) or hear (the woman of inferior condition) the words *Blackstone* and *coverture*. *She* learned perhaps, that 'the English courts and their processes were what they were', and did not blame Blackstone

---

[1]   A shorter version of this chapter was published in Anthony Page and Wilfrid Prest (eds.), *Blackstone and His Critics*, Hart, Oxford, 2018, pp. 133–52.

[2]   Charles Percy Sanger, *The Structure of Wuthering Heights*, Hogarth Essays XIX, Hogarth Press, London, 1926; the website www.wuthering-heights.co.uk/wh/sanger.php reproduces the book in full.

[3]   Susan Staves, *Married Women's Separate Property in England, 1660–1833*, Harvard University Press, Cambridge, MA, and London, 1990, p. viii.

because she had never heard of him.[4] A woman of more elevated degree
had the bourgeois heroine of her novel *Maria* rail against the law of marriage, and all 'the partial laws of society' which 'had bastilled [her] for
life'. In Mary Wollstonecraft's *The Wrongs of Woman; or Maria* (1798), the
abused wife of the title says that all married women are 'as much a man's
property as his horse, or his ass'; not one of them has anything 'she can
call her own'. All husbands can do what hers has done: 'use any means
to get at what the law considers as his, the moment his wife is in possession of it...and, all this is done with a show of equity, because, forsooth,
he is responsible for her maintenance'. Then Wollstonecraft has a poorer
woman than she or her heroine state the case in the simplest terms: the
landlady of the lodging house where Maria seeks refuge explains her
reluctance to take her in with 'Madam, you must not be angry if I am
afraid to run any risk, when I know so well, that women have always the
worst of it, when law is to decide'.[5]

Blackstone's audiences were composed of men, women, and children, of high degree and of inferior condition. Magistrates and attorneys and farmers and cooks (as in the epigraphs to this chapter) may
not have read the *Commentaries* – some may never have 'heard of
Blackstone' – but in their reception of his legal doctrines, or what
were purported to be his doctrines, they played a part in making the
'Blackstone' inherited by the twenty-first-century Atlantic world. So
too did many social and political theorists make 'Blackstone'. Long
after his death, Blackstone was arraigned by feminist thinkers (male
and female) for the doctrine of coverture; it was sometimes implied
that it was his invention. Modern historians have readjusted the
accounts of Blackstone's nineteenth- and twentieth-century critics.
They have pointed out that strict application of the law of coverture
would have made it impossible to manage – to live – everyday life,
within households and outside them.[6] This chapter continues their
work in acknowledging the complex socio-economic and legal realities of eighteenth-century England in which men and women lived
their lives and understood the law. Here are traced out some of the

---

[4] Thomas P. Gallanis, 'Introduction', in William Blackstone, *Commentaries on the Laws of England: Book III of Private Wrongs* (1768), Oxford University Press, Oxford, 2016, pp. x–xi.

[5] Mary Wollstonecraft, *The Wrongs of Woman; or Maria: A Fragment in Two Volumes, Posthumous Works of the Author of a Vindication of the Rights of Woman, in Four Volumes,* Joseph Johnson, London, 1798, Vol. 2, pp. 34, 45, 99.

[6] Tim Stretton and Krista J. Kesselring (eds.), *Married Women and the Law: Coverture in England and the Common Law World*, McGill-Queen's University Press, Montreal, 2013, passim, and pp. 3–22.

pathways of knowledge, transmission and critique of what Blackstone wrote and was reputed to have written about women. At the end, we shall briefly see Blackstone as a judge administering the law he had commented on in the 1760s, in the everyday world of assizes and the London high courts, in the everyday world of women, in a state of coverture.

★★★

Understood as an educational innovation from its first publication, Blackstone's *Commentaries* was summarised, extracted from and anthologised by the printers and booksellers of England from the 1770s onwards.[7] At the booksellers' annual dinner, they toasted Blair's *Sermons*, Buchan's *Domestic Medicine*, and the Burns' *Justice of the Peace* – 'The Three Bs' – for the immense profits their manuals had brought them. They should have toasted *Four* Bs says William St Clair, for they had done just as well out of the *Commentaries*.[8] In his preface to Book I, Blackstone mentioned the 'friends' who thought his 1750s Oxford lectures to law students (in which the *Commentaries* originated) 'not wholly unworthy of the public eye'. No such modest deprecation for the booksellers, who puffed the *Commentaries* in all the versions they produced. Law students may have been seen as their target readership, but the booksellers' abridged versions for use in schools and in the education of young ladies found a wider market in parents and schoolteachers. Simon Stearn has found Blackstone in handbooks and guides and encyclopaedias; Blackstone appeared in Knox's *Elegant Extracts* and in the *Beauties of English Prose*.[9] The first, from 1784 right through to the new century, included passages from the *Commentaries* on the history of juries, on the law of the manor, and on the origin and right of exclusive property.[10] The beauty perceived in Blackstone's account of 'The Feodal System. History of its Rise and

---

[7] Wilfrid Prest, *William Blackstone: Law and Letters in the Eighteenth Century*, Oxford University Press, Oxford, 2008, p. 310.

[8] William St Clair, *The Reading Nation in the Romantic Period*, Cambridge University Press, Cambridge, 2004, p. 270. For the American reprint market, where Blackstone kept company with, not 'the Bs', but Adam Smith and the historian William Robertson, see p. 389.

[9] Simon Stearn, 'Introduction', in William Blackstone, *Commentaries on the Laws of England: Book II Of the Rights of Things* (1766), Oxford University Press, Oxford, 2016, p. xxii.

[10] Vicesimus Knox, *Elegant Extracts; Or, Useful and Entertaining Pieces of Poetry, Selected for the Improvement of Young Persons*, Johnson, Baldwin and 12 others, London, 1803.

Progress' was resolutely reproduced from 1772 onwards in copies of *Beauties*, on both sides of the Atlantic.[11]

Blackstone's 'patriotic history of civil liberties', the stories he told about Anglo-Saxon freedoms, the Norman Yoke, and Alfred the Great and Edward the Confessor as great lawgivers, mapped onto many common tales of 'our ancient constitution', and how we got to be the English people we were.[12] His observations on language history might be found in amusing guides to local history; his account of the sumptuary laws ended up in a handbook for apprentice hairdressers.[13] The historical tales told in the *Commentaries* were repeated in books for children; they also resonated in the introduction to many guides for magistrates administering the law. Here too, was a history that *explained* to a justice of the peace what he was doing as he wearily recorded yet another bastardy examination, or heard out a woman craving the peace against her husband, or a domestic servant seeking a settlement.[14] The history recounted by Blackstone and reproduced for children and young people was always history *for something*: his Alfred and Atlestan, his William and all his Edwards explained the present by a story of the past. The girls and young women who, in Jane Austen's *Mansfield Park* (1814) and *Northanger Abbey* (1817), complain about the *boringness* of history – that mere list of kings' names – could have found history with a purpose in the *Commentaries* and all their extracted reprints.

Literature for children *instructed* and *educated* in the ways of civil society and its history; great political and legal principles might be expounded in a household tale. In Dorothy Kilner's *Life and Perambulations of a Mouse* (1783) Mouse Nimble (an early – and great – anthropologist of the nursery) overhears a mother castigate an appallingly behaved little girl who has just been extremely rude to her nursemaid, and slapped her too: "'And who do you think will

---

[11] *The Beauties of English Prose: Being A Select Collection of Moral, Critical, and Entertaining Passages, Disposed in the Manner of Essays*, Vol. 2, Hawes Clarke and Collins and 3 others, London, 1772.

[12] William Blackstone, *Commentaries on the Laws of England: Book I Of the Rights of Persons* (1765), Intro. David Lemmings, Oxford University Press, Oxford, 2016; Wilfrid Prest, *General Editor's Introduction*, pp. xiii–xiv.

[13] Thomas Wilson, *An Accurate Description of Bromley, in Kent, Ornamented with Views of the Church and College*, for the author, Bromley, 1797; James Stewart, *Plocacosmos; Or, the Whole Art of Hair Dressing; Wherein is Contained, Ample Rules for the Young Artizan, More Particularly for Ladies Women*, for the author, London, 1782, p. 127.

[14] History-as-a-guide for magistrates in their everyday administration of the law had been common at the beginning of the century. After 1770, new handbooks and guides increasingly used Blackstone in their prolegomena and introductions – but very rarely in the body of the text, which was designed to offer practical advice and case law to hard-pressed justices of the peace.

do anything for you, if you are not good, and do not speak civilly! Not *I*, I promise you, neither shall nurse or any of the servants, for though *I pay her wages to do my business for me*, I never want them to do anything, unless they are desired in a pretty manner'".[15] Quite apart from the surprise (which could have been felt by nineteenth-century Atlantic-world suffragists, suffragettes and many a twentieth-century historian) of finding a married woman *in her coverture* contracting with servants for their labour and matter-of-factly talking about 'my business', there is the astonishment of her exposition of the legal and political philosophy of John Locke to a four-year-old. Really, 'in strictness every body ought to transact his own affairs', advised John Barry Bird in1799; 'it is by the favour and indulgences of the law that he can delegate the power of acting for him to another'.[16] Bird (and the fictional mother from 1784) repeated John Locke's lesson, about what happened, legally speaking, when a person 'make himself a servant to another by selling him, for a certain time, the service he undertakes to do in exchange for wages he is to receive'. In that moment of hiring (in such an act of contract), the labour becomes the master's (or the mistress's, as in Nimble's household and countless others across the country). Blackstone may not have agreed with Locke over the 'original compact' inaugurating civil society, but on the question of labour transfer and labour as formative of property, he endorsed the view from the 1690s, explaining (as Bird was to do) that the relationship between master and servant was 'founded in convenience, whereby a man is directed to call in the assistance of others where his own skill and labour will not be sufficient to answer the cares incumbent upon him'. Blackstone further agreed with Locke that 'bodily labour, bestowed upon any subject which before lay in common to all men, is universally allowed to give the fairest and most reasonable title to an exclusive property therein'.[17] Married women whose own skill and labour were not sufficient to answer the cares of cooking and child-care and the cash crop growing beyond the garden wall contracted with servants for their labour as if they had never heard of coverture. Magistrates in their justicing room listening to disputing men, maids

---

[15] Dorothy Kilner, *Life and Perambulations of a Mouse*, John Marshall, London, 1784, p. 31. My italics.

[16] John Barry Bird, *Laws Respecting Masters and Servants, Articled Clerks, Apprentices, Manufacturers, Labourers and Journeymen*, 3rd ed., W. Clarke, London, 1799, p. 6.

[17] John Locke, *Two Treatises of Government* (1690) (Book Two, Chapter 5, Section 26); Blackstone, *Commentaries I*, p. 271; *Commentaries II*, p. 3. For the remarks on the original contract, *Commentaries I*, pp. xxix, 38–41.

and mistresses never inquired into *who*, on the employer's side, made the contract, for the only point of interest was the nature of the hiring agreement: what the contracting parties had agreed to do.[18]

***

Shall we agree to imagine the (fictional) little girl from *Perambulations* some years on, at the age of thirteen perhaps? She has encountered Sir William and his *Commentaries* many times, anthologised in literature designed to educate her into what she must become. Were she to hold an actual volume of the *Commentaries* in her hands, she would not find it difficult to read, for all the reasons of style and grammatical construction his most recent editors have noted.[19] Anyway, she'd been encountering fragments of it all through her reading life. On the Woman she was (by some accounts) so relentlessly being inducted into being, she might think, *How fine to be a Queen*! for the fourth chapter of *Commentaries I* tells her that 'the queen is of ability to purchase lands, and to convey them, to make leases, to grant copyholds, and to do other acts of ownership, with out the concurrence of her lord; which no other married woman can do: a privilege as old as the Saxon aera'.[20] There is fascinating detail about queens and sturgeons and whalebone and stays (were she twelve or so, she was probably wearing her first pair of stays as she read). To be sure, the dark shadow of coverture falls, for the same passages tell her that a queen is 'not, like other married women, so closely connected as to have lost all legal or separate existence so long as the marriage continues'; but our (legal-fictional) girl would have to read far into Book I to learn how very great the difference was between a queen and the rest of English married womankind.[21] If it's now, say, 1795, and she gets that far, she may be surprised at Blackstone's comment on Coke upon Littleton, stating that 'the very being or legal existence of the woman is suspended during the marriage, or at least incorporated and consolidated into that of her husband: under whose wing, protection, and *cover*, she performs every thing: and is therefore called in our law-french a *feme-covert*... her

---

[18] Or: they never *recorded* asking whether husband or wife had made the agreement in the dozens of extant justices' notebooks from the eighteenth-century. Carolyn Steedman, *Labours Lost: Domestic Service and the Making of Modern England*, Cambridge University Press, Cambridge, 2009, pp. 172–98.

[19] See comments of Simon Stearn and Ruth Paley, in *Commentaries II*, p. xiv, and William Blackstone, *Commentaries on the Laws of England: Book IV of Public Wrongs* (1769), Intro. Ruth Paley, Oxford University Press, Oxford, 2016, pp. vii–xxvi, passim.

[20] *Commentaries I*, 'Of the King's Royal Family', pp. 142–6.

[21] *Commentaries I*, Chapter 15, 'Of Husband and Wife', pp. 279–87.

condition during her marriage is called her *coverture*'. It had not been much repeated in the law reports, newspapers, crime sheets, crim. con.-lit. or in guides to everyday life, these twenty years past. Her parents, concerned as all bourgeois parents must be, about the onerous task of getting her settled in marriage in a few years time, with control over her own property, moveable and real, as well-protected as it might be, may have purchased the anonymous and estimable *Laws Respecting Women* (1777), in which coverture was discussed in great detail, following directly on quotation from the *Commentaries*.[22] Its anonymous author was praised two centuries on for devoting '449 pages compared to the meagre nine Blackstone devoted to the law concerning husband and wife'.[23] A law dictionary of 1791, targeted at students and attorneys of a philosophical bent, repeated Blackstone word for word; *An Exposition of the Hair Powder Act, Setting Forth its Legal Operation* of 1795, did the same.[24] But Blackstone's exposition of the law of coverture was not recycled for the educational market in the way of his legal and constitutional history.

If our fictional girl got as far as the end of *Commentaries I*, she would have found a stronger statement of coverture than the one she may have encountered in guides to learning for the fair sex and in pocket primers on the law. (She is protean! She is a figment of the imagination. She is a reading fiction.) An *English Expositor* of 1641, teaching the 'interpretation of the hardest words used in our language' explained that *Coverture* 'signifieth all the time, that a man and wife are coupled in marriage'; or it meant 'a married wife: a woman subject to a husband...In our

---

22 *The Laws Respecting Women, as they Regard their Natural Rights, or their Connections and Conduct; in which their Interests and Duties as Daughters, Wives, Wards, Widows, Heiresses, Mothers, Spinsters, Legatees, Sisters, Executrixes, &c. Are Ascertained and Enumerated*, J. Johnson, London, 1777, pp. 65–6.

23 Nicola Phillips, *Women in Business, 1700–1850*, Boydell Press, Woodbridge, 2006, p. 35. Its author was a practising attorney (maybe a barrister), as not only does a footnote reveal, but his style: no elegant and balanced s+v+o sentences here, for which Blackstone is rightly lauded by Stephen Stearn and Ruth Paley, but the entangled grammar of the scissors-and-paste job, and a wild generosity of footnote references to Blackstone and the Reports. It is much more like the majority of magistrates' handbooks than its major source. For the identity-revealing footnote, p. 142. Useful, though: it lets us imagine Mr Bennet holed up in his library not just avoiding Mrs Bennet, but acquiring *really useful knowledge* for getting *five* daughters well and equitably settled in marriage. Jane Austen, *Pride and Prejudice* (1813), Chapters 3, 8, 15, 20, 49, 55, 57, 59.

24 *A Law Grammar; Or, An Introduction to the Theory and Practice of English Jurisprudence, Containing Rudiments and Illustrations*, G. G. and J. Robinson and 4 others, London, 1791; *An Exposition of the Hair Powder Act, Setting Forth its Legal Operation; with A Full Abstract of the Act; by a Barrister*, G. G. and J. Robinson, London, 1795.

Common Law ... [the word] is sometime taken for marriage'.[25] In 1694, *coverture* was explained to the ladies both legally and etymologically: French word – a bed covering – but 'in Law ... particularly apply'd to the Estate and Condition of a married Woman, who by the Laws of the Realm is in *potestate viri*, under *Coverture* or *Covert-Baron*, and therefore disabled to make any bargain or contract, without her Husband's consent or privity, or without his Allowance or Confirmation'.[26] Whole treatises, directed at the popular market, were devoted to the topic.[27] You could learn *something* of coverture from a stage play of 1675.[28] Guides to coverture for the legal and writing clerk market usually cited the statement of Coke upon Littleton for their many expositions of coverture in relation to property law, but like their authority, gave no definition or statement of its principle.[29] If you reduced 'the principles of law' to everyday 'practice', the strong implication was, that the law, being what it was, practical readers should just *get on with it*.[30]

From the 1730s onwards there was an explosion of books accounting for coverture with 'law' in the title, all of them referring in some way or other to Coke upon Littleton.[31] Law dictionaries; scriveners' guides; guides for attorneys, law students and clerks; handbooks to

---

[25] J. B., *An English Expositor Teaching the Interpretation of the Hardest Words Used in Our Language; with Sundry Explications, Descriptions and Discourses*, John Leggatt, London, 1641, no pagination. For a similar etymological approach, intended for law scriveners and students, John Cowell, *The Interpreter, Or, Book Containing the Signification of Words Wherein is Set Forth the True Meaning of All ... Words and Terms as are Mentioned in the Law-writers or Statutes ... Requiring Any Exposition or Interpretation; A Work Not Only Profitable But Necessary for Such as Desire Thoroughly to Be Instructed in the Knowledge of Our Laws, Statutes, or Other Antiquities*, F. Leach, London, 1658.

[26] N. H., *The Ladies Dictionary, Being A General Entertainment of the Fair-sex; A Work Never Attempted Before in English*, John Dunton, London, 1694.

[27] The Assigns of Richard and Edward Atkyns, *Baron and Feme; A Treatise of the Common Law Concerning Husbands and Wives*, John Walthoe, London, 1700; *A Treatise of Feme Coverts: Or, the Lady's Law: Containing All the Laws and Statutes Relating to Women*, B. Lintot, London, 1732.

[28] *The Woman Turn'd Bully A Comedy, Acted At the Duke's Theatre*, T. Dring, London, 1675.

[29] Edward Coke, *An Abridgement of the Lord Coke's Commentary on Littleton Collected by an Unknown Author; Yet by a Late Edition Pretended to be Sir Humphrey Davenport, Kt. and in this Second Impression Purged From Very Many Gross Errors Committed in the Said Former Edition, With a Table of the Most Remarkable Things Therein*, W. Lee, D. Pakeman, and G. Bedell, London, 1651.

[30] W. Phillipps, *The Principles of Law Reduced to Practice*, Hen. Twyford, Thomas Dring, John Place, London, 1660.

[31] An explosion if you search Eighteenth-Century Collections On-line, which is a good guide to tremors and tendencies in the print market. https://historicaltexts.jisc.ac.uk/, accessed 2 January 2019.

the law for clergymen, landlords, and tenants; abridgements of the law and the statutes, and the 'whole law' of property and trusts for conveyancers; attorneys' pocket books; a clerks' magazine; a justice of the peace's complete practice book... all stated *coverture*, and *baron* and *feme-covert*, and all without reference to the philosophical principle – or the history – of the thing, not even if an author promised the 'Grounds and Rudiments of Law and Equity'.[32] There was similar law self-help material for readers in the American colonies and the Sugar Islands, also making coverture as plain as a writer could, mostly by reference to Coke upon Littleton. Blackstone was (probably) the first to *explain* coverture by reference, not so much to legal philosophy but to history, or 'history' *as* a form of legal philosophy. It is because he *explained* coverture historically that he made a stronger statement of it than his authorities.[33]

Under the influence of 'the penetrating acuteness, and elegant pen of Sir William Blackstone', the author of *Laws Respecting Women* provided even plainer history lessons than his model. *How fine the life of an Anglo-Saxon woman!* thinks our law-reading fiction; *how deleterious the law of women imposed by Conquest!* And if she did not think that, then there are modern historians to do it for her: 'Coverture, the author [of *Laws of Women*] ... concluded, was the product of foreign Norman invasion in the eleventh century – not, as Blackstone would have it, a time-tested "English" legal practice. This was a reading of British history... that put a decidedly feminist twist on the idea of the "Norman Yoke"'.[34]

★★★

Young elite women and their parents needed to know about coverture; knowledge was their armoury for the marriage market. No room here for the embarrassment felt by one of Blackstone's later editors, or the outrage of many male feminists of the nineteenth century, John Stuart

---

[32] *Gentleman of the Middle Temple, The Grounds and Rudiments of Law and Equity; Alphabetically Digested; Containing a Collection of Rules or Maxims... with Three Tables... The second edition*, T. Osborne, London, 1751.

[33] Furthermore Blackstone's statement in the *Commentaries* was stronger than the one made in his *Analysis* (1757) where coverture was presented as affecting men and women equally: 'By Marriage the Husband and Wife become one Person in Law; which Unity is the principal Foundation of their respective Rights, Duties, and Disabilities'. *An Analysis of the Laws of England*, Clarendon Press, Oxford, 1756, p. 25.

[34] *The Laws Respecting Women*, Chapter 2, 'Of the Condition of Women; their Privileges and Obligations'; Phillips, *Women in Business*, pp. 23–4; Arianne Chernock, *Men and the Making of Modern British Feminism*, Stanford University Press, Stanford, CA, 2010, pp. 97, 126.

Mill among them.[35] Families bought hard, printed, practical advice about coverture; they were probably not in the market for abstract propositions about the suspension of 'the very being or legal existence of the woman' during marriage.[36] So too did magistrates need practical advice about coverture and the different classes of women who came before them. They had needed it in the seventeenth century before the eighteenth-century proliferation of statute law affecting poorer women created an even bigger print enterprise.[37] But few guides to administering the poor laws and the laws of settlement of the later eighteenth century cited Blackstone on coverture: they provided case law, and references to Coke and to Matthew Hale's *Analysis of the Law*, especially to the indexed version of 1713.[38] If we look to a clerical magistrate writing a guide for his brethren a century on, we find no reference to Blackstone in his detailed account of coverture as it affected married women and men of the poorer sort.[39]

Every magistrate writing a guide like this promised something new by way of arrangement and referencing. In 1818, Revd Clapham noted his own innovations and explained to country justices how to use his bulky two volumes: he will refer to Tomlins' *Law Dictionary* – 'a book of easy purchase' – to save the reader time; he will refer to Blackstone using the Christian edition of 1809; marginalia will refer to earlier editions. He has indexed the everyday language used to refer to common cases of life; he explains cross-referencing and how 'Apples' might lead you to

[35] 'By 1809, his [posthumous] editor Edward Christian had added substantial footnotes "apologising" for Blackstone's position on many facets of married women's law, and in particular for his assertion that women were "a favourite of the law", because of the many exemptions provided by the "protection" of coverture. Christian added two pages of notes disputing Blackstone's position and … a further note on a wife's ability to sue as if feme sole in equity'. Phillips, *Women in Business*, pp. 34–5. *Commentaries on the Laws of England in Four Books. By Sir William Blackstone … the Twelfth Edition, with the Last Corrections of the Author; and with Notes and Additions by Edward Christian*, A. Strahan and W. Woodfall for T. Cadell, London, 1793–1795.

[36] St Clair, *The Reading Nation*, p. 203.

[37] Joseph Keble, *An Assistance to Justices of the Peace, for the Easier Performance of Their Duty*, for the author, London, 1683.

[38] *Being An Abstract, of the Several Titles and Partitions of the Law of England, Digested into Method. Written by a Learned Hand*, John Walthor, London, 1713; *An Analysis of the Law, Being a Scheme or Abstract, of the several Titles and Partitions of the Law of England, Digested into Method. By Sir Matthew Hale, Kt., late Lord Chief Justice of the Court of King's Bench. The 2nd edition corrected. With the Addition of an Alphabetical Table*, Strahan, Tonson and four others, London, 1713.

[39] Rev. Samuel Clapham MA, *A Collection of the Several Points of Sessions' Law, Alphabetically arranged; contained in Burn and Williams on the Office of a Justice, Blackstone's Commentaries, East and Hawkins on Crown Law, Addington's Penal Statutes, and Const and Nolan on the Poor Laws, in two volumes*, Butterworth, Clarke, London, 1818, Vol. 1, pp. 347–8.

'Forcible Entry', and how, if a magistrate needs to know about selling beer in unlicensed premises, Clapham's system will in a trice lead him to two references in Addington, Burn, and Williams; one in Hawkins; and one in the *Law Dictionary*. 'A lawyer', he says, 'would, doubtless, have produced a publication more systematically arranged, and much better adapted to the utility of the profession; but perhaps less service-able to the country gentlemen who cannot be expected to discover the various sources from which subjects are drawn, and to which a person who has had a legal education would, naturally be directed'.[40]

What did a magistrate need to know about a married woman in her coverture? If one appeared before him, he may need to know how far she might be a bankrupt; – how she can join her husband in deal-ing with her own estate or jointure; – about the legal position on her chattels, in life and after it; – that if, for example, she got her fortune without the oversight of a court of equity, she has no recourse to such a court later on; – that she was not entitled to her jewels and so on, if she had barred herself before marriage out of everything she could claim of her husband's personal estate. And more: the magistrate needed to know the position of *femes soles* and *femes coverts* on contracting debt – when indeed, the high courts had directed a *feme covert* on a charge of debt to represent herself as a *feme sole*, or 'to plead coverture'. The magistrate needed to know about *femes coverts* making wills and about husbands leaving personal property. A *feme covert* can't bring an action in law or be sued alone, but she can be sued with her husband when she is made a defendant … And what magistrates most needed to know for management of interpersonal violence in the everyday life of the poorer sort was that a 'feme-covert may have security of peace against [her] husband'.[41]

A poor or pauper feme-covert was the most likely to be encountered in a justice's parlour, for coverture also operated in the lives of poor women – and men – interpellated by the Laws of Settlement. If they had 'married' in a way unauthorised by the Marriage Act (1753), their union was illegitimate: the woman is deemed 'not married' and cannot gain a settlement through her husband, for she actually does not have a husband. Marriages contracted beyond the seas are valid and the wife takes her husband's settlement; if it prove impossible to discover a hus-band's settlement, the woman reverts to her maiden settlement (there are particular problems with marrying a Scot or an Irishman, for the Act of Settlement does not apply in their homelands). The question of a

[40] Clapham, *Several Points of Sessions' Law*, Vol. 1, iii–ix.
[41] Clapham, *Several Points of Sessions' Law*, Vol. I, pp. 347–8.

married women being removed to her husband's settlement by herself is discussed in detail; if a widow has gained settlement in her own right, it cannot be altered by her marrying a second husband whose settlement is not ascertained. And much, much more.[42]

However heavy-handed, the Revd Clapham thought his two volumes an improvement on Richard Burn's three or four, which had dominated the legal advice market for the previous half-century. In the early editions of the eighteenth century's best-selling justices' manual, Burn had provided information on married women's legal status under the headings of 'coverture', 'feme covert', 'feme sole', and 'wife'. Magistrates needed to know about the position of married women in relation to the laws governing bastard children, and the production and sale of cambrick, among other topics, but above all, in relation to 'Poor: Settlement by Marriage'. The tenth edition (1766) abandoned the term *coverture* except in this case, and – for this was the function of such magistrates' guides – introduced them to new legislation and case law affecting married women, including on 'Larceny', 'Leather' (might the widow of a tanner carry on her husband's business?) and 'Lewdness'.[43] In the entry 'Excise', Burn told of 'a woman ... convicted for selling gin, and it appearing that she was a feme covert, it was objected that she could not be convicted, for as she could make no contract, it must be taken to be her husband's sale; or if she could be convicted, the husband ought to have been joined for conformity. It was answered that, where the crime is of such a nature, as can be committed by her alone, she may be prosecuted without her husband ...'[44]

There were multiple circumnavigations of coverture, and not only by wealthy parents using equity to ensure a young woman's financial independence in marriage.[45] In the fifteenth edition of Burn's manual (1785), there were no references to Blackstone and his *Commentaries* in discussing married women and their legal disabilities and one use of 'feme-sole' to provide a historical example under the heading 'Wife'; the greater part of the entries now covered the poor law, and settlement and removal.[46] John Burn, who continued his father's work into the

---

[42] Clapham, *Several Points of Sessions' Law*, Vol. II, pp. 279–83.

[43] Richard Burn, *The Justice of the Peace and Parish Officer: The tenth edition, in Four Volumes*, Woodfall and Strahan, London, 1766, Vol. 3, pp. 66, 78, 91, 334–5.

[44] Burn, *The Justice of the Peace* (1766), Vol. 2, p. 135.

[45] Cordelia Beattie and Matthew Frank Stevens (eds.), *Married Women and the Law in Premodern Northwest Europe*, Boydell & Brewer, Woodbridge, 2013; Phillips, *Women in Business*, pp. 23–47.

[46] Richard Burn, *The Justice of the Peace and Parish Officer: The fifteenth edition, in Four Volumes*, Strahan and Woodfall, London, 1785, Vol. 2, p. 206.

new century, included an even greater number of examples of married women and the laws concerning the poor.[47]

In Burn's *Justice*, *coverture* lingered as a word, a concept, and a legal formulary in relation to poor women and their families, not in relation to elite or middling-sort women. By far the largest number of justicing-room incidents recorded by Nottinghamshire magistrate Sir Gervase Clifton Bart between 1770 and 1815 related to the poor laws.[48] He needed to know about coverture (or whatever stood in for it) in regard to poor women, not in relation to all the middle-class Marias of the neighbourhood, their fortunes leeched away by their grasping husbands. He may well have encountered such a woman in his social life (and he had daughters to protect in marriage), but never in the parlour at Clifton Hall, which was crowded weekly by poor women craving the peace against their husbands, servants arguing contract with their mistresses, and working people whose employers said they had not finished the task they had contracted to perform.

Women craving the peace against their husbands – and interpersonal violence in general – preoccupied magistrate Clifton less than the poor-law business and the law of labour and employment. Yet 34 of the 217 of the cases he noted between 1770 and 1815 involved interpersonal, non-lethal violence, and a further 29 involved sexual and domestic violence; the majority of the last related to women asking for protection against their husbands and partners. In the *Commentaries*, Blackstone had historicised the question of how far a husband might 'give his wife moderate correction'; he had cited Hawkins; he was describing 'the old law' he said. The reason why, in former times, 'the law thought it reasonable to intrust... [a husband] with... power of restraining her, by domestic chastisement' was that, as with his servants and children, 'the master or parent is also liable in some cases to answer'. The power of correction had always been confined 'within reasonable bounds', he said. Some civil law had indeed sanctioned severer punishment *in the remote past*, but now, in a happier and more polite era 'a wife may... have security of the peace against her husband'; indeed, the ability of a husband to beat

---

[47] *The Justice of the Peace, and Parish Officer. By Richard Burn, LL.D. Late Chancellor of the Diocese of Carlisle. Continued to the Present Time by John Burn, Esq. His Son, The Eighteenth Edition: Revised and Corrected. In Four Volumes*, Strahan and Woodfall, London, 1793, Vol 3.

[48] Carolyn Steedman, *An Everyday Life of the English Working Class: Work, Self and Sociability in Early Nineteenth-Century England*, Cambridge University Press, Cambridge, 2013, pp. 127–8; Barbara J. Todd, '"To Be Some Body": Married Women and The Hardships of the English Laws', Hilda Smith (ed.), *Women Writers and the Early Modern British Political Tradition*, Cambridge University Press, New York, 2010, pp. 343–62.

his wife had been questioned as far back as the reign of Charles II.[49] He then threw the same dark light on working-class husbands, as nineteenth-century feminists and twentieth-century historians were to do, remarking (perhaps satirically) that 'the lower rank of people, who were always fond of the old common law, still claim and exert their antient privilege...'[50] Many Clifton wives and girlfriends complained to the magistrate about being most brutally used; whether they or their partners thought they were exerting an ancient privilege in hitting them is an imponderable question. What is clear is that they knew they *could* ask the local magistrate to restrain their men; what Sir Gervase knew was that the poor women complaining to him had the legal ability to crave the peace against them.

But Blackstone's statement on domestic chastisement figured not at all in the legal imagination of Sir Gervase Clifton or of the women who trudged up the avenue from the village to Clifton Hall. When – if – the magistrates' handbooks provided guidance on the marital chastisement question, they cited *seventeenth-century* authorities. What a *modern* magistrate needed to know was to do with a married woman's ability to crave the peace, not her husband's beating of her. The case was somewhat different in the United States, as we shall see. The internet is alive to the sound of Francis Buller, Justice of King's Bench, 1778–1794, allegedly opining in 1782 that a wife might be beaten with a stick no bigger than her husband's thumb, with many careful accounts of the case law Buller *did* actually refer to on that occasion, and a great many reproductions of Gillray's very funny depiction of 'Judge Thumb'. There was no such journey of dark hilarity though the magistrates' handbooks to attribute to Blackstone the 'rule of thumb', although those who saw the Gillray print were at liberty to make the connection (and one judge with a name beginning with 'B' sounds pretty much like another).[51]

***

[49] Blackstone, *Commentaries Book I*, pp. 286–7.
[50] Reva B. Siegel, '"The Rule of Love": Wife Beating as Prerogative and Privacy', *Yale Law Journal*, 106 (1996), pp. 2117–207; Joanne Bailey, '"I dye by Inches": Locating Wife Beating in the Concept of a Privatization of Marriage and Violence in Eighteenth-century England', *Social History*, 31:3 (2006), pp. 273–94; Jo Aitken, '"The Horrors of Matrimony among the Masses": Feminist Representations of Wife Beating in England and Australia, 1870–1914', *Journal of Women's History*, 19 (2007), pp. 107–31.
[51] National Portrait Gallery, NPG D12316, Sir Francis Buller, 1st Bt ('Judge Thumb'), by James Gillray, published by William Humphrey, hand-coloured etching, published 27 November 1782; James Oldham, 'Buller, Sir Francis, first baronet (1746–1800)', *Oxford Dictionary of National Biography*, Oxford University Press, Oxford, 2004. Accessed 5 March 2017.

I once thought to ask if my hypothetical law-reading girl of the 1790s felt angry at Blackstone's account of coverture, but now the question does not seem worth the asking, and *not* because she was one who preferred 'the compilation of receipts to that of records' so condescendingly figured by the *Caledonian Bee*. 'Coverture' had implications for women of wealthy families and for those of the very poor sort, not for a girl like her. But the pathways of the *Commentaries* through print culture and civil society in the new United States were different, and criticism of Blackstone's position on women was loud and vociferous. And it *was* seen in the United States as a 'position' on wives and wife-beating – no matter how anachronistic the term – not a mere restatement of what 'everyone knew' anyway, and had known, from at least the seventeenth century, about women and the law. Blackstone's statement of the doctrine of coverture has enraged many, says Nicola Phillips. It was a rage fomented in the United States, which then made its way back across the Atlantic to twentieth-century Britain.[52] All commentators on this process, including Blackstone's severest critic, the US historian Mary Ritter Beard, pointed out that the *Commentaries* were fundamentally important to the shaping of the US constitution, and played a role in US legal education in a way they never did in the United Kingdom.[53] Early nineteenth-century US legal treatises *discussed* the 'chastisement prerogative', ambivalently to be sure, but loudly, in a way that was not the case in England.[54]

Ritter Beard's 1946 critique of the *Commentaries* focussed on the way in which 'Blackstone Extinguished the Married Women's Personality'.[55] The subjection of women was writ large throughout history, she said; all historians had done similar work to Blackstone in ignoring the multiple

---

[52] Phillips, *Women in Business*, pp. 24–5; The Papers of Elizabeth Cady Stanton and Susan B. Anthony Project, http://ecssba.rutgers.edu/index.html, accessed 20 July 2018; Berenice A. Carroll, 'Mary Beard's *Women as a Force in History:* A Critique', Caroll (ed.), *Liberating Women's History: Theoretical and Critical Essays*, University of Illinois Press, Champaign, IL, 1976, pp. 26–41.

[53] Phillips, *Women in Business*, pp. 34–5; Mary Ritter Beard, *Woman as Force in History: A Study in Traditions and Realities*, Macmillan, New York, 1946 (repr. 1962); Raymond and Colin Polin, *Foundations of American Political Thought*, Peter Lang, Pieterlen, 2009; Prest, *William Blackstone*, p. 291.

[54] Siegel, 'The Rule of Love'. And still do discuss it: John E. B. Myers, *Myers on Evidence in Child, Domestic, and Elder Abuse Cases*, 2 vols, Aspen, New York, 2005, Vol. 1, p. 763.

[55] Beard was a much more severe critic of Blackstone as a person: she claimed that 'his thinking and writing about law were visibly influenced by his acquired sentiment of class' and that, 'like many a commoner, [he] ... outdid the gentleman in his effusive praises of the ruling class in State and Church'. Beard, *Women as a Force*, p. 91.

ways in which women *could* and *did* act. Blackstone had played his part in effacing women's agency by concentrating on the common law rather than on equity which, said Beard, 'enforced trusts and other understandings that assured to married women rights of property denied to them by the Common Law'.[56] 'Blackstone was savagely attacked...by the American feminist Mary Beard for his omissions, particularly over women's legal rights in equity', says Phillips.[57] She goes on to discuss the feminist position in which 'law' is held responsible both for 'causing women's subordination and being a reflection of the patriarchal attitudes that lay behind it'; 'the claim that the common law reduces women to mere objects of property is...still a common one among modern feminists'.[58] In the 1970s, a wave of feminism transported Blackstone and his US reputation back to Britain. In the United Kingdom, Beard's critique was joined to new readings of John Stuart Mill's feminist argument in *The Subjection of Women* (1869), and to early twentieth-century suffrage-inspired histories, like Alice Clark's.[59] A particularly important text for British feminism was the 1983 reissue of Mill's pained and painful account of violence perpetrated against women by men and the law, by the feminist publishing house Virago.[60] Ray Strachey's *The Cause*, first published in the United Kingdom in 1928, appeared as a US imprint for the first time in 1969 and was reissued by Virago Press for the UK market in 1978. Strachey used the term *coverture system* when describing the parliamentary campaign for women's property

---

[56] Beard, *Women as a Force*, pp. 92–105; Cordelia Beattie and Matthew Frank Stevens, 'Introduction: Uncovering Married Women', Beattie and Stevens (eds.), *Married Women and the Law*, pp. 1–10.

[57] Phillips, *Women in Business*, p. 35.

[58] Ibid., p. 25.

[59] This brief account of Blackstone's transatlantic journeys owes much to Nicola Phillips' brilliant disentanglement of them in *Women in Business*. Kate Soper, 'Introduction', John Stuart Mill, *The Subjection of Women*, Harriet Taylor Mill, *The Enfranchisement of Women*, Virago, London, 1983, pp. i–xvi; Alice Clark's, *The Working Life of Women in the Seventeenth Century* was published in 1919. For the feminist movement in historical writing, June Hannam, 'Women's history, feminist history', www.history.ac.uk/makinghistory. Also June Purvis, 'From "Women Worthies" to Post-structuralism? Debate and Controversy in Women's History in Britain', Purvis (ed.), *Women's History: Britain, 1850–1945 – An Introduction*, Routledge, London, 1995, pp. 1–19. For the way in which Beard's account 'misleads on the subject of equity' (and makes Blackstone and Mill 'strange bedfellows'), Eileen Spring, *Law, Land, and Family: Aristocratic Inheritance in England, 1300 to 1800*, University of North Carolina Press, Chapel Hill, NC, 1993, p. 116.

[60] For John Stuart Mill as a nineteenth- and twentieth-century feminist, Kate Soper, 'Introduction'.

rights. By this route, British readers learned of *Blackstone* and *coverture*, terms previously not in their historical lexicon.[61]

We have now a more complex and contradictory picture of ordinary women's economic lives than the one put in place by Blackstone's nineteenth-and twentieth-century Atlantic-world critics. There were many circuitous routes by which different sections of the law allowed married women to trade without changing the doctrine of coverture. Wealthy families might have some access to a court of equity in its protection of a woman's property in marriage. Margot Finn has described the proliferation of courts of conscience ('Courts of Request' or 'Small Debts Courts') from the 1780s onwards. These were equity courts which allowed the small debtor to circumnavigate the common law, and they were, according to Finn and one of their first Birmingham commissioners William Hutton (encountered in the last chapter), full of women, married, unmarried, and who-knows-what, pursuing their own economic ends.[62] All eighteenth-century legal treatises explained the exceptions to coverture, with a particular emphasis given to married women *feme-sole* traders.[63] Recently, Amy Erikson has dramatically reversed the older historical picture by claiming that England developed an extensive capitalist economy earlier than did mainland Europe *because of* the gender structure of English property law. A 'cash economy, the debt-credit markets, and public investment' spread so completely throughout the society because of 'the flipside of coverture', that is, because unmarried women (*femes-soles*; the never-married, widows) enjoyed a position unique in Europe as legal individuals in their own right, with no requirement for a male guardian... married English women had fewer resources at their disposal but single English women had more resources at their disposal than elsewhere... England was unique in considering unmarried adult women... as legal individuals'. That is half, or more than half, of the adult female population, at any point

[61] Ray Strachey, *The Cause: A Short History of the Women's Movement in Great Britain*, Bell, London, 1928; reprint: Port Washington, NY, Kennikat Press, 1969; reprint: London, Virago, 1978, pp. 270–1; p. 15 for Blackstone and the legal disabilities of women.

[62] William Hutton, *Courts of Request; their Nature, Utility, and Powers described, with a Variety of Cases, determined in that of Birmingham*, Pearson and Rollason, Birmingham, R. Baldwin, London, 1787; Margot Finn, *The Character of Credit: Personal Debt in English Culture, 1740–1914*, Cambridge University Press, Cambridge, 2003, pp. 202–5.

[63] Phillips, *Women in Business*, p. 30.

in time.[64] In 1992, Linda Colley said the same. She rehearsed the conventional story of women and property and coverture to conclude that, as far as property ownership was concerned, 'female Britons were in much the same position as the majority of their male countrymen'.[65]

Historians have uncovered some of the complex arrangements – some say, stratagems – by which men and women, and attorneys and magistrates, made the laws respecting women work for the purposes of everyday life during the long eighteenth century, but as yet we posses only one extraordinary account of how coverture operated in the heart and mind of an eighteenth-century American woman. Abigail Bailey (b. 1746, New Hampshire) struggled with the idea of coverture and what it implied about her marriage to a violent and abusive man who knew the law and lawyers much better than did she, all through the 1780s and 1790s.[66] Her memoirs have been read by Hendrik Hartog for her 'common sense assumptions about law and marital power and personal transformation'. Her struggles on the page suggest that coverture did not so much 'extinguish the married woman's personality' (as Ritter Beard had it); rather, it enhanced knowledge of her own spiritual being, of herself as one of God's creatures, and thus as a social creature, too. The recent collection *Married Women and the Law* emphasises throughout what Abigail Bailey learned so painfully (yet in Hartog's account, so triumphantly): that eighteenth-century Anglo-American law 'considered a married woman's soul...her own'.[67]

Nineteenth-century novelists (Emily Bronte remains our example here) explored similar propositions in their characterisation of femescoverts – and their husbands. Bronte's modern critics sometimes link Blackstone to coverture and wife beating, all over again. A 2009 article on *Wuthering Heights* discusses Bronte's knowledge of coverture and

[64] Amy Louise Erickson, 'Coverture and Capitalism', *History Workshop Journal*, 59 (2005), pp. 1–16. She further argues that the 'multiplicity of different solutions to the problems presented by coverture, and...a plethora of lawsuits to clarify the legality of those solutions' led inevitably to 'increasingly complex legal/financial instruments and an increased willingness to litigate' (6–8); this stimulated a capitalist economy characterized by confidence in property law. See also Sally Wheeler, 'Going Shopping', Linda Mulachy and Sally Wheeler (eds.), *Feminist Perspectives on Contract Law*, Glasshouse, London, 2005, pp. 22–49.

[65] Linda Colley, *Britons: Forging the Nation, 1707–1837*, Yale University Press, New Haven, CT, 1992, p. 39.

[66] Henrik Hartog, 'Abigail Bailey's Coverture: Law in a Married Woman's Consciousness', Austin Sarat and Thomas R. Kearns (eds.), *Law in Everyday Life*, University of Michigan Press, Ann Arbor, MI, 1993.

[67] Stretton and Kesselring, 'Introduction', *Married Women and the Law*, p. 12; Barbara J. Todd, 'Written in Her Heart: Married Women's Separate Allegiance in English Law', idem, pp. 163–91; 164.

the 'prerogative of chastisement', demonstrated in her depiction of Heathcliff: 'While before his marriage... [he] confesses to the violent fantasy of turning Isabella's "blue eyes black, every day or two", after his marriage he knows that he must exercise a certain restraint. He remains within the accepted code of conduct for the *baron*, which grants him, according to William Blackstone, the power of restraining her, by domestic chastisement'.[68] Knowing more about the law of marriage than any twenty-first-century historian possibly can, Emily Bronte nowhere mentioned Blackstone or coverture. Nelly Dean's stunned, disaligned stoicism, as she relates the violence she has seen perpetrated against her several mistresses and the children of the Heights' household, is perhaps a measure of the knowledge that Bronte bestowed on her characters.[69]

★★★

He made the strongest eighteenth-century statement of the principle of coverture, yet it is unlikely that we will ever discover Blackstone's own opinion on the matter – or that it would be very illuminating if we could. A sight of the personal legal advice he provided for family and friends in regard to marriage settlement and women's property would be interesting, but it would probably only reveal a lawyer and a friend doing the best he could with the law *as it was* in regard to elite women, just like everyone else.[70] We have to look to his practice rather than any imputed opinion on the matter of coverture. Wilfrid Prest says that a detailed reconstruction of Blackstone's Westminster Hall activities may well be beyond our reach.[71] And though our reach may extend to the interstices of its everyday functioning, in the assessed taxes appeal system, for example, in poor law settlement appeals to King's Bench, we learn little more. We can see what he said and what he did within the appeal system, just as we can find him making judgement at county assizes, but he spoke as 'the court', not as a person. And yet his words

[68] Judith E. Pike, '"My name *was* Isabella Linton": Coverture, Domestic Violence, and Mrs Heathcliff's Narrative in *Wuthering Heights*', *Nineteenth-Century Literature*, 64 (2009), pp. 347–83, 368. The most recent restatement of coverture/rule-of-thumb is by Samantha Ellis, *Take Courage: Anne Bronte and the Art of Life*, Chatto and Windus, London, 2017, p. 213; which is (also) a brilliant account of the domestic violence Bronte figured in *Agnes Grey* (1847) and *The Tenant of Wildfell Hall* (1848).

[69] Carolyn Steedman, *Master and Servant: Love and Labour in the English Industrial Age*, Cambridge University Press, Cambridge, 2007, pp. 193–216.

[70] Prest, *William Blackstone*, pp. 122–3.

[71] Ibid., p. 167.

are an indication of the experience of those few married women whose coverture was a matter for discussion in court. In the spring of 1779, for example, at Kent Assizes, the court heard an action of trespass and assault for criminal conversation with a plaintiff's wife. Blackstone, assize judge, wondered whether or not the court should proceed, for there had been a misdirection in point of evidence. This was to do with the consequences of the Marriage Act of 1753, and the very great difficulties all courts, high and low, had over the next thirty years in determining whether a couple was actually married or not. The cause was tried again at the next Assizes, when a verdict was found for the plaintiff – the husband.[72] No space here for even the shadow of an 'opinion' to be discerned by the historian, for Blackstone was not on circuit at the Kent Summer Assizes.[73]

It mattered much to a woman that she was legally married. In London in the same year, at the Old Bailey, London, Mary Adey was tried before three judges of King's Bench (not Blackstone; he was not present) for the wilful murder of a London peace officer. He had been attempting to take into custody a Sgr Farmello with whom she lived. The question was, as noted by the reporter, whether 'a woman, who in a transport of passion, kills a peace officer who is about to take the man she cohabits with to prison, under a warrant which turns out to be illegal, is guilty of murder or manslaughter?' The ill-worded warrant was not the point, said counsel. The case might have been of 'a different complexion in the eye of the law if Mary Adey had been the lawful wife of Farmello; but standing in the light she does, she must,

---

[72] Sylvester Douglas, *Reports of Cases argued and Determined in the Court of the King's Bench in he Nineteenth, Twentieth, and Twenty-first years of the Reign of George III, The Third Edition, Part I*, Strahan and Woodfall, London, 1790; 3 May 1779, Birt against Barlow; Lawrence Stone, *Road to Divorce: England 1530–1987*, Oxford University Press, Oxford, 1990, p. 233, for civil suits for criminal conversation at assizes. It is interesting that Blackstone was unimportant to Stone's story of marriage breakdown. The only reference to 'coverture' is in his chapter on 'contract marriage', where he draws a distinction between sixteenth-century canon and common law and their courts. He does describe 'the ancient legal concept that a married woman had no legal personality and lacked powers to borrow, sue, or transact any legal business' (p. 150); this suggests that conventional use of coverture to describe a married woman's disabilities developed among twenty-first-century historians.

[73] He was at Berkshire Assizes, at Abingdon, determining, among other points of law, that under 9 Geo I c. 22 ('The Black Act') horses *were* cattle, *if* they had been maimed and killed. See above, p. 80. Thomas Leach, *Cases in Crown Law, Determined by the Twelve Judges; by the Court of King's Bench and by Commissioners of Oyer and Terminer, and General Goal delivery from the Fourth Year of George the Second [1730] to the Fortieth Year of George the Third, the Third Edition with Corrections and Additions, in Two Volumes*, Butterworth, Cadell and Davies, London, 1800, Vol. 1, p. 72, King v John Paty.

not withstanding her cohabitation with him be considered as an absolute stranger, a meer stander bye; a person who had no right to be concerned in any degree whatever for Farmello. She therefore, being to all
intents and purposes a stranger, and having...stabbed the deceased,
she... [was in his] opinion guilty of murder'. Which is what the court
found.[74] A married woman deemed to have acted under the coercion of
her husband might have received a different verdict, as did Margaret
Chesser in 1784, though this was not a case of murder but of breaking and entering. 'Counsel for the prisoners contended...that the part
which [she]...had acted in this business, shewed that what she did was
by the coercion of her husband, and that, therefore, she could not be
found guilty...The Jury acquitted.... [her], and found her husband
guilty of stealing goods...to the value of forty shillings'.[75]

In his own *Reports*, Blackstone noted the opinion of Common Pleas
on married women, as, for example, in 1763 (long before he was a judge),
when a feme sole arrested for debt turned out to be a feme covert. The
court thought the shopkeeper bringing the case to blame: he should
have made better inquiries into her marital circumstances, and anyway,
'When a tradesman gives credit to a woman of genteel appearance for
articles of dress not much beyond her level...and he does not know
her to be a married woman, nor does she inform him so, nor is her
coverture of such sufficient notoriety as upon reasonable enquiry he
might find out; – if in such a case he brings his action and arrests her
as a feme sole, the Court will not interpose in this summary way...but
will leave her to plead her coverture'.[76] Judge Blackstone commented
again on tactically incurious traders (but how else did you make a sale?)
in 1776 when he saw 'no hardship in a man's losing his money, that
avows upon the record, that he furnished a coach to the wife of a player,
whom he knew to have run away from her husband. If this were universally known to be law, it would be difficult for such a woman to gain
credit; and this would consequently reduce the number of wanderers
[strolling players]'. He quoted his own *Commentaries* to say that 'the

---

[74] Leach, *Cases in Crown Law*, Vol. 1, pp. 245–50.
[75] Ibid., pp. 386–90.
[76] Sir William Blackstone, *Reports of Cases Determined in the Several Courts of Westminster-
hall, from 1746 to 1779; by the Honourable Sir William Blackstone, Knt, One of the
Justices of the Court of Common Pleas; with Memoirs of his Life*, 2nd ed., *revised and
corrected with copious notes and references, including some from the mss of the late Mr
Sergt. Hill, by Charles Heaneage Elsley, Esq; in two volumes*, S. Sweeney, R. Pheney and
A. Maxwell, London, 1828, Vol. 2, p. 902. For Blackstone's movement between the
Courts of Common Pleas and King's Bench, 1770–1780, Prest, *William Blackstone*,
pp. 255–61.

contrary doctrine militates against the first principles of English law, which considers that a woman's powers, – nay, almost her very being, as suspended during the coverture'.[77] He recorded nine cases involving femes-coverts in his own Reports (he was involved as barrister or judge in two of them, as we have seen), all of them making plainer the law of bankruptcy, bail, debt and credit, and the position of married women trading as femes-soles. All but one of the cases involving femes-coverts were heard in Common Pleas.

Here was some kind of interaction with married women of property – even if it consisted only of a tray of laces for street sale or was stolen from someone else. He encountered (on paper) some few women of the employing classes in the work he did at King's Bench as part of the Servant Taxes appeal system. Under this assessed-tax legislation, employers had a right of appeal to the judges if they believed that local commissioners had incorrectly charged them for servants ... *who weren't really servants.*[78] Between July 1778 and August 1780, the judges considered 95 appeals, or requests for the judges' opinion, or for a 'case to be stated' against the decision of local commissioners. Blackstone was present to consider 62 of these 95 appeals, at six of the judges' 11 assessed taxes appeal meetings (he died in February 1780).[79] Women employers were involved in five of these 95 appeals. At Woodstock in July 1777, Mrs Heywood of Sandford appealed against the local commissioners' assessment in respect of her coachman. He had lived with her eight years 'and has always been retained as a day-man, employed in driving the team at plough and doing other husbandry business'. The Servant Tax Act exempted husbandry servants. Yes: he did sometimes drive her coach, and she fed him on these occasions, but *really*, he is day-labourer, she says; not a servant. The Oxfordshire Commissioners had admitted her appeal, but the Crown Surveyor wanted a case stated by the Judges, which was that the Commissioners (and Mrs Heywood) were wrong. Martha Brooks, landlady of the Kings Head Inn in Hounslow, sent her son to the Middlesex commissioners appeal meeting in August 1778 with her argument about why she shouldn't have been charged for her gardener. The local commissioners agreed her appeal; the Crown Surveyor disagreed with them. He appealed to the Judges, who were 'of the opinion that the determination of the Commissioners is wrong'. In August 1779 Mrs Elizabeth Butler, matron of the Magdalen Hospital,

[77] Blackstone [Elsley], *Reports of Cases*, Vol. 2, 1080, 'Hatchett ... vs Baddeley'.
[78] For the Servant Taxes, Steedman, *Labours Lost*, pp. 129–63.
[79] [By Permission of the Honourable Commissioners of Excise], *Cases of Appellants relating to the Tax on Servants, with the Opinion of the Judges thereon*, London, 1781.

Southwark, appealed against assessment for the hospital's steward and messenger on the grounds that she shouldn't have been assessed in the first place: the Committee of Governors appointed servants and as a corporation for charitable purposes they were not within the description of 'master' or 'mistress'. The Crown Surveyor desired that a case be stated by the Judges; their opinion was that the Commissioners had been right in allowing her appeal. Some time in the same year, in the Leeds Division of Skyrack, Elizabeth Strother appealed against a surcharge on her footman and gardener. Yes, she keeps a horse – she sometimes rides double with Joseph Walker saddled in front of her; yes, he takes care of the horse, which is also used for loading coals and in husbandry: 'he hath the care of her spring woods, and manages her husbandry business, and can quit her service when he pleases'. She thought this made him *not a servant* as defined by the Act. The Commissioners did not admit her appeal; they thought she should be assessed but that the surcharge should be lowered. The Crown Surveyor disagreed. At their meeting (no date given) the Judges, including Blackstone, opined that the Commissioners had been right. At the same Skyrack meeting, the Revd James Brooke appeared on behalf of his widowed mother. Her 'servant' was only part-time! He worked for her but two months a year! The Commissioners agreed that he was 'not a servant, within the meaning of the Act'. Again the Crown Surveyor thought otherwise, as did the Judges, Blackstone among the nine at their meeting: the Commissioners had been wrong. But the Judges were determining whether or not *Commissioners* had acted correctly in assessing an employer for having a servant, not whether employers were right or wrong, and in no case did the question of coverture arise. Sometimes, a woman's marital status was given (she was a widow, for example), but the act of Parliament inaugurating the Servant Tax (1777) had not figured employers as men or women, or *femes-soles* or *femes-covert*; it had interpellated *employers*, plain and simple and gender-neutral. In these circumstances the question of whether or not a married woman could make contract with a day-labourer or a footman did not arise – and married women did make contract, everyday, all over the country.

Blackstone approved the principle underlying the Poor Laws; the way in which they demonstrated how law furnished everyone 'with every thing necessary for their support. For there is no man so indigent or wretched, but he may demand a supply sufficient for all the necessaries of life, from the more opulent part of the community by means of the several statutes enacted for the relief of the poor'.[80]

---

[80] Blackstone, *Commentaries I*, p. 234.

As recorder of Wallingford, in the 1750s, he attended some Berkshire Quarter Sessions meetings and was occasionally part of QS committees listening to appeals against poor rate assessments.[81] He made practical attempts to bring some order to the laws of settlement and removal beyond the statement of their administrative efficiency.[82] As a member of Parliament (MP) – and lawyer – Blackstone was nominated to the House of Commons committee whose report formed the basis of the much-later Poor Law Act (1782); this provided for the organisation of poor relief on a county basis – *yet another* attempt to bring some order to the vast, sprawling succubus of the poor law system, though Gilbert's Act was not achieved until after his death.[83] But he was rather less involved in poor law and settlement appeals than his fellow judges who spent more time in King's Bench; his own experience of coverture and its ramifications *in court* was in relation to women of property, moveable and real, however small and meagre that property may have been.

★★★

Our law-reading girl is married now; let us say that it is 1810. Married – best-case scenario – to an amiable man who will, in his later years, heartily endorse the political philosophers' cry of *Shame!* against the very idea of coverture. He will not have heard the term since the day the attorney called on his father-in-law way back in 1805 with the marriage settlement papers. He will not be reminded of it when in 1825, he reads the excoriating account of married women's disabilities under the law that was William Thompson's *Appeal on Behalf of One Half of the Human Race, against the Pretensions of the Other Half, Men...*, for Thompson

---

[81] He noted a case from 1766 which involved a woman who had purchased a tiny estate when sole; her husband had gained a settlement by marrying her; he then communicated that settlement to his wife. But the decision of the court was that she actually had *not* gained a settlement by purchase when sole, for the estate was worth less than the £30 required by legislation. Blackstone (ed. Elsley), *Reports of Cases*, Vol. 1, p. 598; Kings Bench, Ilmington v Mickleton.

[82] See the King's Bench statements of Blackstone and Lord Chief Justice Mansfield in 1770 in the *Rex v. Inhabitants of Kirkby Stephen* [15 June 1770] on the organisation of parishes and townships: an 'Order of removal to a Parish, consisting of several Townships, is binding upon the Township, to which it is delivered, if not appealed from'; a township *was as* a parish for the purpose of removal to it. James Burrow, *Decisions of the Court of King's Bench upon Settlement Cases; from the Death of Lord Raymond in March 1732, to June 1776, inclusive ...* Second Edition, His Majesty's Law-Printers for E. Brooke, 1786, Vol. 1, p. 598, pp. 664–9.

[83] Prest, *William Blackstone*, pp. 74, 228. The Relief of the Poor Act 1782 (22 Geo.3 c.83), known as Gilbert's Act, was drafted with Blackstone's help. Samantha A. Shave, 'The Welfare of the Vulnerable in the Late 18th and Early 19th Centuries. Gilbert's Act of 1782', *History in Focus*, 14 (2008); www.history.ac.uk/ihr/Focus/welfare/articles/shave.html, accessed 4 July 2017.

nowhere used it.[84] It is unlikely that either of them will live long enough to read Barbara Bodichon's *A Brief Summary, in Plain Language, of the most important Laws concerning Women* (1854). Bodichon will mention coverture once in her pamphlet, but she will not associate it with Blackstone's name.[85] They may both have once read *Tristram Shandy*, in their childhood, or in a new early nineteenth-century edition, and noted how the ladies of Shandy Hall and its environs are always reading over their marriage settlement – to comic ends: *three whole pages* of the indenture of marriage for Mrs Shandy – Elizabeth Mollineux – to the end of just 'three words, – My mother was to lay in, (if she chose it) in London'.[86] Later and in a different house, the Widow Wadham goes to 'her bureau, and having ordered Bridget to bring her up a couple of fresh candles...she took out her marriage-settlement and read it over with great devotion...from all which it was plain that widow Wadham was in love with my uncle Toby'.[87]

In 1810, our (fictional) young married woman remembers *something* of Blackstone on coverture but much more of his history lessons. In her married state, she hires and fires the servants as needed; there are many guides to help her devise yet another, new *parole* contract that might ensure they do *something* of what she wants before they up and leave (she has not slapped a servant since 1784). Really (impossibly) the couple would agree with the most recent twenty-first-century scholarship on coverture: that it did not form unitary, hegemonic system in law

[84] William Thompson, *Appeal on Behalf of One Half of the Human Race, against the Pretensions of the Other Half, Men, To Retain them in Political, and Thence In Civil and Domestic Slavery; in Reply to A Paragraph of Mr. Mill's Celebrated "Article on Government"*, Longman and eight others, London, 1825. For Thompson's importance to nineteenth-century feminism and its twentieth-century reconstruction, and to the struggle for women's property rights, see Kate Soper's 'Introduction' to Mill's *Subjection of Women*; also Carol Pateman, *The Sexual Contract*, Polity Press, Cambridge, 1988. Thompson was graphic in his depiction of domestic cruelty to women – physical and psychological – but he nowhere mentioned coverture, or the rule of thumb for that matter.

[85] Barbara Leigh Smith Bodichon, *A Brief Summary, in Plain Language, of the most important Laws concerning Women, together with a few Observations thereon*, Chapman, London, 1854, p. 3. Her one observation on Blackstone anticipates that of Ritter Beard a century on: he was, she said, 'an admirer of, rather than a critic on, every law because it was *law*' (p. 8). Now, in the 1850s, that admiration has been exchanged for 'a bolder and more discriminating spirit'. She then footnotes Edward Christian's observation (1823 edition of the *Commentaries*), that propertied women are taxed without political representation.

[86] Laurence Sterne, *The Life and Opinions of Tristram Shandy, Gentleman* (1759–1767), Penguin, Harmondsworth, 1967, pp. 66–9 (Vol. I, Chapter 15). She was to do this 'at her own will and pleasure, notwithstanding her present coverture, and as if she was a *femme sole* and unmarried, – '.

[87] Sterne, *The Life and Opinions of Tristram Shandy*, p. 523 (Vol. VIII, Chapter 9).

or in everyday life.[88] And we may add: Blackstone's powerful historical-philosophical statement of coverture was not much circulated, in the press, in the Reports, in handbooks and guides to the law of everyday life in the way more matter-of-fact seventeenth-century statements continued to be repeated, right through to the nineteenth. (The case was different in the United States, as we have seen.) The term *coverture* was revived by early twentieth-century campaigners for women's rights and late twentieth-century historians.

And yet, with or without the name, 'coverture' mattered to eighteenth- and nineteenth-century people. The law of women and marriage law circumscribed the lives of women and men. Though their use of the actual legal term *coverture* appears to have declined during the eighteenth century, magistrates had to know about it for their administration of the law as it applied to the poor. Novelists showed a high level of awareness of its circumstance. In the next chapter we shall explore the idea of coverture in the writing (and writing life) of an eighteenth-century woman, Mary Wollstonecraft. Her last novel was *about* the laws of women and of marriage; its production and posthumous publication was also inflected by the law of copyright – the law concerning literary property.

---

[88] Stretton and Kesselring, 'Introduction: Coverture and Continuity', *Married Women and the Law*, pp. 3–22.

5   Who Owns Maria

Property may with equal Reason be acquired by mental, as by bodily Labour. This, the Exertion of animal Faculties, and common both to Us and the Brute Creation, in their *Nests, Caves, &c*: That, the Exertion of the rational Powers, by which we are denominated Men; and which therefore have as fair a Title to confer Property, as the other.

Reports of Cases Determined in the Several Courts of Westminster-hall,
from 1746 to 1779: by the Honourable Sir William Blackstone,
2 vols, His Majesty's Law Printers for W. Strahan,
T. Cadell, London, 1781, Vol. 1, pp. 321–2.

LARBOARD.   First pay me the hundred guineas you have lost.
SIR SOLOMON.   I'd as soon give you the honor and copyright of all my poetry and biography.
LARBOARD.   Expect to answer for this insult.

Thomas Hurlstone, *Just in Time; A Comic Opera, in Three Acts: As Performed*
at the Theatre-royal, Covent-garden, Debrett, London, 1792, p. 30.

This chapter's title is not a question (as "Who owns Maria?" is a question); it is not in the interrogative mode. The unidentified pronoun 'Who' is the subject of a noun phrase; 'Maria' is its object. If I were adopting eighteenth-century title style, I might write 'On Who Owns Maria' and you would expect my discourse to follow, which is about 'Maria', the central character of Mary Wollstonecraft's *The Wrongs of Woman; or Maria,* and about the book itself: *Maria.* It's not a question, because for all interested parties at the time of its publication, it was obvious who owned it, legally speaking. Wollstonecraft started to write *The Wrongs* shortly before she married William Godwin; she died before completing it. As memorial to her, her distraught husband edited the fragmentary manuscript for publication. It was his, as were all her possessions and all her debts, under the laws of marriage (under coverture) as described in the last chapter. During the five months of her marriage (and the last five months of her pregnancy)

Wollstonecraft laboured with her pen on her novel, but she did not own it, for she was in the married state: she was *feme-covert*, and all that she possessed and made during that marriage, and had made before it, was her husband's.

Wollstonecraft's long-standing publisher Joseph Johnson took *The Posthumous Works of the Author of the Vindication of the Rights of Woman*, out of loyalty and affection for a writer whose career he had nurtured since the 1780s, and as a way of clearing some of the debts to him she had accrued over the years. Loyalty was in equal measure to obligation and its rewards: William St Clair points out that Wollstonecraft had been Johnson's acting editor, compiler, reviewer, proofreader and translator (and his lodger too).[1] His agreement with Godwin was also made to support the bereaved husband and the two small children he was left with. Johnson registered copyright at Stationers Hall, as was required by law and the practice of the vast majority of publishers (or printers/booksellers) of the time.[2] This gave him the legal ability to reprint *The Posthumous Works* for a limited term and prevented any other (British) publisher from reproducing it without permission and fee. The English laws of copyright did not extend to the United States, and a one-volume version of *The Wrongs* was published at Philadelphia in 1799.[3]

Under the famous Statute of Anne (1710), which established copyright in its modern form, publishers had got most of what they wanted: the law now held that copyright came into existence with an act of composition by an author, that is, with the writing of a text, in manuscript, on paper. That right was then available to be ceded by the author to the publisher, with or without payment. For the rest of the eighteenth century and beyond – the period St Clair calls publishers' 'High Monopoly' – the book industry was able to operate with a legal intellectual property right enforceable in the courts. Booksellers/publishers had hoped for copyright in perpetuity,

[1] 'The Wrongs of Woman, or Maria; a Fragment', *Posthumous Works of the Author of A Vindication of the Rights of Woman. In Four Volumes*, J. Johnson, London, 1798; William St Clair, *The Reading Nation in the Romantic Period*, Cambridge University Press, Cambridge, 2004, p. 163, note 31: 'when her affairs were finally wound up, ten years after her death, her estate owed her publisher over £75'.

[2] The Stationers Company Archive, TSC/1/E/06/133, Register of entries of copies, 1795–1799. Adam Matthew, Marlborough, 'Literary Print Culture: The Stationers' Company Archive', www.literaryprintculture.amdigital.co.uk/Documents/Details/TSC_1_E_06_13, accessed 20 April 2018.

[3] Mary Wollstonecraft Godwin, *Maria: Or, the Wrongs of Woman. A Posthumous Fragment. By Mary Wollstonecraft Godwin. Author of A Vindication of the Rights of Woman*, Printed by James Carey, Philadelphia, 1799.

claiming that such was a common law right, not limitable, as 8 Anne c. 19 actually limited it, to a renewable 14 years.[4] Ignoring the statute, many booksellers drew up contracts for terms 'unlimited', and 'forever'.[5] And from the mid-century onwards, the booksellers lobbied Parliament to extend the copyright term provided by the act. In the battle of the booksellers, the London-based fought the Scottish over the right to reprint works falling outside the protection of the 1710 act. Scottish booksellers argued that there was no common law copyright in an author's work; the London booksellers argued that the Statute of Anne was only a supplement to pre-existing common law copyright. The English booksellers promoted the doctrine of common law copyright to support their case for perpetual copyright. All of this was argued, in a series of notable cases heard in the high courts, throughout the 1750s. Another high-profile case reached the House of Lords in 1774 (Donaldson v Beckett) in which the decision was against perpetual copyright. The Lords confirmed that the copyright *did* expire, according to statute. The Donaldson v Beckett ruling confirmed that a large number of books first published in Britain were now in the public domain, either because the copyright term granted by statute had expired, or because they were first published before the 1710 act. The ruling opened the market for cheap reprints and changed the reading landscape of the nation.[6] But none of this had much to say to a woman *in her coverture*, making property with her pen, for it was not (legally) hers to have and to hold in the first place.

What Godwin appropriated, or added, or made, as he worked on the unfinished *Maria* (and he did a good deal of creative, thoughtful, innovative editorial work, though designated 'naiveté and ineptitude' by some) was not a subject for question: what he worked on was his own property (all that was hers was now his, and had been since the day

---

[4] John Feather, 'The Book Trade in Politics: The Making of the Copyright Act of 1710', *Publishing History*, 19:8 (1980), pp. 19–44.

[5] William St Clair, *The Reading Nation in the Romantic Period*, Cambridge University Press, Cambridge, 2004, pp. 91–5.

[6] St Clair, *Reading Nation*, pp. 103–21; Mark Rose, *Authors and Owners: The Invention of Copyright*, Harvard University Press, Cambridge, MA, 1993, pp. 92–112; Joasiah Brown, *Reports of Cases, upon appeals and writs of error, in the High Court of Parliament; from the year 1701, to the year 1779*, 7 vols. (1779–1783), Vol. 7, P. Uriel, London, 1783, pp. 88–111; Gentleman of the Inner Temple, *The Cases of the Appellants and Respondents in the Cause of Literary Property, Before the House of Lords: Wherein the Decree of Lord Chancellor Apsley Was Reversed, 26 Feb. 1774 … with Notes, Observations, and References*, J. Bew and 3 others, London, 1774.

they exchanged their marriage vows).[7] In Lockeian terms, he worked in the field of Wollstonecraft's prose – her notes, her fragments, her discarded and crossed-through sections – mingled his editorial and imaginative labour with it, and brought forth something new: his literary property. Blackstone had written that this thing called writing (ideas clothed in certain words) was a 'species of property'. Being 'grounded on labour and invention', it (the product) was probably best considered as occupancy, 'since the right of occupancy itself is supposed by Mr Locke, and many others, to be founded on the personal labour of the occupant'. Occupancy was the right which an author may be supposed to have in his own original literary compositions, said Blackstone, 'so that no other person without his leave may publish or make profit of the copies. When a man by his rational powers has produced an original work, he has clearly the right to dispose of that identical work as he please, and any attempt to take it from him, or vary the disposition he has made of it, is an invasion of his right of property'.[8] But in this particular case, Godwin did not have to labour in the field of Wollstonecraft's prose to bring forth his property, for he owned it already.

It was the printers/booksellers/publishers who had the interest in copyright; it protected the investment they made in producing the book. Their promotion of the 'author' and his or her rights and interests actually served *them*, as 'the ultimate proprietors of copyrights'. The property that the writer 'nobly, brought into being, quickly passed into the hands of the booksellers'.[9] It was they who, for the main part, registered copyright. In this period most authors 'sold the copyright' to their publisher, which meant that they exchanged a manuscript with the publisher for a sum of money and sometimes the promise that they

---

[7] For Godwin's editorial work Tilottama Rajan, 'Framing the Corpus. Godwin's "Editing" of Wollstonecraft in 1798', *Studies in Romanticism*, 39:4 (2000), pp. 511–31. For her last days of writing, and the aftermath, Janet Todd, *Mary Wollstonecraft: A Revolutionary Life*, Weidenfeld & Nicholson, London, 2000, pp. 418–57; Lyndall Gordon, *Vindication: A Life of Mary Wollstonecraft*, Virago, London, 2006, pp. 370–81, 385; Charlotte Gordon, *Romantic Outlaws: The Extraordinary Lives of Mary Wollstonecraft & Mary Shelley* (2015), Penguin, London, 2016, pp. 396, 494, 512–18.

[8] William Blackstone, *Commentaries on the Laws of England: Book II Of the Rights of Things* (1766), Oxford University Press, Oxford, 2016, pp. 274–5, 405–6; Rose, *Authors and Owners*, pp. 5–8; William Enfield, *Observations on Literary Property* (for the author, London, 1774), *The Literary Property Debate: Eight Tracts, 1774–1775*, Stephen Parks (ed.), Garland, New York, 1974; William Thomas Ayres, *A Comparative View of the Differences between the English and Irish Statute and Common Law: In A Series of Analogous Notes on the Commentaries of William Blackstone*, for the author, Dublin, 1780, Vol. 1, pp. 315–16.

[9] Rose, *Authors and Owners*, p. 120.

would be given a share of any profits made from selling copies.[10] Joseph Johnson sometimes wrote to tell a new author that his or her book had been entered at Stationers Hall. Any slip made in doing this 'would allow competing publishers to print with impunity'.[11] One of Johnson's typical arrangements was sent to Erasmus Darwin in 1799 when the bookseller was planning second and third editions of works he had earlier published: 'if any errata occurs in the Bot. Gard. [*The Botanical Garden*] please send them in a fortnight. The agreement proper put in 20 January. As you have had trouble add 100£ for improvements in *Zoonamia* & fifty for Plan of Edn [*A Plan for the Conduct of Female Education in Boarding Schools*] as I must have all your copyrights, but I shall not print it in 8o [*volume made up of one or more full sheets, printed with 16 pages of text, and then folded three times to produce eight leaves*]. before the end of the year that you may have all this for the sale of present edn. Account of it in a fortnight ...'[12] He was reminding Darwin and himself that the new, prospective editions would also need to be registered at Stationers Hall. Sometimes Johnson fended off would-be authors by telling them that the writer they wanted to quote or extract from retained their own copyright.[13] Occasionally he recorded a contract, mentioning copyright, as in a letter to Thomas Beddoes in March 1800: 'I hereby undertake to furnish Dr Tho Beddoes with such books as he may order to the amount of £250 & to pay him 250£ in money twelve months after the day of publication for the copyright of a work to be written by him... on Physiology and Preventative medicine &c and to fulfill the same terms for a 2d vol or continuation of the said work'.[14]

In 1803, he told Maria Jackson that he would offer her £30 for 'a 2d ed... £50 for the copy right' of her *Botanical Dialogues*, the first edition of which he had published in 1797.[15] In 1806 he talked terms with the Irish novelist Sydney Owenson: 'Madam... You have been offered a very liberal sum; not much more, say a hundred pounds per Volume

---

[10] St Clair, *Reading Nation*, pp. 43–5, 57–8; Rose, *Authors and Owners*, p. 57: 'in seeking to establish the author's property in his work, the booksellers were of equally seeking to establish their own claims'.

[11] John Bugg, *The Joseph Johnson Letterbook*, Oxford University Press, Oxford, 2016, pp. xxxii–xxxiv.

[12] Ibid., p. 55.

[13] Ibid., p. 19, to Revd Maurice re John Aikin's *England Delineated* (1788), 8 January 1796, 'he retains his own possession of the copyright of his book'. Maurice probably wished to use some of Aiken's illustrations for his own work.

[14] Bugg, *The Joseph Johnson Letterbook*, pp. 68–9.

[15] Ibid., p. 94.

is the most, as far as my knowledge extends, that has been given to the most popular writers after their characters were established, for works of this nature and size'. But she too was a canny negotiator: three weeks later Johnson agreed 'to give ... [her] three hundred pounds, British, for the copyright of ... [her] work, entitled the *Wild Irish Girl*, on condition that it make three large volumes in duodecimo [*volume in which each leaf is one-twelfth of the size of the printed sheet*]'.[16] Sydney Owen was *feme-sole* – not to be Lady Morgan for another six years – and all the evidence is that she did her own negotiating.[17] A writing daughter or sister might be a valuable economic unit of a household; having a brother, or the local clergyman, negotiate on her behalf (as several of Johnson's female authors did) or doing it herself would make no difference to the domestic dispersal of her literary earnings.[18] And they may not have been that great, were she in the novel-writing business: 'the average copyright fee from one novel was roughly equivalent to the annual wages of a laundry, scullery, or dairy maid', says Cheryl Turner. She would have had to publish ten novels a year to make the genteel income of £50.[19]

Copyright was a game for the booksellers, not authors, though many of the latter complained about the legal regime under which they wrote and made a living. In all the adjustments to the 1710 Statute of Anne that Edward Law had seen, and in all the arguments about copyright in Parliament and the press he had read, the 'benefit of either Author or Reader seems not to be really consulted so much as that of a few Booksellers; who, 'tis apprehended, have been in no small degree oppressive to both'.[20] Many were concerned about the iron grip of the book industry on 'the private fortunes of many hundred families ... [and] on the progress of Science and Literature in this

---

[16] Ibid., pp. 131, 133.
[17] Dennis R. Dean, 'Morgan, Sydney, Lady Morgan (bap. 1783, d. 1859)', *Oxford Dictionary of National Biography*, Oxford University Press, 2004, accessed 3 August 2017. In 1840, she published the excoriating *Woman and Her Master*, which, being an account of women's oppression in Biblical times and the Hellenic era, did not *textually* confront Blackstone. But he provided Morgan's killer epigraph: '"As the old law-phrase runs, Baron et Feme – the master and his woman." – BLACKSTONE'. Lady Morgan, *Woman and Her Master*, 2 vols, Henry Colburn, London, 1840.
[18] Cheryl Turner, *Living by the Pen: Women Writers in the Eighteenth Century* (1992), Routledge, London, 1994, p. 116.
[19] Ibid., p. 116.
[20] Edmund Law, *Observations Occasioned by the Contest about Literary Property*, for the author, Cambridge, 1770, pp. 3, 4, 6, 9.

Country'.[21] There were affecting stories from history about the widow's mite of a copyright on which she had to live after her husband's death.[22] This is why the true insult in the pre-duel scene of *Just in Time* (in the second epigraph to this chapter) is the idea that the copyright of all Sir Solomon's poetry cannot answer *anything*, let alone a debt. Copyright, says this text, is a perfectly useless thing to authors.[23]

The ever-enterprising Revd John Trusler attempted *to do something about it* (as he attempted for so many aspects of common life and civil society). In 1780, he revived the twenty-year-old The Literary Society 'whose object was to print works of reputation, giving authors all profits arising from the same, and leaving them in full and free Possession of their copyright'. It was a crying shame that 'in the present enlightened age, so little encouragement should have been given to Literature, and that Authors should be obliged to accept a price for their works very inadequate to their worth... not only they, but their families after them, have been deprived of the fruits of their labour'.[24] Trusler's *DNB* (*Oxford Dictionary of National Biography*) entry says that his aim was to 'abolish publishers'.[25] His proposals constituted a variant of what St Clair calls vanity publishing (though Trusler is not mentioned in St Clair's *Reading Nation*), an arrangement by which some provincial writers funded the

[21] Francis Hargrave, *An Argument in Defence of Literary Property: By Francis Hargrave, Esq.*, for the author, London, 1774. Both Hargrave and Law were agitating about the 1774 House of Lords judicial decision which led to a competitive market in out-of-copyright texts. Much tighter copyright controls were introduced in the 1790s. St Clair, *Reading Nation*, pp. 43–65; Joseph Harrison, *The Accomplish'd Practiser in the High Court of Chancery. Shewing the Whole Method of Proceedings,...Together with a List of the Officers and Their Fees...the Seventh Edition...with Additional Notes and References...by John Griffith Williams,...in Two Volumes...*, Vol. 2, T. Whieldon and R. Pheney, London, 1790, p. 251; *Points in Law and Equity, Selected for the Information, Caution, and Direction, of All Persons Concerned in Trade and Commerce; with References to the Statutes, Reports, and Other Authorities, Upon Which They Are Founded*, T. Cadell, London, 1792, pp. 55–6; Barrister at Law, *Legal Recreations, Or Popular Amusements in the Laws of England*, 2 vols., J. Bew and 11 others, London, 1792, Vol. 1, pp. 33–131. The Burns thought that at least *some* magistrates needed to know this law: Richard Burn, *A New Law Dictionary: Intended for General Use, As Well As for Gentlemen of the Profession...And continued to the present time by John Burn, Esq. his son,...In two volumes*, Vol. 1, T. Cadell, London, 1792, pp. 121–2, 224.

[22] Mark Noble, *Memoirs of the Protectorate-house of Cromwell; Deduced from an Early Period, and Continued down to the Present Time:...Together with an Appendix: and Embellished with Elegant Engravings*, for the author, Birmingham, 1784, p. 282.

[23] Thomas Hurlstone, *Just in Time; A Comic Opera, in Three Acts. As Performed at the Theatre-royal, Covent-garden*, Debrett, London, 1792, p. 30.

[24] Figaro, *The Novelties of A Year and A Day, in A Series of Picturesque Letters on the Characters, Manners, and Customs of the Spanish, French, and English Nations...by Figaro*, for the author, London, 1785.

[25] Emma Major, 'Trusler, John (1735–1820)', *Oxford Dictionary of National Biography*, Oxford University Press, 2004, accessed 4 December 2017.

printing of their sermons, poetry and cookery manuals, paying the print operatives, the presser, the sewer, the binder…, and distributed the books themselves. Vanity publishing, or publishing on commission, made the author the investor, with the publisher taking the royalties. It is not known what kind of financial deal The Literary Society offered authors, though Trusler mentioned a group of 'Literary Men', who would print and publish, at their own risk all works they thought worthy of it.[26] Many like Trusler pointed out the enormous benefit to families in having a surer route to profit after the death of the author than provided by the publishers, who had effectively alienated the breadwinner's copyright – and his earnings – from widows and orphans.

Writing was often a family business, whilst publishing was a form of monopoly capitalism. Whatever which way writing men and women came to arrangement and contract with the booksellers, their interests were divergent – to say the least.[27] Writing by men and women supported families; but to designate Sydney Owenson as a *feme-sole*, or to raise the question of coverture in Wollstonecraft and Godwin's marriage, is to use modern historians' terms, learned from nineteenth-century campaigns for women's suffrage.[28] Nevertheless, Godwin *was* operating (writing, editing, selling, publishing) under the laws of coverture. His thoughts and actions in the months following Wollstonecraft's death underline William Blackstone's view from the 1750s, that coverture was the legal situation of both (married) men *and* women.[29] Godwin and Wollstonecraft are a good example of the multitude of the unphilosophical couples who *just got on with it*, living a life, earning a living in which the law did not figure until it was evoked. But it was certainly the case that 'novels by married women were legally the property of their husbands, as were any profits from publication', as Cheryl Turner confirms. She points to the very great irony of Caroline Norton's profits from her 1839 pamphlet condemning the child custody

---

[26] St Clair, *Reading Nation*, pp. 165–7; G. E. Fussell, 'The revd John Trusler', *Notes and Queries*, 156: 9 (1929), pp. 148–51. The Literary Society published in small way. ECCO shows 14 titles between 1785 and 1800, 1 comprising five volumes, 2 of three volumes, and 1 of two volumes – so 23 items in all. One was Trusler's own *Modern Times; Or, the Adventures of Gabriel Outcast. Supposed to Be Written by Himself. In Imitation of Gil Blas* (3 vols., 1785). In the same period, ECCO attributes near 2,000 titles to Johnson, either publishing alone or with other booksellers.

[27] St Clair, *Reading Nation*, p. 167.

[28] See above, Chapter 4.

[29] See above, p. 92. The focus on *women* in their coverture came in the *Commentaries*, not in Blackstone's earlier William Blackstone, *An Analysis of the Laws of England*, Clarendon Press, Oxford, 1756; William Blackstone, *Commentaries on the Laws of England. Book I of the Rights of Persons (1765)*, Oxford University Press, Oxford, 2016, p. 285.

laws being paid directly to her estranged husband.[30] Coverture entitled a husband to alter or destroy his wife's work and to 'arrogate to himself the authorship of a successful or potentially successful publication'. There is no evidence to show that writers, husbands, publishers and the reading public didn't treat a married woman's *writing* as their own. Much more problematic were the literary *earnings* of married women; they had no legal control over the profits of publication and husbands had a legal claim to them.[31]

Godwin never used the term *coverture*; neither was it used by his wife. In her unmarried state – writing the *Vindication* – Wollstonecraft made no mention of coverture; that is, she did not use the word, affirms Mary Sokol. However, its legal circumstance was a major topic of her writing.[32] In the *Vindication of the Rights of Woman* (1792) she promised to discuss 'the laws respecting woman … in a future part', pausing to observe that the law made 'an absurd unit of a man and his wife; and then, by the easy transition of only considering him as responsible, she is reduced to a mere cypher'. In the *Vindication* she was concerned with the political, civic and human (natural) rights of women (or the rights they lacked); the law was the looming background to their disabilities, not a focus of her polemic: to make a woman 'really virtuous and useful' a (married) woman 'must not, if she discharge her civil duties, want, individually, the protection of civil laws; she must not be dependent on her husband's bounty for her subsistence during his life, or support after his death – for how can a being be generous who has nothing of its own? or, virtuous, who is not free?'[33] *The Wrongs of Woman, or Maria*, is one long discourse on the legal disabilities of married women, in which Kristen Kalsem believes that Wollstonecraft made reference to Blackstone on coverture, or at least engaged intertextually with his *Commentaries'* pronouncement, as when Maria cannot 'sometimes help regretting [her] … early marriage; and that, in my haste to escape from a temporary dependence, and expand my newly fledged wings, in an unknown sky, I had been caught in a trap, and caged for life' (Vol. 2, 118). Once, 'wings' had

[30] Turner, *Living by the Pen*, p. 100; Caroline Norton, *A Plain Letter to the Lord Chancellor on the Infant Custody Bill*, James Ridgway, London, 1839.
[31] Turner, *Living by the Pen*, pp. 100–2; Cheri Larsen Hoeckley, 'Anomalous Ownership: Copyright, Coverture, and *Aurora Leigh*', *Victorian Poetry*, 36:2 (1998), pp. 135–61.
[32] Mary Sokol, *Bentham, Law and Marriage, A Utilitarian Code of Law in Historical Contexts*, Continuum, London and New York, 2011, p. 56.
[33] Mary Wollstonecraft, *A Vindication of the Rights of Woman* (1792), Penguin, London, 1992, pp. 240–52; Chapter 9, 'Of the Pernicious Effects which Arise from the Unnatural Distinctions Established in Society'.

signified freedom to Maria rather than the ironically evoked 'wing and protection' of a husband as promulgated by Blackstone.[34]

Maria was written, says Wollstonecraft in her preface, to exhibit 'the misery and oppression, peculiar to women, that arise out of the partial laws and customs of society'. She tells her readers not to think of Maria as a person, or an individual (maybe not even as a character) but as Woman in general.[35] But whether or not she's a character in the sense established by modern (post-Romantic) literary criticism, she certainly is 'an extraordinary woman'. It is her attendant in the madhouse where she has been incarcerated by her husband, who thinks this. But Jemima, who knows some of Maria's story, who knows about her odious husband and the suckling babe snatched from her mother's breast, must also consider that "'this may only be one of... [her] lucid intervals'":

> Nay, the very energy of Maria's character, made... [Jemima] suspect that the extraordinary animation she perceived might be the effect of madness. 'Should her husband then substantiate his charge, and get possession of her estate, from whence would come the promised annuity, or more desired protection? Besides, might not a woman anxious to escape, conceal some of the circumstances which made against her? Was truth to be expected from one who had been entrapped, kidnapped, in the most fraudulent manner?' (Vol. 1, 24–5)

Jemima knows about coverture. The madhouse is full of women like Maria, suffering under the brutal laws of marriage. There's the poor, mad warbler, singing behind bars, to start with. 'Jemima could only tell... [Maria], that it was said, "She had been married, against her inclination, to a rich old man, extremely jealous (no wonder, for she was a charming creature); and that, in consequence of his treatment, or something which hung on her mind, she had, during her first lying-in, lost her senses"' (Vol. 1, 120). "'What a subject of meditation – even to the very confines of madness'" thinks Maria. She tells the

---

[34] Kristin (Brandser) Kalsem, 'Looking for Law in All the Wrong Places: Outlaw Texts and Early Women's Advocacy', *Review of Law and Women's Studies*, 13:2 (2004), pp. 273–325; also *Faculty Articles and Other Publications*, Paper 12 (2003) http://scholarship.law.uc.edu/fac_pubs/12; William Blackstone, *Commentaries on the Laws of England: Book I Of the Rights of Persons* (1765), Intro. David Lemmings, Oxford University Press, Oxford, 2016, Chapter 15, 'Of Husband and Wife', pp. 279–87. The term *wing and protection* was well used in the eighteenth century. From Psalm 91 and Jeremiah 5, 10, it was often employed to describe the protection provided by the British state's armies and fleets. A vast, comfy hen may not have been the foremost image in eighteenth-century readers' minds when 'protection' was provided by some coercive power or other: God, the British Navy, a husband.

[35] *The Wrongs of Woman, or Maria*, Vol. 1, Author's Preface. Volume and page numbers henceforth noted in text.

increasingly sympathetic and engaged Jemima her story (though not
before, in an extraordinary authorial and political move to be later discussed, Jemima has told hers). She tells Jemima about the courtship
of Mr Venables and the early days of her marriage. The first tremor
of anxiety had come when Maria suggested to her husband that some of the
£5000 settled on him by her loving but unworldly uncle be given to Maria's
two sisters. "'I had the simplicity to request, speaking with warmth
of their situation, that he would give them a thousand pounds apiece,
which seemed to me but justice''', she tells Jemima. "'He asked me, giving me a kiss, 'If I had lost my senses?' I started back, as if I had found
a wasp in a rose-bush. I expostulated. He sneered; and the demon of
discord entered our paradise...''' (Vol 2, 2). Then she reports on the
next five years of her marriage: the way in which Venables forced her
to get yet more money from her uncle 'to save my husband, to use his
own words, from destruction' – his declining credit – the refusal of his
bills – the bailiffs at the door. Slowly, she began to think that 'he would
have made more exertions of his own to extricate himself, had he not
relied on mine' (Vol. 2, 9). She sank into depression: a 'baleful corrod-
ing melancholy took possession of my soul. Marriage had bastilled me
for life... fettered by the partial laws of society, this fair globe was to
me an universal blank' (Vol. 2, 34). She was obliged to contract debts
which she 'had too much reason to fear would never be paid'. She tells
Jemima that she 'despised [the] ... paltry privilege of a wife', to have the
courts blame the tradesman who, as in one of the judgements delivered
by Blackstone, sold goods to a married woman whose husband could
not pay.[36] A legal judgement like this can 'only be of use to the vicious or
inconsiderate', believes Maria, and she was 'determined not to increase
the torrent that was bearing... [her husband] down'. But, of course, she
'was then ignorant of the extent of his fraudulent speculations, whom I
was bound to honour and obey' (Vol. 2, 35). Her conclusion was general, as 'Maria' herself is a general proposition and argument:

> Such are the partial laws enacted by men; for, only to lay a stress
> on the dependent state of a woman in the grand question of the
> comforts arising from the possession of property, she is (even in
> this article) much more injured by the loss of the husband's affec-
> tion, than he by that of his wife; yet where is she, condemned to the
> solitude of a deserted home, to look for a compensation from the
> woman, who seduces him from her? She cannot drive an unfaithful
> husband from his house, nor separate, or tear, his children from

[36] Above, pp. 104–5.

him, however culpable he may be; and he, still the maker of his own
fate, enjoys the smiles of a world, that would brand her with infamy.
(Vol. 2, 36–7)

Property is the master key to understanding a married woman's circumstances under the partial laws of British society: a wife is as 'much
a man's property as his horse...she has nothing she can call her own',
says Maria. A husband may use any means 'to get at what the law considers his, the moment his wife is in possession of it'. Venables had done
this, forced the lock, searched for notes in her writing desk – 'and, all
this is done with a show of equity, because, forsooth, he is responsible
for [a wife's]...maintenance' (Vol. 2, 45–6).

Maria imagines a time before such laws were framed; shouldn't
the decision to enact them have been made by The People? Shouldn't
'impartial lawgivers have first decreed, in the style of a great assembly,
who recognized the existence of an Être suprême, to fix the national belief,
that the husband should always be wiser and more virtuous than his wife,
in order to entitle him, with a show of justice, to keep this idiot, or perpetual minor, for ever in bondage [?]' (Vol. 2, 45–6). The fictional Maria
does not ask *when did this thing happen? When were married women made
perpetual children by the law of the land?* Had she read the *Commentaries on
the Laws of England*, or *The Laws Respecting Women* from 1777, she would
have had a legal-fictional history of Anglo-Saxon freedoms and the
imposition of the Norman Yoke as her answer; as it was, Wollstonecraft
modelled Maria's legal history on her own experience of France in the
years of the National Constituent Assembly. (Wollstonecraft had been
in France from December 1792 to April 1794.) Maria was made as confused about the law as most people were. She tells Jemima that when she
attempted to leave her husband, he shouted that she did so at her peril.
She had no legal resource, he told her: she 'could not swear the peace
against him! – I was not afraid of my life – he had never struck me' (Vol.
2, 57). In real time, real-life Nottinghamshire and in other places across
the country, magistrates *did* hear married women who craved the peace
against their husbands. Sometimes magistrates believed a woman who
said she was in fear of her life even though she had no injuries to show.
Venables (fictionally) exercises the hegemony of superior (though inaccurate) legal knowledge here, as did Abigail Bailey's, in another common
law system on the other side of the Atlantic.[37]

Maria takes up with the highly romantic (and deeply dubious) fellow
madhouse inmate Darnford. He too has been incarcerated by his family,

[37] Above, p. 101.

for his radical and democratic views. As Christine Krueger points out, few have noticed what his 'madness' is alleged to consist of, which are opinions close to Maria's – and Wollstonecraft's – own.[38] These threaten his family's reputation as well as their estate. He lends Maria Rousseau's *La Nouvelle Heloise* to fuel all her fantasies – and Wollstonecraft's readers' fantasies – of a sensitive man who will treat every heroine as an equal. Aided by Jemima, the couple escape the madhouse. Venables commences an action against Darnford for seduction and adultery. No actual, historically existing woman appeared in an eighteenth-century court to defend herself in such a case, not least because the charges were not against the woman, but against the man who had seduced and alienated the husband's property: his wife. Neither does Maria appear in court; she writes a statement for her counsel to read on her behalf. But in a fine piece of textual slippage (maybe Godwin's; maybe the simple effect of punctuation when copy-edited by two hands) Maria's voice *is* heard in court. She reveres marriage, she says to the Judge; it is an institution which fraternizes the world. What she protests against are 'the laws which throw the whole weight of the yoke on the weaker shoulders, and force women, when they claim protectorship as mothers, to sign a contract, which renders them dependent on the caprice of the tyrant, whom choice or necessity has appointed to reign over them'. She points out that during her marriage and after she left it, she had incurred no debts, and demanded no maintenance. Certainly, as presently constituted, marriage leads to immorality – 'yet, as the odium of society impedes usefulness, she wished to avow her affection to Darnford, by becoming his wife according to established rules'. She wants to marry Darnford (Vol. 2, 141–55). The trial scene is staged in a divorce court that will not exist for a century and a half.

But it makes better sense not to dwell on confusion about legal proceedings and the high courts displayed in the novel; better sense, says Kreuger, to read *Maria* as deliberately modelled by Wollstonecraft on Chancery lunacy proceedings. What Wollstonecraft wrote about was the case against Darnford, not a case against Maria Venables. What is at stake is not Darnford's action in escaping the madhouse with another man's wife, but Maria's mental competence in defending his and her actions. In this regard, her deposition *would* have been allowed in Chancery (though not in person) as part of determining her status as *compos mentis*. She defends Darnford by insisting on her power as a rational agent in the disposal of her own body and affections.[39]

[38] Christine L. Krueger, *Reading for the Law: British Literary History and Gender Advocacy*, University of Virginia Press, Charlottesville, VA, 2010, pp. 117–18.
[39] Krueger, *Reading for the Law*, pp. 118–20.

A writer and her characters may not use – possibly not know – the term *coverture* yet be highly aware of the way in which it circumscribed the lives of women, including the writing sort. In Britain, The Married Women's Property Committee, founded in the late 1840s, was the first to describe the effects of coverture on married women writers, using its terms.[40] The arguments it employed, and those of its historians, emphasise as much as eighteenth-century commentators, the contribution of married women writers to the household economy. And this we may see preoccupying William Godwin, in all his grief and distress, as he worked on his dead wife's prose. He was responsible for her debts, to Johnson and to others. This is the taken-for-granted of the correspondence between Godwin and Johnson over the publication of the *Posthumous Works*.[41] They discussed their obligations towards Wollstonecraft's first child, daughter of Gilbert Imlay and four years old when her mother died. Johnson helped Godwin in discovering the status of Imlay's provision for Fanny; he helped Godwin negotiate with Wollstonecraft's creditors besides himself. Johnson approved a letter in which Godwin assured a creditor's agent that he had 'surrendered the whole property of Mrs Godwin's posthumous works, without deriving a penny advantage from them', that he had paid his own agent to settle her small debts. His plea in this letter was that 'I was married to her for five months; & that I have taken upon myself the care and support of her two children. More than this, under my circumstances, cannot, I think, be expected of me'.[42] Married for only five months! What any 1790s husband landed with a deceased wife's debts might say, however fond of her he was. Johnson was concerned for little Fanny and took practical steps regarding her future security, which included the settling of her family's debts. When he died in 1809, his will provided the fifteen-year-old with £200, which Godwin was to give her to pay her father's, Godwin's, debt to Johnson's estate. Lyndal Gordon notes that 'Fanny was not given this bequest', but it was always intended for the benefit of the family.[43] The child of a writing household who did not write herself, she was nevertheless part of the family business and the network of debt and credit by which its members, dead and alive, were sustained.

---

[40] Hoeckley, 'Anomalous Ownership'.

[41] Oxford, Bodleian Libraries, MS. Abinger c. 15, 22 April n.y., Joseph Johnson to William Godwin, Fol(s).: 20r & 21v.; William Godwin to? Joseph Johnson, 2 January 1797 [for 1798], Fol(s).: 86–7.

[42] MS Abinger William Godwin to? Joseph Johnson, 2 January 1797 [for 1798], Fol(s).: 86–7; Bugg, *The Joseph Johnson Letterbook*, p. 50.

[43] Gordon, *Vindication*, p. 414.

Another writer of the age, more celebrated than Wollstonecraft, equally as scandalous in her way of living, had much to say about writing, copyright, authorship and ownership. The notable republican historian Catharine Macaulay (1731–1791) was particularly attentive to the legal and parliamentary debates that brought to a close what William St Clair has called the booksellers' era of high monopoly.[44] She was scathing about depictions of 'true' authors as ethereal spirits who would not condescend to bargain with a 'dirty bookseller' for a living.[45] It was no degradation, she said, 'to traffic with a bookseller for the purchase of their mental harvest, as the opulent traffic with monopolisers in grain and cattle for the sale of…the product of their land'.[46] And in any case, literary merit could scarce get her the price of a shoulder of mutton, or prevail with 'sordid butchers and bakers to abate one farthing in the pound of the exorbitant price which meat and bread at this time bear'. Neither the booksellers and butchers, or authors and householders doing the shopping, were low, or 'sordid' or 'dirty' for taking their part in the marketplace. But Macaulay did not care for arguments that writers/ authors were just some kind of worker, or artisan, *making something* like a pair of shoes, or a loaf of bread – or a book. A major argument of the copyright wars of the early 1770s had been that authors were simply that – artisans, with a right to profit of their invention, just as if their book were a new kind of knitting frame, or screw and bolt, or periscope. Macaulay thought that there was something more to authors than there was to inventors of 'inferior order', and the difference lay in the work their inventions did in the national culture: 'Every common capacity can find out the use of a machine; but it is a length of time before the value of a literary publication is discovered and acknowledged by the vulgar'.[47] She was taken to task for proposing a 'pretended difference between AUTHORS and ARTIFICERS, regarding a right of property in their respective inventions…It is therefore very inconsequentially inferred, that the one hath a greater or less natural right to the fruits of his industry and ingenuity than the other', said one of her critics.[48]

---

[44] St Clair, *Reading Nation*, p. 112; Rose, *Authors and Owners*, pp. 97–107.

[45] Catharine Macaulay, *A Modest Plea for the Property of Copy Right*, Edward and Charles Dilly, London, 1774; Jane C. Ginsburg, 'Exceptional Authorship: The Role of Copyright Exceptions in Promoting Creativity', Susy Frankel and Daniel Gervais (eds.), *The Evolution and Equilibrium of Copyright in the Digital Age*, Cambridge University Press, Cambridge, 2014, pp. 15–28; 25–6.

[46] Macaulay, *A Modest Plea*, pp. 14–15.

[47] Ibid., p. 18.

[48] William Kenrick, *An Address to the Artists and Manufacturers of Great Britain; Respecting an Application to Parliament for the Farther Encouragement of New Discoveries and Inventions in the Useful Arts*, Domville and 5 others, London, 1774, pp. xii, 6–7, 12.

Macaulay had been a widow for six years when she wrote her pamphlet on copyright. She was between husbands, marrying for the second time in 1778.[49] She was a widow, feme-sole, with full disposal of her earnings and the ability to buy a shoulder of mutton whenever she pleased. She was a married woman for much longer periods of time than Wollstonecraft was, but she wrote nothing about the law of women or of marriage as Wollstonecraft did, in both the *Vindication* and *Maria*. Macaulay's interest was in the legal theory of copyright – in the arguments in the House of Lords and the high courts, between copyright as a common-law right, founded on precedent, and the idea of literary property as founded in equity and the moral fitness – of booksellers – to possess it.[50] Wollstonecraft deeply admired Macaulay, celebrated her in the *Vindication* ('the woman of the greatest abilities, undoubtedly, that this country has ever produced') and there is evidence of admiring correspondence between the two.[51] To point out that Wollstonecraft had no need to be exercised by the copyright question when her writing was steered by Johnson, and her income, bread and board provided by him, is not to reduce a woman's interest in the law to the press of her personal circumstances. Macaulay had more knowledge of the law – and the legislation on copyright – than did Wollstonecraft, not least because her writing career coincided with febrile national debate on it in the early 1770s. She was interested in the *persona* 'Catherine Macaulay' that earned a living by the pen, in a way that Wollstonecraft was not interested in 'Mary Wollstonecraft'. She certainly knew more of the history of the British state and parliamentary legislation than did her admirer. She was much more of the modern individual author brought into being by the copyright debates than was Wollstonecraft. The burdens of copyright and coverture fell on Wollstonecraft's husband, for many years after their brief marriage.

And what of Jemima, madhouse attendant? Sometime prostitute and servant? What of she, who has, it seems, a clearer grasp of the laws of marriage, or at least of its vocabulary, than does her charge, the middle-class Maria? Despite the condescension and disgust with which Wollstonecraft wrote about working-class women across all her publications, 'Jemima' is an extraordinary textual innovation, and perhaps

---

[49] Bridget Hill, 'Macaulay, Catharine (1731–1791)', *Oxford Dictionary of National Biography*, Oxford University Press, 2004, accessed 2 October 2017.

[50] Macaulay, *A Modest Plea*, pp. 6–7, 11–12.

[51] Wollstonecraft, *A Vindication* (1992), p. 210; Bridget Hill, 'The Links between Mary Wollstonecraft and Catharine Macaulay: New Evidence', *Women's History Review*, 4:2 (1995), pp. 177–92.

a legal one too. The final shape of Wollstonecraft's novel owes a lot to Godwin's editorial hand, especially in terms of structure. He swapped sections of text around as he determined plot and sequence; he provided rows of asterisks when he judged a scene was missing; he made a decision as to its ending by providing readers with Wollstonecraft's brief drafts of all its possible ones. But the narrative structure of *Maria*, the timing and placing of the two life stories that compose it, could not – cannot be – altered or reversed. The first story of a woman's life told, is Jemima's. Her tale comes before Maria's, and we must read it before we encounter hers. It is only after – it is only *because* – Maria has heard Jemima's harrowing record of physical and sexual abuse, rape, abortion, prostitution, starvation, and all the failures of the law to relieve her suffering, that Maria's autobiography emerges. Wollstonecraft has the bourgeois heroine *only able* to narrate her own childhood, *only able* to interpret her own story as one of women's suffering under a legal system of extraordinary misogyny, through the previous articulation of Jemima's terrifying tale. As readers, then and now, we simply cannot have Maria's narrative, in any shape or form, without its framing by Jemima's. Certainly, the early pages of the novel show Maria attempting to alleviate the boredom and anxiety of incarceration by writing of 'the events of her past life', which 'might perhaps instruct her daughter' – should the baby live to read her mother's words (I, 21). But the autobiography does not materialise until Jemima has delivered hers. We know nothing of Maria's theme until it actually emerges, seven chapters long, between inverted commas, and explicitly related to what Jemima has already told: 'thinking of Jemima's peculiar fate and her own, she was led to consider the oppressed state of woman ... she dwelt on the wretchedness of unprotected infancy, till sympathy with Jemima changed to agony, when it seems probable that her own babe might even now be in the very state ... so forcibly described' (I, 228). In textual terms, there is no story of Maria without Jemima's being in place first.

Wollstonecraft's stated political purpose in writing *The Wrongs of Women* was to describe a sisterhood of suffering, shared by *all* women under the laws of England, under the 'partial laws enacted by men'.[52] But Maria has trouble with the plebeian Jemima, just as her creator had trouble with servants and other working women: their hardness of demeanour, coarseness of language, want of sensibility, all their distasteful habits and manners. Her disgust at the *poissardes* (market-women;

---

52 'The Wrongs of Woman, or Maria; a Fragment', *Posthumous Works*, Vol. 1, Author's Preface and Vol. 2, pp. 36–7, for 'the partial laws'.

fishwives) who she saw screaming and rioting during the period of the Terror in France, was palpable.[53] Nevertheless, Wollstonecraft thought that a middle-class woman was to be judged by her treatment of working women, condemning that 'weaknesses of mind, which often pass for good nature' in a middle-class wife: 'she who submits, without conviction, to a parent or husband, will as unreasonably tyrannise over her servants; for slavish fear and tyranny go together'. But that woman's children, left in the care of servants, could only imbibe mean and vulgar notions: most working women were artful as well as 'ignorant and cunning'; 'we must consider their characters, if we would treat them properly, and continually practise forbearance'.[54] In the introduction to the *Vindication of the Rights of Women* she explained that women of the middling sort were in the most natural condition of reason and sensibility: working women had been corrupted by great poverty, aristocrats by pleasure and high living.[55] But she was willing to teach children (fictional and real) lessons about sympathy for servants and other working women.[56] She said that 'the good sense which I have met with, among the poor women who have had few advantages of education, and yet have acted heroically, strongly confirmed me in the opinion that trifling employments have rendered [upper-class] woman a trifler'.[57] She oscillated then, in her writing at least, between contempt, disgust and sympathy for lower-class women. Was it easier for Wollstonecraft to find fellow-feeling with a young woman originating outside the class and status structures of her own society? The French nursemaid Marguerite Fournée, whom she took into service after the birth of her first daughter in 1794, was satirised and ridiculed in Wollstonecraft's letters to lover Imlay.[58] The actually existing Marguerite was not – could not be conceived of as – any kind of heroine, or as a sister in law or suffering.

---

[53] Mary Wollstonecraft, *An Historical and Moral View of the Origin and Progress of the French Revolution; and the Effect it has Produced in Europe*, 2 vols., J. Johnson, London, 1790, p. 289; Emma Major, *Madam Britannia: Women, Church and Nation, 1712–1812*, Oxford University Press, Oxford, 2012, pp. 262–3.

[54] Mary Wollstonecraft, *Thoughts on the Education of Daughters: With Reflections on Female Conduct, in the More Important Duties of Life*, J. Johnson, London, 1787, pp. 63, 13–14, 118; also pp. 14, 60, 125–6.

[55] Mary Wollstonecraft, *A Vindication of the Rights of Woman: With Strictures on Political and Moral Subjects*, J. Johnson, London, 1792.

[56] For lessons in sympathy for the poor, *Original Stories From Real Life; with Conversations, Calculated to Regulate the Affections, and Form the Mind to Truth and Goodness*, J. Johnson, London, 1791; and 'Fragment of Letters on the Management of Infants', *Posthumous Works*, Vol. 4, pp. 55–60.

[57] Wollstonecraft, *A Vindication*, p. 167.

[58] Carolyn Steedman, 'Where Have You Been?', Pal Brunnstrom and Ragnhild Claesson (eds.), *Creating the City. Identity, Memory and Participation*, Conference Proceedings, Institute for Studies in Malmo's History, University of Malmo, 2019, pp. 18–34.

Maria's story has been designated an outlaw narrative, as was Wollstonecraft's writing of it her own outlaw act. The text itself *and* Maria's narrative told of the law and its effects in places where law's stories are not usually looked for. To say it another way: *The Wrongs of Woman* is not a conventional legal text; it is outwith the purview of legal inquiry, but it is a text in which '"law" is an integral signifying system'.[59] In this view, Maria's story is one told from a position *outside* the law, written *against* the laws of marriage and of coverture. But Jemima's outlaw tale – if it is one – tells of a woman whose personality and *persona* has been made by the law – specifically the Poor Laws. She may be outside them, but they are also within her: a shaping force on how, as a character, she is made, by Wollstonecraft her author, to see and understand the world.

Jemima's story focuses on a wretched childhood: 'An insulated being' thinks Maria. 'From the misfortune of her birth, she despised and preyed on the society by which she had been oppressed... [she] loved not her fellow-creatures, because she had never been beloved. No mother had ever fondled her, no father or brother had protected her from outrage; and the man who had plunged her into infamy, had deserted her when she stood in greatest need of support' (I, 22–3). Much later, in Chapter 5 of the second volume, Jemima gives much detail to this picture of neglect, abuse, and violence – though not the half of it, she has earlier informed Maria: 'I will not attempt to give you an adequate idea of my situation, lest you, who probably have never been drenched with the dregs of human misery, should think I exaggerate' (I, 88). Helplessness and hopelessness frame the narrative of her young womanhood; there is nothing and no one to help her. She knows about the laws of Settlement and Removal – her story is a condemnation of them – but even living on the streets, destitute, hungry and ill, she does not access the Poor Law for fear that she should be Removed – 'lest they should have passed me, I knew not whither' (I, 120). Once, 'exhausted by hunger and fatigue,... [she] sunk down senseless at a door where... [she] had vainly demanded a morsel of bread'.

> I was sent by the inhabitant to the work-house, to which he had surlily bid me go, saying, he 'paid enough in conscience to the poor', when, with parched tongue, I implored his charity. If those well-meaning people who exclaim against beggars, were acquainted with the treatment the poor receive in many of these wretched asylums, they would not stifle so easily involuntary sympathy, by saying that they have all

---

[59] Kalsem, 'Looking for Law', pp. 273–95.

parishes to go to, or wonder that the poor dread to enter the gloomy walls. What are the common run of workhouses, but prisons, in which many respectable old people, worn out by immoderate labour, sink into the grave in sorrow, to which they are carried like dogs!. (I, 123)

Really, here, we must bow to the fact of fiction, in a somewhat obvious way: Wollstonecraft invented 'Jemima'; knowledge of the poor laws, and the laws of marriage and women displayed in the pages of *Maria* is Wollstonecraft's knowledge, not that of an eighteenth-century plebeian woman.

Wollstonecraft has Maria learn something of the psychology of deprivation and poverty from Jemima: Maria achieves the insight that Jemima cannot love because she has never been loved. She hopes that by witnessing the delicate transports of her and Darnford's *amour*, Jemima will find her own sensibility within – and help Maria, for she calculates that she must cultivate Jemima's sympathy to effect her own escape and find her abducted baby. The figure of Jemima serves Wollstonecraft's purpose: to find a sisterhood of suffering among all women, high and low (except perhaps for aristocrats).

In the next chapter, we shall consider some actually existing eighteenth-century working-class woman suffering under the 'partial laws' of eighteenth-century Britain. Their stories and destinies, like Jemima's, were made by the laws relating to the poor.

6   Sisters in Law

Exhibiting the misery and oppression, peculiar to women, that arise out of the partial laws and customs of society.

Mary Wollstonecraft, *The Wrongs of Woman; or Maria* (1798)

Some – not all – of the working women discussed in this chapter were domestic servants whose claims for the right to settlement by domestic service were the subject of dispute between two parishes and sent on appeal from a county court of quarter sessions to the court of King's Bench. What happened to these women and the judgements made in their cases give some insight into the ways in which eighteenth-century law operated in the lives of the poorer sort.[1] In settlement and other poor law appeal cases, we shall see the social relationships of everyday life come face-to-face with laws that were not particularly equipped to deal with the real forms of work and family; the judges had to force them into the grid of statutory provision (they often complained long and hard about statute law relating to the poor). They did not have a free hand to do what they thought was correct. They were lumbered with a system, the effects of which they might dislike, but which did give them some room for manoeuvre. They sometimes discussed the policy implications of their appeal court decisions, especially in regard to their varying views on public morality.[2]

Under the complex of sixteenth- and seventeenth-century legislation that set the old poor law in place, there emerged a dominant mode of operation: a poor or indigent person claiming relief from parish authorities was required in various ways to demonstrate his or her 'settlement', that is, that

[1] For an earlier account of some of the women discussed in this chapter, Carolyn Steedman, 'Lord Mansfield's Women', *Past and Present*, 176 (2002), pp. 105–43. For magistrates, the appeal system and King's Bench, Peter King, *Crime and the Law in England, 1750–1850: Remaking Justice from the Margins*, Cambridge University Press, Cambridge, 2006, pp. 1–69, esp. 31–4.

[2] Joanna Innes, 'Parliament and the Shaping of Eighteenth-Century Social Policy', *Transactions of the Royal Historical Society*, 5th Series, 40 (1990), pp. 63–92.

they 'belonged' to that place and were among its settled poor. Settlement could be acquired in a variety of ways, most commonly by being born to a father who possessed it and by never moving from a natal parish, though it still had to be confirmed by magistrates by examination of an applicant for poor relief, for it to be legally activated. 'Earning' it by service was the next most common route, and it certainly produced the most litigation. A man or a woman hired to work in a particular place and fulfilling the agreement to serve for a calendar year had an important claim to parish settlement and thus to relief. 'Serving' meant many kinds of work done for a master or mistress under a hiring agreement, but in the eighteenth century the most common kind of service agreement was to work as a domestic. Settlement through service was something that a woman could 'earn' out of her own labour, and, in certain circumstances, pass on to her children. The cases discussed here are examples of many workers whose attempts to acquire settlement were challenged by disputing parish authorities and local courts, and sent to King's Bench on appeal.

William Murray, first Earl of Mansfield (1705–1793), chief justice of the court of King's Bench from 1756 to 1788, heard many poor law appeal cases concerning plebeian women. As chief justice, his was the permanent presence among his fellow judges, so his adjudication had critical importance in the way the poor laws were interpreted. He was a severe critic of the law the judges exercised in poor law appeal cases. He frequently lambasted 'the litigious zeal of public bodies', eager to see every disputed settlement case 'travel through every stage which the law allow[ed]'. In disputes like these, where parish ratepayers were responsible for the relief and maintenance of the poor, the collective financial resources of a county often led them to defy 'the salutary menace of costs', that is, to ignore the considerable outlay of county funds (ratepayers' money) involved in briefing attornies for a dispute between two quarter sessions, and the even greater expense involved in preparing a case for the high courts. 'The litigation of the poor laws … are … a disgrace to the country'; Mansfield thought them 'a dropsey … swollen to monstrous proportions' by 'the invitation offered to each parish to cast its burden upon its neighbours'. He believed that many magistrates acted solely in regard to the local case before them, with no generalizable legal principle at work; this amounted to saying 'there was no Rule at all'; he thought it 'important in most Cases that the Law shou'd be certain than what the Law is'.[3]

[3] Cecil Fifoot, *Lord Mansfield*, Clarendon Press, Oxford, 1936, pp. 206–7, citing *Rex* v. *Inhabitants of Newington* (1786). Also Scone Palace, Murray Family Papers, Earls of Mansfield, NRA(S) 0776, box 68, King's Bench Papers, 1782–5; Mansfield's remarks in the case of *Rex* v. *Inhabitants of Harberton [Devon]* (1786) are discussed by James Oldham, *The Mansfield Manuscripts and the Growth of the English Law in the*

'There ought to be no litigations at all in the settlement of the poor', wrote an equally exasperated Thomas Ruggles in 1793: '"le jeu ne vaut pas la chandelle;" [the game isn't worth the candle/it isn't worth it] there should be no attornies' bills on overseers' accounts; it is cheaper to relieve them than to remove a family by a suit to the [quarter] sessions, which, if the overseers are peculiarly astute in watching over the interests of their parishes, or in other words, are tenacious in their opinions, will go into the King's Bench'.[4] The costs inherent in the developing adversarial legal procedures to which the poor laws were yoked was not mentioned by any of these commentators, though they noted with disapproval the number of attorneys and barristers employed by disputing local authorities at quarter sessions.[5] In 1840, in a comparative history of poverty in France and England, Eugène Buret was shocked to note how an English settlement dispute between two parishes 'has often cost more money than would have been needed for the relief of all the poor of both of them', but he made no mention of the adversary system that provoked

Eighteenth Century, 2 vols, University of North Carolina Press, Chapel Hill, 1992, Vol. 1, pp. 108–10; John Impey, *The New Instructor Clericalis. Stating the Authority, Jurisdiction and Modern Practice of the Court of the King's Bench; With Directions for Commencing and Defending Actions, Entring up Judgements, Suing out Executors and Proceeding in Error*, W. Strahan and W. Woodfall, London, 1782; *An Attorney's Practice Epitomized; or, The Method, Times and Expenses of Proceeding in the Courts of King's Bench and Common Pleas*, 8th ed., Henry Lintot, London, 1757. For an account of the procedures that followed on King's Bench 'general superintendency over all inferior magistrates and courts', and the peculiar consequences of the 'judgement of justices of the peace in questions on the poor laws [being] not conclusive on the parties', William Hands, *The Solicitor's Practice on the Crown Side of the Court of the King's Bench, with an Appendix Containing the Forms of the Proceeding*, J. Butterworth, London, 1803, pp. 27–31.

4 Thomas Ruggles, *The History of the Poor: Their Rights, Duties and the Laws Respecting Them*, 2 vols., J. Deighton, London, 1793, Vol. 2, p. 91. See also H. C. Jennings, *A Free Inquiry into the Enormous Increase of Attornies, with Some Reflections on the Abuse of Our Laws. By an Unfeigned Admirer of Genuine British Jurisprudence*, Debrett, London, 1785.

5 A comic turn in Parliament on the increase: an MP proposes 'a tax on gentlemen of the bar and solicitors' with 'a droll account of the great increase of barristers, declaring that where he lived in the country, there formerly appeared but two or three at every quarter sessions, but that the black gowns were so numerous now on such occasions, that the old town hall was large enough to hold them, and they had been obliged to build a new one on their account'. *The Parliamentary Register*, Vol. XVII, p. 229 (9 May 1785); *A View of Real Grievances, with the Remedies proposed for redressing them; humbly submitted to the Consideration of the Legislature*, for the author, London, 1772, p. 47, describes how 'each Parish always has an Attorney and generally several Witnesses to pay, so that the Expence which attends these unnecessary Disputes, are upon an Average 9 or 10 Guineas each'. For the adversarial system implicated here, John H. Langbein, *The Origins of Adversary Criminal Trial*, Oxford University Press, Oxford, 2003.

this vast expense of money across the country. With the best will in the world (for he deeply admired the English system of poor relief), he found legal comparisons of the treatment of the poor in France and England difficult, for in France, as he stated, the poor were not noticed by the state but left either to charity or to fend for themselves.[6]

Judges criticizing the poor laws did not achieve the satiric heights of Richard Burn (1709–1785), vicar of Orton in Westmorland, justice of the peace (JP) for Westmorland and Cumberland, and author of the best-selling and long-running *Justice of the Peace and Parish Officer* (1st ed., 1756). Familiarity and fury guided his pen as he recorded the activities of overseers of the poor in far northwestern villages:

> [I]n practice, the office of an overseer of the poor seems to be understood to be this: To keep an extraordinary look-out, to prevent persons coming to inhabit without certificates, and to fly to the justices to remove them ... to warn [all inhabitants], if they will hire servants, to hire them half yearly, or by the month, or by the week, or by the day, rather than by any way that shall give them a settlement; or if they do hire them for a year, to endeavour to pick a quarrel with them before the year's end, and so to get rid of them: To maintain their poor as cheap as they possibly can.... to hang over them *in terrorem* if they shall complain to the justices for want of maintenance.... To move heaven and earth if any dispute happens about a settlement; and in that particular, to invert the general rule, and stick at no expense. ...[7]

Magistrate Henry Zouch agreed: 'It would be highly meritorious in the heads of parishes, to discourage all frivolous suits, those chiefly respecting settlements, which are often set on foot from interested motives, and prosecuted with a spirit of malevolence which ought

---

[6] Eugène Buret, *De la misère des classes laborieuses en Angleterre et en France*, 2 vols., Paulin, Paris, 1840, Vol. 1, p. 144. He calculated the cost of such removals in the way Keith Snell was to do in 1985 in *Annals of the Labouring Poor: Social Change and Agrarian England, 1660–1900*, Cambridge University Press, Cambridge, 1985, p. 18, and note 5. Also David Eastwood, *Governing Rural England: Tradition and Transformation in Local Government, 1780–1840*, Oxford University Press, Oxford, 1994, pp. 76–7. For a twentieth-century comparative history of the poor laws, Joanna Innes, 'The State and the Poor: Eighteenth-Century England in European Perspective', John Brewer and Eckhart Hellmuth (eds.), *Rethinking Leviathan: The Eighteenth-Century State in Britain and Germany*, Oxford University Press, Oxford, 1999, pp. 225–80.

[7] Richard Burn, *A History of the Poor Laws: With Observations* (1764), Augustus M. Kelly, Clifton, NJ, 1973, pp. 211–12. Also John A. Conley, 'Doing It by the Book: Justice of the Peace Manuals and English Law in Eighteenth-Century America', *Journal of Legal History*, 6:3 (1985), pp. 257–98.

everywhere to be repressed'.[8] A modern conclusion is that 'Settlement cases ... [were] the bread and butter of a provincial lawyer's office'.[9] The adversarial system not only cost money; it made money, too – for the booksellers. There was a brisk trade in the informal codification of law (statute and common law judgement) relating to the management of domestic and other workers in the second half of the century, in handbooks for magistrates, advice books for employers, legal instruction ('friendly advice') for servants, and tracts and stories for servants and children.[10]

Chief Justice Mansfield thought the poor law to be bad law; some think his King's Bench animadversions unworthy of attention because they contributed so little to the development of the eighteenth-century legal system.[11] But law is made not only in striking formulations and innovatory judgement (about commercial and shipping law, for example, where the chief justice made important contributions), but also in the routine and irritated adjudication of local disputes. If 'the writing was on the wall by the 1780s' for the old poor law as a 'generous, flexible and humane' relief and welfare system, then adjudication of settlement disputes in the high courts contributed to its decline.[12] There were no

[8] Henry Zouch, *Hints Respecting the Public Police: Published at the Request of the Court of Quarter Sessions Held at Pontefract*, John Stockdale, London, 1786, p. 8. Also *A View of Real Grievances, with the Remedies proposed for redressing them; humbly submitted to the Consideration of the Legislature*, for the author, London, 1772, pp. 45–7, 53–7. These writers thought settlement litigation mostly to do with attorneys ferreting out fees in country places.

[9] Roger L. Brown, 'John Hughes, Attorney', *Montgomeryshire Collections*, 92 (2004), pp. 79–85.

[10] *The Laws Relating to Masters and Servants: With Brief Notes and Explanations to Render Them Easy and Intelligible to the Meanest Capacity. Necessary to Be Had in all Families*, Henry Lintot, London, 1755; Jonas Hanway, *Virtue in Humble Life: Containing Reflections on the Reciprocal Duties of the Wealthy and the Indigent, the Master and the Servant...*, 2 vols., J. Dodley, Brotherton & Sewell, London, 1774, Vol. 1, pp. 361–2; *A Present for Servants, from their Ministers, Masters, or Other Friends*, 10th ed., John Rivington for the SPCK (The Society for the Promotion of Christian Knowledge), London, 1787; John Huntingford, *The Laws of Masters and Servants Considered*, for the author, London, 1792; James Barry Bird, *The Laws Respecting Masters and Servants, Articled Clerks, Apprentices, Manufacturers, Labourers, and Journeymen*, 3rd ed., W. Clarke, London, 1799; *Domestic Management; or The Art of Conducting a Family with Instructions to ... Servants in General, Addressed to Young Housekeepers*, H. D. Symonds at the Literary Press, London, 1800; *Reflections on the Relative Situations of Master and Servant, Historically Considered*, W. Miller, London, 1800; *A Familiar Summary of the Laws Respecting Masters and Servants*, Henry Washbourne, London, 1831.

[11] Oldham, *The Mansfield Manuscripts*, Vol. 1, p. 108.

[12] Paul Slack, *The English Poor Law, 1531–1782*, Cambridge University Press, Cambridge, 1996, p. 40, for the writing on the wall; also Snell, *Annals of the Labouring Poor*, p. 107.

reporters regularly at work in any of the trial courts before the end of the eighteenth century; instead, notes made by an individual judge often became the predominant source for the statement of facts in the printed reports of cases, and it is from these that we may estimate how many disputed settlement cases, forwarded by litigation-happy courts of quarter sessions, passed before the judges.[13]

Joseph Burchell's *Arrangement and Digest of the Law in Cases Adjudged in the King's Bench and Common Pleas*, which covered the years 1756–1794, reported on more than a hundred disputed settlements. Over a third of these involved questions of hiring and service, or entitlement to settlement by service.[14] Other means of gaining settlement (by birth, apprenticeship, marriage, office-holding, property ownership, paying rates) did not give rise to anything like as much litigation. Francis Const's 1793 revision of Bott's standard *Decisions of the King's Bench upon the Laws Relating to the Poor* devoted the most space to the question of 'Settlement by Hiring and Service', in that 'late and most active period' in the making of 'law positive' (statute law, parliamentary legislation) and legal judgement, in the 1770s and 1780s.[15] In 1989, James Taylor used 985 settlement examinations to produce an account of poverty and migration during the early Industrial Revolution, 679 of which had hiring and service as the basis of settlement.[16] These last were cases settled locally, some of them not even forwarded from parishes to quarter sessions for adjudication; had they gone on appeal to King's Bench, he would not have found them in the local records. But the number of settlements by service he *did* find underlines the point made by Burchell and Const

---

[13] Oldham, *The Mansfield Manuscripts*, Vol. 1, pp. 164–8; and for unreported cases (a 'lively repository of social history' of little use to the legal historian), pp. 183–5.

[14] Joseph Burchell, *Arrangement and Digest of the Law in Cases, Adjudged in the King's Bench and Common Pleas from the Year 1756 to 1794, Inclusive*, T. Jones, London, 1796.

[15] *Francis Const, Decisions of the Court of the King's Bench, upon the Laws Relating to the Poor. Originally Published by Edmund Bott Esq. of the Inner Temple, Barrister at Law; Revised ... by Francis Const Esq. of the Middle Temple*, 3rd ed., 2 vols., Whieldon and Butterworth, London, 1793, Vol. 2, pp. 315–541. The remark about legislative activity in the second half of the eighteenth century is Joseph Burchell's: *Arrangement and Digest of the Law*, Preface. See also *The Parliamentary History of England, from the Earliest Period to the Year 1803, XIX, Comprising the Period from January 1777 to ... December 1778*, London, 1814, Preface; Oldham, *The Mansfield Manuscripts*, Vol. 1, p. 163.

[16] James Stephen Taylor, *Poverty, Migration and Settlement in the Industrial Revolution: Sojourners' Narratives*, Society for the Promotion of Science and Scholarship, Palo Alto, CA, 1989, p. 188, note 2.

in the 1790s: it was through settlement legislation that the poor laws had the greatest effect on the largest number of lives in the last quarter of the century. Settlement by service produced more litigation than any other aspect of the poor laws since their sixteenth-century inauguration.[17]

Keith Snell referred to some thousand settlement examinations in *Annals of the Labouring Poor*. For the early part of the century, he emphasised the importance of being hired for a year as 'virtually the only method to gain one's own settlement', from which followed the typical pattern of leaving home at about fourteen years of age, and then moving from one annual hiring to the next. Many settlements might be gained by working and receiving wages in a parish for a full 365 days, with each new settlement supplanting the last. On getting married, a man might shift from being a yearly servant to being a labourer, hired (and paid) by the week or the day.[18] Women could gain their own settlement in exactly the same way as men, by a series of annual hirings. For women as for men, the contract of service was practically the only way of doing this. Indeed, it is likely that more women than men sought settlement in this way in the period 1750–1790 – certainly more disputed women's cases reached King's Bench. On marriage, a woman took her husband's settlement. Modern historians draw our attention to the difficulties of proving settlement for groups like women or children needing to show a 'derivative' settlement from husband or parents, and for married women claiming relief for whatever reason, on their 'maiden settlement' – the settlement held before marriage.[19] Appeal cases often involved marriage law

[17] Taylor, *Poverty, Migration and Settlement*, p. 24; Robert Pashley, *Pauperism and the Poor Laws*, Longman Brown Green & Longman, London, 1852, pp. 268–9. Also James Willis, *On the Poor Laws of England: The Opinions of Blackstone, Addison, Wimpey, Winchelsea, Young, Rumford, Estcourt, Gilbert, Stewart, Eden, Pitt, Nasmith, Townsend, Pew, Davies, Colquhoun, Weyland, Bate, Rose, Monck, Malthus, Whitbread, and the Society for Bettering the Condition of the Poor*, John Lambert, London, 1808, pp. 67–9.

[18] Snell, *Annals of the Labouring Poor*, pp. 73, 105–8, pp. 17–18 for settlement legislation; also Pamela Sharpe, *Adapting to Capitalism: Working Women in the English Economy, 1700–1850*, Macmillan, Basingstoke, 1996, pp. 109–21; 51–6.

[19] For the case of Rachel Clark of Colchester, married to a Scot who, having no settlement in England, appealed for relief through his wife, see Sharpe, *Adapting to Capitalism*, pp. 118–20, and notes. For Richard Burn's analysis of the difficulties arising from there being 'not the same measure of justice between the two kingdoms of England and Scotland', see Burn, *A History of the Poor Laws*, pp. 283–4.

and the coverture of propertyless women.[20] Judge Blackstone's own *Reports* noted a poor law removal case from 1762 which hinged on the question of whether Susannah and John Meredith of Herefordshire were legally married. No banns appeared to have been published, and under the Marriage Act of 1753, banns were 'now as much essential to a marriage, as livery to a feoffment, or attestation to a will of lands'. However, Lord Mansfield thought that whilst in the ecclesiastical courts it might well be 'necessary prove, that all the solemnities of the Marriage Act have been punctiliously … complied with: but, God forbid, that in other cases (the legitimacy of children and the like) the usual presumptive proofs of marriage should be taken away by this statute'. Anyway, there was abundant evidence that there *had* been banns; the church minister had been highly blamable in not *publishing* them. All orders of removal for the couple and their children were quashed by King's Bench.[21]

Coverture was not a question in the case of *Rex* v. *The Inhabitants of Newstead* (May 1770). The court consisted of Lord Mansfield, Mr Justice Willes, and Blackstone, who was standing in for Lord Aston, engaged that day at the Court of Chancery. The case concerned the question of settlement by service, and its subject was Frances Downey, who had hired herself to a householder of Holy Island (now Northumbria, then County Durham) at Whitsuntide 1767. She was stated to be a single woman, which was important, for all questions of her right to settlement by domestic service devolved on the non-derivative settlement which she had acquired by a year's work in one place. She had served her time; taken her wages; had gone home to Newstead, Balmbrough, in Northumberland. Two justices had made an order for her removal back to Holy Island, where they believed she had earned a settlement by her year's service. The argument between the two parishes was about whether or not, under the antique way of calculating a year that pertained in the northeast, she had actually served the 365 days at Holy

---

[20] Kim Kippen, 'Poor Law, Coverture, and Maintaining Relations in King's Bench, 1601–1834', Tim Stretton and Krista J. Kesselring (eds.), *Married Women and the Law: Coverture in England and the Common Law World*, McGill-Queen's University Press, 2013, pp. 64–87.

[21] William Blackstone, *Reports of Cases Determined in the Several Courts of Westminster-hall, from 1746 to 1779; by the Honourable Sir William Blackstone, Knt, One of the Justices of the Court of Common Pleas; with Memoirs of his Life*, 2nd edn, revised and corrected with copious notes and references, including some from the mss of the late Mr Sergt. Hill, by Charles Heaneage Elsley, Esq; in two volumes, S. Sweeney, R. Pheney and A. Maxwell, London, 1828, Vol. 1, p. 366.

Island that the legislation specified. She had, said the Judges: 'this is stated to be the usual Way of hiring Servants in this County, and such Service always deemed to be a Year's Service. There are many of the Clergy, in Durham: They compute from ecclesiastical Days. It is stated as a Hiring "to serve for a Year ... from Whitsuntide to Whitsuntide".'[22] Had she married someone from her home parish of Newstead on her return, she would have taken his settlement and would not have had to return over the county border to a place where she had no job, though some entitlement to poor relief. But this was not about Frances Downey, or her single status, or her being feme sole, nor her own right to settlement, but about two parishes refusing financial responsibility for her, as Lord Mansfield frequently observed. He had a great many opinions – trenchant, widely known – about the poor law; he outspoke the rest of the judges put together at King's Bench appeal meetings. His fellow judge William Blackstone's opinion of the poor laws was much the same as Mansfield's: 'notwithstanding the pains that has been taken about them [the Poor Laws], they still remain very imperfect, and inadequate to the purposes they are designed for'. This, he said was 'a fate, that has generally attended most of our statute laws, where they have not the foundation of the common law to build on'. Things had been much better for the poor under the Great Alfred.[23]

★★★

Tabitha Reynolds had been a servant (whether domestic or not is unclear), had been married, had children in and out of wedlock. Her settlement struggles of the late 1760s never went further than Doncaster quarter sessions; the dispute occasioned by her chequered marital career was resolved without any appeal to King's Bench. Mrs Reynolds and her three youngest children (Sarah, five years old; John, aged three, and Mary, one year) were removed to Leeds from Doncaster on the

---

[22] James Burrow, *Decisions of the Court of King's Bench upon Settlement Cases; from the Death of Lord Raymond in March 1732, to June 1776, inclusive ... Second Edition*, His Majesty's Law-Printers for E. Brooke, 1786, pp. 669–71. *Rex v. The Inhabitants of Newstead* [May 1770]: 'Hiring and Service from Whitsuntide to Whitsuntide, according to the Custom of the Country, will gain a Settlement'. Whitsun was a moveable feast. In some years there might not be 365 days between one Whitsun and the next.

[23] William Blackstone, *Commentaries on the Laws of England. Book I of the Rights of Persons* (1765), Oxford University Press, Oxford, 2016, p. 234; William Blackstone, *Commentaries on the Laws of England. Book IV of Public Wrongs* (1769), Oxford University Press, Oxford, 2016, p. 20.

order of two West Riding magistrates at the end of December 1767. The family was received by the Leeds overseers.[24] Before she married in the late 1740s, she had gained her own settlement by hiring herself for a year to William Pookett of Methley, in the triangle between Leeds, Castleford and Wakefield: 'About 1742, when she was a spinster, she was hired for a year... & served such year Service & consequently was then legally settled there', ran the brief prepared by Leeds attorneys for the Doncaster quarter sessions to be held in January 1768. Seven or so years later, she had married Joseph Turner of Garforth (some five miles north of Methley) and had had one or two children by him (she, or more likely the attorney's clerk recording her story, was uncertain on this point). When Turner left her in 1752 and she applied for parish relief, it was on her husband's settlement. But where Turner's 'legal Settlement was she never knew for a Certainty, otherwise than as she has heard him say yt (that) it was at Hepelstone or some such like Place in Staffordshire'; and that was where she was removed, sometime in 1752. This could have been Eccleshall, or Mucklestone, or indeed any one of a dozen Staffordshire places, though there is no Hepelstone in the county. The point is that she did not know where she was going, but it didn't matter that she didn't, because 'the Officers of the Place, to which she had been so removed agreed with the Officer who conducted her thither, to bring her [back] to Methley, which he did accordingly, and... she was received at Methley'. The attorneys were alarmed to find that 'This Order seems not to have been appealed from – We have applied to the Officers of Garforth & endeavoured to possess our selves of this Order but in vain – Indeed they alledge there was no such Order, but the Pauper says otherways, & will acquaint the Court, if proper to touch upon this Matter'.

Sometime after her turnaround journey to – *somewhere*, Tabitha Turner heard that her husband was dead, and in June 1755 married Jonathan Reynolds of Leeds, sometime boatman and sometime porter, by whom she had the three children named above, all of them born in the township of Leeds. Then, nine years after his disappearance and not dead at all, Joseph Turner turned up in Leeds '& findg. the Pauper in the Possession of Reynolds as his Wife, demanded her of him, but at last Turner & Reynolds came to an Agreement touching her whereby the

[24] West Yorkshire Archives Wakefield District, Wakefield Record Office, West Riding of Yorkshire Quarter Sessions, Doncaster Sessions, January 1768, Quarter Sessions Rolls, QS1/107/3-7, Orders; Order of Removal for Tabitha Reynolds... from Doncaster to Leeds Wedon, 26 December 1767.

former pretended to sell, and the latter to buy her, & so Reynolds still continued in Poss'ion, till he ran away & left her some 20 or 30 Weeks ago', that is, in the summer of 1767.[25] There were strenuous attempts made by the firm of Bridges, Solicitors, to trace Turner and Reynolds, and, more to the point, to discover whether either of them 'did any Act whereby to gain a Settlement at Leeds'. It appeared that as a young man Reynolds had hired himself for a year to a miller at Castleford 'and served for a year, indeed 'tis said, Reynolds served … for sevl. years successively as … hired Servt for a year', in which case, the township of Castleford close by Castleford Mills, would have been responsible for Tabitha and the children. But soon into the preparation of the case, Tabitha Reynolds's own marital and settlement status became the principle of drawing up the brief: 'As it appears, ye Woman has acquired a Settlement at Methley in her own Right, & the Settlement of her real Husband cannot be ascertained & the 3 children ment'd in the order are Bastards'. None of the adults in the case had their settlement at Leeds, neither Turner, nor Tabitha nor Jonathan Reynolds. There was a further point to take into consideration: 'altho' the Children may, possibly, be Bastards, & the Place of their legal Settlement may be [at Leeds] as being the Place of their Birth', they had not, in fact, been removed to Leeds on those grounds. Until they were bastardized by a justices' order they had to be assumed legitimate. Thinking through the technicalities of the case, the attorneys thought that 'even admitting them Bastards, for Argument sake' was not to the point, for they were supposed in law 'to be inseparable from their Mother, being all Nurse Children under the Age of 7 years, & ought to have been removed with her to her Place of Settlement, as a necessary Appendage of hers, & not she with them'. In other words, Tabitha Reynolds and her children ought to have been removed to Methley, the place of her maiden settlement.[26]

When it came to court, the argument on behalf of the township of Leeds rested on two points: proof that the proper place of settlement for Tabitha Reynolds and her children was in Castleford Township (where her second husband had gained a settlement) *and* her settlement

---

[25] Pamela Sharpe, 'Bigamy among the Labouring Poor in Essex, 1754–1857', *Local Historian*, 24:3 (1994), pp. 139–44.

[26] West Yorkshire Archives, Bradford Record Office, 16D86/1150, Sharp Bridges Accounts, 'Brief to Doncaster Sessions 20 Janry 1768'. For the ways in which a woman's settlement might apply to her children and grandchildren, Edmund Bott, *Digest of the Laws Relating to the Poor, by Francis Const*, 3 vols., Strahan, London, 1800, Vol. 2, pp. 161–2, 164–6.

'at Methley in her own Right' – though where mattered less than its not being at Leeds, but *somewhere else*, outwith the town. The West Riding magistrates found for Leeds at their Doncaster meeting on 20 January. The attorneys' fee, the flurry of paperwork in Leeds (the letters sent vainly seeking removal orders twenty-odd years old, or persuading former employers to appear as witnesses), the maintenance of the children in Leeds Workhouse, and the price of legal opinion and representation, cost some £4. It is not clear whose determination of settlement removed Tabitha Reynolds and her children from the responsibility of Leeds: her own, or that of her second husband, Jonathan. It seems likely though, that it was her maiden settlement rather than her derivative one that determined the next place to which she was sent off in the waggoner's cart, as the evidence to support Jonathan Reynolds's settlement at Castleford was not very compelling.[27] Women's complicated legal personae are exemplified by Tabitha Reynolds, in her relationship to a body of law (the poor laws and laws of settlement) in which it mattered very much what kind of body *she* possessed, in all its dramatic mutability. The legal status of this woman rested on her having, in succession, a pregnant body, a parturient body, a lactating body; on the body she exercised in labour (in both its meanings); and on the connection of that body to men, as feme-covert and as feme-sole. As a legal person, Tabitha Reynolds was perpetually being covered and uncovered.

One of the tendencies of ratepayers, satirized by Richard Burn, scandalized everywhere, was that 'if they will hire servants...for a year, [they] then endeavour to pick a quarrel with them before the year's end, and...get rid of them'.[28] But courts of quarter session had also to deal with the question of the employer's right to dismiss his servant, his

---

[27] Bott, *Digest of the Laws*, Vol. 2, pp. 161–2, 164–6; West Yorkshire Archives Wakefield District, Wakefield Record Office, West Riding of Yorkshire Quarter Sessions, Doncaster Sessions, January 1768, Quarter Sessions Rolls, QS1/107/3–8, Miscellaneous, 'Expences of the Maintenance of Tabitha Reynolds and her Three Children in Leeds Workhouse from Decr 29th 1767 to Jany 9th 1768 being 3 Weeks'; Quarter Sessions Order Books, 1767–1769, QS10/25, entry for 20 January 1768.

[28] Burn, *A History of the Poor Laws*, p. 211; Snell, *Annals of the Labouring Poor*, p. 757. Magistrates in quarter sessions in Buckinghamshire in 1782 hearing the case of a farmer telling a farm servant at the hiring that '"he should not belong to Mursley"...stated that they were of the opinion that all such transactions on the part of masters are fraudulent to prevent servants gaining settlements by virtue of their service': Charles Durnford and Edward Hyde East, *Term Reports in the Court of the King's Bench*, 7 vols., Butterworth and Cooke, London and Dublin, 1817, Vol. 1 (1785–1787), *Rex* v. *Inhabitants of Mursley*. Mr Justice Grose commented that 'if the opinion of the Court of Sessions amount to anything, it goes to the length of saying that all hirings for less than a year are fraudulent'.

general authority over a female servant, and how it was to be exercised, under the complex and antique body of laws that regulated domestic work. For example, magistrates in their sessions had long been advised that 'if a woman who is a Servant shall marry, yet she must serve out her Time and her Husband cannot take her out of her Master's Service'; the law of service overrode marriage law in this regard; a working-class husband's absorption of his wife's legal personality did not take effect until her year's service contract finished.[29]

There was much debate over the question of whether or not the Elizabethan legislation that gave the resolution of disputes between employers and their servants in husbandry (farm workers) to magistrates was also applicable to domestic servants. There was also the thorny question of whether the provisions of 20 Geo. II, c. 19, giving such jurisdiction to *two* magistrates, actually extended to household servants.[30] A servant hired according to 5 Eliz. c. 4 was not to leave his or her service unless allowed to do so by a magistrate, and there was a similar jurisdiction exercised by magistrates as far as the employer's dismissal of a servant before time was concerned.[31] The weight of contemporary advice was that this legislation applied only to farm servants. Many regretted this. A 'Gentleman of the Inner Temple' who published his *Laws Concerning Masters and Servants* in 1785, noted 20 Geo. II c. 19 (1747) and 31 Geo. II c. 11 (1758), remarking that 'if instead of Servants in Husbandry... [they] had said servants in general, it would have extended the Law to all Domestic servants whatever, and have subjected them as well as their Masters and Mistresses, to have their Misconduct and Misbehaviour and Disputes about Wages, etc. to be inquired into. The Body of Domestic Servants is very large, and at present without Regulation'. These two statutes were missed opportunities for the policing of household service.[32]

---

29 Michael Dalton, *The Country Justice: Containing the Practice, Duty and Power of the Justices of the Peace, as well as in as out of Their Sessions*, Henry Lintot, London, 1742, p. 139; Samuel Clapham, *A Collection of Several Points of Sessions Law, Alphabetically Arranged*, 2 vols., Butterworth and Clarke, London, 1818, Vol. 2, pp. 83–86; *Familiar Summary of the Laws*, p. 4.

30 *The Laws Relating to Masters and Servants*, p. 40. The legislation referred to was 5 Eliz., c. 4, 'An Act Containing Divers Orders for Artificers, Labourers, Servants of Husbandry and Apprentices' (1562); and 20 Geo. II, c. 19, 'An Act for the Better Adjusting and More Easy Recovery of Wages of Certain Servants and for Better Regulation of Such Servants' (1747).

31 Clapham, *A Collection of Several Points of Sessions Law*, p. 5.

32 Gentleman of the Inner Temple, *Laws Concerning Masters and Servants*, His Majesty's Law Printer, London, 1785, p. 40.

Nevertheless, county justices, sitting alone, *did* act as if they had jurisdiction over the domestic service relationship.[33] James Bird said that the original legislation related 'particularly to artificers and servants of [sic] husbandry, but it is imagined that it may well be construed to give justices a general jurisdiction over servants of every description, and such jurisdiction is in fact exercised by them'.[34] Collating *The Whole Law Relative to the Duty and Office of a Justice of the Peace* in 1812, Thomas Waller Williams thought that in the previous century, magistrates had simply assumed the legal fiction that all servants 'were servants in husbandry, and thus exercised jurisdiction'.[35] Part of the irresolution over a magistrate's ability to intervene in the domestic service relationship was founded in the nature of women's *actual work* in service, which throughout the century had effectively rendered useless the legal distinction between husbandry work and domestic work – when performed by a woman. All over the country, young women in single-servant households did all sorts, indoors and out: dusting and getting the dinner on the table, washing the baby's clouts, milking the house cow, putting down peas and beans in the kitchen garden, helping bring in the cash crop the family grew in the field beyond the garden wall, and much, much more. Debating a proposed tax on the employment of female servants in 1785, Members of Parliament (MPs) recognized that many women servants were kept 'for the double purpose of doing the work of... [a] house and... [a] farm'.[36] Things continued in this way, well into the new century: in 1824, Richard Stileman, JP of Winchelsea in Sussex, recorded in his notebook 'the complaint of Mercy Lacy of the Parish of Beckley... hired by Mrs Stonham... at Conster to serve her as an Indoor Servant and Dairymaid... and tht John Stonham & his Wife neglect & refuse to pay her the sum of eight shillings on account of her Wages'.[37]

---

[33] Carolyn Steedman, *Labours Lost: Domestic Service and the Making of Modern England*, Cambridge University Press, Cambridge, 2009, pp. 172–98. Also John Beattie, *Crime and the Courts in England, 1660–1800*, Oxford University Press, Oxford, 1986, pp. 268–81, quoting Sir John Hawkins, *Charge to the Grand Jury of Middlesex*, Edward Brooke, London, 1780, pp. 26–7.

[34] Bird, *The Laws Respecting Masters and Servants*, p. 3.

[35] Thomas Waller Williams, *The Whole Law Relative to the Duty and Office of a Justice of the Peace*, 4 vols., John Stockdale, London, 1812, Vol. 3, pp. 887–93. See also Richard Burn, *A New Law Dictionary: Intended for General Use, as Well as for Gentlemen of the Profession, Continued to the Present Time by His Son, John Burn*, 2 vols., Strahan and Woodfall, London, 1792, Vol. 2, pp. 325–8; Ruggles, *The History of the Poor*, Vol. 2, p. 255.

[36] *Parliamentary History of England*, Vol. XXV (1785–1786), pp. 559–60, 9 May 1785.

[37] East Sussex County Record Office, Lewes, AMA 6192/1, notebook of Richard Stileman of Winchelsea, JP, 1819–1827, 115–16, entry for 3 June 1824.

Examples of this kind of work, performed by women inside and outside the house, litter the fragmented records of local justice.

The court of King's Bench discussed the point (indoor servant and dairymaid in one person) many times, in 1795 in relation to a disputed settlement. At Michaelmas 1793, Elizabeth Lamb had been hired to serve Joseph Scrivener of Potterspury in Northamptonshire 'to work in the Dairy, but not to milk the cows'. She worked until May 1794 'when becoming insane her Master took her before ... one of His Majesty's Justices of the Peace'. The magistrate declared her unfit for service and discharged her from her hiring. She was removed to the parish where she had gained a prior settlement. The removal was disputed, and her case went before quarter sessions, which decided that she was indeed a servant in husbandry, who *could* be discharged by a magistrate, and the order of removal was confirmed. The appeal case actually hung on the question of whether or not the order of a justice removing someone like Elizabeth Lamb had to state, *in writing*, that she was actually a farm servant; this the Northamptonshire justice had failed to do. In Westminster Hall, 5 Eliz. c. 4, s. 6 was discussed yet again: the wording of the act was pondered. It was *general* wording, it was declared; it specified a 'person who shall retain *any servants*'. In the event, the judgement was given on the grounds that Elizabeth Lamb was indeed a farm servant (in the manuscript notes of the hearing, the telling phrase 'but not to milk the cows' is underlined, as if that might be the dividing line between domestic and husbandry work). The judges' doubts about what Elizabeth Lamb actually did as a servant were discussed in full, with one remarking to his colleagues that magistrates had always exercised this kind of jurisdiction over all manner of servant. But the decision was that the order of removal was void 'because it did not appear on the order itself to be a case within the jurisdiction of a magistrate ... [so] the order of Sessions must be quashed',[38] thus leaving the distinction between farm and domestic work for women

---

[38] Lincoln's Inn Library, Dampier Manuscripts, L.P.B., 104, King agst. Inhabitants of Hulcott, argued on Wednesday 10 June 1795; Durnford and East, *Term Reports in the Court of the King's Bench*, Vol. 6, pp. 583–7. This was the kind of case that Samuel Glasse used to urge his readers to secretarial caution, telling them that Dr Burn himself 'enumerates not less than twenty instances, in which an Order of Removal has been, or is liable to be, quashed on account of some apparently insignificant error in the mere matter of form'. County Magistrate [Samuel Glasse], *The Magistrate's Assistant; or, A Summary of Those Laws Which Immediately Respect the Conduct of a Justice of the Peace*, R. Raikes, Gloucester and London, 1788, pp. xii–xiii.

as unclear as it had been for seventy years past. So uncertain was the position that the 1793 edition of Burn's *Justice* could only advise magistrates that 'whether the jurisdiction of justices extends to servants in general or is confined to servants in husbandry ... does not seem to be fully and absolutely settled'.[39] *Domestic/husbandry* and *indoor/outdoor* were legal distinctions that related uncertainly to what people actually *did* in everyday life.[40]

The case of Hannah Wright from 1776 to 1777 did nothing much by way of clarification. In February 1777, Lord Mansfield and his fellow King's Bench judges heard the case of Rex v. The Inhabitants of Brampton, Derbyshire. The year before, Hannah Wright had been removed from Ashover, also in Derbyshire, to Brampton. Brampton parish had appealed to quarter sessions, where the removal order was confirmed on the grounds that Hannah Wright had earned her legal settlement there through a year's hiring and wage-earning. The settlement in Brampton was not in question, but rather it was whether or not it might have been superseded by one worked for at Eyam, another Derbyshire village some fifteen miles west of Brampton along the Chapel-en-le-Frith road. Wright had hired herself to Mr Longsdon of that place for a year and had worked under the hiring until, just three weeks before the year was up, when 'her master discovering her to be with child, turned her away, and paid her year's wages, and half a crown over; whereupon she went home to her father's at Ashover, from whence she was removed'.[41] Examined at quarter sessions, Hannah Wright said that she 'was willing to have staid her year out, if she might; but ... it was not material to her whether she staid or went, as she had received her whole year's wages; and that she was not half gone with her child when she left her service; and hoped that she could have done

---

[39] Richard Burn [John Burn], *The Justice of the Peace, and Parish Officer. By Richard Burn, LL.D. Late Chancellor of the Diocese of Carlisle. Continued to the Present Time by John Burn, Esq. His Son, The Eighteenth Edition; Revised and Corrected. In Four Volumes*, Strahan and Woodfall, London, 1793, Vol. 3, p. 199. John Burn (now continuing his father's work) here transliterates Thomas Caldecott, *Reports of Cases Relative to the Duty and Office of a Justice of the Peace, from Michaelmas Term 1776, Inclusive, to Trinity Term 1785, Inclusive*, 3 vols., P. Uriel, London, 1786, Vol. 2, p. 11.

[40] Michael Roberts, 'Wages and Wage-Earners in England: The Evidence of the Wage Assessments, 1563–1725', D. Phil. thesis, University of Oxford, 1982, pp. 168–76.

[41] Derbyshire County Record Office, Quarter Sessions Records, Q/SO 1/9, Translation Sessions, 1776, 'Ashover v. Walton [Brampton]'; The National Archives (TNA) KB 16/18/1, Records of Orders Files, 17 Geo. III, 1776–1777: the Order – 'the Writt' – demanding the production of documents in the case from Derbyshire magistrates is dated 23 February 1777.

the work of her place to the end of the year'. Andy Wood's account of the culture of Peak Country lead-mining communities leads us to expect Hannah Wright's cheerful (at least, cheerful-seeming) independence of mind.[42]

The questions debated at Derbyshire Quarter Sessions were asked again in Kings Bench: had the contract between her and her master been dissolved before the end of the year for which Hannah Wright had been hired? Had her employer acted 'either arbitrarily or fraudulently'? An employer surely had a right to dismiss his servant if he had 'just and reasonable cause'; there could be no doubt 'but that a criminal conduct like [hers] amounts to a reasonable cause'. To be sure, there was earlier case law to say that 'a maid-servant, got with child' can't be dismissed from her service, but that surely meant that she could not be removed by *parish officers* before the contract was dissolved. In this case, Hannah Wright's misconduct was a very good reason for her master to dissolve the contract. There were those who said that a magistrate should have been applied to; 'but in the first place, this [was] not the case of a servant in husbandry, and therefore a justice of the peace had no jurisdiction ... or if he had, it was in this case unnecessary, as the servant consented [to her own dismissal]', for had she not said that she really wasn't *very* pregnant and could easily have worked up to her confinement? – that 'it was not material to her whether she staid or went, as she had received her whole year's wages'? The wage question was important: did her master give her her full wages (and that extra half-crown) because he assumed that the contract was to last until the end of the year? No; because it has been 'again and again ... determined that a deduction of wages does not prove a contract dissolved within the year'. The arguments on the other side were that 'all the authorities say, that when dismission of a servant is accompanied ... with the payment of the whole wages, it shall be considered as a ... constructive continuance of it to the end of the year'. To argue in this way meant denying the servant's consent to the dissolution of the contract and seeing the extra 2s. 6d. as a substitute for her board and lodging; indeed, if you followed this train of thought, 'the only object of the master was to defeat the settlement of the servant in his parish'.[43]

[42] Andy Wood, *The Politics of Social Conflict: The Peak Country, 1520–1770*, Cambridge University Press, Cambridge, 1999. Hannah Wright's movement across the Peaks lead-field parishes can be reconstructed from the maps on pp. 31, 32, 34, 35.

[43] Caldecott, *Reports of Cases*, Vol. 2, pp. 11–14.

Now Lord Mansfield moves with lightning speed from the ruminations of his fellow judges into the role identified by his first biographer, as *custos morum* [moral guardian] of the people'.[44] He agrees that Hannah Wright's saying that she could have worked out her time is not the point: 'it is not her ability but her criminal conduct that must be the test; or otherwise a master might be obliged to keep a woman in the house for many months, though he were a clergyman, or had a wife and daughters'.[45] His fellow judges make the point that she has committed no crime: that 'an unmarried woman by being with child is not guilty of any crime, or even misdemeanour at common law'; but the chief justice focuses on the question of hiring, and, referring to 8 & 9 Will. III, c. 30 (1697), says that 'there must be a hiring for a year, and a continuance for a year in that service, to gain a settlement'.[46] Service by its very nature 'admits often of questions upon the circumstances … but these questions have always been brought to this point. Whether the contract was put an end to within the year'. This could not be done by dismissing the servant without good cause, so the solution to the problem of Hannah Wright rests on asking a different question: 'has the master done right or wrong in discharging his servant for this cause?' – 'I think he did not do wrong', says Mansfield. Certainly, if an employer agreed under these circumstances to the continuance of contract (that is, agreed to keep on a pregnant servant) 'the overseers it is true, shall not take her away, because she is with child'.[47] But did this then mean, pursues Mansfield, that 'the master therefore be bound to keep her in his house'? To do that 'would be *contra bonos mores* [against morality]; and in a family where there are young persons, both scandalous and dangerous'. His fellow judges agree that if the master had daughters, it would 'not be fit that he should keep such a servant'.[48]

The removal orders were affirmed, a point for case law and the justices' manuals, but not for Hannah Wright. For by the time the case came to Westminster Hall in February 1777, matters – following a different timetable from that of the appeal system – had proceeded apace in Derbyshire. Hannah's daughter Mary had been born, and baptized

---

[44] John Holliday, *Life of William Late Earl of Mansfield*, P. Elmsly and D. Bremner, London, 1797, p. 214.

[45] Caldecott, *Reports of Cases*, Vol. 2, pp. 11–14.

[46] 'An Act for Supplying Some Defects in the Laws for the Relief of the Poor'; Const, *Decisions of the Court of King's Bench*, Vol. 2, pp. 516–18.

[47] Keith Snell, 'Pauper Settlements and the Right to Relief in England and Wales', *Continuity and Change*, 6:3 (1991), pp. 375–439; 384.

[48] Williams, *The Whole Law*, Vol. 3, pp. 902–3.

in July 1776 at Ashover, her grandfather's village.[49] This was where, three years later Sarah, Wright's second 'Base Dr', was also christened. John Bower, Ashover forgeman, was named as Sarah's father.[50] Wright's case was cited as late as 1812, for the benefit of justices of the peace, to advise that 'a master may of his own authority, and without the intervention of a magistrate, dismiss [a] servant for moral turpitude; even though it be not such for which the servant may be prosecuted at common law'.[51]

What was determined between the lines of Hannah Wright's insouciant and marvellous resistance of Lord Mansfield's disapproval (though it's unlikely she ever heard of it – or him – and had indeed shown confidence in her own capacities before he uttered it) was a judgement that convinced servants and their employers, for the next fifty years, that a pregnant, unmarried servant, 'not guilty of any crime, or...misdemeanour at common law', might be dismissed her place. Commenting on the likelihood of dismissal for a pregnant servant (and the contingent, but clearly likely, 'new born child murder' in which he is interested), Mark Jackson points out that servants were 'in theory protected by law from summary dismissal'.[52] But such protection afforded under 5 Eliz. c. 4 extended only to servants in husbandry, and, as a legal fiction cuts both ways, many a pregnant woman, who worked indoors and out, found herself called an indoor servant, who might be dismissed after Mansfield's judgement in the case of Hannah Wright.[53]

The judges behaved differently a year later when in the case of Ursula Owens of St Bartholomew's by the Exchange, London, they supported the settlement of a servant seven days short of her year's service (but

---

49   Derbyshire County Record Office, Parish Records, M77 vol. 2, Ashover Parish Register, 'Christenings at Ashover 1776 July: Mary Base Dr of Hannah Wright'.

50   Her mother had not named her sister Mary's father. Derbyshire County Record Office, Parish Records, M77 vol. 2, Ashover Parish. Register, 4 July 1779; Quarter Sessions Records, Q/SO 1/9, Order Books, 1774–1780, Easter Sessions 1779.

51   Williams, *The Whole Law*, vol. 3, pp. 902–3.

52   Mark Jackson, *New-Born Child Murder: Women, Illegitimacy and the Courts in Eighteenth-Century England*, Manchester University Press, Manchester, 1996, pp. 48–9.

53   You did not *have to* dismiss your pregnant servant. There may have been many like the amiable and ancient Reverend Murgatroyd of Slaithwaite, West Yorkshire, who spent much effort in 1802 trying to get the archetypal bad lot George Thorpe to marry his pregnant servant Phoebe Beatson; who resisted all the complaints of his scandalized neighbours worried about what *visitors would think* if he let her lie in in his house; who adored the baby, and left mother and child well provided for. Carolyn Steedman, *Master and Servant: Love and Labour in the English Industrial Age*, Cambridge University Press, Cambridge, 2007.

she was not pregnant). Her employer went to Manchester to purchase a factory, on his return telling his servants that he would soon be moving there, 'but he did not mention any time & that they might look out for other services if they chuse and might stay with him till he went to Manchester'. One evening in June 1777 he abruptly paid Owens the whole of her wages and half a guinea over, and left for the North. She quickly found a new job in a different London parish, but a year later found herself removed back to St Bartholomew's. In King's Bench on appeal, in disagreement with Mansfield, Judges Dunning and Sylvester spoke of Owens' loss of settlement, 'her only one, which she deserves so well'; 'Justice as well as reason of the thing are here with the Settlement' they said. 'Service wanted 7 days of a Year but whole years wages pd gains a Settlement', run the notes on the back of the papers in the case. Indeed. But not for Hannah Wright.[54]

The case of Hannah Phillips demonstrated that even when a year's service was not mentioned at the hiring, and even when the concept of hiring was imperfectly understood by the contracting parties, then the law would assume that it was a 'general hiring' for a year: a true hiring, that brought with it settlement rights. Some time in 1792, Hannah Phillips was removed from St Leonard's, Bridgenorth, Shropshire, to Worfield, where her father was legally settled. The Bridgenorth overseers were evidently attempting to make her claim relief on a derivative settlement in her natal village. She had been a servant in Bridgenorth for about seven years. For Shropshire quarter sessions, no less than the court of King's Bench (to which the case was forwarded for opinion from the April 1793 sessions), it raised important questions about settlement by service, including the much debated issue of whether the payment of wages at all, never mind for a year, was necessary for the right of settlement.[55] In 1789 (or thereabouts; she was uncertain about dates), Phillips had gone to live with the Smith family in Bridgenorth 'and served... near a year, but was not hired to... [Mr Smith] as she knows of'. She was approached by one John Jones of St Leonard's parish, Bridgenorth, who asked her if she had hired herself again to Andrew Smith for the coming year. When she said she had not, Jones

---

[54] Lincoln's Inn Library, Dampier Manuscripts, A.P.B., 19, Easter Term, 1778; Caldecott, *Reports of Cases*, Vol. 2, pp. 48–51, *Rex* v. *Inhabitants of St Bartholomew by the Exchange*.

[55] Shrewsbury, Shropshire Record Office, *Orders of Shropshire Quarter Sessions*, 5 vols., Shrewsbury, n.d., Vol. 3, Sir Ofsey Wakeman and R. Lloyd Kenyon (eds.), 'April Sessions, 1793, *Worfield* v. *St Leonard Bridgenorth*. Adjourned; the opinion of the Court of the King's Bench to be taken'.

invited her to come and live with his family 'and take care of his child, to which she consented', arriving at Christmas-time 1790. A few days into her new place, Mr Jones asked her if it would be all right to pay her in kind – to 'find her meat, drink and clothes' – and she agreed. She said that he had been willing to pay her in cash, but 'it was better for her to have clothes, as she was connected with bad friends, who would take her money'.[56] She stayed for two and a half years on these terms, leaving in May 1792 after Mrs Jones told her that 'the child was old enough not to require any further attendance, and dismissed her'. The case turned on whether or not she had ever actually been hired for a year. A very long argument, including much quoting of precedent on behalf of the two parishes in conflict, was cut through in Westminster Hall by Lord Chief Justice Kenyon (Mansfield had retired his post in 1788), who said that 'it has been so long settled, that a general hiring is for a year, that it ought not to be controverted. In my opinion in this case there was a hiring for a year'. His fellow judges agreed: 'clothed by the master the day after she went into the service, could it have been the intention of the parties that she might have left the service immediately [?] ... both parties meant that the service should be permanent ...'. The order was quashed, and Hannah Phillips gained her Bridgenorth settlement, the appeal court judges confirming that neither wages for any period of time nor wages for a full 365 days were always needed for a woman to gain her own settlement.[57]

Pregnancy removed you from the benignity of legal interpretation that Hannah Phillips (Shropshire) experienced, and so did the uncertain legal status of the slave and servant Charlotte Howe, who had her application for poor relief tossed between the parishes of Thames Ditton in Surrey and St Luke's, Chelsea (London) all through 1784 and 1785. Charlotte Howe had been brought to England in 1781 when very young, by Captain Tyringham Howe, who settled in Thames Ditton with his wife.[58] She had been purchased in America as 'a negro slave', perhaps

---

[56] Durnford and East, *Term Reports in the Court of the King's Bench*, Vol. 5, pp. 224–6.

[57] For the reception of this judgement, Shropshire Record Office, Quarter Sessions Records, QS/3/1, 1708–1800, Sessions Minutes, July 1793. For its continued importance, see County Magistrate, *A Letter Addressed to the Agriculturalists in General, and to the Magistrates and Clergy in Particular throughout the Kingdom, on the Subjects of Hiring, Service and Character*, Longman and Whittaker, London, 1821, p. 7.

[58] Sylvester Douglas, *Reports of Cases Argued and Determined in the Court of the King's Bench*, 4 vols., Sweet & Stevens, Milliken, London and Dublin, 1813–31, Vol. 4, pp. 301–2; TNA, ADM 25/101, Half-Pay Registers July–December 1781; ADM 1/1906, Captains' Letters 1780–1781, 28, Tyringham Howe; ADM 36/10121, Navy Transports 1 January 1775 – 27 March 1785. For Captain Howe's Atlantic passage,

out of the maelstrom of war in which slaves, the goods and moveable property of the rebels, were stolen back and forth by both sides, and the British could not make up their mind about a half-hearted, never-official policy – strategy – of subverting the rebels by recruiting their slaves as soldiers or simply as runaways.[59] Howe's ship, the *Thames*, was at anchor off Sewell's Point, Virginia, in January 1781 when 'Came on board Several Negroes who had made their escape from the rebels' and the to-be-named Charlotte may have been among them, but it is more likely that the young woman (or child, perhaps) was acquired in the more sedately managed slave markets of the North, where Captain Howe was on sick leave from February to June 1781.[60]

Having been transported across the Atlantic, she continued in the Howes' service in Surrey until the death of Captain Howe in June 1783.[61] His dying evidently brought about a change in the household's perception of its circumstances – as the death of a master often did – for Charlotte (or perhaps her mistress arranged it) got herself baptized in December of that year, the Thames Ditton churchwarden recording in the register that she was 'Charlotte, an african servant to Mrs How'.[62] Some time in the new year, Mrs Howe moved to Chelsea, London taking her black servant with her. In June, Charlotte walked out (we cannot tell whether this was done with encouragement) thus – perhaps – making herself free. Douglas Lorimer has suggested that this was the major route to the end of slavery in Britain, brought about by slave-servants themselves, rather than by the conventionally evoked

---

recorded in Admiralty records and which nowhere indicate the presence of a young woman, Carolyn Steedman, 'Lord Mansfield's Women', *Past and Present,* 176 (2002), pp. 105–143. She was almost certainly transported on Howe's ship, the *Thames*. A muster roll may account for every last cockroach (only joking!), cat, and nameless supernumerary acting as cabin boy, but this young woman was a personal possession of its captain, and not to be mustered, listed, or accounted for.

[59] Sylvia R. Frey, *Water from the Rock: Black Resistance in a Revolutionary Age,* Princeton University Press, Princeton, NJ, 1991, pp. 64, 95, 134; James A. Rawley, *The Transatlantic Slave Trade: A History,* Norton, New York, 1981.

[60] TNA, ADM 51/982, Captains' Logs, pt 10, pp. 20, 22, 38, 42. Howe departed for New York on 7 February, on board *HMS Charles Town*. Parties of slaves had got on board the *Thames* before. National Maritime Museum, Greenwich, ADM L/T84, Lieutenants' Logs, *HMS Thames*, 10 September 1780–20 November 1780, Montagu Blackwell, 1st Lieutenant, entry for Monday 22 November 1780.

[61] She was not mentioned as person or property in Tyringham Howe's will: TNA PROB 11/1106.

[62] Surrey History Centre, Thames Ditton Parish Records, Baptisms, entry for 17 December 1783. See Taylor, *Poverty, Migration and Settlement*, pp. 67–8, for Ann Clossen, brought to England by a Captain Moore in the 1770s (from Africa, say the overseers' records) and whose fortunes 'improved dramatically after baptism and a new master'.

abolition inaugurated by legislation.[63] She may have freed herself (and no one went after her), but she was without means of subsistence and, in the late summer of 1784, applied to St Luke's (Chelsea) parish officials for poor relief (she does not appear to have been examined by the magistrates as to the state of her settlement). She next turned up in Thames Ditton, from whence in October she was removed back to St Luke's (this was on the order of two magistrates) and was placed in the parish workhouse.[64] In January 1785, the Thames Ditton authorities paid St Luke's 1s 5d for three months' keep of Charlotte Howe.[65] The Chelsea parish won its case against Surrey, and in January 1785, Charlotte Howe was carted back to Thames Ditton. At the end of the month, the vestrymen determined to take the opinion of King's Bench, a decision that was to cost them over £50, and which brought no one much satisfaction, for what churchwardens and magistrates learned from Lord Mansfield and his fellow judges was that their attempts to deal with Charlotte Howe in terms of her settlement, or lack of it, had been completely erroneous.

It had been argued most eloquently at quarter sessions and again in King's Bench that, as she had 'lived as a servant from year to year, and therefore is to be considered a servant as far as the laws of England will permit…it would be hard if a person of this description should not be maintained and taken notice of by the law'.[66] She had acted as a servant; she had displayed a clear understanding of the nature of her obligation 'as she never thought of quitting the service of the family

---

[63] Douglas Lorimer, 'Black Slaves and English Liberty: A Re-Examination of Racial Slavery in England', *Immigrants and Minorities Review*, 3 (1984), pp. 121–150; but see Norma Myers, 'Servant, Sailor, Soldier, Beggarman: Black Survival in White Society, 1780–830', *Immigrants and Minorities*, 12:1 (1993), pp. 47–74.

[64] Thames Ditton paperwork ended up in King's Bench records: TNA, KB 16/19/5, Records of Orders Files, 25 Geo. III, 1784–1785, including the removal order signed by two Surrey justices.

[65] London Metropolitan Archives, St. Luke's Chelsea, P74/LUK/111, Workhouse and Discharge Register, January 1782–December 1800, entries for 25 October 1784, 20 January 1785. Charlotte Howe's name was the only one on these two lists with a recorded age of twenty, signalling not necessarily that she was below the age of majority ('21' only signalled that someone was a legal adult, not an actual age) but that she had the status of a child, or some other category of minor, and was certainly not a full legal subject. She was most likely in her teens when she arrived in England in 1781. Surrey History Centre, Thames Ditton Parish Records, 2568/8/4, Overseers Accounts, 1773–1805, entries for 10 December 1784, 2 April 1785, and undated entries 1786; 2568/7/4, Poor Rate Assessment and Vestry Minutes, 1778–1796, entry for 31 January 1785; Surrey Quarter Sessions Order Books, QS2/6/.

[66] TNA, KB 16/19/5, Records of Orders Files, 25 Geo. III, 1784–1785; Douglas, *Reports of Cases*, Vol. 4, p. 301.

till her master's death: [and] that to deprive her of her settlement, the court must hold that she might have gone away at any time...'[67] But Mansfield cut briskly through the narration of her circumstances with the observation that 'it cannot be contended that this was a voluntary hiring, and [it is] therefore not a service'.[68] Whether she had been paid wages or not was irrelevant, for wages were not necessary to make a settlement (as the case of Hannah Phillips was to emphasize a few years later); indeed, there was no entitlement to wages anyway whether cash was handed over or not, 'because there never was a contract for wages'. All of this – with whom and how she had lived, how the parties had behaved towards each other, the money she may have received – was irrelevant, and so were clever arguments by attorneys from Chelsea and Surrey, that the English legal system recognized the condition of slavery, or at least serfdom, and should thus recognize Charlotte Howe.[69] None of this would do, said Mansfield; for although the poor law was a 'subsisting positive law [statute law], enforced by statutes which began to be made about the time of Queen Elizabeth, when villeinage was not abolished, and villeins [might]...in point of law...subsist to this day', nevertheless 'the statutes do not relate to them, nor had they them in contemplation'. For Charlotte Howe to 'bring herself under a positive law, she must answer the description it requires'. Further, 'her colour or [her] being a slave, or [her] having become such will not affect the question'. Her case was indeed 'very plain', said Mansfield. 'The statute says there must be a hiring, and here there was no hiring at all. She does not come within the description'; or, as another transcription has it, 'There is nothing in it'.[70] An unfree person, without description, she had never been in a position to make contract in the first place. As the notes on the back of the King's Bench papers tersely summarize: 'Easter term 25th Geo: 3d a black who was purchased abroad and continues to live with Mar [Master] or his Exectr for years in England without any Hiring does not gain a Settlement'.[71] The case of Charlotte Howe thus became no case at all;

---

[67] Caldecott, *Reports of Cases*, Vol. 3, pp. 515–20.

[68] Douglas, *Reports of Cases*, Vol. 4, p. 301.

[69] Granville Sharp, *A Representation of the Injustice and Dangerous Tendency of Tolerating Slavery; or of Admitting the Least Claim of Private Property in the Persons of Men, in England. In Four Parts*, Benjamin White & Robert, London, 1769, pp. 108–11, suggests that these arguments were widely known among lawyers.

[70] Douglas, *Reports of Cases*, Vol. 4, p. 301; Caldecott, *Reports of Cases*, Vol. 3, p. 520.

[71] Lincoln's Inn Library, Dampier Manuscripts, B.P.B., 377, 'Surrey: The King agt the Inhabitants of Thames Ditton'.

neither Thames Ditton nor Chelsea was responsible for her; she disappears from the records, leaving behind fragments of a story made for her by the legal system.[72]

A couple of days after the appeal was heard *The Times* reported on this 'curious case' heard in King's Bench, engaging readers' attention by the strange conjunction of 'slave' and 'parish'. The case had turned on a question, the reporter said: 'whether a negro slave can obtain settlement in a parish?'[73] It related Charlotte Howe's story – the American, sea-journey and Thames Ditton parts. This newspaper report is important for being the most immediate and perhaps most revelatory of the legal understandings at work in court that Tuesday morning than, for example, the tired repetition of the Howe case in the 1831 edition of Douglas's Reports was to be. (Anyway, three years on from then, settlement-by-service case law, the very purpose for telling again and again the narrative of Charlotte Howe, would be rendered quite redundant by the Poor Law Amendment Act.) It had been said in court that 'she had gained a settlement under the rule of law that, all general hiring is hiring for a year'. It had been claimed that, although 'having been a slave in America, [she] became on her arrival here to a certain degree free'. She was called 'the pauper' in court (as if for all the world she really was one: a poor person claiming her rightful relief, and actually getting what Tabitha Reynolds and Hannah Wright got, which was a lot of time on the road in parish carts). The 'great hardship and inconvenience' of the case had been urged on the judges (Willes, Ashurst and Buller sat that day with Mansfield), and so had the unfairness of things: 'if, after many years of service, a negro could not obtain that asylum and relief afforded to others'. 'Asylum', 'relief' – and entitlement to both these things – were at work in the court's language-in-common.[74] Lord Mansfield, according to this account, had made his point about statute law and about having to

---

[72] Carolyn Steedman, 'Enforced Narratives. Stories of Another Self', in Tess Cosslett, Celia Lury and Penny Summerfield (eds.), *Feminism and Autobiography. Texts, Theories, Methods*, Routledge, 2000, pp. 25–39.

[73] 'Law Reports', *The Times*, 29 April 1785, p. 2.

[74] For 'entitlement' relevant to these cases, W. M. Spellman, *John Locke*, Macmillan, Basingstoke, 1997, p. 115; Thomas A. Horne, *Property Rights and Poverty: Political Rights in Britain, 1605–1834*, University of North Carolina Press, Chapel Hill, NC, 1990, pp. 130–1, 141, 201–3; Lynn Hollen Lees, *The Solidarities of Strangers: The English Poor Laws and the People, 1700–1948*, Cambridge University Press, Cambridge, 1998, pp. 7–22, 29–33, 177; Taylor, *Poverty, Migration and Settlement*, pp. 18–19, 42.

bring yourself within its terms if you sought its application. but using a vocabulary nowhere else recorded, he said (according to *The Times*) that 'the poor law [is] a system of positive law established by several acts of Parliament... whoever comes to *claim benefit* under them must exactly answer the description given in them, that of being hired and serving for a year... in this case there was no hiring at all' (my italics). In 1800, reporter Thomas Caldecott also noted this language of benefits, rights and entitlement from twenty years before: 'where a party is in a condition to perform and bound also to perform in the parish where his master lives, he seems to be directly an object of these acts; and if he performs such service, justly entitled to the benefits they hold out'. Furthermore, the words 'deprive her of her settlement' had also been used that day, according to Caldecott.[75]

Benefit, right, justly entitled, her settlement: perhaps for those involved in the case or reporting on it in their various ways, these terms were the echoes of a political philosophy that still – just about – encompassed the poor laws. They had, after all, been inaugurated as a kind of bulwark against the law of necessity that John Locke had so clearly delineated: it was the first duty of any of God's creatures to sustain the life He had given them, and to stay alive, an injunction which, in social terms, might involve the poor and indigent in just taking what they needed to fulfil their duty to the Creator.[76] But these were probably not Mansfield's words; perhaps we can only be sure that they were the words of a newspaper reporter in 1785, and of Thomas Caldecott fifteen years on. The interest of the case for the lord chief justice (or rather, the interest attributed to him by generations of commentators) was the clarification it allowed him of the judgement he himself had made in the famous Somerset slavery case of 1771.[77] That earlier judgement, that a master had no right to remove a slave from England against his or her will, had allowed Mansfield to expiate on the 'odious' condition of slavery, so odious that it could not be inferred from, or be

[75] Caldecott, *Reports of Cases*, Vol. 3, pp. 517–520.
[76] Horne, *Property Rights and Poverty*, pp. 4–9; Spellman, *John Locke*, pp. 83–115; Lees, *The Solidarities of Strangers*, p. 19; David Lieberman, *The Province of Legislation Determined: Legal Theory in Eighteenth-Century Britain*, Cambridge University Press, Cambridge, 1989, pp. 56–67.
[77] Lorimer, 'Black Slaves and English Liberty'; Seymour Drescher, 'Manumission in a Society without Slave Law', *Slavery and Abolition*, 10 (1989), pp. 85–101; Oldham, *The Mansfield Manuscripts*, Vol. 2, pp. 1221–38; 'New Light on Mansfield and Slavery', *Journal of British Studies*, 27 (1988), pp. 45–68; Dana Rabin, 'In a Country of Liberty?' Slavery, Villeinage and the Making of Whiteness in the Somerset Case (1772), *History Workshop Journal*, 72 (2011), pp. 5–29.

taken to be supported by natural law, common law, or political philosophy. Indeed, it was so horrible a condition that it could only be upheld by statute law.[78] Contemporary abolitionists and Mansfield's modern historians have judged him kindly over his judgement in the Somerset case, pointing to the courage with which he implicitly found against the West Indian and commercial pro-slavery lobbies. Indeed, the end of British slavery is still sometimes dated from 1771.[79] But on 29 April 1785, in the case of Charlotte Howe, Mansfield made his famous earlier judgement a very small thing indeed. It is his qualification that will echo through the law reports, down to the 1830s: all he had done fourteen years before, he said, in the case of James Somerset the slave, was to go no further than 'to establish, that the master had no power to take the slave by force out of the Kingdom'.

Just as manumission was a difficult thing in a society without slave law, so was any legal procedure that needed knowledge of what kind of legal entity stood there, in a court of law. It was not so much that Charlotte Howe was a slave or not, or a person or not; her problem in King's Bench (as it had been in all the lesser tribunals she had actually stood in) was that there was no legal category for her condition of existence. *The Times* reporter understood the perfect uselessness of the terms of the debate since 1771: did slavery exist in England? Could it? Was William Blackstone right (or the opinion attributed to him correct) that a slave was free the moment he or she breathed Albion's air?[80] The anonymous reporter devised his own contradictory category to describe Charlotte Howe: she 'became on her arrival here to a certain degree free' – which was as perfectly useless to Howe as everything else that was said about her in King's Bench that day.

---

[78] Not the opinion of James Ramsay: 'slavery ... being the negation of law, cannot arise from law, or be compatible with it'. This was because society was *about* law: 'its prime design ... the extension of the operation of law, and the equal treatment and protection of its citizens'; 'slavery can never have been ended for the social state'. James Ramsay, *An Essay on the Treatment and Conversion of African Slaves in the British Sugar Colonies*, T. Walker and five others, Dublin, 1784, pp. 18–19, 173.

[79] We could add the biopic *Belle*, dir. Amma Asante, DJ Films, Isle of Man Film, Pinewood Pictures, BFI, 2013, to recent historiographical assessments of Mansfield on slavery. Also Paula Byrne, *Belle: The True Story of Dido Belle*, William Collins, London, 2014.

[80] For the much-quoted formulation, *Commentaries on the Laws of England: Book I Of the Rights of Persons* (1765), Oxford University Press, Oxford, 2016, pp. 411–13. For Mansfield's involvement in all these questions, Ruth Paley, 'After Somerset: Mansfield, Slavery and the Law in England, 1772–1830'; Norma Landau (ed.), *Law, Crime and English Society, 1660–1830*, Cambridge University Press, Cambridge, 2002, pp. 165–84, p. 177 for Howe.

According to the 'Gentleman of the Inner Temple' who published his *Laws Concerning Masters and Servants* later in 1785, the problem with young people like Charlotte Howe was that, having been brought to England as cheap servants, 'they put themselves on a Footing with other servants, [become] intoxicated with Liberty... and either by Persuasion of others, or from their own Inclinations, begin to expect Wages according to their own Opinion of their Merits'. They would deliberately get themselves dismissed (never mind the legal impossibility of that); then they would 'enter into Societies, and make their Business to corrupt and dissatisfy every fresh black Servant that comes to England'. They would persuade new arrivals to get themselves baptized, or married, 'which they inform them makes them free' (insolently ignoring what 'England's most able lawyers' told them: that baptism altered the master's property in them not one jot) because it got 'the Mob on their side'.[81] There is no evidence – as yet – of these support networks among the eighteenth-century black poor, but it is good to think of Charlotte Howe, who was without a settlement, and without legal personhood, in connection with friends like these.

The interest of Charlotte Howe for lawyers and legal theorists was not to be what her story said about slavery. For Michael Nolan, writing his careful scrutiny of the poor laws and the laws of settlement twenty years later, her case showed the elevation of statute law and contract law above common law and customary practice; for, as he told his readers, there was 'a presumption which might have arisen from her service', that is, from her relationship with Captain and Mrs Howe and in its 'reciprocal acts of service and maintenance': a presumption that she had obtained settlement through the relationship and the actions and deeds it involved. But in this case 'the situation of the woman, previous to her arrival in England, negatived the presumption'. She had been 'in the condition of a slave in America'; she had worked without reference to a contract; there was no – could not be a – contract for service in a case like hers.[82] No hiring, no settlement.

All the women discussed in this chapter have much to say to these questions of law, contract and personhood, not least from their position and status as domestic servants, that enormous and ubiquitous

---

[81] Gentleman of the Inner Temple, *Laws Concerning Masters and Servants*, pp. 28–30. Slaves and servants, black and white, persisted in believing that baptism constituted a form of manumission. This was probably because the courts positively refused to pronounce on the question and had been refusing since the late seventeenth century.

[82] Michael Nolan, *A Treatise of the Laws for the Settlement of the Poor*, 2 vols., J. Butterworth, London, 1805, Vol. 1, pp. 191–2.

section of the eighteenth-century workforce. They were women workers, who on the fragmentary and faint evidence of their narratives, believed that their energies exercised in labour brought them money, sometimes clothes and keep, sometimes a settlement. We may dimly discern a belief in their entitlement (especially on the part of Charlotte Howe) to the major benefit that domestic service brought, inaugurated by act of Parliament in 1662.[83] Tabitha Reynolds and Hannah Wright may also have known what differences illegitimacy made to the legal ability of their children to inherit their mother's settlement.[84] And they must have known what their historians have only recently understood, that the Law of Settlement was 'in fact, the most important branch of law, if judged by the number of lives affected and lawyers' hours expended' (and the reason why a manual like Burn's *Justice of the Peace* had to go through so many editions, in the attempt to keep up with the high court judges' almost daily adjustment of it).[85]

They had argued in King's Bench that the law should take note of Charlotte Howe, and it did, despite the manifold impossibilities of doing so, which Lord Mansfield outlined. This is the fine paradox that all of his women show: that the law admitted them to consideration and to discourse, even though it said it didn't; and, because it did admit them, the State came face-to-face with the poor law: saw how it worked, and what kind of thing it was – through its effect on women in far-flung and provincial places, those effects described in written words, and heard in London through the appeal system. These marvellous girls spoke out in courts of law: 'not half gone with her child... could have done the work of her place to the end of the year'... 'better for her to have clothes'... 'connected with bad friends'... 'the Pauper says otherways, & will acquaint the Court', knowing what and who they were, as women and workers, as legal persons.

But not, of course, Charlotte Howe. It is not possible to retrieve her spoken voice from the court transcripts. Through the fifty years in which her story is repeated, it is always written in a way that makes it impossible to recover the first-person singular.

★★★

[83] The amending acts of 13 & 14 Car. II, c. 12, and 3 Will. III, c. 11, establishing the rule of hiring and contract for 365 days, were more important to these women.

[84] See Bott, *Digest of the Laws*, Vol. 2, pp. 164–6.

[85] Taylor, *Poverty, Migration and Settlement*, pp. 18–19. Constant adjustment was a feature of term time, of course, that is, for less than half the year.

One nineteenth-century commentator was bemused by 'former times' (the eighteenth century) when 'an imagined, but mistaken analogy between a settlement and a right of property' had preoccupied both claimants and high court judges, when 'as it appears in the Law Reports ... judges used to speak of a settlement as a thing to be favoured in the law, and when they seemed to consider it ... as a peculiar privilege of the poor'.[86] Modern historians of the old poor law tend to emphasise this view, that 'the settlement ... [was] a property right for the poor'.[87] At the same time (the later twentieth century) there was a fierce debate among social and economic historians about the purposes of the poor laws in general, and the laws of settlement and removal in particular. Was this legislation inaugurated and used as a means of controlling the labour supply and managing internal migration?[88] Was it a form of police? A form of surveillance and management of the poor, indigent and vagrant?[89] Were the poor laws a system provoking pride in the English law that furnished everyone 'with every thing necessary for their support', as Blackstone once said? That there was no one so indigent or wretched that they might not 'demand a supply sufficient for all the necessaries of life, from the more opulent part of the community'?[90]

Social historians of the poor law rarely discussed settlement law *as law*: looking at law's effects on wretched and indigent lives (which is what most social historians did and do) could only confirm the view that the law is uncertain, imponderable, and arbitrary in its judgements

---

[86] Pashley, *Pauperism and the Poor Laws*, p. 269.

[87] Horne, *Property Rights and Poverty*, p. 141; Lees, *The Solidarities of Strangers*, pp. 29–33, 117; Sharpe, *Adapting to Capitalism*, p. 34; Snell, *Annals of the Labouring Poor*, pp. 71–4; Pamela Sharpe, '"The Bowels of Compation": A Labouring Family and the Law, *c*. 1790–1834', Tim Hitchcock, Peter King, and Pamela Sharpe (eds.), *Chronicling Poverty: The Voices and Strategies of the English Poor, 1640–1840*, London, 1997, pp. 87–108; Taylor, *Poverty, Migration and Settlement*, p. 42, calls settlement 'an important patrimony of any poor child, for good or ill'.

[88] Snell, 'Pauper Settlements and the Right'; Norma Landau, 'Going Local: The Social History of Stuart and Hanoverian England', *Journal of British Studies*, 24:2 (1985), pp. 273–81; 279; 'Laws of Settlement and the Surveillance of Immigration in Eighteenth-Century Kent', *Continuity and Change*, 3 (1988), pp. 391–420; 'The Eighteenth-Century Context of the Laws of Settlement', *Continuity and Change*, 6:3 (1991), pp. 417–39.

[89] Nicholas Rogers, 'Vagrancy, Impressment and the Regulation of Labor in Eighteenth-Century Britain', *Slavery and Abolition*, 15 (1994), pp. 102–13; Douglas Hay, 'Patronage, Paternalism, and Welfare: Masters, Workers and Magistrates in Eighteenth-Century England', *International Labour and Working-Class History*, 27 (1998), pp. 27–47; Byung Khun Song, 'Landed Interest, Local Government, and the Labour Market in England, 1750–1850', *Economic History Review*, 2nd ser. 51 (1998), pp. 465–88.

[90] Blackstone, *Commentaries I*, p. 234.

in courts high and low. Then, labour and legal historians turned their attention to the poor laws; they pursued questions of labour as property by discovering the permeable boundaries between labour/employment law and the poor laws.[91] In the disembodied legal encounters discussed in this chapter (no pauper or poor person actually *appeared* in King's Bench when the judges considered their claim to settlement), bodies of legislation were used together because of the particular kinds of body before the judges.

'Sisters in law' (sufferers from 'the misery and oppression, peculiar to women') have historical existence because stories were told about them, by contemporary writers and by later historians. This chapter has focussed on the stories that the law and legal encounters wrote for them. But there were brothers too. Another poor law settlement case, which Judge Blackstone published in his own *Reports of Cases*, had been heard in back in 1763 when he was still a barrister. It involved an Oxfordshire man whose settlement derived from his father. At the King's Bench appeal meeting, Mansfield took time to animadvert, as he so often did, upon the inadequacies of 'the present system of the Poor Laws'. Here, he said 'is an Instance where the Parties have been at much more Expence than the *keeping* of the Paupers would amount to: They have been before … two Justices; then at the Sessions; then before this Court, after a Removal of the Orders by *Certiorari*; and here are three Counsel on one Side: And all this, in a Case where [the disputing parish has] … had the Labour of the Father for 36 Years and the Son from his Birth'.[92] After much deliberation on the distinction between settlement right and the father's right not to be removed from own estate, it was determined that the father really had no settlement to communicate to his son, and the original removal order, away from the pauper's birth village, was confirmed. The interest here is not so much

[91] For legislation governing labour relations from the medieval period onwards, Douglas Hay, 'England, 1562–1875: The Law and Its Uses', Paul Craven and Douglas Hay (eds.), *Masters, Servants and Magistrates in Britain and the Empire, 1562–1955*, University of North Carolina Press, Chapel Hill, NC, 2004, pp. 59–116. For eighteenth-century 'law of master and servant', Simon Deakin and Frank Wilkinson, *The Law of the Labour Market: Industrialization, Employment and Legal Evolution*, Oxford University Press, Oxford, 2005, pp. 62–3. The first modern Master and Servant legislation was enacted in 1747: nineteenth- and twentieth-century use of 'Master & Servant' was to describe a complex of laws regulating the employment relationship, and providing criminal sanctions against workers (not against employers) for failing to perform what had been agreed at the hiring.

[92] Burrow, *Decisions of the Court of King's Bench*, pp. 516–19, 'Hilary Term 4 Geo. 3. *Rex v. Inhabitants of Salford*'; Blackstone, *Reports of Cases*, Vol. 1, pp. 432–4.

the judges' exasperation with the poor laws, but in the conceptual space opened up (if only for historians) by the judges and barristers in King's Bench to see the law concerning poor women on a continuum with other elisions of legal identity. To be sure, the man from Salford was not married; no one came near the law of coverture in their long wranglings about where he 'belonged'; but his legal identity derived from *someone else*: from his father.[93] He too, was *covered*.

---

[93] See also Blackstone as counsel in the case of *Rex* v. *Inhabitants of Walpole St Peter (Norfolk)*, reported by Burrow, *Decisions of the Court of King's Bench*, pp. 638–9.

7   Hating the Law: Caleb Williams

> Once we have discovered the proper clue … [the] labyrinth is easily
> pervaded. We inherit an old Gothic castle, erected in the days of chiv-
> alry, but fitted up for a modern inhabitant. The moated ramparts,
> the embattled towers, are magnificent and venerable, but useless.
> The inferior apartments, now converted into rooms of convenience,
> are chearful and commodious, though their approaches are winding
> and difficult.
>
> William Blackstone, *Commentaries on the Laws of England*,
>   III (1768), 2016, p. 178.[1]

William Godwin (1756–1836) – husband of Mary Wollstonecraft, philosopher, author of *Political Justice* and the novel *Things As They Are* and
much else besides' owner, as has been discussed, of *Maria* – hated well
the law. It was the certain, forensic, determined hatred that is ascribed
to God, as when in *Proverbs* VI we are told of the six things which the
Lord hates.[2] It is not the hatred of Kevin the Teenager ('I HATE you!
I wish I was dead! That is SO unfair!'[3]), though some of the literature
on Godwin's relationship with the law comes perilously near evoking
Kevin, especially when his profound antagonism is explained by his
childhood experience of Calvinism. Godwin's depiction of the all-
seeing, awe-ful parental power of Squire Falkland, one of the central
characters of *Things As They Are…Caleb Williams*, is a transposition of

---

[1] For Blackstone's many architectural meanings and metaphors, in the *Commentaries*
and elsewhere, Wilfrid Prest, 'Blackstone as Architect: Constructing the
Commentaries', *Yale Journal of Law & the Humanities*, 15:1 (2003), pp. 103–31.

[2] 'These six *things* doth the Lord hate: yea, seven *are* an abomination to him: A proud
look, a lying tongue, and hands that shed innocent blood, An heart that deviseth
wicked imaginations, feet that be swift in running to mischief, A false witness *that*
speaketh lies, and he who soweth discord among brethren'. *Proverbs*, VI, 16–19.

[3] Kevin ('The Teenager') Patterson is a character created and played by the British
comedian Harry Enfield. He was broadcast widely on television and in film
between 1990 and 2000. http://harryenfield.wikia.com/wiki/Kevin_the_Teenager,
accessed January 2019. His long-suffering parents, sole recipients of his ire, were
Sheila and Dave.

'all the contrary feelings of respect and horror which he felt as a child for the Calvinist God' as promulgated by parents and schoolteachers.[4] (Kevin hates well his parents.) In fact, Godwin's hatred was in familiar eighteenth-century emotional form, as when Hester Lynch Piozzi (Hester Thrale as was) remembered Dr Johnson saying of a deceased acquaintance that he had been 'a man to my very heart's content; he hated a fool, and he hated a rogue, and he hated a *whig*: He was a very good *hater*'.[5] The furious intelligence involved in *hating well* the law comes very close to loving it. Both are shadowed – perhaps propelled – by the anxious intimation that the law does not love you back, or in the first place; that, indeed, the law doesn't even know you exist. And hating brings you no nearer to understanding it than does a helpless, hopeless love for it.

And to evoke a child's – or Kevin's – hatred may not be inapposite or insulting to Godwin. It may well describe an emotional stance towards the law inculcated in childhood. Consider this fulmination of Godwin, from Book III, Chapter 2 of *Political Justice* ('Principles of Government... Of the Social Contract'):

> So numerous are the varieties of human understanding, in all cases where its independence and integrity are sufficiently preserved, that there is little chance of any two men coming to a precise agreement about ten successive propositions that are in their own nature open to debate. What then can be more absurd than to present to me the laws of England in fifty volumes folio, and call upon me to give an honest and uninfluenced vote upon their whole contents at once?[6]

'The laws of England' is suggestive of Blackstone; the 'fifty volumes folio' may be ironic hyperbole as Blackstone had only four to the *Commentaries*. Did some earlier expositor of 'The Laws of England' pen *fifty* folios? If you search Eighteenth-Century Collections Online (ECCO)

---

[4] Peter Marshall, *William Godwin: Philosopher, Novelist, Revolutionary* (1984), PM Press, Oakland, CA, 2017, pp. 8–16, 146–8.

[5] Hester Lynch Piozzi, *Anecdotes of the Late Samuel Johnson, LL.D. during the Last Twenty Years of His Life*, T. Cadell, London, 1786, p. 83. Also Chris Salvesen, 'Hazlitt and the French Revolution', C. C. Barfoot and Theo D'haen (eds.), *Tropes of Revolution: Writers Reactions to Real and Imagined Revolutions, 1789–1999*, Rodopi, Amsterdam and Atlanta, GA, 1991, pp. 55–71; 70.

[6] William Godwin, *An Enquiry Concerning Political Justice* (1793), ed. with an Introduction and Notes by Mark Philp, Oxford University Press, Oxford, 2013, p. 83. This is the edition used in this chapter. It reproduces the first edition, published by G. G. J. and J. Robinson, London, in February 1793 – with one important typographical omission – see below, pp. 169–70.

with 'fifty volumes folio', the only hits are *Political Justice* and the mysteriously authored *Little Goody Two-Shoes*, first published and promoted to the parents who bought books for children, by John Newbery in 1766.[7] At the beginning, the author (or 'Editor') discourses upon how difficult it is to get law if you're a poor farmer with a large family like Margery Meanwell's father. The Meanwell family is subject to the 'wicked persecutions' of landowner Sir Timothy Gripe and the 'overgrown' and engrossing Farmer Graspall, who wish to turn the family off their smallholding. In his connivance with Sir Timothy, Graspall *is* the law in this neck of the woods:

> Judge, oh kind, humane and courteous Reader, what a terrible Situation the Poor must be in, when this covetous Man was perpetual Overseer, and every Thing for their Maintenance was drawn from his hard Heart and cruel Hand. But he was not only perpetual Overseer, but perpetual Churchwarden; and judge, oh ye Christians, what State the Church must be in, when supported by a Man without religion and Virtue... Complaints indeed were made, but to what Purpose are Complaints, when brought against a Man, who can hunt, drink, and smoak with the Lord of the Manor, who is also the Justice of Peace?

Parents driven to their grave, two orphaned children, Little Margery and her brother cast upon the wide world... 'Ah, my dear Reader, we brag of Liberty, and boast of our Laws – but the Blessings of the one, and the protection of the other seldom fall to the Lot of the Poor; and especially when a rich Man is their Adversary... Where is he to find Money to see Council, or how can he plead his Cause himself... when our Laws are so obscure, and so multiplied, that an Abridgment of them cannot be contained in fifty Volumes in Folio'? And should you, Reader, wonder about the propriety of all this in a tale for children; should you ask 'Do you intend this for Children, Mr. NEWBERY?', the answer is that it 'may Come from another Hand. This is not the Book, Sir, mentioned in the Title, but the Introduction to that Book; and

---

[7] *The History of Little Goody Two-Shoes; Otherwise called Mrs. MARGERY TWO-SHOES. With the Means by which she acquired her Learning and Wisdom, and in consequence thereof her Estate; set forth at large for the Benefit of those,*
  Who from a Start of Rags and Care,
  And having Shoes but Half a Pair;
  Their Fortune And their Fame would Fix,
  And gallop in a Coach and Six.
See the Original Manuscript in the Vatican at Rome, and the Cuts by Michael Angelo. Illustrated with the Comments of our great modern Critics, John Newbery, London, 1766. Attributed to Newbery himself (he produced many children's books), to Oliver Goldsmith and others. For Newbery, John Townsend Rowe, *Trade and Plumb-cake for Ever, Huzza! The Life and Work of John Newbery, 1713–1767: Author, Bookseller, Entrepreneur and Pioneer of Publishing for Children,* Colt, Cambridge, 1994.

it is intended, Sir, not for those Sort of Children, but for Children of six Feet high'.[8] *Everyone* knew *Little Goody Two-Shoes* if its reprint and adaptation history is anything to go by.[9] In 1793, long before Godwin ran his own bookshop specialising in children's literature, he was as likely to have known it as well as the next person – or child.

In regard to *Political Justice*, that he *simply didn't understand the law* was the major charge of Godwin's contemporary critics, most of them professional lawyers, as we shall see. They did not say that had he known it better, he might have grown fonder of it, for their critical project was not to have him befriend or like the law, but to stand condemned and alone as its implacable enemy. Two centuries on, in the 1980s, when controversy over Althusserian theory and the idea of the *state apparatus* was much in the air, it was possible to convincingly conclude a major – brilliant – study of Godwin with the explanation that he hated the law … because he hated it: Godwin 'systematically rejected government and its coercive apparatus of standing armies, courts and prisons. Although intended to suppress injustice, the effect of government has been to perpetuate it'.[10] In place of government Godwin proposed 'a pluralistic commonwealth' with something very much like existing parishes as basic units of organisation (there was no getting away from the parish in eighteenth-century England, not even by William Godwin).[11]

Brought up and educated by radical dissenters, a dissenting minister himself in his twenties, Godwin was perhaps not familiar with the parish as an ecclesiastical entity, but as familiar as anyone else with the parish as a fundamental unit of state and government.[12] Like all middle-class families, his had paid the parish rates and other local taxes and thus supported the parish poor and maintained the local road network; Godwin knew the parish as a unit of *civil* administration

---

[8] *The History of Little Goody Two-Shoes*, pp. 4–12.

[9] Peter Hunt (ed.), *International Companion Encyclopedia of Children's Literature*, 2nd ed., 2 vols, Routledge, Abingdon, 2001, Vol. 1, p. 247.

[10] Marshall, *William Godwin*, p. 399. In a famous polemic against Althusserianism and the idea of 'level' and 'apparatus', E. P. Thompson claimed to have found the law 'at every bloody level' in eighteenth-century England. *The Poverty of Theory and Other Essays*, Merlin, London, 1978, pp. 288–9.

[11] K. D. M. Snell, *The Parish and Belonging: Community, Identity and Welfare in England and Wales, 1700–1950*, Cambridge University Press, Cambridge, 2006.

[12] For Godwin as dissenter, Marshall, *William Godwin*, pp. 1–55; Rowland Weston, 'William Godwin's Religious Sense', *Journal for Eighteenth-Century Studies*, 32:3 (2009), pp. 407–23; James Grande, 'The Roots of Godwinian Radicalism: Norfolk Dissent in the Diary', *Bodleian Library Record*, 24:1 (2011), pp. 35–43; Mark Philp, *Godwin's Political Justice*, Duckworth, London, 1986, pp. 15–37.

as well as any other man. In the vastly changed legal order of things
he proposed, a parish would act as a self-governing commune; popular
juries would be convened to deal with injustices; in times of national
emergency, there would be assemblies of federated communes to orga-
nise against in invasion – but there would be no law: 'Free intercourse
in society, unrestrained by the fetters of codes' was the better way, he
thought.[13]

At this juncture, it is worth considering what other law-experience
the author, now in his late thirties, had when he wrote *Political Justice*
and *Caleb Williams; or, Things As They Are*. Family experience of the
parish as a civil law unit been noted. As a boy, he was interested enough
in the law to take himself off to the Sessions House in Norwich during Assizes. Neither the occasion nor the setting appear to have provoked anything but a sense of his own worth and merit: he later told
of having stood immediately next to the Bench where the then–lord
chief justice William de Grey, 1st Baron Walsingham, was presiding.
He stayed some hours, he recalled, at one point shifting his position
to get comfortable 'by leaning my elbow on the corner of the cushion
placed before his lordship'. Soon, the Judge 'laid his hand gently on
my elbow and removed it ... I recollect having silently remarked, if his
lordship knew what the lad beside him will one day become I am not
sure that he would have removed my elbow'. He was thirteen or fourteen years old.[14] At sixteen or so, as pupil-teacher near Holt, Norfolk,
he read the *Gentleman's Magazine* in his leisure time 'paying particular attention to the records of the parliamentary debates', which were
records of statute (positive) law and its making, though he disliked very
much the intemperance of the debates that raucously accompanied
bills into acts of Parliament.[15] He also read widely in constitutional history. He spent much time with lawyers in the 1790s, including several
involved in the Treason Trials.[16] Later, it is said, he learned much from
his friend Thomas Holcroft about marriage law: 'marriage is law, and

---

[13] Godwin, *An Enquiry Concerning Political Justice* (1793), p. 403.
[14] Godwin appears to have high confidence in his understanding of assize courts. He
altered his descriptions of magistrates' sessions in later editions of *Caleb Williams*,
but assize-scenes were kept the same. See Caleb's careful, knowledgeable critique
of his own non-appearance at county assizes. Godwin, *Things As They Are; or The
Adventures of Caleb Williams*, p. 196.
[15] Marshall, *William Godwin*, p. 29.
[16] Benjamin Pauley, '"Far from a Consummate Lawyer": William Godwin and the
Treason Trials of the 1790s', Ulrich Broiche et al. (eds.), *Reactions to Revolutions:
The 1790s and Their Aftermath* (Kulturgeschichtliche Perspektiven, 2), Lit, Münster,
2007, pp. 203–30; Philp, *Godwin's Political Justice*, pp. 99–119.

the worst of all laws... the most odious of all monopolies', he wrote in *Political Justice*.[17] The encounter between Godwin and the law most discussed is his involvement through friends and compatriots in the 1794 Treason Trials. Here, the law at issue was very high law indeed, that of seditious treason.[18] Godwin chose the publication date of 12 May 1794 for *Things As They Are*, the day on which the Habeas Corpus Suspension Act (34 Geo. III, c. 54), as devised and promulgated by William Pitt, came into force. *Caleb Williams* then, was conceived and published when law terror 'was the order of the day'.[19]

But Godwin's first charge against the law (and his remedies) was presented in 1793 in the *Enquiry Concerning Political Justice*. 'Book VII. Of Crimes and Punishments', contained the chapter 'Of Law', and the majority of Godwin's accusations and complaints are to be found here. Earlier writers had discussed law as the opposite of despotic power; in all societies calling themselves civilised 'law had been conceived as the measure by which to judge all offences and irregularities disapproved of by the public'. But Godwin does something different in this book; he investigates the merits of this thing called law and searches out 'the most eligible principle that may be substituted in its place.'[20] You could tell a society in which people were content with the rules of justice (though Godwin did not name one of them) by the fact that its law was not continually being distorted and added to: in those other societies, 'law was evidently a less necessary institution'. His arguments were against the huge heap of clutter that was English law; common law, statute law – all a jumble. Its accretions, its eternal *bricolage*, troubled him.[21]

Law was endless. It never stopped: 'One result of the institution of law is, that the institution once begun, can never be brought to a close. Edict is heaped upon edict, and volume upon volume'. He outlined the process by which this happened: 'As new cases occur, the law is perpetually found deficient. How should it be otherwise? Lawgivers have

---

[17] Marshall, *William Godwin*, pp. 88–9.

[18] For 'high' and 'low' law, above, p. 1.

[19] Marshall, *William Godwin*, pp. 144–54.

[20] Godwin, *Enquiry* (2013), pp. 402–3.

[21] 'The parliaments of George III legislated at over four times the rate of the parliaments of William III', says David Lieberman, *The Province of Legislation Determined: Legal Theory in Eighteenth-Century Britain*, Cambridge University Press, Cambridge, 1989, p. 13; James Oldham, *The Mansfield Manuscripts and the Growth of English Law in the Eighteenth Century*, 2 vols., University of North Carolina Press, Chapel Hill and London, 1992, Vol. 1, p. 479: 'The legislative process was active during the eighteenth century – more statutes of a regulatory nature were passed than is commonly supposed. But it was an undisciplined process'.

not the faculty of unlimited prescience, and cannot define that which is infinite. The alternative that remains, is either to wrest the law to include a case which was never in the contemplation of the author, or to make a new law to provide for this particular case'. Lawgivers and law practitioners made new laws, piling one upon the other. Lawyers made him particularly angry, as they did many less radical men. Lawyers were active in the making of what, in the twentieth century, would be called a total institution:

> The quibbles of lawyers and the arts by which they refine and distort the sense of the law, are proverbial...the very education that enables the lawyer, when he is employed for the prosecutor, to find out offences the lawgiver never meant, enables him, when he is employed for the defendant, to find out subterfuge, that reduce the law to a nullity. It is therefore perpetually necessary to make new laws. These laws, in order to escape evasion, are frequently tedious, minute and circumlocutory. The volume in which justice records her prescriptions is for ever increasing, and the world would not contain the books that might be written.

There was just...so much of it.[22] How was a person to study it? You must begin with the volumes of the statutes – add a strict enquiry into the common or unwritten law – maybe enter the byways of civil, ecclesiastical and canon law – discover the character and view of earlier lawmakers – the whole history of its interpretation, use and adjustment. Then, to understand how it might be used in a court of justice, the student must trace out 'the whole collection of records, decisions and precedents'. Lawyers did this no better than the industrious enquirer: 'law was originally devised that ordinary men might know what they had to depend upon, [but]...there is not at this day a lawyer existing in Great Britain, presumptuous and vain-glorious enough to pretend that he has mastered the code'. All the diligence and determination in the world will not help you: 'time and industry, even were they infinite, would not suffice. It is a labyrinth without end; it is a mass of contradictions that cannot be extricated'. From all of this, we must conclude that 'law is an institution of the most pernicious tendency'.[23] Had he read the *Commentaries on the Laws of England* before publishing *Political Justice* he could have noted that, as in the epigraph to this chapter, Judge Blackstone never said that it was going to be easy.[24]

---

[22] Godwin, *Enquiry* (2013), pp. 403–4.

[23] Ibid., p. 405.

[24] In a diary entry made in August 1826 when he was working on *The History of the Commonwealth*, Godwin noted 'çala...Blackstone' – that is, dipping in and out of Blackstone. In September 1819, he had noted 'Paragraph on Blackstone'.

It was not that things would change dramatically in an altered state of society; you wouldn't notice much difference, wrote Godwin: 'The juridical decisions that were made immediately after the abolition of law, would differ little from those during its empire. They would be the decisions of prejudice and habit'. But habit would have lost its centre; law would be much less used. The panels of parishioners convened to consider misdemeanours – actions that violated community norms – would ask themselves questions about the old law: 'their understandings would grow enlarged, in proportion as they felt the importance of their trust, and the unbounded freedom of their investigation'. Then would begin 'an auspicious order of things, of which no understanding of man at present in existence can foretell the result, the dethronement of implicit faith and the inauguration of unclouded justice'.[25]

Modern readers may wonder at the appeal of Godwin's abstract utopianism to nineteenth-century Atlantic-world radicals and labour activists.[26] His proposals did not, on the face of it, have much purchase on the law experience of the poor, in magistrates' sessions, or in a justice's application of labour law. In *Political Justice*, Godwin's focus was the criminal law, not the law of everyday life. He listed common law, civil, ecclesiastical and canon law in his despairing account of what you needed to read in order to know the law, but his focus was statute and criminal law. Something that is omitted from modern editions of *The Enquiry Concerning Political Justice* may explain enthusiasm for it during the next century. If you read the marginalia – which carried the story or the argument 'Of Law' as it did for many time-pressed, uncertain readers of popular and religious literature from the seventeenth century onwards – then Godwin is very plain. Run together the marginal notes read: *Arguments by which it [law] is recommended – law is endless – particularly in free states – causes of this disadvantage – uncertain – instanced in the question of property – Mode in which it must be studied – pretends to foretel future events – Laws are a species of promises – check the freedom of opinion – are destructive of the principles of reason – Dishonesty of lawyers – An honest lawyer mischievous – Abolition of law vindicated on*

---

http://godwindiary.bodleian.ox.ac.uk, entries for 1 September 1819, and 10 August 1826. In the second entry, he mentions having met a lawyer acquaintance, perhaps to discuss Blackstone. But his acquaintance with the *Commentaries* was actually earlier than this. See below, p. 171.

[25] Godwin, *Political Justice*, p. 409.

[26] Marshall, *William Godwin*, pp. 118–43; 389–408.

the score of wisdom – of candour – from the nature of man – Future history of political justice – Errors that might arise in the commencement – Its gradual progress – Its effects on criminal law – on property.[27]

Political Justice was well received by the British press, as an expression of pure democracy, or as a communication of the highest moral and political sentiments. There was conservative condemnation of its French Enlightenment and Revolutionary principles, but in general, reviewers read and praised the book as a whole and did not focus on one short chapter concerning the law, as I have done here – though on reading it a very young Henry Crabb Robinson is said to have given up the study of the law, albeit temporarily, wrote a critique of lawyers which was essentially an abridgment of Godwin's thesis, and discoursed enthusiastically on Godwin's political philosophy in the radical press.[28] Neither have modern commentators dwelled much on Godwin's account of the law *as law*. The focus has rather been rather on the elaboration of the idea of *justice* Godwin provided, and in full conviction of his lessons: that justice is not something found in laws – not something that humanity receives passively; justice is an activity.[29]

In the months after publication of *Political Justice*, during the Treason Trials and in company with many lawyer friends, Godwin wrote up another encounter with the law: the high law of high treason. Members of the London Corresponding Society and other organisations designated 'jacobin' by government were held in the Tower all through the summer of 1794 whilst the case against them was prepared. In October,

---

[27] William W. E. Slights, *Managing Readers: Printed Marginalia in English Renaissance Books*, University of Michigan Press, Ann Arbor, MI, 2001; Femke Molekamp, '"Of the Incomparable Treasure of the Holy Scriptures": The Geneva Bible in the Early Modern Household', Matthew Dimmock and Andrew Hadfield (eds.), *Literature and Popular Culture in Early Modern England*, Ashgate, Farnham, 2009, pp. 121–35. For Godwin's thoughts on *Political Justice* being read slowly, read later and read democratically by people with time for reading, Christina Lupton, *Reading, Codex and the Making of Time*, Johns Hopkins University Press, Baltimore, MD, 2018, pp. 135–44.

[28] Mark Philp, 'Introduction'; Godwin, *Political Justice* (2013), pp. xxii–xxiii; Marshall, *William Godwin*, p. 122 – though this account of Crabb Robinson giving up articles after reading a book persuading him of 'the duty of not living to oneself, but of having for one's sole object the good of the community' does not tally with Robinson's law studies as described in the *DNB*. Vincent Newey, 'Robinson, Henry Crabb (1775–1867)', *Oxford Dictionary of National Biography*, Oxford University Press, 2004, accessed 6 November 2017.

[29] Ian Ward, 'A Love of Justice: The Legal and Political Thought of William Godwin', *The Journal of Legal History*, 25:1 (2004), pp. 1–30; Sue Chaplin, 'Before the Law – Godwin's *Caleb Williams*', Chaplin (ed.), *The Gothic and the Rule of Law*, Palgrave Macmillan, New York, 2007, pp. 125–42, the remarks on *Political Justice* are on p. 125.

Lord Chief Justice Eyre delivered the charge against the prisoners to the grand jury of Middlesex, advancing the view that the Privy Council had spent long months devising: that the prisoners' activities and publications had constituted an attempt to subvert both Parliament and government. Eyre devoted much of his charge to the question of high treason; he argued that the question should be answered by trial of the men, and urged the grand jury to find a true bill, which it did.[30] They said then, as some say now, that Godwin simply didn't understand this law, in particular the distinction between substantive and constructive treason. It is said that Godwin's respect, learned from Blackstone, for the ancient statute defining treason (25 Edw. III) was mere posture: 'his uncertain grasp of the equally uncertain argument of the charge, seems to have encouraged him to direct against Eyre a battery of criticism which, intellectually if not strategically, would have been better directed against the statute itself'. Godwin quoted Blackstone's chapter on high treason at length, on the invention of 'new and strange treasons...new-fangled crimes' during the bloodier passages of England's history.[31] Godwin was convinced that he had caught Chief Justice Eyre out in inventing the law, or that in discoursing upon the meaning of 'encompassing' or 'imagining' the king's death as laid out in 25 Edw. III, Eyre had himself imagined new crimes, and new-fangled law.[32] In autumn 1794, Godwin was modern witness to the legal bricolage he had described in *Political Justice*.

---

[30] William Godwin, *Cursory Strictures on the Charge delivered by Lord Chief Justice Eyre to the Grand Jury, October 2, 1794. First Published in the Morning Chronicle, October 21*, C. and G. Kearsley, London, 1794, pp. 20–1; *Answer to Cursory Strictures...First published in The Times, 25 Oct, 1794*, D. L. Eaton, London, 1794; William Godwin, *A Reply to An Answer to Cursory Strictures, Supposed to be Wrote by Judge Buller, by the Author of Cursory Strictures*, D. L. Eaton, London, 1794; Philp, *Godwin's Political Justice*, pp. 177–79; John Barrell, *Imagining the King's Death: Figurative Treason, Fantasies of Regicide, 1793–1796*, Oxford University Press, Oxford, 2000, pp. 300–17; John Barrell and John Mee (eds.), *Trials for Treason and Sedition, 1792–1794*, 8 vols., Pickering and Chatto, London, 2006–2007.

[31] Barrell, *Imagining the King's Death*, p. 303; Godwin, *Cursory Strictures on the Charge delivered by Lord Chief Justice Eyre to the Grand Jury*, pp. 20–1; William Blackstone, *Commentaries on the Laws of England: Book IV of Public Wrongs* (1769), Intro. Ruth Paley, Oxford University Press, Oxford, 2016, pp. 49–61 ('Of High Treason').

[32] Barrell, *Imagining the King's Death*, pp. 303–4; Randa Helfield, 'Constructive Treason and Godwin's Treasonous Constructions', *Mosaic*, 28:2 (1995), pp. 43–62; 44: 'Godwin argued that judges should not be allowed to "construct" new laws in the process of interpreting old ones, and that such judicial constructions belonged to the realm of fiction, not legal fact. In support of this contention, Godwin quoted Blackstone as having stated that the original purpose of codifying the common law of treason was to provide clear cut and limited guidelines by which to define this law in order to protect the people from arbitrary accusations and executions'.

The law in *Political Justice* was not taken much notice of, but the lawyers who read Godwin's novel, *Things As They Are; or, The Adventures of Caleb Williams*, published a year later, came out in force with their sharp pens, as we shall see. 'Reading *Caleb Williams* is like entering a nightmare', said Peter Marshall; many readers, from 1794 to the present day, have found it to be so.[33] Of late, the peculiar psychological workings of the literary Gothic and Godwin's deliberate use of it have been used to explain the novel's uncanny power to frighten its readers with a vision of an England – then and now – in which each familiar thing is made terrifyingly strange. This, it is said, was the mission of the Gothic in the 1790s: to interrogate a modern juridical mythology of power.[34] What happens to Caleb, and to many other victims of the English legal system whom the novel brings before our dream eye, does not belong to the everyday. We, like Caleb, are utterly alone, no help to be found, anywhere. The true terror of the book, from which you cannot awake, is that, in a nightmare dream sequence, you come to recognise this horrifying England as *true*; then and now.[35]

The novel 'was intended to supplement the intellectual and political project of the *Political Enquiry*, to make plain the violence and irrationality of late eighteenth-century law'.[36] Do you need a plot summary?[37] On a landed estate, somewhere in a remote part of southern-ish England, landowner Fernando Falkland takes a poor eighteen-year-old orphan into his employ. Caleb Williams has received enough of an education to be designated the squire's secretary and librarian; he is to file Falkland's papers, order his books, and transcribe the literary notes his master spends his days compiling.[38] Much later, when Caleb is before one of the several arrogant and sadistic magistrates he encounters as the result of this fateful service contract, he explains his employment thus: 'Mr Falkland is a gentleman of six thousand per annum. I lived with him as his secretary.' – 'In other words, you were his servant?' says the

---

[33] Marshall, *William Godwin*, p. 148.
[34] Chaplin, 'Before the Law', p. 126.
[35] Marshall, *William Godwin*, p. 148.
[36] Chaplin, 'Before the Law', p. 133.
[37] There are excellent and shorter ones available. Try Andrew Pepper, *Unwilling Executioner: Crime Fiction and the State,* Oxford University Press, Oxford, 2016, pp. 57–8.
[38] Late in his career of so-called criminality and outlawry, in retreat with an accommodating Robber Band, Caleb reads his pocket Horace on the pleasures of rural tranquillity. He contemplates the sunrise through his window, falls asleep, wakes to find the Robbers' housekeeper standing over him with a meat-cleaver. In prison he meets a common soldier with a taste for Horace and Virgil. Reading competence in Latin could be acquired in many eighteenth-century parochial schools.

magistrate. 'As you please', replies Caleb.[39] Godwin disliked the very idea of servants; their abjection and passivity bothered him a great deal; he wrote some of his most searing social and class critique of English society by following a footman (in imagination) to his dank lair in the basement of a grand London house. The thought of a wealthy man maintaining a household inhabited by 'two different classes of being' enraged him.[40] His political anger in the 1799 'Of Servants' essay was – possibly – only achieved by imagining a depressed and humiliated *man*; it is not clear that he had any political position on the female servants who helped him bring up his little household of orphan daughters.[41] But in a legal and contractual universe that does not once appear in the novel, Caleb *is* a servant, though Godwin had him appear less of one in later editions by changing the designation of Falkland from 'master', which he is in 1793, to 'patron', which he became in 1796.

When young Caleb comes to the Big House, he enters a new world: 'in place of the hard-favoured and inflexible visages I had been accustomed to observe', his master's countenance seemed 'in inconceivable degree pregnant with meaning' (p. 7). He is entranced by Fernando Falkland: by his brilliance, his sweet and engaging air of sympathy, his mysteriously attractive melancholy. He notices that the other servants do not often go near him: 'they regarded him upon the whole with veneration, as a being of a superior order' (p. 9). Falkland has a secret, which it is Caleb's fate to discover. He learns from a fellow servant about Falkland's altercations with a neighbour, a brutal, philistine John-Bull of a country squire, Mr Tyrrel. After many perceived slights and somewhat condescending reprimands from Falkland, Tyrrel redirects his anger to one of his own household, his niece Emily Melville who, like Caleb (and the whole county) admires Falkland very much indeed. Tyrrel forces her engagement to an odious fiancé. When she escapes his house, he casts her into a debtors' prison for not paying her keep whilst she was living in it. (Godwin's critics were to highlight these events as one of the many, many troubles – inaccuracies – with the law Godwin

[39] William Godwin, *Things As They Are; or The Adventures of Caleb Williams* (1794, 1831), Penguin, London, 1987, p. 286. Henceforth, page numbers noted in text. This chapter employs the Penguin edition (which uses the 1831 Standard Novels series) for ease of reference. Significant alterations to the first edition (which Godwin made from 1795 onwards) are described later in this chapter.

[40] William Godwin, 'Of Servants', Essay IV of *The Enquirer: Reflections on Education, Manners and Literature. In a Series of Essays*, G. G. and J. Robinson, London, 1797, pp. 201–11.

[41] There *was* a man among the band of female servants who helped rear his children. Miranda Seymour, *Mary Shelley*, John Murray, London, 2000, pp. 35–55.

depicted in the novel.) Emily dies. Tyrrel is outraged at Falkland's public condemnation of his behaviour; they have a very public fight. Later that evening Tyrrel is found murdered. Falkland denies his guilt; he is exonerated; he allows local tenant farmers – in fact, Tyrrel's tenants – Hawkins and his son, to go to the gallows for the crime.

This is Falkland's secret. The curious Caleb, convinced in his heart of his master's guilt, takes the opportunity of a house fire to open a mysterious trunk which Falkland has hitherto been angry to see him approach. Falkland discovers him in the act; he confesses to the murder of the Hawkinses; he extracts an oath of secrecy and loyalty from the young man. Caleb flees, is apprehended and indicted for theft upon planted evidence. He twice escapes prison; he joins a band of robbers, managed by the Gentleman (and Philosophical) Thief, Mr Raymond. Caleb feels himself to be constantly under Falkland's eye, not only because his story has been widely disseminated in chapbook and criminal broadside, but because he actually *is*: at one meeting, Falkland tells him that 'I had my eye upon you in all your wanderings. You have taken no material step though their whole course with which I have not been acquainted'. 'Did his power reach through all space, and his eye penetrate every concealment?' Caleb asks himself. 'Was he like that mysterious being, to protect us from whose fierce revenge mountains and hills we are told might fall on us in vain? No idea is more heart-sickening and tremendous than this...' (p. 249). The young man disguises himself; he moves about the country a hunted man until apprehended by one of Falkland's omniscient agents, Gines (Jones in the first edition). He breaks his self-imposed silence; but no magistrate will countenance even listening to his story. He is sent back to jail to await trial and then released when Falkland declines to appear against him. Caleb appears to be free. He begins a new life in Wales, and briefly settles down to teaching applied maths to the locals and to his own private 'etymological study of the English language' (pp. 289, 294).[42] Jones/Gines arrives and distributes an old broadside telling of the notorious criminal

---

[42] 'What is this about?' asks Martin A. Kayman, 'Trials of Law and Language: Caleb Williams and John Horne Tooke', Monika Fludernik and Greta Olson (eds.), *In the Grip of the Law: Trials, Prisons and the Space Between*, Peter Lang, Frankfurt, 2004, pp. 83–104; and answers the question by reference to a comparative linguist tried for murder in 1759, who conducted his own defence with his own antiquarian studies, pitting language against law; and to John Horne Tooke's (one of the accused in 1794) earlier trial for seditious treason. In 1777, Tooke (then known as John Horne) turned the accusation against him into an indictment of the law and its language, as Godwin did with Judge Eyre and 25 Edw. III in *Cursory Strictures*. Godwin had a footnote reference to Eugene Aram and Horne Tooke in *Things As They Are*, p. 236.

'Caleb Williams'. Caleb is informed that Falkland intends the whole of England to be his perpetual prison. He writes a full and circumstantial account of his 'adventures' for Falkland: he writes the novel you are now reading.

There are several unpublished endings and postscripts, from 1793, from 1795, and later; in all of them Caleb finds himself to be truly miserable only when he learns of Falkland's death: 'I thought that, if Falkland were dead, I should return again to all that makes life worth possessing. I thought that, if the guilt of Falkland were established, fortune and the world would smile upon my efforts. Both these events are accomplished; and it is now only that I am truly miserable' (p. 336). The narrative ends where Caleb had (in the fictional realm of his own writing) begun his story: 'My life has been for several years a theatre of calamity. I have been a mark for the vigilance of tyranny, and I could not escape', he said at the start. 'My fairest prospects have been blasted. My enemy has shown himself inaccessible to entreaties, and untired in persecution' (p. 5). Godwin's terrifying sublime of writing in *Caleb Williams* haunts his modern critics, so that of this end it can be said that Caleb is 'the living dead thing that must be kept alive at the margins as reminder of the law's own transgressions'. In this way Godwin shows that 'the law *is*...the demonic presence that possesses the body and "haunts" the mind'.[43]

The novel is, above all else, a relentless, unceasing, exhausting account of the law's transgressions. The law is on every page, experienced by its many characters, misunderstood (or so Godwin's critics were to say) by everyone, including their author. That *no one* understands its Gothic edifice, or how to make their way through its dank, rambling passages, contributes much to the novel's oppressive atmosphere. But in fact, Caleb is given a working understanding by his author, of the kind of everyday law on which Godwin as political philosopher made no comment: Caleb is given the vocabulary to write about parish, borough and county; Caleb knows what a vestry is; he knows enough of will making and the role of attorneys to write intelligible commentary on Falkland's (pp. 24, 35). He can tell a story that figures: equity, coverture, Emily Melville's inheritance, and primogeniture, though to be sure, this is a law lesson delivered by the kindly steward Mr Collins, before his voice is incorporated in Caleb's (p. 40). Caleb does not appear to know much about the law concerning domestic servants, but then, as we have seen, he does not believe himself to be one (p. 41). Neither does his

---

[43] Chaplin, 'Before the Law', pp. 129, 137.

employer Falkland know much about service law and the reciprocal rights of notice and warning. When Caleb has resolved to quit his service, Falkland cries out, '[Y]ou are desirous to quit my service. To that I have a short answer, You shall never quit it with life. If you attempt it, you shall never cease to rue your folly as long as you exist. That is my will; I will not have it resisted' (pp. 153–62). Caleb then reflects that 'every man is fated to be more or less the tyrant or the slave'. Later, when Caleb *has* left and is in the thieves' lair, we appear, for the space of just one utterance, to enter the bright modern world of contractual relations, where things can be explained and Captain Raymond *does* understand the law of service. 'The poor lad's story is a long one' he tells his band of robber brothers:

> [I]t is as clear as the day, that, because he wished to leave the service of his master, because he had been perhaps a little too inquisitive in his matter's concerns, and because, as I suspect, he had been trusted with some important secrets, his master conceived an antipathy against him. This antipathy gradually proceeded to such a length, as to induce the master to forge this vile accusation. He seems willing to hang the lad out of the way, rather than suffer him to go where he pleases or get beyond the reach of his power. (p. 232)

Raymond believes Caleb; he explains that Falkland's other servants and a relative of the Squire (also a magistrate), who were all called in to hear the accusation against Caleb, all appeared to think him guilty; 'gave it on...[Falkland's] side with one voice, and thus afforded Williams a sample of what he had to expect in the sequel'.[44] No wonder Caleb is on the run. 'If no other person have the courage to set limits to the tyranny of courts of justice, shall not we?' Raymond asks his *confrères* (pp. 232–3). Does not their fraternity of thieves exist 'to counteract the partiality and iniquity of public institutions'? They, who are 'thieves without a licence, are at open war with another set of men, who are thieves according to law', he continues. 'If any one disapprove our proceedings, at least we have this to say for ourselves, we act not by choice, but only as our wise governors force us to act' (pp. 224–5).

Hatred of the idea of service permeates *Caleb Williams*: one of the reasons for the Hawkinses coming to grief is the implacable refusal of Farmer Hawkins to let his son go to Tyrrel's service. (Favouring the Hawkinses is one way for Tyrrel to undermine Falkland.) But 'I cannot bear to think that this poor lad of mine should go to service', Father Hawkins says. 'For my part, I do not see any good that comes

---

[44] For Falkland's relative, Magistrate Forester, see below, p. 180.

of servants...I will lose all that I have, and go to day-labour, and my
son too, if needs must; but I will not make a gentleman's servant of
him' (pp. 72–4). Tyrrel threatens to turn father and son off their farm;
Hawkins responds that he has a lease 'and I shall not quit it o'thaten.
I hope there is some law for rich folk, as well as for poor ones' (p. 75).
Tyrrel is unused to being thwarted: 'God damn my blood!' he bellows
'but you are a rare fellow. You have a lease, have you? You will not quit,
not you! A pretty pass things are come to, if a lease can protect such fellows as you against the lord of a manor!' We enter, in darker mode, the
pre-plot of *Little Goody Two-Shoes* (and that is dark enough).

The logic of the service relationship dictates that it *must be* one of
Caleb's fellow servants who speaks truth to law. Visiting him in prison
as he languishes long months waiting for the next assizes, Thomas
exclaims:

> Zounds, how I have been deceived! They told me what a fine thing it
> was to be an Englishman, and about liberty and property, and all that
> there; and I find it is all a flam. Lord, what fools we be! Things are
> done under our very noses, and we know nothing of the matter; and
> a parcel of fellows with grave faces swear to us that such things never
> happen but in France, and other countries the like of that. Why, you
> han't been tried, ha' you? No. And what signifies being tried, when
> they do worse than hang a man, and all beforehand? (p. 210)

Caleb has much earlier confirmed this view: 'Wealth and despotism easily know how to engage those laws, which were perhaps at first intended
(witless and miserable precaution!) for the safeguards of the poor, as
the coadjutors of their oppression' – one tiny echo, in a very long text,
of Blackstone's assertion that in the distant land of once-upon-a-time,
under the great Alfred, for example, things had been better for the poor
(p. 75). It is also an echo of the editorial outrage at the law expressed in
Little Goody Two-Shoes; of course there is no evidence that Godwin had
read either by 1793, but as suggested above, *Little Goody Two-Shoes* is
as likely a source as Blackstone. We shall return to the Hawkinses and
their fate in order to discuss the major legal change Godwin made to his
text between 1793 and 1795.

Every single attorney in the text who serves a landed master is at one
with him in his scheming and blatant manipulation of the law; there
are pen-portraits here very much like those of William Hutton – or any
eighteenth-century satirist of the law trade.[45] True gentlemen despise
their attorneys: 'when you came in I had just finished making my will',

[45] See above, p. 74.

says Falkland to a neighbour; 'I did not choose in my present situation to call an attorney. In fact, it would be strange if a man of sense ... should not be able to perform such a function for himself' (p. 35). Tyrrel on the other hand – boor, bully; not a true gentleman – urges his attorney to employ whole series of procedural tactics in the Hawkins affair, telling him, by affidavits, motions, pleas, demurrers, flaws and appeals, to protract the question from term to term and from court to court. 'It would ... be the disgrace of a civilized country, if a gentleman, when insolently attacked in law by the scum of the earth, could not convert the cause into a question of the longest purse, and stick in the skirts of his adversary till he had reduced him to beggary' (p. 35).

Attorneys apart, the law's personnel are wavering uncertain figures in *Caleb Williams*, because the reader cannot map them on to any known legal history. What *is* Jones/Gines? Thief taker, yes; but a Bow Street Runner, a constable, a court bailiff? None of these, though he behaves like such law personnel. His menace is considerably increased for any moderately informed modern enquirer by having nothing to imagine him *with*. He is a sometime member of the Robber Band, headed up by Mr Raymond. He is also Falkland's private agent (or servant) of vengeance. Other private police officers object to being so used: when Tyrrel instructs his steward Mr Barnes (who had been 'for several years the instrument of Mr Tyrrel's injustice') to arrest Emily Melville, the servant cries out:

> 'Your worship? – I do not understand you! – Arrest Miss! – Miss Emily!'
>
> 'Yes, I tell you! What is the matter with you? Go immediately to Swineard, the lawyer, and bid him finish the business out of hand!'
>
> 'Lord love your honour! Arrest her! Why, she does not owe you a brass farthing; she always lived upon your charity!'
>
> 'Ass! Scoundrel! I tell you she does owe me, owes me eleven hundred pound. – The law justifies it. – What do you think laws were made for ? – I do nothing but right ... and my rights I will have' (p. 85).

But the magistrates are the most uncanny law personnel in the book. There is nowhere to place them; their courts – the justicing room at home, their petty courts, quarter sessions – are not present in the text. They sit – nowhere, nowhere that can be located in a sociolegal history of eighteenth-century England. It is as late as halfway through Volume II that we learn that Fernando Falkland is himself a justice of the peace. But there is nothing to do with that knowledge (p. 131). For where *is* he one? In the case of a young peasant accused of murdering a friend, he appears to be at home, for he and his steward and Caleb are present in what is called a 'room'. He is called upon to act on this occasion, Caleb tells us, because 'two or three of the neighbouring justices were all of them from home at once...he was the only one to be found in a circuit of many miles'. The terms *evidence* and *examination* (of the peasant lad) are used; 'the accused is called upon for his defence'; witnesses are called. In these circumstances and sitting alone, a magistrate might commit the accused for trial at quarter sessions or assizes. Here Falkland dismisses the case, having cried silently for half an hour because, Caleb thinks, he is reminded of his own murder of the Hawkinses (by letting them hang for his own crime). Moreover he does not dismiss the peasant lad in person but, having fled the room, sends his steward Mr Collins with word that he is indisposed. 'At the same time, the accused was ordered to be discharged' – but by whom? A household servant? It is not so much that the law narrative is inaccurate as that it swims disconcertingly in and out of sociolegal history in the manner – it has to be said again – of a bad dream (pp. 131–5). But perhaps we should recognise the many, daily irregularities of magistrates' proceedings (the sort on which Lord Mansfield regularly expiated), recognise that the examination scene may represent very well how the law was *experienced* – *Things As They Just Are* – by poor plaintiffs and defendants and pleaders (for poor relief; for some community justice of which a magistrate had no cognisance). And its not that actually existing magistrates weren't told – by one of their brethren no less – the following:

> The individuals who are brought before [a magistrate] are almost universally his inferiors; and commonly in the lowest ranks of society. The principal share of his business is transacted in his own house, before few spectators, and those in general indigent and illiterate. Hence he is liable to become dictatorial, brow-beating, consequential, and ill-humoured; domineering in his inclinations, dogmatical in his opinions and arbitrary in his decisions.[46]

The magistrates in *Caleb Williams* provoked the reviewers' ire – as did almost every other legal aspect of the novel. In the *British Critic*, in July 1794, the complaint was that in 'this extraordinary performance,

---

[46] Thomas Gisborne, *An Inquiry into the Duties of Men in the Higher and Middle Classes of Society in Great Britain, Resulting from Their Respective Stations, Professions and Employments*, 2nd ed., 2 Vols., B. & J. White, London, 1795, Vol. 1, p. 410. This is from Chapter 10, 'On the Duties of Justices of the Peace and Municipal Magistrates'. Lord Mansfield described what happened when 'justices of the peace at their sessions, or even out of sessions, are...erected into chancellors'; 'it cannot but happen but that on the same facts very different decisions must be made'. Oldham, *The Mansfield Manuscripts*, p. 108.

every gentleman is a hard-hearted assassin...every Judge is unjust, every Justice corrupt and blind'.[47] But...not *every* justice; this reviewer did not notice Mr Forester, the relative of Falkland who, along with the household servants, appears to believe in Caleb's guilt. Forester is a reasonable man, and a reasonable magistrate with a confidence in the law that dictates much of the pursuit of Caleb. Caleb often attributes to Falkland a persecution that is in fact inaugurated by Forester, who thinks that Caleb will be treated fairly by the law once he stands before a magistrate.[48] This is not a 'belief' in the law as in something good, imbricated in a fictional character; it is not that Forester is presented as *believing* in Caleb's version or not believing it; it is perhaps Godwin's understanding of the adversarial nature of the common law system and how the law trial – not witnesses, not accused, plaintiffs, defendants, but the trial itself – produces the truth in the verdict given at the end. It is the verdict that 'retrospectively reinterprets hitherto ambivalent or conflicting evidence into a singular meaning'.[49] Seventy years on, Anthony Trollope will expound on this point through the entire length of his novel *Orley Farm* (1862), in the conversations and soliloquies of his large cast of lawyerly and lay characters.[50] But only the vulgar, uneducated in the law, use the word *story* to describe a defendant's prepared testimony (though attorneys and barristers *think story* throughout).[51] *In Things As They Are*, before Caleb's first trial for theft, Godwin has magistrate Mr Forester use *story* in his advice to the young man:

> Make the best story you can for yourself; true, if truth, as I hope, will serve your purpose; but, if not, the most plausible and ingenious you can invent. That is what self-defence requires from every man where, as it always happens to a man upon his trial, he has the whole world against him, and has his own battle to fight against the world (p. 169).

'Behind the clever arguments spun from the pages of a law book, there is always a human tale', says twenty-first-century former barrister Sarah Langford. 'It is my job to help my clients fit their lives, in all their messy

---

[47] 'Novels. ART. 20. *Things As They Are; or, the Adventures of Caleb Williams. By William Godwin*. In 3 Vols., 12mo. 9s. Crosby. 1794', *The British Critic*, 4 (July 1794), pp. 70–1.

[48] Philp, *Godwin's Political Justice*, p. 113.

[49] Kayman, 'Trials of Law', p. 104.

[50] Anthony Trollope, *Orley Farm* (1862), Oxford University Press, Oxford, 1985, esp. Vol. I, pp. 118, 251, and Vol. II, pp. 165, 213, 225, 303–305, 331.

[51] Trollope, *Orley Farm*, Vol. II, p. 213.

shades of grey, within the black and white of the law by telling their *story* and telling it well'.[52] In 1794, in the *British Critic* reviewer's mind, Forester's clear-eyed advice to Caleb may have aligned Mr Forester with all the other corrupt and blind magistrates in the book; but neither Forester nor his law advice was mentioned.

The reviewer's problem with the novel was rather that Godwin had set out to 'render the laws of his country odious', and the manner in which he had effected this – putting Caleb in a jail that he had found in *The Newgate Calendar*! – from as long ago as the reign of George I! – was given a narrow smile of contempt. The much kinder *Critical Review*, which reported in the same month, took no notice of the law, being much more interested in the psychosocial drama of enmity between 'two neighbouring gentlemen... one governed by all the vulgar passions predominant in unformed minds, pride, interest, love of power, and envy; the other... externally amiable, but... internally directed, not by true principle, but by... the love of fame'. Long extracts tell a story of misdirected passion. Twentieth-century critics who named Godwin as a first master of psychological fiction could have learned from this review that eighteenth-century readers got there first, albeit without a twentieth-century vocabulary. The reviewer simply *couldn't put it down*: 'few readers will have sufficient coolness to lay down the book before they have concluded it'. With a readerly urbanity, he or she concluded that 'instead of "Things as they are," the novel might perhaps... have been intitled, "Things as they ever have been"'.[53]

The *British Critic* review was an excoriating account of the sociolegal world depicted in *Caleb Williams*. A correspondence ensued, Godwin replied, and was further chastised for his pains. (This exchange took place between April and August 1795.) 'I beg it may be observed', said the anonymous reviewer (he reported to have had his critique from 'a friend'), that 'though I have a high veneration for law in general, and a particular affection for the laws of my own country, I have not

---

[52] My emphasis. Sarah Langford, *In Your Defence: Stories of Life and Law*, Doubleday, London, 2018, p. ix. The book is made up of defendants' stories, many as agonised and uncomprehending as the one Caleb tells. Langford tells how she studied for an English degree because she 'loved the way that words transported me into someone else's life so that I could better understand them. And this, I later discovered, is exactly what barristers do'.

[53] '*Things As They Are; or, the Adventures of Caleb Williams. By William Godwin*. 3 Vols. 12mo. 10s 6d sewed. Crosby. 1794', *The Critical Review, or The Annals of Literature*, 11 (July 1794), pp. 290–6.

undertaken to show that they ought to be what they are, but simply, that they are very different from the picture exhibited in Caleb Williams'.[54] He (this was certainly a barrister, or a man with barrister friends) had been urged to make this point: that in *Caleb Williams* Godwin had made a statement with 'respect to the law of England, absolutely false'. He gave a blow-by-blow account of exactly what was wrong with the Hawkinses story: had Godwin investigated whether a landlord was justified in turning out his tenant in the circumstances described in the novel? No, he had not. And, anyway, law apart, would a landlord put himself to the trouble of losing his income and finding a new tenant? No, he would not. Godwin had claimed that the incident by which the Hawkinses are ruined – when the odious Tyrrel floods his tenants' farm, destroys their crops, breaks down fences and poisons their cattle, all to get them out – is one for which legal redress is too expensive for a person of 'the degree of farmer to resort to'. Wrong! 'The fact is notoriously the reverse'. In sociolegal reality the Hawkinses' remedy would have been simple and cheap. And no attorney would have been able to protract the case as described in the novel. Moreover, Godwin supposes that the fact of poisoning cattle 'is only ground for a civil action'. Wrong! 'It is a capital Felony under several Statutes. By the Black Act, unlawfully to kill or maim any cattle is felony without benefit of Clergy...'[55] There are more corrections to the scenes in which Tyrrel makes further attempts to distress Farmer Hawkins by blocking off the road from the farm to town. Young Hawkins removes the obstacle, breaks the padlocks, opens the gates. He is carried before 'a Bench of Justices, who commit him to take his trial for *Burglary* at the next assizes'. Wrong! What young Hawkins did was merely trespass. It was no ground for criminal proceedings, unless it had been done in the company of others with violence and outrages so as to constitute a riot. The rioters would be bailable, and punishment would have been either a fine or imprisonment depending on the circumstances. 'It could in no case constitute a capital offence, much less a Burglary, of which the legal definition... is a breaking into

---

[54] For the exchange between Anon. and Godwin, 'Correspondence', *The British Critic*, 5 (April 1795), pp. 444–7; W. Godwin, 'Correspondence: To the Editor of the British Critic', 6 (July 1795), pp. 94–5; 'Correspondence: To the Editor of the British Critic', 7 (August 1795), pp. 213–15. The quote above is from the last.

[55] From its medieval origins (when clergymen could claim that they were outside the jurisdiction of the secular courts and be tried in an ecclesiastical court) 'the benefit of clergy' evolved into a legal fiction by which first-time offenders could receive lesser sentences for some crimes.

a dwelling house, in the night time, with intent to commit a Felony'. (Godwin took particular note of these points, particularly the one about the Black Act, as we shall see.)

His pen sharpened by use, Anon. turned his attention to Emily Melville's arrest, imprisonment and death. Improbable! Who would do such a thing 'at the risk of incurring the penalty for murder'? And Falkland acquitted for the murder of Tyrrel? *Not* improbable: 'there is no evidence to bring the fact home to Mr Falkland, and the jury set his high reputation against the very slight presumption of his guilt'. Moreover, 'the circumstances stated against the Hawkinses are so strong as almost to amount to positive proof. There is no tribunal by which they would not probably have been condemned'. Yes; he knows that *Caleb Williams* is a fiction and that these law errors are failure of the novelist's imagination; Godwin has not been able to account for the murder of Tyrrel and has produced a narrative that exceeds all the bounds of probability. For some few lines of the review, Godwin's failures come not from want of legal knowledge but are rather a failure of writing: of plot, characterisation and motive.

The worst failure was over the many magistrates in the book: 'it should appear...that Mr Godwin is utterly ignorant of the nature of the office of a Justice of the Peace'. Murder can only be determined by a jury ('the only judges of fact which the law of this country knows'), not by a weeping magistrate who has vacated his parlour. And anyway, a magistrate is 'bound to commit a man charged before him, by the oath of credible witnesses', not dismiss the case, as Falkland did with the peasant lad. 'It is not material whether a Justice of the Peace ought to have the discretionary powers attributed to him by Mr Godwin. The Law of England does not give it'. Godwin was either ignorant of the law or consciously determined to misrepresent it. And then to Caleb's time in prison – it was for such a long time the reviewer noted: 'this also is impossible to have happened under the law of this country'. And then, the worst offence – 'the most extraordinary falsehood concerning the law of England' – when 'the author all along affects to believe that a man [Caleb] may be tried twice for the same offence'; it is 'universally known, that a verdict of acquittal upon a criminal charge, is a complete bar to a further trial for the same offence'. What was Godwin *doing*? This is another failure of writing: the law error is the less excusable for being 'no use in carrying on the Fable'. The letter ends with a P.S. about 'one of the most daring misrepresentations in the book', to do with Caleb's time in jail when he is provided with stinking water to drink taken from the nearest puddle, his jailers telling him that this

what they must do, by law. Godwin may cite Volume 2, page 217 of
the *State Trials* in the margin of the novel, but he has completely mis-
read the explanation given by Lord Coke therein. But what can you
expect? – 'Such is the candour of this writer'.[56]

Who would not be hurt by such a review? Who would not be confirmed in her or his view that the law is endless, infinite, mystifying; that
'the consequence of the infinitude of law is its uncertainty'? Godwin
could have done with a good publisher's reader, competent in the law,
and a fact checker; the evidence is that he set about finding one (or
more) from among his friends. He also treated Anon. *as* a publisher's
reader, albeit a cruel one. But his first response was defensive. He had
not intended to cast an odium upon the laws of his country, he said; he
had a much larger purpose in view, which was to 'expose the evils which
arise out of the present system of civilized society' and by novelising
them, to launch readers 'upon the sea of moral and political inquiry'.
Caleb Williams was set in England because he knew it, but he did not
suppose that its laws were worse than those of any other country. It
wasn't the business of a novel like his to determine whether a rich man
was authorised, for example, to destroy the crop of a poor one; it was
enough that similar oppressions were practised everyday, and everyone
knew it. Could any reader with a smidgen of history of the squirearchy
and its tenantry not recognise in the Hawkinses episode 'what he has
himself heard and seen'? As for the statement that a person acquitted
of a criminal charge may not be tried again for the same offence – had
Anon. not read *The Newgate Calendar*? Godwin footnoted his letter with
cases that showed his critic to be wrong.[57] He had consulted professional lawyers who *had* told him that a second trial *could* take place
on appeal from the family of a murdered man; 'whether this be so or
not, I have not yet had leisure to examine'. Time would tell whether or
not Anon.'s attack were discreditable to him or to William Godwin.
That was it: just two of the criticisms answered. The letter was dated
7 June 1795.

Anon. returned to the fray a month later in August with a detailed
refutation of Godwin's points; 'in my opinion, he ought to have gone
further, and to have stated his ignorance of the law of England,
that his readers might take nothing in his book, but as a matter of

---

[56] *British Critic*, April 1795.
[57] Godwin, 'Correspondence' (July 1795). The footnote, p. 95, reads 'Case of
Christopher Slaughterford, 1708. Newgate Calendar, Vol. I, p. 118 – Case of James
Cluff, 1719. Lives of the Convicts. Vol. II, p. 199.'

invention'. He was scornful of the very idea that *he*, the reviewer, should read *The Newgate Calendar* or *Lives of the Convicts* – such low literature! Surely Godwin was indulging himself in 'a little merriment'? 'I suppose that this is a sort of sneering at my learning'. It must be a joke, a bad joke, 'for no man surely can fall into the ridicule of quoting such books seriously'. 'I never have read the books in question ... and oh, spare my blushes; but it must come out; I never shall'. Godwin had put many of his characters in legal situations they could not possibly, ever, legally find themselves in; it did not matter how many learned friends he had consulted, he had had Falkland stand trial twice, put his character in a situation 'which is impossible, as the law of England stands; and thus exhibited a false picture of the law itself'. A little Latin, a quotation from Cicero on why we should cherish the law – knowledge of law and the classics (not that Godwin didn't know them too) wielded as power – and Anon. signed off and ended the correspondence.[58]

Godwin learned a lot from this exchange and altered lot of practical law information for the second edition of *Caleb Williams*, published in 1796.[59] These changes endured in all subsequent editions of the novel, right through to the 1831 Standard Novels edition which is used for most modern reprints. For a start, he got to work on magistrates, and tidied up his vocabulary. In 1794, the magistrates who were obliged to take some steps upon the subject of Tyrrel's murder and suspicion of Falkland send for him to 'appear before them at one of their meetings' in 1794. By 1796, the 'meeting' is called 'a trial', and there are other changes of detail of procedure. In 1794, at the acquittal of Falkland, there is 'a general murmur of applause and involuntary transport burst forth in the court' when 'the verdict of the jury was given'. In 1796 (and subsequently), the applause bursts out when 'the decision of the magistrates was declared'. These changes do not exactly make what happened to Falkland at his two 'trials' much clearer, and the charge that he had not the slightest idea 'of the nature of the office of a Justice of the Peace' probably still stood, but they do show Godwin attempting to heed the lessons in the law so publicly delivered in 1795. In 1796, Caleb himself is a character much cannier about magistrates and what they can and cannot (or choose to) listen to than he was in his original shape. But the striking and major textual change between 1794 and 1796 is to

---

[58] 'Correspondence: To the Editor of the British Critic' (August 1795), pp. 213–15.
[59] William Godwin, *Caleb Williams; or, Things As They Are*, 2nd ed., G. G. & J Robinson, London, 1796.

do with the Hawkinses' story, and the account of burglary, felony, riot, malicious damage and the Black Act, given to Godwin in the pages of the *British Critic*.

In 1794, young Hawkins was 'carried before a bench of justices, and by them committed to the county jail, to take his trial for the burglary at the next assizes'. The narrative voice then continues: 'This was the finishing stroke to Hawkins's miseries . . .' By 1796, and Godwin having done some hard work on the Black Act, a long new passage is inserted between these two sentences:

> Mr Tyrrel was determined to prosecute the offence with the greatest severity; and his attorney, having made the proper inquiries... undertook to bring it under that clause of the act 9 Geo. I commonly called the Black Act which declares that "any person, armed with" a sword or other offensive weapon, and having his face blacked, or being otherwise disguised, appearing in any "warren or place where hares or conies" have been or shall be usually kept, and "being thereof duly convicted, shall be adjudged guilty of felony, and shall suffer death, as in cases of felony, without benefit of clergy."

Godwin further provides an explanation for his use of the statute:

> Young Hawkins, it seemed, had buttoned the cape of his great coat over his face as soon as he perceived himself to be observed; and he was furnished with a wrenching-iron for the purpose of breaking the padlocks. The attorney further undertook to prove, by sufficient witnesses, that the field in question was a warren in which hares were regularly fed. Mr. Tyrrel seized upon these pretences with inexpressible satisfaction. He prevailed upon the justices, by the picture he drew of the obstinacy and insolence of the Hawkinses, fully to commit the lad upon this miserable charge; and it was by no means so certain as paternal affection would have desired, that the same overpowering influence would not cause in the sequel the penal clause to be executed in all its strictness.[60]

This is really most efficiently done, though Godwin had to do that unsatisfactory thing in a novel, which is tag on a plot item in order to make sense of a revised narrative. But it is a fine recommendation for plagiarising one's readers' reports in revising a manuscript. And what reader, over two hundred years, has noticed that young Hawkins had masked

---

[60] Godwin, *Things As They Are*, 2nd ed. (1796), Vol. 1, pp. 123–4. Besides consulting lawyer friends for his narrative of the Black Act, Godwin could also profitably have read the government 'newspaper' *The Gazette*. Stories of how the law, including the Black Act, was infringed all over the country were a monthly feature. See above, pp. 80–1.

his face with a cape collar in 1796 that he hadn't had in 1794? Just one reader.[61] The pleasure of this moment – this change – is relief from the oppressions of the text; briefly, you can vacate the nightmare and contemplate the pantomime form, or more appropriately, an unwritten episode of *Blackadder* (dark night, hooded villain, wrenching-iron in hand). Disconcerting scenes in which furniture shifts position, people appear in clothes they were not wearing in the last frame, or where the sky is a different colour from what it was before, *are* the *mis-en-scène* of modern dreams, not of nightmares. Godwin's change appears benign – because it is rational; it is about an actual act of Parliament; it evokes its use in the higher courts from 1723 onwards; it is an inscription of an actual social history, by a historian.

But this text can never be *just a dream*. Soon it will leave history, or society, rejoin the inchoate nightmare of the law: no end in sight, no way out of the Gothic edifice. On publication of the *Commentaries on the Laws of England*, William Blackstone was praised – still is praised – for shining the clear light of day upon the common law's 'impenetrable jumble of antiquated forms and obscure procedures'. It has always been recognised that he did this by the elegance of his prose and the telling of a particular kind of historical narrative, in which there is no place outside the *reasonableness* of the explanations it provides.[62] He – like many writers – like William Godwin – found great imaginative resource in the literary and architectural Gothic, as in the epigraph to this chapter, where the common law is represented as both a labyrinth and an old Gothic castle. The moat, ramparts, and battlements have been preserved, though they are unused, though they are perfectly useless. The smaller interior chambers – *not* the Great Hall – have been converted into 'rooms of convenience' – bright and cheerful, easy to live in – but the dark winding corridors are still there; it is difficult to find – we must imagine this – the sunlit parlour, the pretty private dining room with its new sash windows. It is Blackstone's mission to guide the brightly engaged enquirer through these labyrinthine passages.[63] But it is not

---

[61] *Collected Novels and Memoirs of William Godwin ... Volume 3 ... Caleb Williams*, Pamela Clemit (ed.), William Pickering, London, 1992, p. 288. In this account of 'Variants from Manuscripts and Editions 2–5', the Black Act is explained but not why young Hawkins's buttoning his greatcoat cape over his face is an infringement of it.

[62] See above, pp. 90–2. William Blackstone, *Commentaries on the Laws of England: Book I. Of the Rights of Persons* (1765), Oxford University Press, Oxford, 2016, General Editor's Introduction, p. x; Editor's Introduction, pp. xvii–xl.

[63] William Blackstone, *Commentaries on the Laws of England*, III (1768), 2016, Oxford University Press, Oxford, p. 178.

at all clear that Godwin wished to be so guided. The common law appeared on the list of law categories you had to learn that he produced in *Political Justice*, but for the purposes of this novel, Caleb must remain trapped in the long dark corridor of the Gothic castle. There is no light here, so he might as well be outside, where skies are always dark and lowering, or rusty, bloody red. The only sunlight in the entire novel is in Caleb's memory of childhood, or in a memory of a nature poet's effusions, or after a reading of Horace. But throughout the long dark story he tells, Caleb retains what is possibly some small faith in the law: that it might let him into the light. He seeks out magistrates all over England and Wales to whom to tell his mangled tale ('mangled tale' is the end stop in 1794, preserved in later editions); it is in a magistrate's justicing room that Caleb confronts Falkland with his crime, and his own love and admiration for his former master. The actual proceedings in this magistrate's parlour are as dodgy to this historian's tedious little mind as they have been throughout: Where *is* it? What kind of sessions is this? Can I find proceedings like these in Burns' *Justice of the Peace*?...Yet Caleb appears to have developed in his legal understanding and explains that 'I met Mr. Falkland in the presence of the magistrate to whom I had applied...The audience I met at...[his] house...consisted of several gentlemen and others selected for the purpose the plan being to find a medium between the suspicious air of a private examination, and the indelicacy as it was styled of an examination exposed to the remark of every accidental spectator' (p. 329).

Falkland makes his confession before this magistrate – 'I have spent a life of the basest cruelty to cover one act of momentary vice and to protest myself against the prejudices of my species. I stand now completely detected. My name will be consecrated to infamy, while...[Caleb's] heroism...patience and...virtues will be for ever admired'. Caleb has inflicted on him 'the most fatal of all mischiefs', but Falkland blesses the hand that wounds him. And '–turning to the magistrate' – 'do with me as you please', says he. He is prepared to 'suffer all the vengeance of the law' – 'You cannot inflict on me more than I deserve. You cannot hate me more than I hate myself. I am the most execrable of all villains...' He does not appear to be committed on a charge of murder. Then, three days later, in some place outwith the text and outwith the law, he dies. Now Caleb can call himself a murderer, in tragic emulation of the man he so loved: 'I endure the penalty of my crime. His figure is ever in imagination before me. Waking or sleeping I still behold him. He seems mildly to expostulate with me for my unfeeling behaviour. I live the devoted victim of conscious reproach' (pp. 336–7).

Caleb ends by accepting – dwelling within – his own abjection and exile from life. He loves the man who has taken his life (any normal life) away from him. Throughout, in a blind and uncomprehending way, he has sought shelter in the law that has failed him. He retains a faith that some magistrate, somewhere, might, like a good father, listen to his story (the fatal chest – Falkland's secret – the murder – the hanging of the Hawkinses) and comfort him. He may not understand the technicalities of the justicing room, but he knows what he wants from the magistracy. Indeed, we could speculate that Caleb's ignorance is a fine piece of characterisation on his author's part, not Godwin's ignorance, at all – though the *British Critic's* lawyerly Anon. would not have allowed such speculation. And indeed, Caleb's author suggests that his attenuated faith in the law is puerile.

Earlier, Caleb listens to a law lesson in the Robber's Lair. It is not directed at him, but at one of the band who has returned from a marketing (or shoplifting) trip to a town 'at some distance'. They bring back with them a printed reward sheet offering a payment for information about the notorious criminal *Caleb Williams*. It is shown to Captain Raymond with the words: 'a prize! I believe it is as good as a bank-note of a hundred guineas'. Mr Raymond asks what they need money *for*. They are not in distress or want, and the price of the prize would be treachery and violation of the rules of hospitality. The man who comes home with the handbill changes his name between 1794 and 1796, becoming Larkins rather than Wilson, but he justifies himself in the same way over the years: Caleb is a true criminal; he, Wilson/Larkins is not; Wilson/Larkins is a highway robber who only takes money from those who can afford to lose it. Just because he laughs at 'assizes and great wigs and the gallows, and because I will not be frightened from an innocent action when the lawyers say me nay, nay, does it follow that I am to have a fellow-feeling for pilferers, and rascally servants, and people that have neither justice nor principle?' Moreover, Caleb is a mere interloper in the trade of thieving (pp. 230–1).[64]

'You are wrong, Larkins!' thunders Mr Raymond. 'You certainly ought not to employ against people that you hate, supposing your hatred to be reasonable, the instrumentality of that law which in your practice you defy. Be consistent! Either be the friend of law, or its adversary!'. Caleb listens from his corner, and remembers when he writes his

---

[64] The change from 'Wilson' to 'Larkins' was probably because there is a Dr Wilson earlier in the book who could (in some wild imagining) be confused with him. Dr Wilson attends Emily Melville in her last days.

narrative – his half-told and mangled tale. He remembers too, the wider lessons taught by the Captain: 'Depend upon it that, wherever there are laws at all, there will be laws against such people as you and I. Either therefore we all of us deserve the vengeance of the law, or law is not the proper instrument of correcting the misdeeds of mankind'; but he can scarcely be said to heed them. Caleb's inability to be a philosopher of the law – Caleb's failure to hate it well and reasonably – is his very point.

'Be consistent! Either be the friend of law, or its adversary!'
William Godwin, *Things As They Are* (1795), Vol. 2, p. 90.

They conceived the daring idea of reducing all the laws of England, all that was necessary for the preservation of the state, or the police of civil society, into a certain number of plain aphorisms, to be comprised in the bigness of a pocket-volume.
William Godwin, *The History of the Commonwealth of England,
From the Death of Charles the First to the Protectorate, Volume
the Third*, Henry Colborn, London, 1827, p. 573.

Thirty years on from the publication of *Caleb Williams*, as a historian now rather than a political philosopher, Godwin appears to be just a little enamoured of the law, or, interested in, informative on, engaged with the law, as it reveals the deep structure of the events narrated in *The History of the Commonwealth of England* (1824–1828). Some biographers claim that he had always wanted to 'be a historian' – to be read and understood *as a historian*. Peter Marshall says that, his whilst his boyhood passion had been for poetry, by his twenties he felt almost a vocation for history; he spent the greater part of his life studying and writing history.[1] In the 1790s, when he published both *Political Justice* and *Things as They Are*, he did not see a conflict between the writing of history and the writing of poetry (poetry in the Aristotelian sense; 'poetry' as fiction/romance/*roman*; literature in general).[2] In 'Of History and Romance' (1797), he declared that a good historian was also a poet, that is, a writer unafraid of exercising the 'sublime licence'

---

[1] Peter Marshall, *William Godwin: Philosopher, Novelist, Revolutionary*, Foreword by John P. Clark, PM Press, Oakland, CA, 2017, p. 38; Marshall is informative on the works of historical biography Godwin produced before *Commonwealth*.

[2] For the eighteenth-century's febrile discussions of the relationship between history and poetry (literature), see Carolyn Steedman, *Poetry for Historians; or, W. H. Auden and History*, Manchester University Press, Manchester, 2018, pp. 12–16.

of imagination.[3] Readers of discrimination will surely reach the end of his essay preferring the 'reality of romance' to the 'falseness and impossibility of history'.[4]

In 'History and Romance', Godwin considered history and history writing under two headings: the history of collectivities (of nations and societies, of humankind 'in the mass'); and the history of individuals. Historians producing the first kind of history investigated progress, nation formation and the formation of property; they made comparisons between societies at different stages of development. There were subdivisions of this first type: histories of literature, rhetoric, and the arts; of capitalism, trade, commerce, taxation and state formation. Historians of this bent traced the effect of climate and environment on societies. Some applied themselves entirely 'to the examination of medals and coins' (H&R 360).[5]

It was perfectly possible to write this kind of history without considering individuals at all; the historian producing it 'disdain[ed] the records of individuals'. They thought it soppy (Godwin wrote: 'a symptom of effeminacy') to write – to even think – about the personal: 'Their mighty minds cannot descend to be busied about anything less than the condition of nations, and the collation and comparison of successive ages'. They over-value the history they had themselves produced because it *took so long* and it was *so very hard to do*.[6] They try to persuade their readers of their own excellencies. But 'the mind of man does not love abstractions'; children and the unlearned – perhaps all of us – are interested in *people*. If you study 'the history of nations abstracted from individuals whose passions and peculiarities are interesting to our minds, ... [you] will find it a dry and frigid science'; the reader cannot

---

[3] Ian Ward, 'A Love of Justice: The Legal and Political Thought of William Godwin', *The Journal of Legal History*, 25:1 (2004), pp. 1–30; 28.

[4] Marshall, *William Godwin*, p. 38; The Penguin Classics edition of *Caleb Williams* (1987) was the first to include Godwin's 1797 manuscript essay. William Godwin, *Things As They Are; or The Adventures of Caleb Williams* (1794, 1831), Penguin, London, 1987, pp. 359–73 (in this chapter 'History and Romance' [1797] is referred to as 'H&R'). According to a note in the manuscript, Godwin wrote it 'while the *Enquirer* [1797] was in the press, under the impression that the favour of the public might have demanded another volume'. The *Enquirer* was published in February 1797 – so it was probably in press between December 1796 and January 1797.

[5] What *is* it with coins and medals (and weapons) as the mark of the most hidebound empiricism in a historian? See W. H. Auden pondering this question in 1955, in Steedman, *Poetry for Historians*, pp. 161–206.

[6] Making things hard in the sense of 'difficult' (and also in its lewd meaning) was an important aspect of disciplinary formation in the English nineteenth century. For an early account of the masculinisation of English studies, Chris Baldick, *The Social Mission of English Criticism, 1848–1932*, Oxford University Press, Oxford, 1983.

make it cohere in her mind; it 'crumbles from ... [our] grasp, like a lump of sand'. It is quite different when historians write of individuals; we readers compare them to ourselves; the handful of sand coheres, and 'we return home to engage in the solemn act of self-investigation' in the light of other individualities (H&R 361). The history of other people – the history of *their* self-formation – can obviate depression, especially when the course of an individual life is traced:

> The excellence ... of sages, of patriots and poets, as we find it exhibited at the end of their maturity, is too apt to overwhelm and discourage us with its lustre. But history takes away the cause of our depression. It enables us to view minutely and in detail what to the uninstructed eye was too powerful to be gazed at; and, by tracing the progress of the virtuous and the wise from its first dawn to its meridian lustre, shows us that they were composed of materials merely human (H&R 362).

We must not content ourselves with the first sort of history – of 'society in the mass'. We must endeavour to see how a particular society is shaped by the individuals composing it. Then, 'he that would prove the liberal and spirited benefactor of his species, must connect the two branches of history together, and regard the knowledge of the individual, as that which can alone give energy and utility to the records of our social existence' (H&R 363). He, Godwin the historian, is not content to observe an historical actor upon the public stage:

> I would follow him into his closet. I would see the friend and the father of a family, as well as the patriot. I would read his works and his letters, if any remain to us. I would observe the turn of his thoughts and the character of his phraseology. I would study his public orations. I would collate his behaviour in prosperity with his behaviour in adversity. I should be glad to know the course of his studies, and the arrangement of his time. I should rejoice to have, or to be enabled to make, if that were possible, a journal of his ordinary and minutest actions. I believe I should be better employed in studying one man, than in perusing the abridgement of Universal History in sixty volumes (H&R 364).[7]

Godwin had much to say about the historical heroes of classical antiquity and about Thucydides and Livy compared with modern historians like Hume and Voltaire. With the ancient historians, we *as readers* feel the feelings with which they recorded their heroes: 'the ancients were not ancients to their contemporaries'. He quoted Rousseau on this

---

[7] Godwin was fond of rhetorical hyperbolic intensifiers like 'fifty volumes in folio' (see above, pp. 163–4) and 'universal history in sixty volumes'. Discriminating readers will note that in its verbosity, history come off worse than the law.

point (H&R 366). But modern historians 'neither experience such emotions nor excite them'. We should just take it for granted that ancient history is a fable; we should not inquire too closely into 'the facts' of it; rather, we should ask ourselves if we can learn from it and use its lessons to enhance ourselves as moral beings (H&R 367).

He pursued the distinction between fable (story/romance/novel) and history by asserting that 'nothing is more uncertain, more contradictory, more unsatisfactory than the evidence of facts'. He pondered the slipperiness of 'facts' in the operation of the law compared with history: 'in courts of justice…truth is sometimes sifted with tenacious perseverance' to make one version of it. That is the case with the historian also; but he 'can administer no oath…cannot issue his precept… [or] summon his witnesses from distant provinces, he cannot arraign his personages and compel them to put in their answer'. He must take what they choose to tell: the broken fragments, 'the scattered ruins of evidence' (H&R 367). To be sure, the most 'truthful' history was the mere chronicle of 'facts, places…dates' – and it was very boring: the historian and the reader who 'knows only what day the Bastille was taken and on what spot Louis XVI perished, knows nothing. He professes the mere skeleton of history'. In sum, 'the reader will be miserably deluded if, while he reads history, he suffers himself to imagine that he is reading facts' (H&R 368, 370). Even with the most up-to-date kind of history – modern critical history – the 'main body of the composition consisting of a logical deduction and calculation of probabilities', was no better, for 'the narrative is sunk in the critic'.

Really, what historians should aim to do is write 'romance under a graver name', that is 'a composition in which, with a scanty substratum of facts and dates, the writer interweaves a number of happy, ingenious and instructive inventions, blending them into one continuous and indiscernible mass' (H&R 368). In this way, modern romances (novels) can be thought of as a species of history. But there *were* differences: 'the historian is confined to individual incident and individual man, and must hang upon that his invention or conjecture as he can'. The novelist, on the other hand, 'collects his materials from all sources, experience, report, and the records of human affairs; then generalises them; and finally selects, from their elements and the various combinations they afford, those instances which he is best qualified to portray, and which he judges most calculated to impress the heart and improve the faculties of his reader'. That is why 'romance… [is] a bolder species of composition than history' (H&R 370). 'True history consists in a delineation of consistent, human character, in a display of the manner in which such a character acts under successive circumstances, in showing how character increases and assimilates new substances to its own, and how it decays, together with the catastrophe into which by its own gravity it naturally declines'. The novelist can do this, not least because he understands 'the character which is the creature of his own fancy'. The writer of romance is 'the writer of real history'. The formerly so-called 'historian' might attempt to 'step down into the place of his rival' and do what the novelist does. He will still labour under a disadvantage: of being a kind of romance writer 'without the arduous, the enthusiastic and the sublime licence of imagination, that belong to that species of composition'. But his discriminating readers will love him for it; they will cry out in approbation: '"Dismiss me from the falsehood and impossibility of history, and deliver me over to the reality of romance"' (H&R 371, 372). This exhilarating argument about the possibilities of writing history loses its focus on the idea of the individual, and *writing individuality*, towards its end, though that is the aspect of 'History and Romance' to which most attention is paid by modern commentators, who are particularly interested in how Godwin brought his thesis about the individual as the proper study of the historian to bear on his major work on the English Commonwealth.[8]

In comparing the writing and reading of history and romance, Godwin did not take the final conceptual step of declaring that 'the facts of imaginative literature are as hard as the stone that Dr Johnson kicked'. 'We must always take the novelist's and the playwright's and the poet's word, just as we are almost always free to doubt the biographer's or … the historian's', says Janet Malcolm. Reading the romance – the novel – we are 'constrained from considering alternative scenarios – there are none. This is the way it is [*Things Are*]. Only in nonfiction does the question of what happened and how people thought and felt remain open'.[9] These ideas and this distinction *were* available in the new century – a lesson for children by the 1840s, when an anonymous contributor to a *Juvenile Miscellany* has a 'young girl … reading a fairy tale'. She looks up at the adult sitting beside her and asks: 'Is it true?' Some one else in the room tells her that it is both true and untrue. 'Oh I know what you mean', says she. 'You mean that the story teaches what is true,

[8] Porscha Fermanis, 'William Godwin's "History of the Commonwealth" and the Psychology of Individual History', *The Review of English Studies*, 61:252 (2010), pp. 773–800; John Morrow, 'Republicanism and Public Virtue: William Godwin's History of the Commonwealth of England', *The Historical Journal*, 34:3 (1991), pp. 645–64.

[9] Janet Malcolm, *The Silent Woman: Sylvia Plath and Ted Hughes* (1993), Picador, London, 1994, pp. 154–5. For Dr Johnson kicking the stone, see above, p. 14.

though the things did not happen'.[10] In 1843, it is too late for imagining Godwin reading this charmingly philosophical tale for children before he sold it to a customer of the Juvenile Library, for he died in 1836.

Back in the 1790s, did he, one wonders, discuss this idea – these ideas – with Mary Wollstonecraft? Godwin said he wrote 'Of History and Romance' in early 1797, though there is no indication of when it was started. He and Wollstonecraft became lovers in August 1796 and married in the month the *Enquirer* was published (February 1797). They were by now living together – in their fashion. Wollstonecraft was pregnant and working on *Maria; Or, The Wrongs of Woman*. One bridles a little at the thought that *Maria* was written with the 'help' of Godwin, beyond his provision of *Caleb Williams* which she asked for a copy of in February 1797.[11] For she did not need help to make a conceptual leap in theorising the relationship of the individual and society, in history *and* the novel: right at the beginning of *Maria* she tells the us that, in reading her history (she labels *Maria* a history), it 'ought...to be considered, as of woman, than of an individual'. Godwin is wonderfully aware of his readers in 'History and Romance', as we have seen, but he produced a *theoretical* piece about writing history rather than an introduction *to* a history/romance/novel, as did Wollstonecraft. In his essay he had no need to instruct readers in how they were to read a history of an individual in relation to society-in-the-mass. Wollstonecraft explained that she had invented her story because she wished to exhibit 'the misery and oppression, peculiar to women, that arise out of the partial laws and customs of society'.[12] 'Maria' was to be herself, an

---

[10] *The Juvenile Miscellany of Facts and Fiction, with Stray Leaves from Fairy Land, Volume I*, Houlston and Stoneman, London, 1844, pp. 143–4.

[11] Janet Todd (ed.), *The Collected Letters of Mary Wollstonecraft*, Allen Lane, London, 2003, pp. 342–437. There is a first reference to *Maria* in July 1796 (343); Todd says that the manuscript Wollstonecraft gave Godwin to read on 26 August 1796 was a draft of *Maria* (354); in February 1797 Wollstonecraft asked Godwin for a copy of *Caleb Williams* – Todd says for inspiration for her work in progress (399). The idea of 'help' comes from Lyndall Gordon, *Vindication: A Life of Mary Wollstonecraft*, Virago, London, 2005, p. 341: 'Wollstonecraft began the book with help from Godwin in the second half of 1796, at the time of her delayed recovery from Imlay'. He certainly offered to help Wollstonecraft with her writing style, and provided lessons in English grammar based on Latin exercises (Todd, 357); Ralph M. Wardle, *Godwin and Mary: Letters of William Godwin and Mary Wollstonecraft*, University of Kansas Press, Lawrence, KS, Constable, London, 1967, pp. 27–35. Madly in love she must have been, to accept criticism of her prose style. Godwin probably 'helped' another woman writer in the same way: Elizabeth Inchbald, *A Simple Story* (1791), Oxford University Press, Oxford, 2009; See M. S. Tomkins, 'Note on the Text', p. xxi.

[12] Mary Wollstonecraft, *Posthumous Works of the Author of A Vindication of the Rights of Woman: In four volumes*, J. Johnson; and G.G. and J. Robinson, London, 1798, Vol. 1 ('Author's Preface').

(invented) individual, who also embodied a much more general state of affairs. But to know whether or not Godwin was aware of this formulation before he read and edited Wollstonecraft's manuscript for publication after her death, we would need a detailed writing timetable from the author ('a journal of... [her] ordinary and minutest actions' would be very useful indeed) and these we do not have. And anyway, there is the somewhat obvious point to make, that both writers of history and writers of romance must create, or invent, their subjects; that 'Oliver Cromwell' in *Commonwealth* and 'Maria' in *The Wrongs of Woman* issue from their authors' minds and imaginations (as well as all their other sources, out there in the world); that they are the objects and subjects of *writing*, a point on which Godwin was eloquent. When in *The History of the Commonwealth in England*, Godwin wrote that 'the historian treats of facts, not of fictions', he was not contradicting the points he (may just have) made in 1797.[13] He was talking about something more mundane than the writing of a novel: about the proper reticence of a historian contemplating the might-have-been (in regard to Oliver Cromwell) and what is nowadays sometimes called counterfactual or subjunctive history.[14]

In the *Commonwealth in England*, Godwin did indeed consider his individual historical actors as embodying wider principles and developments in their own (historical) society-in-the-mass; their individuality was *for* something, in writerly and philosophical terms. But that is not the factor that makes *Commonwealth* as exhilarating a read as 'Of History and Romance', even though exhilaration is harder to sustain through four volumes and two thousand pages. The excitement comes in episodes as you, the reader, learn of a history obfuscated by most of modern English education in history. Having read it, I now know more than I ever have known, or really have a use for, about the period 1640–1660 in the British Isles. This history has been absent for most of my life. In England, only if you have studied early modern English history as an undergraduate do you live your life with much knowledge of the English Republic and Commonwealth. My own access to the years 1640–1660 was obtained at primary school, though R. J. Unstead's *Looking at History: From Cavemen to Present Day* (1955) provoked the hot topic of playground debate about the advantages of drawing a Roundhead's helmet over a Royalist's lace

---

[13] William Godwin, *History of the Commonwealth of England, From Its Commencement, to the Restoration of Charles the Second, Volume the Second*, Henry Colborn, London, 1826, pp. 7, 303.
[14] Steedman, *Poetry for Historians*, p. 233.

collar in your project book. (The very great bother of drawing all those feathered hats and furbelows and all that facial hair was what provoked the declaration that quite a few of us were Commonwealth Girls.[15]) At secondary school, about the age of twelve, we were asked to write about whether or not we would, personally, have signed the death warrant for Charles I. But apart from voluntary reading of Christopher Hill's work on the world turned upside down and the experience of defeat, I was as ignorant as the next woman of the English Republic, and that with two degrees in history. At twenty, by way of contrast, I could have recited to you a day-by-day timetable of the French Revolution, and discoursed powerfully on the *meaning* and *historical import* of each event for the making of the modern world. (I had not Godwin to tell me that she who 'knows only what day the Bastille was taken and on what spot Louis XVI perished, knows nothing'.) I wilfully misinterpreted Edmund Burke's pronouncement that 'all circumstances taken together, the French revolution is the most astonishing that has hitherto happened in the world' as 'the greatest revolution', using 'greatest' according the lexicon of the 1960s *(it was just great!)* and ignoring what I knew about the common meaning of 'revolution' in the 1790s.[16] However, I believed I knew the *meaning* of my ignorance of the Interregnum, and also from the age of twenty could bore mightily anyone who would listen to my theories of state and educational *conspiracy,* to explain why we all knew so very little about our very own Republic. Having read Godwin, I now know a good deal about it and am particularly grateful for his account of its playing out in Ireland.[17] The anti-(Irish) Catholicism he displays is as disgusting and shameful to read as it always is, but no reader from the

---

[15] Carolyn Steedman, 'Battlegrounds: History and Primary Schools', *History Workshop Journal,* 17 (1984), pp. 102–12.

[16] Edmund Burke, *Reflections on the Revolution in France, and on the Proceedings in Certain Societies in London Relative to That Event. In a Letter Intended to Have Been Sent to a Gentleman in Paris,* J. Dodsley, London, 1790, p. 1. But Godwin interpreted Burke in this way too, claiming of his *History of the Commonwealth* that 'it relates to a great and interesting topic, a series of transactions perhaps not to be surpassed in importance by any thing that has occurred on the theatre of the world'; *The History of the Commonwealth of England* 'constitutes a chapter in the records of mankind, totally unlike any thing that can elsewhere be found'. Godwin, *History of the Commonwealth* II, pp. vii, 1.

[17] Complete silence about Ireland throughout the historical education I experienced between eight and eighteen: there was a vague feeling on the vague left that it was improper for an English person/historian to discuss the history of Britain's conquest and repression of it, because of the weight of historical guilt we carried as UK citizens, even if only ten years old.

sixteenth to the twenty-first century in England could claim that she wasn't used to encountering it in a very wide variety of historical texts (and in everyday life, too).[18]

But that is not the source of exhilaration; neither is Godwin's dignified attraction to the law (which will be discussed later in this chapter). The reason for a historian's enchantment with *The History of the Commonwealth in England* is that Godwin writes *as a historian*; about his working method, his historical assumptions, what he did and didn't do with the material he was able to find; about his use of archives; about what history *is*, as a form of thinking and writing. These things are very rare. Modern historians do not, in general, say much about how the written artefact you have in your hands came into being. No more did they in the eighteenth century. Historiographers may speak of the *style* of historical texts, and they may discuss history as a form of writing, but this does not generally encompass questions of form, authorial voice, or history writing as literary artefact.[19] Many prefer to use an impersonal, omniscient, historical voice; then and now they attempt a seamless narrative to mask the constructed nature of historical inquiry

---

[18] Carolyn Steedman, *Landscape for a Good Woman*, Virago, London, 1986, pp. 33, 140. And a strange, arbitrary comment about the dirtiness of the Scottish people makes the modern reader think 'racism' as well as 'what *is* he up to?' William Godwin, *History of the Commonwealth of England, From the Death of Charles the First to the Protectorate, Volume the Third*, Henry Colborn, London, 1827, pp. 313–14. Dirty, and suffering under a notoriously corrupt justice system, it seems. But Scottish dirt and judicial corruption were commonplaces of eighteenth-century observation, as in the travel journals of Celia Fiennes, *Through England on a Side Saddle in the Time of William and Mary, Being the Diary of Celia Fiennes ... (1662–1741) with an introduction by Emily Wingfield Griffiths*, Field and Tuer, London, 1888; Boswell thought Edinburgh the dirtiest place imaginable; there was contemporary evidence about the dubious partiality of the judges of the Edinburgh Court of Sessions. Historical Manuscript Commission, *Report on the Manuscripts of Lord Polwarth Preserved at Mertoun House, Berwickshire. ... Presented to Parliament by Command of His Majesty*, Volume 5, HMSO, London, 1961. I am grateful to Wilf Prest for pointing out that Godwin's account of the Scots was a typical one.

[19] Steedman, *Poetry for Historians*, pp. 163, 221, 240. Philippe Carrard, 'History as a Kind of Writing: Michael de Certeau and the Poetics of Historiography', *South Atlantic Quarterly*, 100:2 (2001), pp. 465–83. But see Michael Bentley, *Modern Historiography: An Introduction* (1999), Routledge, London, 2005, for 'an obsession with how to write history books' among the generation of European historians born during the Revolutionary period; also Noelle Gallagher, 'Don Quixote and the Sentimental Reader of History in the Works of William Godwin', *Historical Writing in Britain, 1688–1830. Visions of History*, Palgrave Macmillan, Basingstoke, 2014, pp. 162–181 – which deals with *genre* rather than style. For Godwin the novelist not trusting 'the tale of the historian, the cold and uncertain record of words formed upon paper', Mark Salber Phillips, *Society and Sentiment: Genres of Historical Writing in Britain, 1740–1820*, Princeton University Press, Princeton, NJ, 2000, p. 326.

and writing. But Godwin did not write in this way. He presented himself as *A Historian* throughout the four volumes, and was concerned that his readers should understand what that *meant (where he was coming from)*: he didn't want to be thought objective; he didn't want anyone to think that he was indifferent to what he wrote about: 'I have no desire to be regarded as having no sentiments or emotions, when any thing singularly good or singularly evil passes under my review. I wish to be considered as feeling as well as thinking'.[20] His impartiality consisted of a fair and just examination of the evidence. Only by doing this would the historian have a right to an opinion: 'I will inform my readers what impartiality I aim at, and consider as commendable'; he will not suffer 'any respect of persons, or approbation of a cause, to lead... [me] to misapprehend or misrepresent the nature of facts. If I have failed in this, I desire to be considered as guilty of a breach of the genuine duties of an historian'.[21]

Sentiment and sympathy are on display in his account of Ireland. Back in 1800, debating the proposed Acts of Union of Ireland and the United Kingdom, John Fitzgibbon, then Lord Chancellor of Ireland, had accounted for Cromwell's massacre and removal of the Irish population in favourable terms. As Godwin reached chapter twenty of his third volume, he remembered reading the pamphlet version of Fitzgibbon's speech to the House of Lords. In a very long footnote and in a fine example of using the evidence of hostile historical witnesses, Godwin the historian told of reading the speech – dropping his pen at the great diorama of destruction displayed before his eyes – endeavouring to imagine the whole of Ireland 'without an inhabitant – no soul left through its cities, uplands, its farm-houses, and its granges, but the English invaders and their families'. He could not take it in; he had not the imagination to understand what he saw in his mind's eye: 'All the natives of Ireland, all the Catholics who were in a manner the nation', leaving for a narrow strip of county Connaught, leaving behind them their 'immoveable property', carrying with them the moveable, 'in carts, on their shoulders, hands, what they were able, or what they were permitted, to take away with them perhaps a few cattle... Such was the rapacity of their conquerors' that most of them left with nothing, most of them 'like Hagar and Ishmael in the desert, with a loaf of bread and

---

[20] For the production of sentiment among eighteenth-century historians and their readers. Mark Salber Phillips, '"If Mrs Mure Be Not Sorry for Poor King Charles": History, the Novel, and the Sentimental Reader', *History Workshop Journal*, 43 (1997), pp. 110–31.

[21] Godwin, *History of the Commonwealth* I, p. viii.

a bottle of water'.[22] He feels, as he said he would; he speaks in his own voice, as he said he would; he makes it clear what he thinks – and the agonised audience of history's horror is several hundred pages away from the casual anti-Catholic he had earlier (textually) been.

'The present work calls itself a History; and the author will not knowingly suffer it in any respect to forfeit that appellation. "Nothing extenuate, nor set down aught in malice,"' is a text that shall forever be before his eyes.[23] Neither royalist, nor presbyterian, nor republican, shall be described by him as pure or corrupt until 'his character and his actions shall have been carefully scrutinised'.[24] He had much to say about the duty of the historian throughout the four volumes of *Commonwealth* – 'to glean up incidental points of information, that may throw light upon the real state of things in greater transactions' – and also much discourse on the failings of duty in other historians – in that 'careless and imitative set of men that we call historians'; he corrected their errors.[25] He was particularly concerned that no historian – no reader – should *ever* rely on Edward Hyde, 1st Earl of Clarendon's version of events.[26] Anyone who did so, using *The History of the Rebellion and Civil Wars in England* (1702–1704), was in dereliction of duty. 'It is time that the character of Clarendon as an historian should be understood', he said; 'he is perhaps a good deal to be relied on for the things which passed under his own inspection; for the rest his information was neither ample nor accurate, and he was not always very scrupulous what he said respecting them'.[27] He advised that a source emanating from the pen of a bitter opponent of a regime might be more useful than one of a supporter. 'Though a high-church bigot', he said of Laurence Echard,

[22] Godwin, *Commonwealth IV*, pp. 436–7; Ann Kavanaugh, 'FitzGibbon, John, first earl of Clare (1748–1802), lord chancellor of Ireland', *Oxford Dictionary of National Biography*, 2008, accessed 6 November 2017; *Speech of the Right Honourable John, Earl of Clare, Lord High Chancellor of Ireland, in the House of Lords of Ireland, on a Motion Made by Him, on Monday, February 10, 1800*, J. Milliken, London, 1800; Fermanis, 'William Godwin's "History"', pp. 795–6; Genesis 21, 8–21 for Hagar and Ishmael.

[23] From William Shakespeare, *Othello*, Act V, Sc. 2. Godwin knew his audience. He did not need to provide a reference for his quote.

[24] Godwin, *History of the Commonwealth* I, pp. vii, 6

[25] William Godwin, *History of the Commonwealth of England*, p. 78; Godwin, *History of the Commonwealth* I, pp. 64–5, 115, 356, 359, 397–8; Godwin, *History of the Commonwealth* II, pp. 303, 345.

[26] Paul Seaward, 'Hyde, Edward, first earl of Clarendon (1609–1674), politician and historian', *Oxford Dictionary of National Biography*, 2004, for Clarendon as chancellor before, during and after the Civil War and Commonwealth, accessed 22 January 2018.

[27] Godwin, *Commonwealth* I, pp. 64–5, 115, 396, 397–8.

'his work is nevertheless the best general collection of facts respecting this period under the name of a history, that has yet been published'.[28]

Moreover, Godwin corrected his own mistakes, sometimes in a footnote, when he pondered whether or what he said in the text was actually true; or when he knew he had earlier made an error of judgement.[29] He delivered, with clarity and authority, the hardest of all advice to follow: to remove yourself as far as possible from your own times. 'We cannot do justice to the deeds of former times, if we do not in some degree remove ourselves from the circumstances in which we stand, and substitute those by which the real actors were surrounded', he said.[30] Historians do not (or rather must not) 'judge the past by the present: Nor is it reasonable for us to require, that men of other times, and subject to different impressions, should in all cases see with our eyes, and judge with our judgments'.[31] But in pursuit of the modern (twenty-first-century) social historian's question *How did they feel?* (the 'sentiment by which they were actuated'), Godwin inscribed the pitfalls of seeing with historical actors' eyes: you come to take part in the complex feelings of those who killed a king, for example: 'they deemed it an awful act of justice they had to perform. The engagement of a king to his people is infinitely the most solemn, and pregnant with the most various and lasting consequences, of any that can be contracted by a human being to his fellows'.[32] You begin to share feelings and convictions that you, the modern philosopher and historian, may not actually want to have.

Godwin's account of his sources, his advice about archives, their history and how to use them, and about the reading of documents, is wonderfully informative trade knowledge, passed from one artisan to another, and might be read with profit by any modern post-graduate student of history.[33] Right at the beginning of the project, his major source had been 'the Journals of the Two Houses of Parliament'. He had been 'astonished to find that this source had been so little explored', but

---

[28] Godwin, *Commonwealth* III, pp. 121, 465. R. T. Ridley, 'Echard, Laurence (bap. 1672, d. 1730), historian', *Oxford Dictionary of National Biography*, 2004, accessed 10 November 2017. Laurence Echard, *The History of England: From the Beginning of the Reign of King Charles the First, to the Restoration of King Charles the Second. Containing the Space of Above 35 Years. Volume the Second*, Jacob Tonson, London, 1718.

[29] Godwin, *Commonwealth* II, p. 219; Godwin, *Commonwealth* III, p. 345.

[30] Godwin, *Commonwealth* I, p. 84.

[31] Ibid., p. 77.

[32] Godwin, *Commonwealth* II, p. 692.

[33] For a very long footnote on what you need to know to read a document, Godwin, *Commonwealth* II, pp. 179f. He was an instructive *aficionado* of the footnote. He sometimes qualified his own argument by means of a footnote: Godwin, *Commonwealth* II, p. 219. For historians and footnotes, Steedman, *Poetry for Historians*, p. 236.

soon discovered why: they were not printed until 1742, 'nor those of the Lords till 1767; too late to allow of their being incessantly consulted by Hume and our most considerable historians'.[34] Later, when researching the period from the Civil War to the Protectorate, he encountered 'the copious and almost perfect collection of tracts published between 1640 and 1660, called the King's Tracts, in the British Museum', and told his readers about them.[35] By the time he started work on the actual Commonwealth era for Volume III, he had encountered the Order Books of the Council of State, then deposited at the State Paper Office in Great George Street, Westminster (this was before the establishment of the Public Record Office).[36] His appreciation of the 'singular merits of Mr. Robert Lemon, the Deputy Keeper' was politic, and also constitutes good advice about the utility to the working historian of cultivating your archivist: 'previously to the period of his superintendence, these records were in a state of absolute chaos, incapable of being used or consulted by any one. By the labour of years, by an industry and application indefatigable and unparalleled', Robert Lemon had made them available and usable.[37]

As a writer (of history), Godwin is constantly aware of his readers, and what they need to know about the text in front of them. He explains how the volumes of *Commonwealth* are structured: Ireland, for example, is not mentioned until the very end of Volume I: it will work better for

---

[34] Godwin, *Commonwealth* I, p. x. Godwin was highly aware of seventeenth- and eighteenth-century developments in print capitalism and how they created the sources he used. He pointed out that there was no publication of parliamentary debates until the reign of George III. Godwin, *Commonwealth* II, pp. 75–6.

[35] Godwin, *Commonwealth* III, p. 345. British Library, Thomason Collection of Civil War Tracts, www.bl.uk/books/thomason/thomasoncivilwar.html, accessed 18 January 2018; *Catalogue of the Pamphlets, Books, Newspapers, and Manuscripts Relating to the Civil War, Commonwealth, and Restoration, collected by George Thomason, 1640–1661*, Trustees of the British Museum, London, 1908, repr., Ann Arbor, 1977. This collection, made between 1640 and 1661, was formerly known as 'the King's pamphlets'. George III donated the collection to the new British Museum in 1763. In 1973, the museum transferred the Thomason Tracts (after the original collector, a London printer/bookseller) to the British Library, where they continue to be housed.

[36] The English Council of State, also known as the Protector's Privy Council, was first appointed by the Rump Parliament on 14 February 1649 after the execution of Charles I. Robert C. Brown, 'The Law of England during the Period of the Commonwealth', *Indiana Law Journal*, 6:6 (1931), pp. 359–82; Sarah Barber, 'The Engagement for the Council of State and the Establishment of the Commonwealth Government', *Historical Research*, 63:150 (1990), pp. 44–57; Sean Kelsey, 'Constructing the Council of State', *Parliamentary History*, 22:3 (2003), pp. 217–41.

[37] Godwin, *Commonwealth* III, p. vii; Gordon Goodwin, 'Lemon, Robert (1779–1835), archivist', *Oxford Dictionary of National Biography*, 2004, accessed 20 November 2017.

the narrative and the reader if the Irish question is drawn together 'in a comprehensive view [so that] the reader might the better comprehend the way in which transactions there operated upon what was going on in England'.[38] Without rancour or resentment, he accepts that most of them would have been waiting for Volume IV, in which the 'business…is to delineate the reign of a usurper'. There is the merest hint that fifteen thousand pages describing 'the unavailing efforts of virtuous and magnanimous men in the perhaps visionary attempt to establish a republic in England' is the price the reader has to pay for getting to God's Englishman, his character, his personality, his *individuality*.[39] 'The present volume treats of the Commonwealth, strictly so called', he wrote of the third. It was 'the subject for the sake of which the work was undertaken'; but you should have read the first two; though 'in a certain sense preliminary matter… [they are] indispensable to the understanding of the whole'.[40]

He explains why he starts and stops where he does.[41] He always tells you about the administrative and judicial structure of the society under consideration.[42] He frequently pauses to summarise what has gone before (to say nothing of his masterly overview at the very end).[43] It is a very long read, but not everything is there: Godwin leaves things out (and tells you so); he will summarise rather than quote verbatim from the documents ('The second and third days of the trial were consumed in similar discourses'.)[44] He is open about his own beliefs and predilections. He believes, for example, that 'human passions have nearly at all times been the same', and this despite knowing that 'the characters of men, and the judgments they make respecting questions of right and wrong, depend upon the circumstances in which they are placed; and we must not condemn them for acts inseparably connected with those circumstances'.[45] His practical task is to fill in the gaps ('to fill up this chasm in

---

[38] Godwin, *Commonwealth* I, pp. 213–58.
[39] William Godwin, *History of the Commonwealth of England, From Its Commencement, to the Restoration of Charles the Second, Volume the Fourth, Oliver, Lord Protector*, Henry Colborn, London, 1828, p. vi.
[40] Godwin, *Commonwealth* III, p. V.
[41] Godwin, *Commonwealth* I, p. 6.
[42] Godwin, *Commonwealth* I, pp. 23–5.
[43] Godwin, *Commonwealth* II, pp. 151, 192; Godwin, *Commonwealth* III, p. 528; Godwin, *Commonwealth* IV, pp. 578f.
[44] Godwin, *Commonwealth* II, p. 672.
[45] Godwin, *Commonwealth* II, pp. 416, 78.

our annals'), write about what has been formerly unconsidered, and to rescue those hitherto lost to history by his research and his pen.[46]

All of this discussion of method aside, what makes *The History of the Commonwealth of England* such a joyous and energising (and *very* long) read is Godwin's insistence on doing his own historiography. *He* is not content to leave determination of meaning in his writing to the philosophers of history and cultural theorists, as would become common a hundred and fifty years on. And his historiography is poetic. Not until Jules Michelet and 1868, and in French, would such a resigned and beautiful account of history's traffic with the dead, as is Godwin's, be found:

> ... [H]istory is obliged to grope its way, in treating of the most considerable events. We put together seemings, and draw our inferences as well as we may. Contemporaries who employ themselves in preserving facts are sure to omit some of the most material [facts], upon the presumption of their notoriety, and that they are what every body knows. History in some of its most essential members dies, even as generations of men pass off the stage, and the men who were occupied in the busy scene become victims of mortality. If we could call up Cromwel [sic] from the dead, – nay, if we could call up some one of the comparatively insignificant actors in the time of which we are treating, and were allowed the opportunity of proposing to him the proper questions, how many doubts would be cleared up, how many perplexing matters would be unravelled, and what a multitude of interesting anecdotes would be revealed to the eyes of posterity. But History comes like a beggarly gleaner in the field, after Death, the great lord of the domain, has gathered the crop with his mighty hand, and lodged it in his garner, which no man can open.[47]

Much of the beauty comes from Godwin knowing himself to be a *writer* (of history), one who had earned the poetic right to *say things* in this way. Individual actors, considered in relation to their circumstances,

---

[46] A different view of Godwin as historian: 'Well-documented, original and lucid', says Peter Marshall of the *History of the Commonwealth*. It successfully analyses 'the motives of the leading protagonists and showed a masterly understanding of the period. But [Godwin] ... paid more attention to statutes and battles than to the social and economic conditions of the people. At times, his style trips over dates and authorities, and the narrative founders on the rocks of historical accuracy'. Marshall, *William Godwin*, pp. 359–60. Marshall's view of Godwin's *Commonwealth* as actually rather boring has maybe to do with his being *not-a-historian*. But the enormous literature on the seventeenth century in England, and the ways in which it was written of in the nineteenth, rarely mentions Godwin's work.

[47] Godwin, *Commonwealth* II, pp. 29–30; Steedman, *Poetry for Historians*, pp. 211–13. For Michelet and The Dead, Carolyn Steedman, 'Living with the Dead', *The Craft of Knowledge: Experiences of Living with Data*, Carol Smart and Jennifer Hockley (eds.), Palgrave, 2014, pp. 162–75.

their times, provoked his most elegant and moving historical writing. Of John Lilburne, Leveller and Libertarian, who still calls forth the poetry of contradiction among historians and across the internet, Godwin claimed that he had painted a true picture of 'a vulgar patriot – narrow of comprehension, impassioned, stiff in opinion – seeing nothing, but what he can discern through one small window, and sitting at a distance from that – so that the entire field of his observation, his universe, in the wide landscape of the world, and the immense city of mankind, with all its lanes, its alleys, its streets, and its squares, is twelve inches by twelve'.[48]

He loves this past that he has made – rewritten – conjured – before your eyes. He often stands to one side, stage right, as if for all the world he were the eighteenth-century Clio, *showing*, not *telling*, the drama enacted there. (Godwin was a great theatre-goer.)[49] He knows the ways of pathos; he is not afraid to provoke the tears that a century and a half on would be occasioned by the merest mention of the forgotten, the unconsidered, those condescended to by posterity, as in Edward Thompson's *Making of the English Working Class*.[50] It has to be noted, however, that Godwin was not concerned with the poor men and women who throng the pages of later social history of the seventeenth century in England; they were not his topic and had no role (and thus no character) in *Commonwealth*, though they made one brief entrance as the losers of the legal system, not just during the period 1640–1660 but for all time.[51] From the late twentieth century onwards, the poor, the poor laws and the parish became the focus of historians wishing to understand the politics of the revolutionary period in its effect on everyday life. But in the early nineteenth century, there was no historiography to draw Godwin's attention to them.[52] It was 'the republicans

[48] Godwin, *Commonwealth* II, p. 44. Andrew Sharpe, 'Lilburne, John (1615?–1657), Leveller', *Oxford Dictionary of National Biography*, 2006, accessed 16 January 2018; Morrow, 'Republicanism and Public Virtue', pp. 654–7; F. K. Donnelley, 'The Levellers and Early Nineteenth Century Radicalism', *Labour History Review*, 49 (1984), pp. 24–8.

[49] David O'Shaughnessy, *William Godwin and the Theatre*, Pickering & Chatto, London, 2010.

[50] Renato Rosaldo, 'Elaborating Thompson's Heroes: Social Analysis in History and Anthropology', Harvey J. Kaye and Keith McClelland (eds.), *E.P. Thompson: Critical Perspectives*, Polity, Cambridge, 1992, pp. 103–24; 115; Elizabeth A. Clark, *History, Theory, Text: Historians and the Linguistic Turn*, Harvard University Press, Cambridge, MA, and London, 2004, p. 248.

[51] Godwin, *Commonwealth* IV, pp. 582–3.

[52] Tim Wales, 'The Parish and the Poor in the English Revolution', Stephen Taylor and Grant Tapsell (eds.), *The Nature of the English Revolution Revisited*, Boydell Press, Woodbridge, 2013, pp. 53–80; John Morrill (ed.), *Revolution and Restoration: England in the 1650s*, Collins and Brown, London, 1992.

or commonwealths-men...worthy of our admiration, [but] whose cause has not prospered', who called forth the noble tears of *caritas*; he was certain that 'the tragic termination of... [their] tale will often not on that account render the tale less instructive, or less interesting to a sound and judicious observer'.[53] Later, he wrote that 'many men of the most consummate intellect have doubtless passed away from the stage of life unknown and unheard of, because no combination of favourable circumstances occurred to unfold and give the required impulse to their talents'.[54] He was in the business of rescue and restoration of what was lost to history, the forgotten – and he knew it; he found the idea of both the lost and the forgotten beautiful enough to provoke his beautiful words.[55]

But it is Godwin's relationship with the law in *Commonwealth* that this current book compels us to consider. It develops because, as a historian, he had to *explain* so much to his readers. He discovered *so much* about the legal structure and legal proposals and innovations (many more proposals than innovations) of the Protectorate that he could not tell his historical tale without writing about the law. His discussion of the law, legislation, and legal institutions accelerated through the four volumes. He developed opinions about the judges and the jury system which he (probably) found words for in Blackstone (August 1826 – 'çala...Blackstone' – dipping in and out of Blackstone).[56] Of the latter, he wrote that 'Trial by jury had for many centuries been the peculiar boast and glory of this country. It is a main pillar of our liberties'.[57] A far cry from *Political Justice*! 'Pillar of our liberties' was used of the jury system in several texts of the 1790s, though Blackstone had actually called it their 'bulwark'.[58] When Godwin discussed changes to the judiciary under the Protectorate, he overtly cited Blackstone.[59] He very much admired Judge Mathew Hale, for his independence in 'setting himself in opposition to the will of the chief executive magistrate' (Cromwell).[60] Very early he developed the affection of

---

[53] Godwin, *Commonwealth* I, pp. 5–6.

[54] Godwin, *Commonwealth* II, p. 219.

[55] For Godwin's relationship with his sentimental readers, Phillips, *Society and Sentiment*, pp. 103–28, 322–41.

[56] For Godwin's reading of Blackstone, see above, p. 171.

[57] Godwin, *Commonwealth* III, p. 188

[58] William Blackstone, *Commentaries on the Laws of England: Book III of Private Wrongs* (1768), Intro. Thomas P. Gallanis, Oxford University Press, Oxford, 2016, pp. 349–53; Blackstone, *Commentaries on the Laws of England: Book IV of Public Wrongs* (1769), Intro. Ruth Paley, Oxford University Press, Oxford, 2016, pp. 225–6.

[59] Godwin, *Commonwealth* IV, pp. 24–5.

[60] Ibid., pp. 27–9. Alan Cromartie, 'Hale, Sir Mathew (1609–1676), judge and writer', *Oxford Dictionary of National Biography*, 2004, accessed 22 January 2018. Cromwell appointed him a justice of the court of Common Pleas in January 1654.

utility for Sir Edward Coke (1552/3?–1634) and his *Institutes of the Lawes of England* (1628–1644). He could not do without him, he who was 'universally admitted to be the great oracle of the laws of England'; it was impossible to review the historical events he wrote about without 'feeling that the liberties of Englishmen are perhaps to no man so deeply indebted as to sir Edward Coke' (Coke was Chief Justice of Common Pleas and Kings Bench).[61] He was particularly concerned to examine the appointment and position of the judges before and during the Commonwealth, for you could measure the temper of each regime by its treatment of them.[62] He offered a detailed account of new ways of appointing the judges under the Protectorate, pointing out that they did not by this become a new kind of judiciary. They were appointed for 'a special and temporary purpose', and however 'exemplary and conscientious...their character and dispositions' they could 'fail to have a strong predilection for the views of the government by which they...[were] nominated'. It was the same with all judges; 'the chances of escape therefore for the prisoner are considerably diminished'.[63] And they did not turn into new men, with new feelings and sentiments under a new regime: of the judge presiding at Lilburne's trial, and in order to argue his thesis that 'human passions have nearly at all times been the same', Godwin suggested that 'whatever be a man's title, or however elevated the seat he occupies, he feels that he is but a man. The countenance of the judge instantly reddens, and his muscles involuntarily string themselves, whenever he deems that he is insulted'.[64] But it was important to understand how Commonwealth-era judges were appointed and equally important to understand their tenure, for it related to the 'tenure of liberties and the rights of man in society'.[65] The Long Parliament had done well in this regard, he thought.[66]

---

[61] Godwin, *Commonwealth* I, pp. 27–9; Allen D. Boyer, 'Coke, Sir Edward (1552–1634), lawyer, legal writer, and politician', *Oxford Dictionary of National Biography*, Oxford University Press, 2004, accessed 22 January 2018.

[62] Godwin, *Commonwealth* I, pp. 23–5.

[63] Godwin, *Commonwealth* III, pp. 9, 192.

[64] Godwin, *Commonwealth* II, p. 416. Did he remember Norwich Assizes, way back in the 1760s, the Lord Chief Justice William de Grey removing the teenage Godwin's arm from the bench he was leaning on? See above, p. 166.

[65] Government websites still explain long judicial tenure as an underpinning of democracy and the judiciary's independence. Currently, it is explained how 'the fundamental concept of judicial independence came into being in England and Wales in 1701 with the enactment of the Act of Settlement. This statute formally recognised the principles of security of judicial tenure ...' www.judiciary.gov.uk/about-the-judiciary/the-judiciary-the-government-and-the-constitution/jud-acc-ind/independence/, consulted 25 May 2018. There is a good reading list here, for all interested enquirers: 'Selected lectures, articles and books on judicial independence'.

[66] Godwin, *Commonwealth* III, pp. 497–8.

Godwin showed how law making during the Protectorate was conducted under the shadow of a judiciary that remained much the same in temperament and predilection as it had been before. And so too with lawyers: in the first volume he described 'the character of a lawyer, full charged with all the pitiful tricks of his profession'.[67] By the end, he aligned lawyers with the judges, in the profound conservatism of their legal education. It was lawyers who had produced the most inarguable case for the restoration of the monarchy: 'Men, educated to the profession of the law, will always have a strong partiality to the forms handed down from our ancestors. It had been continually urged by the race of lawyers at this time existing, that the office and name of a king were every where interwoven with our old institutions, and that, unless our whole scheme of legislation were changed, the course of affairs could never run smooth, till that office were restored'.[68] And he took their point, over the immutability of kingship, woven as it was into every institution, into economic base and superstructure, into land-ownership and self-identity in this society in the mass, as we shall see later in this chapter.

Godwin was not much interested in the common law or, at least, it was not a category for his analysis and understanding. On my reading, he used the term twice in the course of four volumes, and then when quoting other scholars. If we consider the common law as promulgated by magistrates as a form of everyday law, or law as affecting everyday life, he appeared uninterested. He briefly mentioned some changes to the law of marriage (and the law of women, though not labelled as such by him). Later historians were to argue that the Commonwealth and Protectorate 'witnessed a slip towards local control [of the poor laws] that was to last for nearly two centuries'; but Godwin nowhere mentioned the poor laws by name, though he was interested in 1652 law reform proposals, which included the suppression of vagabondage and the 'setting to work such as were capable, and providing for the subsistence of such as through age and decrepitude were unable to relieve themselves'.[69] He remained throughout highly sensible of inequitable access to the law in a society ordered by rank and status, though his

---

[67] Godwin, *Commonwealth* I, p. 61.
[68] Godwin, *Commonwealth* IV, p. 345.
[69] A. L. Beier, 'Poor Relief in Warwickshire 1630–1660', *Past & Present*, 35 (1966), pp. 77–100; Godwin, *Commonwealth* III, p. 419; John Morrill, 'The Impact on Society', idem. (ed.), *Revolution and Restoration*, pp. 91–111; David Feldman, 'Settlement and the Law in the Seventeenth Century', Steven King and Ann Winters (eds.), *Settlement and Belonging in Europe, 1500–1930s*, Berghahn, New York and Oxford, 2013, pp. 29–53.

conclusions here revealed the conflicted nature of his own relationship with the idea of law: 'We are told that justice is blind, and the law speaks the same language indifferently to all', he wrote towards the end. 'But this is by no means universally the case. The rich man, and the man of powerful connections will often be successful in the courts, where the poor and the friendless man has a small chance'. And then: 'These however are the exceptions. In the majority of cases law is a rule serving to protect the plain man in his honest undertakings and pursuits'.[70] The law he pursued in *Commonwealth* is high law for the main part: ordinances, acts of Parliaments, and proposals for law reform issuing from committees of the Interregnum Parliaments, which never saw the light of enactment (though many Interregnum failed reforms were enacted later[71]).

The only way of telling the story of the Commonwealth was as a legal story. The war between factions that carried the narrative of the first three volumes recedes as Godwin described the making of a new constitution and legal order of society. He must perforce understand the principle of monarchy and the ways in which it underpinned all hitherto existing law in England – and the very great difficulties of unpacking law and kingship. He suggested that this is why Oliver Cromwell became a king – or that Cromwell convinced himself that he had to be one, given the weight of legal history as lived and experienced across the realm.[72] There was no way out of monarchy. In describing the Commonwealth, Godwin paid full attention to the impact of legislation on the counties; he described church and parochial funding; he told of the new county commissioners appointed for the scrutiny and funding of public preachers: who they were and the summary powers they were given.[73] He described many police measures for the suppression of popular tumult.[74] He had much to explain about the legal structure of the Commonwealth: how, for example, in 1649 'the style of the laws passed by the house of commons was changed; and what had hitherto been called ordinances, were denominated acts of parliament'.[75] The law was placed in a new relationship to the people: 'the new constitution for the political government of England...was by an agreement of the People, to be assented to and subscribed throughout the nation. The Agreement was thenceforth to

[70] Godwin, *Commonwealth* IV, pp. 582–3.
[71] Donald Veall, *The Popular Movement for Law Reform 1640–1660*, Clarendon Press, Oxford, 1970.
[72] Godwin, *Commonwealth* IV, pp. 6–14.
[73] Ibid., pp. 26–39.
[74] Ibid., pp. 231–2.
[75] Godwn, *Commonwealth* III, pp. 8–9.

be considered as sacred, so that the parliament, whose province it was to make laws, such as the public welfare and safety might from time to time require, should yet be held as not having authority to violate these provisions'.[76] He had travelled far from the thesis of *Political Justice*: contemplating the Levellers and their demand for the suppression of the council of state 'and the extinction for the future of all high courts of justice'; he could not imagine what they were *after*: 'the affairs of a nation cannot be conducted without an administration and an executive'.[77] He warmed towards the new law of treason promulgated: the 'principle of this law was undoubtedly founded in reason and justice'; it was in the mould of 'the old wholesome law of England'.[78] It sounds Blackstonian; Blackstone frequently used the term *wholesome* to describe the (old) laws of England, as did many seventeenth- and eighteenth-century legal commentators, and Godwin cites Blackstone a dozen times when discussing the minutiae of legal developments before and during the Protectorate. But in fact Blackstone gave the period 1649–1660 very short shrift in the *Commentaries*: 'I pass by the crude and abortive schemes for amending the laws in the times of confusion...the establishment of new trials, the abolition of feodal tenures, the act of navigation, and some others...were adopted'.[79] For Godwin, there was more to explain, with and without Blackstone: the Committee for Law, the act for reorganisation of the high court of justice, the 1652 act of Parliament for the suppression of vagabondage, measures on behalf of those imprisoned for debt, various marriage acts.[80] He had done this from the beginning: expounded about the law on the episcopacy, provided various technical law terms when they needed to be understood[81], but most of it occurs in the third volume. He told his readers how much they *did* actually understand; he measured the distance between their now (the 1820s) and then (1640–1660) told them how little the historical subjects they were reading about had known: 'we are at this day

---

[76] Ibid., p. 47.

[77] Ibid., p. 65. The Council of State was first appointed by the Rump Parliament in February 1649 after the execution of King Charles I. It was to act as the executive in place of the King and the Privy Council, to ensure the security of the Commonwealth and to direct domestic and foreign policy.

[78] Godwin, *Commonwealth* III, pp. 105–6.

[79] William Blackstone, *Commentaries on the Laws of England: Book IV of Public Wrongs* (1769), Oxford University Press, Oxford, 2016, p. 282.

[80] Godwin, *Commonwealth* III, pp. 180, 187, 238, 419–21, 570; Brown, 'The Law of England', p. 365, for the Committee of Law of the Rump Parliament (1648–1653). It was presided over by Judge Hale; Mary Cotterell, 'Interregnum Law Reform: The Hale Commission of 1652', *English Historical Review*, 83 (1968), pp. 518–22.

[81] Godwin, *Commonwealth* I, pp. 355, 376–7.

more familiar with the principles of a representative government, than our ancestors were in the days of the commonwealth'. So much had been printed and published by 1826 about the workings of Parliament and government; 'publicity has pervaded our courts of law, and all judicial proceedings. Government, in many of its branches, is no longer a mystery...'.[82] It was not the philosopher but the historian who wrote – about crime and punishment, for example. His readers needed working definitions of 'crime' drawn from a seventeenth-century *and* a modern context as 'that act of a human being, in possession of his understanding and personal freedom, which diminishes the quantity of happiness and good that would otherwise exist among human beings; and the greatness of a crime consists in the extent to which it produces this effect' – though many would and would have argued that such a definition owed more to the perspective of *Political Justice* (or to utilitarian legal philosophy) than the English seventeenth century.[83] Godwin's appeal to context faltered over the execution of Charles I, for although 'the great object of punishment upon the principles of jurisprudence, seems to be example, the deterring others from the perpetration of crime... there was no use in this instance in making an example, since the men by whom Charles was tried and condemned, had determined that there should be no more kings in England'.[84] In textual terms, familiarity, the result of the effort to understand and explain the law of the Commonwealth to others, did not breed contempt in Godwin but a kind of approbation and respect.

The most intellectually challenging legal history he encountered was over the question of Cromwell as lawmaker and the right the Lord Protector may – or may not – have possessed to make law. He examined this question in regard to the ordinances issued in regard to the all-important questions of excise and taxation. An ordinance on customs duties had been passed by the Lord Protector in March 1654 (and customs were indeed collected under it for the next four years). But was it lawful? That was the question at the time, and for Godwin the historian. Who had the power to make law? 'It was a maxim among the professional men [lawyers], that the written laws of England were statutes, acts or edicts, enacted by the people assembled in parliament', but this law had been issued by a council whose power depended upon the authority of a document and

---

[82] Godwin, *Commonwealth* II, pp. 73–6.
[83] Patricia Crawford, 'Charles Stuart, that man of blood' (1977), *Parergon*, 32:3 (2015), pp. 43–63; this is a Special Issue: *Religion, Memory and Civil War in the British Isles: Essays for Don Kennedy* (eds.), Dolly MacKinnon, Alexandra Walsham, and Amanda Whiting.
[84] Godwin, *Commonwealth* II, pp. 688–90.

official record called 'The Government of the Commonwealth'. 'But, if
brought into a court of justice, what was this record?' Godwin asked. 'It
was a document, prepared by the council of the army, and sanctioned
by the principal officers of state. This could not for a moment stand the
scrutiny of men bred in the technical habits of the courts, as being of force
to change the essential dicta of the English constitution'. And there had
been other objections in 1654, including that 'those who issued the ordinance had in reality no power to make a law'.[85] He considered the truly
interesting question of what it *meant* for Cromwell to think himself above
the law, and yet he concluded that 'the government of Cromwel was in a
very imperfect degree a government according to law'.[86]

Godwin had all the material for arguing that it could not last; he had
explained the ways in which constitution and legal structure were inex-
tricably bound up in the idea of the king; that all law issued from and
was the king's. He frequently noted the abilities of Commonwealth-era
lawyers, as well as their (already noted) deep conservatism, which he
attributed to their partiality for law handed down from their ancestors. It was they, 'the race of lawyers' that 'continually urged…that
the office and name of a king were every where interwoven with our
old institutions, and that, unless our whole scheme of legislation were
changed, the course of affairs could never run smooth, till that office
were restored'.[87] Again and again he told his readers what he had himself discovered: 'the law of England is technical. All its proceedings
are carried on in the name of the king–; and all public offences among
us are stiled offences against the king'.[88] ('Technical' in the early
nineteenth-century sense of the structure of knowledge pertaining to a
discipline or field of study.) He had already declared that 'the day that
saw Charles perish on the scaffold, rendered the restoration of his family certain'. But that was a historical judgement, not a judgement of the
ardent student of the law Godwin became towards the end of his task.[89]
The political philosopher who had written *Political Justice* appreciated
the project of the Little Parliament to do something about 'the cum-
brous volumes of the statutes, with all their intricacies, accompanied
as they were, illustrated, as some would say, but in the opinion of these
men perplexed and obscured, with a vast accumulation of reports,
cases, and precedents'; they were 'an insupportable grievance' (as they

---

[85] Godwin, *Commonwealth* IV, pp. 176–82.
[86] Ibid., pp. 221, 293, 692.
[87] Ibid., p. 335.
[88] Godwin, *Commonwealth* III, pp. 110–11.
[89] Godwin, *Commonwealth* II, pp. 691–2.

had been to the Godwin who wrote *Political Justice*). To codify it all, 'they conceived the daring idea of reducing all the laws of England, all that was necessary for the preservation of the state, or the police of civil society, into a certain number of plain aphorisms, to be comprised in the bigness of a pocket-volume'; the 'revision and new modelling of the whole body of the law', was a 'daring idea'.[90] The historian then had to explain how this improvement did not come to pass; how 'with a variety of other grand conceptions and improvements', the law pocket-book 'was cut off by the abrupt catastrophe of the parliament'.[91]

Godwin's appreciation of the little law handbook, which all *could have* owned and understood, may have been inflected by British experience of – or experience of reading about – the progress of the Napoleonic Code in the British press.[92] Godwin was deeply interested in Napoleon Bonaparte, 'as man and popular hero'.[93] Although the newspapers kept the British reading public up to date with the progress of the Napoleonic Code from 1804 onwards, there was no lauding of its brevity. Indeed, the first English translation of the Code Napoléon in 1811 was 500 pages long.[94] Before and after translation, the newspapers' tone of voice was sarcasm. There were a few testy exchanges in the letter columns of the provincial press about some of the code's provisions, particularly on debt and debtors, for the purposes of showing up the notorious scandal of the English system.[95] A view from Dublin was that Napoleon 'must hate the name of liberty—. Every page of the Code Napoleon is pregnant with proofs of this'. What made matters worse was that it issued from the hand of a 'living lawgiver', who 'alters, and modifies, and interprets, at his own pleasure. Nothing is certain in it; nothing rests on prescription and ancient usage; but all depends upon the arbitrary will

[90] The Little Parliament (also known as the Barebone's Parliament, the 'Nominated Assembly', and the 'Parliament of Saints') sat between July and December 1653, after which Cromwell was installed as Lord Protector.

[91] Godwin, *Commonwealth* III, pp. 573–6.

[92] Though Stuart Semmel believes that 'few British observers seem to have had all that much to say about Napoleon's Civil Code'. *Napoleon and the British*, Yale University Press, New Haven, CT, and London, 2004, p. 15; also pp. 142–3 for William Cobbett's growing appreciation of it.

[93] Mark Philp, 'William Godwin's Diary', *The Last Stand: Napoleon's 100 Days in 100 Objects*, www.100days.eu/items/show/100, accessed 15 January 2019.

[94] Barrett Bryant, *The Code Napoléon: Verbally Translated from the French*, 2 vols., London, W. Reed, London, 1811 actually clocked up 500 pages; and George Spence, *The Code Napoléon: Or, The French Civil Code*, William Benning, London, 1827, 600 pages. It grew fatter over the century: Charles Sumner Lobingier, 'Napoleon and His Code', *Harvard Law Review*, 32:2 (1918), pp. 114–34.

[95] *Morning Chronicle*, 7 October 1808; *Aberdeen Press and Journal*, 25 October 1809; *Morning Chronicle*, 26 March 1811.

and authority of one man'. It was the law work of a tyrant.[96] Parliament
discussed the Code Napoléon when contemplating questions of criminal evidence raised by the Election Bribery Bill; had it been drafted
'by those speculative persons, who, in comparison between the Laws
of England and the Code Napoleon, are of opinion that, in matters of
evidence, it is impossible to say which abounds with the greatest evils',
one Member of Parliament should not have been so astonished at the
bill before him.[97] The code evidently was discussed, in lawyerly and
governmental circles. The new law journals of the late 1820s (aimed
variously at the practitioner, professional and student market) treated
the code *as history*, tracing its reception across Europe over the past
quarter century. There was controversy over whether or not Napoleon
had only done with 'the indigestible heap of [English] laws and authorities' what Lord Bacon had proposed in the early seventeenth century,
and the Napoleonic Code was described as consisting of 500 'moderate
octavo pages' – but these law journals appeared too late for Godwin
to have taken note of them.[98] Radical British voices lauded the code
for its simplicity and popularity from about 1810 onwards, and for the
way in which, as William Cobbett put it in 1812, it knew 'nothing at
all of all *religious distinctions*'.[99] Comparisons between Napoleon and
Cromwell were made when the English Revolution was compared with
the French – and with the Napoleonic era.[100] But a recent account of

[96] *Saunders Newsletter*, 2 July 1810.
[97] 'United Parliament of Great Britain and Ireland... March 25th', *Morning Chronicle*,
26 March 1811; *Cobbett's Weekly Political Register*, 6 April 1811.
[98] Stefan Vogenauer, 'Law Journals in Nineteenth-Century England', *Edinburgh Law
Review*, 12 (2008), pp. 26–50; 'Codification Controversy – Mis-Statements and
Mistakes of Mr. Humphreys', *Law Magazine; or, Quarterly Review of Jurisprudence*,
1:3 (1828–1829), pp. 613–37.
[99] Semmel, *Napoleon and the British*, pp. 143–5; Stuart Semmel, 'British Uses for
Napoleon', *MLN*, 120:4 (2005), pp. 733–46.
[100] Peter J. Kitson, '"Not a reforming patriot, but an ambitious tyrant": Representations of
Cromwell and the English Republic in the late Eighteenth and early Nineteenth centuries', Timothy Morton and Nigel Smith (eds.), *Radicalism in British Literary Culture, 1650–
1830: From Revolution to Revolution*, Cambridge University Press, 2002, pp. 183–200;
for William Cobbett's Napoleon *as* Cromwell, Jon Mee, 'William Cobbett, John Clare
and the Agrarian Politics of the English Revolution', idem. pp. 167–82. Comparison
between the two was made in a review of John Lingard, *A History of England, from the
First Invasion to the Twenty Seventh Year of Charles II*, in *The Monthly Review from January
to April Inclusive*, 10:43 (1829), pp. 389–95. Here the Napoleonic Code was described as
'one of the noblest and most salutary products of the human mind'; Thomas Babbington
Macaulay's review of *Hallam's Constitutional History of England*, in the *Edinburgh Review*,
1828 (repr. Baron Thomas Babbington Macaulay, *Critical, Historical, and Miscellaneous
Essays and Poems*, Vol I, Carey, Philadelphia, PA, 1841), declared that 'In the general
spirit and character of his administration, we think Cromwell far superior to Napoleon' –
but does not discuss the law of the Commonwealth or the Napoleonic Code.

Napoleon's reception and reputation in turn-of-the-century Britain, does not mention his law making at all.[101] Nevertheless, Godwin's appreciation of the Commonwealth law pocket-book that never was may well have derived from appreciation of a system of law written down, classified, indexed, easy to understand – not *endless*, and incomprehensible, as was English judge–made common law.[102]

Like all historians, Godwin did not know precisely how his own historical tale of the Commonwealth of England would be unravelled to form the new fabric of some later historian's argument (he must have known that it *would be* unravelled, just as he had unravelled so many earlier histories of the period). He did not know that, a century on, the conclusion about the abandoned law reform projects of the Commonwealth would be that although all was undone upon the Restoration, the reforms of Charles II owed much to Commonwealth example; that constitutional developments of the period influenced American and US law making; that though the pocket-book constitution may have been unworkable in England, it had resonances elsewhere, and indeed, that in the United Kingdom the 'negative accomplishments [of the Commonwealth and Protectorate] have been permanent'. These accomplishments were: that there was to be no more absolute monarchy, and that no branch of government stood above the supreme authority of Parliament.[103] Neither were the legal punishments that a succession of Interregnum parliaments sought to do away with the 'few anomalies' of nineteenth-century commentators: 'such things as *peine fort et dure* and the burning of women at the stake', which they proposed to abolish, were more than anomalies.[104] The provisions for torturing a prisoner if he or she did not enter a plea, and the execution by burning of a married woman found guilty of the petty treason of murdering her husband, were not proscribed until the later eighteenth century.

Had Godwin wanted to understand his growing attraction to the law, he might have found it under the rubric of necessity. In the 1650s, lawyers maintained a powerful grip on legal business and on theoretical

---

[101] Peter Hicks, 'Late 18th-Century and Very Early 19th-Century British Writings on Napoleon: Myth and History', *La Fondation Napoléon/Napoleonica. La Revue*, 9:3 (2010), pp. 105–71.

[102] Yet radical historians appear to like the idea of all manner of pocket-book: publicity for *The Permanent Guillotine. Writings of the Sans-Culottes* (ed. and trans. by Mitchell Abidor), PM Press, Oakland, CA, 2018, proclaims 'New Revolutionary Pocket Book!' It is 160 pages long. Which *is* pretty short, compared with the Code Napoléon.

[103] Brown, 'The Law of England', pp. 381–2.

[104] Ibid., p. 381.

arguments in which legal principles manifested themselves as political argument. Lawyers proclaimed that government by a single person (that is, Oliver, Lord Protector) was in accordance with law; juries were instructed that treason was a crime, not only against a king, but also against any supreme magistrate. When Cromwell died, it was said in Parliament that, as rebellion against him was a crime, he had been to all intents and purposes a king. But it was acutely a historian's problem that so many law proposals and projects did *not* come to pass, were *not* actually enacted by the ten parliaments that sat between 1640 and 1661. As a historian, Godwin focused on the law he *could* describe, as event or happening or development; the end of his journey through the historical record was not the historian's but the legal theorist's or philosopher's claim that 'the government of Cromwel was in a very imperfect degree a government according to law'. But discovering the ways in which that was – and was bound to be – the case warmed his historian's heart towards the law, to the measure of a little pocket-book.

An Ending: Not a Story

Amazing, really. The processes of law. So unruffled and so unperturbed. They just go on and on, with the same basic data, no matter what happens after the case is set in motion.

Margaret Drabble, *The Needle's Eye* (1972), Penguin, 1973, p. 334.

But the law of England is technical…

William Godwin, *Commonwealth III*, pp. 100–1.

In the high days of narrative theory and narratology, in the 1980s, when stories were told about stories across all the human and social sciences, there were the most minimum requirements of 'a narrative' to be one.[1] 'The ball bounced' was considered to be a narrative: *Once upon a time there was a ball; it bounced; now it is no longer bouncing/has stopped bouncing/has returned to the state it was in at the beginning, Once Upon a Time. The End.* It hadn't always been there, or existed as a ball, but it did/is now, in this narrative. Then it bounced. Then it ceased to bounce/no longer bounced/bounced no more. You could do the same with the archetypal narrative The Cat Sat on the Mat, or at least as far as *The Cat Sat,* but maybe not with the *on the Mat* part, for that introduced a whole other story element, which was The Story of the Mat, its genealogy and history, the question of its intentionality and will (did The Mat want to be sat on, eternally, by The Cat? Is The Cat still there?). Obeying the laws of physics, a ball does stop bouncing, quite quickly, but a cat might sit there until kingdom come or until the cat expired. *The Cat Sat on the Mat and then Stopped Sitting on the Mat* (just walked away; died) is too wild and complex a series of events for this narratology to contain. What happens to the object, The Mat, when The Cat, the subject of the utterance, dies? And why The Mat? What's

---

[1] The great marker of this interest is Jerome Bruner, *Making Stories: Law, Literature, Life,* Harvard University Press, Cambridge, MA, and London, 2002. Also Anthony G. Amsterdam and Jerome Bruner (eds.), *Minding the Law,* Harvard University Press, Cambridge, MA, 2002.

it doing here? Why this Mat rather than another mat? And once you ask that, you have to ask the same questions about The Cat. Why sit on *this* mat? Why sit on a mat at all? Whilst we're at it, let's question both 'on' (why not 'beside'?) and 'mat' (why not Persian carpet, car bonnet, drain cover, to name but three of the thousand places the cat could have sat?). And why sitting and not lying or lounging? Such minute and troublesome questions – questions concerning the irreducibility of physics and biology: gravity, force, and motion; endurance; growth, decline, and death; to say nothing of will and intention and anthropomorphism…! And in the last alternatives, questions concerning poetics, and the whys and wherefores of the images writers use to conjure the world before the eyes of their readers.

Historians – some historians (maybe *historiographers* would be better, for they were interested in the theory of the thing) – *were* compelled by the idea of narrative and narrative theory. Indeed, by the beginning of the new century, twenty years worth of their fascination with the narratologists and their account of historical thinking and writing could be brought together in a compendious account.[2] We do not know if practising lawyers (solicitors, barristers, judges) were as interested in questions of narrative as legal philosophers and theorists were. The enthusiasm of law *practitioners* for narrative theory appears to have been as muted as it was among practising academic historians, though, like most young historians taking courses in historiography, law students encountered such ideas during their education, from about 2000 onwards.[3] But among rhetoricians, literary theorists, and linguists, interest in the law as narrative was not at all muted. Peter Brooks' and Paul Gewirtz's edited collection *Law's Stories: Narrative and Rhetoric in the Law* (1996) accounts for the law as a form of narrative exchange, explanation, and performance.[4] Here are the competing narratives of prosecution and defence;

---

[2] Alun Munslow, *Narrative and History*, Palgrave Macmillan, Basingstoke, 2007; Anne Rigney, 'History as Text: Narrative Theory and History', Nancy Partner and Sarah Foot (eds.), *The SAGE Handbook of Historical Theory*, London, 2012, pp. 183–201.

[3] Maksymilian Del Mar and Michael Lobban, *Law in Theory and History: New Essays on a Neglected Dialogue*, Hart, London, 2016; Bernard S. Jackson, 'Narrative Theories and Legal Discourse', Cristopher Nash (ed.), *Narrative in Culture: The Uses of Storytelling in the Sciences, Philosophy and Literature*, Routledge, London, 2005; 'Teaching the Narrative Power of the Law: Program in Law and Humanities Sets Legal Study in Broad Context', University of Virginia School of Law, www.law.virginia.edu/html/alumni/uvalawyer/f05/humanities.htm, accessed 5 February 2018; Philip Meyer, *Storytelling for Lawyers*, Oxford University Press, Oxford, 2014.

[4] Peter Brooks and Paul Gewirtz, *Law's Stories: Narrative and Rhetoric in the Law*, Yale University Press, New Haven, CT, and London, 1996. Also Peter Brooks, 'Narrativity of the Law', *Law and Literature*, 14:1 (2002), pp. 1–10; 'Narrative in and of the Law', James Phelan and Peter J. Rabinowitz (eds.), *A Companion to Narrative Theory*, Wiley, Maldon, MA, and Oxford, 2005, pp. 415–27.

appeal courts weighing up evidence to produce new narratives; to say nothing of the narratives told by defendants, plaintiffs and witnesses. Reviewing the book, a chief judge of the United States Court of Appeals first named Brooks' field as 'legal narratology', so this judge did read it, albeit as a sceptic.[5] And actual narratologists (actual narratologists, who work from a theoretical-linguistics perspective on text and transcribed spoken language) have been sceptical as well: They have recognised Brooks' *own* scepticism about whether the law constitutes a narrative, pointing out that he highlighted many problems with narrative reasoning when brought to bear on the business of the law.

'Narratives presume a logic of events that may not exist in real life', says Monika Fludernik. 'By forcing what happened into a Procrustean bed of narrative shape, by imposing the well-formedness of narratives on life, we falsify the real and may base our judgments on fictions that have no purchase on what really was the case'. She concedes that a criminal *trial* may be *thought of* as – may actually be – a narrative. Crime is something done – committed – by an agent; there are witness reports, interrogations and confessions to tell of this; at trial, pleas by prosecutors and defence lawyers, judges' summing up, the delivery of their sentencing remarks and written judgements – all of the language they use constitutes a form of story-ing. But Fludernik has doubts about the law code (in countries that have such a thing) or statute law, as narrative. There maybe a deep structure of narrativity in an act of Parliament, somewhere, but the idea of direct agency is eliminated, particularly by the use of the passive tense. The 'discourse strategy' of a piece of legislation is closer to that of 'instructional texts … scientific or philosophical argumentation' than it is to, say, a fairy-story.[6]

Long ago, on a much grander scale, a lawyer (barrister then judge) William Blackstone made a story about English law by using items of its history (the reigns and proclamations of kings, invasions, conquests, battles) to tell it. There is no narratology that can deal with such a complicated series of events, selected out of time, though you might do something with its smallest component parts, like 'William the Norman usurped the crown'. The laws of England are the subject of Blackstone's discourse, but they are not an agent – do not have agency – and the whole drive of the commentary is to remove them from historical time, make their 'first ground and chief cornerstone … general immemorial

[5] Richard A. Posner, 'Reviews: Legal Narratology', *University of Chicago Law Review*, 64:2 (1997), pp. 737–47.
[6] Monika Fludernik, 'A Narratology of the Law? Narratives in Legal Discourse', *Critical Analysis of Law*, 1:1 (2014), pp. 87–109. Also Jane B. Baron and Julia Epstein, 'Is Law Narrative?', *Buffalo Law Review*, 45 (1997), pp. 142–87.

custom, or common law, from time to time declared in the decisions of the courts of justice'.[7]

Though interest in narratology was muted among historians (as opposed to historical theorists/historiographers) *practitioners* of social history were highly aware of legal proceedings as stories or narrative sources. From the 1960s onwards, magistrates' notebooks, bastardy and settlement examinations, quarter sessions rolls and minute books, assize records, 'trew' confessions of the condemned, prison records, and the strange and bitter testimonary fruits of the Hanging Tree – all allowed social historians to rewrite the history of the poor in England. We knew full well that 'the last dying words' of the maidservant convicted of infanticide were not *her own words*; that often they were printed hours or even days before she mounted the scaffold and had already been read by the crowd waiting to see her swing;[8] that the words 'I told my brother-in-law as soon as I got home that the prisoner had used me very ill, but I did not tell him the particulars. I told my sister the same: two days afterwards I told my sister all the particulars' were written by an assize court reporter.[9] But a young woman said *something like this*; she has a *story* that the court record captures; we can embellish it, fill in the spaces, reconstruct a life lived in historical time; add it to other stories told by poor men and women, in and out of court. Social historians love legal records – a court report, a notebook like the ones a lord chief justice kept – because they allow them to reconstruct a personhood, an identity.[10] Social historians are far more interested in the possibilities this legal record offers for their own narrative – the one they will write, in some history or other – than in the narratological analysis of a few words that were probably not spoken in that way, precisely. Social historians love legal records because they are useful; their love is born of utility.

And recorded legal proceedings are as good an assurance as we can have that something did once happen in the world: a court sat, a young woman appeared and gave her evidence; friends went a-walking

---

[7] William Blackstone, *Commentaries on the Laws of England: Book I. Of the Rights of Persons* (1765), Oxford University Press, Oxford, 2016, p. 55.

[8] *An Account of the Execution of Mary of Shrewsbury for the Murder of Her Bastard Child; God's Judgement Upon False Witnesses*, Alston, London, 1775; Carolyn Steedman, 'Enforced Narratives: Stories of Another Self', Tess Cosslett, Celia Lury, and Penny Summerfield (eds.), *Feminism and Autobiography: Texts, Theories, Methods*, Routledge, London, 2000, p. 30.

[9] See above, p. 67.

[10] Carolyn Steedman, 'Lord Mansfield's Voices: In the Archive, Hearing Things', Stephanie Downes, Sally Holloway, and Sarah Randles (eds.), *Feeling Things: Objects and Emotions through History*, Oxford University Press, Oxford, 2018, pp. 209–25.

of an evening wearing their Sunday best (though whether that was on a Monday or a Sunday in April or May remains in doubt). This, I think, was William Godwin's continuing problems with the law he was so attracted to in *The History of the Commonwealth of England. It didn't happen* (or strictly speaking, didn't happen within the time frame – the historical period – of *Commonwealth*). It has long been argued that the Interregnum left fewer traces on the law than almost any other area of national life.[11] Law reform committees sat and proposed changes to the law were debated by a series of Parliaments; Godwin discussed some of these proposals in very great detail. Many of the reforms *did* come to pass, a hundred, two hundred years later, and thus cannot be seen to have had no legal effect, but they did not come to pass between 1640 and 1660. How can a historian tell of what *didn't happen*? The thing is impossible, as many eighteenth-century reiterations of Aristotle's third-century BCE statement of the case affirmed. Poets and other creative writers might deal in the never-happened, but historians cannot: 'their difference, according to [Aristotle] ... is not in the *form*, or *stile*, but in the very nature of the things. But how so? History only paints what has happened, poetry what might have happened*'; 'It is the end of oratory to persuade, of poetry to please, and history to instruct by the recital of true events'. Or, from another, severe typologist, 'the object of the poet is not to relate what has actually happened, but what may possibly happen, either with probability, or from necessity ... [the historian] relates what actually has been done'.[12] The differences were irreducible. Of course, Godwin the historian could have (though maybe not in the 1820s) devoted his enquiries to the history of law reform, the cultural history and political experience that dictated the ways in which successions of a Member of Parliament (MPs), high court judges, legal theorists and indeed, Oliver Cromwell, thought about the law and their own proposals concerning it. These things certainly happened. But that was not Godwin's chosen historical and scholarly task: He wrote a narrative history of the English Republic 'unfolding, according to the order

---

[11] Alan Cromartie, 'The Rule of Law', John Morrill (ed.), *Revolution and Restoration: England in the 1650s*, Collins and Brown, London, 1992, pp. 53–69; 66–9.

[12] *The Freemasons' Magazine; or, General and Complete Library*, Vol. 5, London, 1793; Vicesimus Knox, *Essays Moral and Literary*, 13th ed., Vol. 1, London, 1793, p. 211; Henry James Pye, *A Commentary Illustrating the Poetic of Aristotle, by Examples Taken Chiefly from the Modern Poets: To which is prefixed, a new and corrected edition of the translation of the Poetics*, John Stockdale, London, 1792, pp. 25–8 ('The Object of Poetry and How It Differs from History'). Carolyn Steedman, *Poetry for Historians; or, W. H. Auden and History*, Manchester University Press, Manchester, 2018, pp. 12–15.

of time, [its] ... causes, principles, and progress ...'¹³ He was a (willing)
prisoner of the narrative protocol he employed (it was the only one –
still is the only one) available, and narrative theory holds out no hope
and cannot help a historian like him. Or help us reading him, or help us
producing this writing – this writing here – about him.

What *has happened* in this here history is many people, from the seventeenth century to the nineteenth, interacted with the law, thought about
the law, talked about the law, joked about the law, loathed the law, used
its institutions and proclamations and statements to make something
happen in their own lives, or to think about their own life stories. Here,
an active relationship with the law has been the province of the poor
and middling sort (including middle-class writers) rather than the high
court judges, magistrates and legal theorists who also figure in these
pages. William Blackstone and William Murray, Earl of Mansfield (for
example), promoted and provoked the law, and wrote about it from a
position of authority. Their relationship to the law was different to that
of the subjects of its dominion and has not been much featured here.
It for those subjects of law's dominion that a historian might love it –
love the law, not as thing or entity in itself, but for the access it gives
to minds and hearts and thinking in the past. Historians love it for the
continual return of surprise at how much those people knew and understood the legal structures that shaped their lives – especially if those lives
were bound up and tied down by the Old Poor Law.¹⁴ Their law thinking is a fine means of access to *mentalité*, to their own understanding
of the structures that shaped their lives. How could historians *not* love
the examination by a magistrate on a complaint of slander? Not love the
formulaic narrative of the settlement examination? Enchantment also
comes from the very great difference between then and now; because
historians grew up and became historians in a polity where this kind of
law consciousness had been lost.

Law mattered to eighteenth-century people out of necessity, because it
was *there* – in their face – shaping and dictating the lives they led, the love
they felt, the labour they exchanged for livelihood. The criminal law and
the coercion of whatever 'police' existed in the eighteenth century apart,
it was available and on display, in magistrates' parlours, at sessions and

---

¹³ James Beattie, 'On Poetry', *Essays. On Poetry and Music, as They Affect the Mind.
On Laughter, and Ludicrous Composition. On the Utility of Classical Learning*, William
Creech, Edinburgh, and E. & C. Dilly, London, 1776, pp. 104–5. Here Beattie dis-
cusses differences between 'historians' and 'poets' (meaning all creative writers).

¹⁴ Samantha Shave's *Pauper Policies: Poor Law Practice in England, 1780–1850*,
Manchester University Press, Manchester, 2018, opens with poor and pauper law
knowledge.

assizes, and above all in the great, grinding operation of the poor law. You could not go down the Coach and Horses Clifton in 1803 without someone going on about some law story, or fragment of a legal tale, that they had heard in Sir Gervase's parlour yesterday, or from someone living over at Ruddington. A conventional way of locating the decline of this kind of law consciousness among ordinary people, by historians, is to look to the Poor Law Amendment Act of 1834.[15] Among its many provisions affecting the life of poor families was the removal of the right to parish settlement by service. We have seen how very much employment (service) contracts and circumstances preoccupied magistrates and pleaders in their parlours.[16] Settlement legislation and the judges' adjustment of it into case law in the higher courts had a great effect on a very large number of people. Settlement by service produced more litigation than any other aspect of the Poor Laws since their sixteenth-century inauguration. But after 1834, the particular kind of relationship to the law and the law consciousness that the poor law and settlement laws provided slowly declined. Another way of putting this is that people stopped knowing as much as they had perforce *had* to know about it to get through life.

Knowing about the law and the poor laws in particular was important; for a very much long time than 1601 (An Act for the Relief of the Poor) and 1834 (The Poor Law Amendment Act), there existed provisions *in* law, for poor people *at* law. However, *in forma pauperis* was not of much relevance to the majority of eighteenth-century poor people who found themselves face-to-face with a magistrate. There was no way of acting *in forma pauperis* – 'in the character or manner of a pauper' – in a magistrate's justicing room, for it applied only when a poor person had *initiated* legal proceedings, not when he or she had been brought there by the constable to hear the complaint of the farmer who said that he or she had not completed the hoeing of his field in the way agreed at the hiring. *In forma pauperis* referred to the ability of an indigent person to proceed in court without payment of the usual fees associated with a lawsuit or appeal. It was of ancient and complex origin; Edward the Confessor, that 'great judicial reformer', was given credit for important developments *in forma pauperis* well into the twentieth century.[17] It is interesting to note that

---

[15] 4 & 5 Will. 4 c. 76. An Act for the Amendment and Better Administration of the Laws Relating to the Poor in England and Wales.

[16] See above, pp. 135–50.

[17] John MacArthur Maguire, 'Poverty and Civil Litigation', *Harvard Law Review*, 36:4 (1923), pp. 361–404, 362. For a detailed history of *forma pauperis*, William Minchin, *An Essay to Illustrate the Rights of the Poor, by Law: Being a Commentary on the Statute of King Henry the VII. Chapter 12. With Observations on the Practice of Suing and Defending In forma Pauperis and Suggestions for Extending the Benefits of Such Practice*, Edward Dunn, London, 1815, pp. 1–13.

William Blackstone, on the other hand, gave *in forma pauperis* very few words in the *Commentaries* and named no kings from whose benevolent hand it sprang.[18] Readers of Henry Minchin's thoughtful 1815 book on the rights of the poor would be puzzled, thought its author, at the great gulf between the practice of modern courts in regard to *in forma pauperis* and the ancient rules on poor people suing and defending in the courts. The income bar was set far too low, he thought. As things were (in the early nineteenth century) a suitor must be 'denudated even so low as Ten pounds before he is permitted to have…benefit'. Why shouldn't he have benefit of *in forma pauperis* simply by showing that 'he has not the ability nor power to sue according to the laws of the land, for redress of injury, without impoverishing his family, and becoming burdensome to the parish'? If he happens to be 'possessed of £100 must he dissipate £95, before he can assert his rights?'[19]

Minchin believed another difficulty with contemporary practice was the position of counsel, attorney and clerk. It was always said that they could not refuse when asked to aid and assist a pauper (without very good reason, to be acknowledged by a court). But these men were unpaid; they were required to 'render advice and assistance without fee or reward'. Was it any wonder that a man with a living to earn and a family to support 'should perform indifferently what he undertakes reluctantly'?[20] Then is told the kind of attorney-story with which we have become familiar: 'a speculative attorney was appointed at his own suggestion to conduct the suit of a pauper, who placed in his hands the only £5 he had in the world, for the purpose of obtaining some official documents to elucidate his right to the matter in question. The attorney kept the £5 and deserted his client alledging that he could not prosecute the suit without advancing money'.[21] Minchin told many such attorney tales, but assured his readers towards the end that 'an exposure of the malpractices of a few, cannot be charged as an attack upon the general body'; but…wouldn't it be nice if such bad-apple examples promoted rectitude and honour in the profession? It was 'the *Poor* [who] are chiefly the sufferers by that spirit of competition in law, which whether encouraged by the designing and dishonest, or resisted by the honorable Attorney, too often involves in certain ruin such as cannot endure the expence of the contest'.[22]

---

[18] William Blackstone, *Commentaries on the Laws of England: Book III of Private Wrongs* (1768), Intro. Thomas P. Gallanis, Oxford University Press, Oxford, 2016, pp. 262–3.

[19] Minchin, *An Essay to Illustrate the Rights of the Poor*, p. 35.

[20] Ibid., p. 36.

[21] Ibid., p. 37.

[22] Ibid., p. 101.

The vocabulary of 'aid' and 'advice' permeates Minchin's book. By the mid-twentieth century, when *in forma pauperis* was still operative, it was discussed as 'legal aid'. The 1945 Rushcliffe Committee provided a truncated history: 'for probably more than 150 years there has existed, in many courts...a system whereby Poor Persons could sue or defend in forma pauperis. Originally, before an applicant could be admitted so to sue, it was necessary for him to swear that "He was not worth more than £5."...At a later date the limit was raised to £25. But it appears unnecessary to give any detailed consideration to these early systems...'[23] There were, however, several twentieth-century accounts of legal aid for the poor that gave detailed consideration to its medieval origins.[24] Visit www.parliament.uk/, and legal aid will be explained to you by reference to the history of the 'right of poor persons to sue in forma pauperis [which] is of very ancient origin...The right to litigate in forma pauperis was abolished by the Legal Aid and Advice Act 1949'.

The Rushcliffe Report detailed the operation of the early twentieth-century system by the Law Society and gave high praise to the way in which it and other voluntary organisations – Poor Men's Lawyer Societies, trade unions, and the settlement movement[25] – had attempted to provide legal advice for the poor from the middle years of the nineteenth century. It was a key proposal of the Report that the Law Society should continue in the operation of the new arrangements proposed.[26] This was to be a scheme administered by the state, local authorities, and 'the lawyers themselves'. Control of the scheme should be in the hands of the lawyers because the management of the present 'Poor Persons System' had been undertaken by the Law Society for many years; along with provincial law societies, it had gained experience which would be of inestimable value in administering the scheme Rushcliffe proposed. The scheme was to be answerable to the Lord Chancellor for its administration, and a central advisory committee was appointed to advise him on matters of general policy.[27]

---

[23] *Report of the Committee on Legal Aid and Legal Advice in England and Wales* [under the Chairmanship of Lord Rushcliffe], Cmd. 6641, His Majesty's Stationery Office, London, 1945, p. 1.

[24] Maguire, 'Poverty and Civil Litigation', pp. 361–404; A. H. Hassard-Short, 'Legal Aid for the Poor', *Journal of Comparative Legislation and International Law*, 23:1 (1941), pp. 27–37; Robert Egerton, 'Historical Aspects of Legal Aid', *Law Quarterly Review*, 61 (1945), pp. 87–94.

[25] The settlement movement was a reformist social movement beginning in about the 1880s and peaking in the 1920s in the United Kingdom and the United States. 'Settlement houses', staffed mainly by university graduates, provided childcare, adult education, and medical and legal services to the poor of a district.

[26] *Report of the Committee on Legal Aid and Legal Advice*, pp. 15–17, 23.

[27] Ibid., p. 24.

The Rushcliffe recommendations were enacted (in part) after four years of regular debate in the House of Commons. A new modern history of legal aid was written there, in Parliament, before and after 1945, in which (on my reading of *Hansard*) *in forma pauperis* was not once evoked – though Magna Carta was. The Rushcliffe report involved no new principle, said one MP: 'It merely reaffirms a principle established 730 years ago in Magna Charta: "To none will we refuse or delay right or justice"'.[28] He went on to explain why he emphasised the word *delay*: every petition for divorce that was currently held up by want of funds on the part of plaintiffs affected 'two, if not three, or more persons. The happiness and well being of thousands of men, women and children are involved'.

The divorce question framed the history of legal aid and advice produced in Parliament from 1940 onwards. Many questions were asked about the system devised in the army, navy and air force for giving 'assistance in litigation to persons in the Fighting Forces', to which the Rushcliffe Report gave wide publicity.[29] Questions about the workers and legal aid were also asked about the Home Front – could men ordered to resign in lieu of dismissal from the Metropolitan and City of London police take advantage of the Poor Person's Rules when taking a case to court? Might a Land Girl insured in her place of work be entitled to legal aid?[30] But the focus of these debates was divorce, sought by men and women of the poor and middling sort, at home and overseas. There were 900 applications per month submitted by the army and Royal Air Force (RAF) Legal Aid Sections in 1945. The number of applications received by the Poor Persons Committee of the Law Society in London during 1944 was 11,137, which was 'treble the figure of 1941. Of these cases, 97 per cent are matrimonial'.[31] One legal

---

[28] Commons Sitting of Friday 26 October 1945, Parliament 1945–1946, *Hansard* Fifth Series, Volume 414, 2349–472. www.legislation.gov.uk/aep/Edw1cc1929/25/9/, accessed 25 January 2019. The Great Charter was to be quoted again in Parliament between 1945 and 1950, but always in this truncated form, about delaying and denying. In full, the passage translates as 'To no one will we sell, to no one deny or delay right or justice'. All the conversation in Parliament was about the cost of the thing: how much it would cost the state to provide legal aid to those of limited income. It had been a long time since a judge had been accused of *selling* justice, to anyone (see above, p. 199, note 18). But the cost of getting before one, in fees to attorneys and counsel, had been considered the purchase of *the route to justice* for a very long time.

[29] Egerton, 'Historical Aspects of Legal Aid', p. 98; 'LEGAL AID FOR POOR PERSONS', Lords Sitting of Monday 18 February 1946, *Hansard*, Fifth Series, Volume 139, 623–66.

[30] Written answers (Commons) of Tuesday, 17 February 1942, *Hansard* Volume 377, 1659–1671; 'AGRICULTURE Women's Land Army (Accidents, Legal Aid)', Commons Sitting of Thursday, 14 October 1943, *Hansard* Volume 392, 1023–182.

[31] Commons Sitting of Friday 26 October 1945, *Hansard* Fifth Series, Volume 414, 2349–472.

historian believes that legal aid would not have been expanded the way it was in the post-war years had there not been such an enormous increase in the number of cases involving the dissolution of marriage, from the 1930s onwards.[32]

Could we please have the Rushcliffe Report implemented by legislation? asked one MP in 1946. The aphorism that 'justice in this country is open to everybody just like the Ritz Hotel' needed to be brought up to date, he said. In 1946, justice was 'open to the destitute, to the very poor and the very rich, but it is not open to those with limited incomes'. He thought of the man earning £5 a week; *he* could not get legal aid. And 'no one can get free legal aid in the county court or the coroner's court, where it is often wanted; but the man with a maximum of £4 a week can get legal aid in the High Court'. But take a £5-a-week man ('not very much today') who finds that his wife has run off with somebody else, leaving him with two two children. 'Perhaps after a time he finds someone else who is willing to make a new home with him. He goes to a solicitor and says he wants a divorce and finds that the cost of an undefended divorce will be anything between £60 and £70. He cannot afford that...If he does not know where his wife is, and has to serve the petition upon her by means of substituted service through the medium of a newspaper advertisement, he finds the cost of that advertisement is something like £25'. The point was that 'Justice simply does not exist for a person like that. He has got a right, but he certainly has not got a remedy'.[33] Moving that the Legal Aid and Advice Bill be read a second time, the Attorney General said that he was inclined to call it a charter: 'It is the charter of the little man to the British courts of justice. It is a Bill which will open the doors of the courts freely to all persons who may wish to avail themselves of British justice without regard to the question of their wealth or ability to pay'.[34]

Many other recommendations of the committee were introduced in stages between 1950 and 1961. But there continued to be many courts in which the Legal Aid and Advice Act did not apply, including county and magistrates' courts. The Rushcliffe Committee recommendations regarding legal advice (as opposed to legal aid) were not

---

[32] Christopher W. Brooks, *Lawyers, Litigation and English Society since 1450*, Hambledon, London, 1998, pp. 117–18; also Richard I. Morgan, 'The Introduction of Civil Legal Aid in England and Wales, 1914–1949', *Twentieth Century British History*, 5:1 (1994), pp. 38–76.

[33] Commons Sitting of Thursday 14 November 1946, *Hansard*, Fifth Series, Volume 430, 235–384.

[34] 'ORDERS OF THE DAY. LEGAL AID AND ADVICE BILL. Order for Second Reading read', Commons Sitting of Wednesday 15 December 1948, *Hansard Fifth Series*, Volume 459, 1177–352.

included in the act.[35] Certain categories of complaint were not allow-
able for legal aid. Unlike Clifton villagers in the early nineteenth century, those believing themselves to be slandered in the post-war years
could not drop in on the local magistrate for a good long moan, or at
least not at the state's expense, and not in a magistrate's court. ('We
think this scheme would be gravely overloaded if every slander which
was uttered across the back garden wall were made an appropriate
subject for litigation at the expense of the State. Similarly, we exclude
action for breach of promise of marriage ... ')[36] In October 1950, the
first month in which the legal aid scheme was operative, 9,060 applications were made for legal aid in the High Court.[37] By the end of the
first year of the legal aid scheme, of the 36,357 certificates issued and
awaiting issue, 29,365 were in respect of matrimonial proceedings in
the Probate, Divorce and Admiralty Division of the High Court.[38]
Most questions asked in Parliament about legal aid between 1950 and
1955 were to do with divorce, though the support of proceedings in
rent tribunals, benefits claims under national insurance and pensions
legislation, and the rights of immigrants and settlers to legal aid also
preoccupied MPs.

Legal historians (and lawyers writing the history of their profession)
as well as journalists discuss legal aid as a pillar of the welfare state.
'The scheme was introduced as part of the post-war welfare state',
says Tamara Goreily.[39] Social historians, on the other hand, do not in

---

[35] Reginald Heber Smith, 'Legal Aid and Advice: The Rushcliffe Report as a Land-
Mark', *American Bar Association Journal*, 33 (1947), pp. 445–7; 'The British Legal
Aid and Advice Bill', *The Yale Law Journal*, 59:2 (1950), pp. 320–44; Tamara
Goreily, 'Gratuitous Assistance to the "Ill-Dressed": Debating Civil Legal Aid in
England and Wales from 1914 to 1939', *International Journal of the Legal Profession*,
13:1 (2006), pp. 41–67.

[36] 'ORDERS OF THE DAY LEGAL AID AND ADVICE BILL Order for Second
Reading read', Commons Sitting of Wednesday 15 December 1948, *Hansard* Fifth
Series, Volume 459, 1177–352.

[37] Commons Sitting of Wednesday 8 November 1950, *Hansard* Fifth Series, Volume
480, 911–1088; Written answers (Commons) of Friday 10 November 1950, *Hansard*,
Volume 480, 101–4.

[38] Commons Sitting of Monday 3 December 1951, *Hansard*, Fifth Series, Volume
494, 1995–2196. 'More than four-fifths of all the High Court cases to which the aid
is applied are matrimonial causes', Lords Sitting of Wednesday 21 January 1953,
Hansard, Volume 179, 1141–94; 1 Eliz. II.

[39] Emma Howard, 'Legal Aid Cuts: "The Forgotten Pillar of the Welfare State" – A
Special Report', *Guardian*, 25 September 2014; Goreily, 'Gratuitous Assistance',
p. 41; Alastair Hudson, 'Regeneration, Legal Aid and the Welfare State (1998)',
www.alastairhudson.com/legalsystem/legalaid&welfarestate.pdf, accessed on 25
January 2019; also *Towards a Just Society: Law, Labour and Legal Aid*, Pinter, London,
1999; Tamara Goreily, 'Rushcliffe Fifty Years On: The Changing Role of Civil Legal
Aid within the Welfare State', *Journal of Law and Society*, 21:4 (1994), pp. 545–66.

general have a place for it in their compendious accounts of the post-war Beveridge reforms.[40] The most recent historical account of the origins of the welfare state mentions legal aid not at all.[41] An earlier history concludes that whilst legal was a small part of a much broader series of reforms – a national system of social security, the National Health Service, educational reform – it was 'an area of social provision without a natural political "constituency" ... unlike issues of education or health, which implicitly concerned the vast majority of the population, legal provision was of much less general concern'. In this situation, the contribution of pressure groups and those with legal expertise became significant; 'policy-making concerning legal aid was left to specialist groups and organizations ... and other bodies largely composed of lawyers and other professionals with a direct interest in the system'.[42]

Similarities between legal aid and other welfare benefits were also discussed by parliamentarians between 1940 and 1950, and they too found the analogy between health and law difficult to sustain, not least because 'The Welfare State' was not yet in their vocabulary. There were always jokes to be made, as when one peer – 'borrowing a metaphor from the Health Service' – expressed his anxiety about 'everybody ... at the same time go[ing] and buy[ing] their legal spectacles at the public expense'.[43] Perhaps legal aid was to do more with the health of the legal system itself than that of the people? Surely it was 'very desirable, if our legal institutions are to develop healthily, that legal principles should be continually applied to the changing conditions of our increasingly complex society, and that all kinds of problems should come before the courts for free ventilation and judicial interpretation. It makes our legal system unreal if it becomes remote from the problems of every-day life ...' Did not the 'evolution and development of our common law and our legal institutions depend upon the fact that for generations the law has been concerned with the social and human problems that arise from the daily round of every-day life by all classes of the community'? But the health analogy *was* useful; the Member for West Derby conceded that 'there might he a flood of litigation as a result of this Bill, but if there is, that will only go to prove that for many years past a great many poor people

---

40 'Legal aid emerged as a small and unobtrusive part of the welfare state, but one in which, when it started in 1950, covered almost 80 per cent of the population', said Nicholas Timmins, *The Five Giants: A Biography of the Welfare State* (1995), Harper Collins, London, 2001, p. 172.

41 Chris Renwick, *Bread for All: The Origins of the Welfare State*, Allen Lane, London, 2018.

42 Morgan, 'The Introduction of Civil Legal Aid', pp. 73–5.

43 'LEGAL AID AND ADVICE BILL', Lords Sitting of Monday 27 June 1949, *Hansard* Fifth Series, Volume 163, 279–344.

have been deprived of the opportunity of access to the courts and of getting redress from grievances, injuries and injustices from which they have been suffering'.[44] It had been said in 1945 that 'legal assistance for ordinary folk... and an adequate scheme of legal aid must be regarded as an essential contribution towards improved social services'.[45]

In the era of decline in legal aid, from the 1990s onwards, legal historians had second thoughts about the pillar-of-the-welfare-state question. Less wary of ascribing purpose to historical actors than most historians are, Alastair Hudson said that it was 'to provide access to [some] few lawyers practising in the UK after the Second World War'. He had come to think that legal aid was not introduced as 'a means of supplying a further welfare benefit. If it had been meant to be a welfare benefit, it could be expected that it would have been linked more closely to the structures applicable to the provision of other welfare state benefits'.[46] Then the Legal Aid, Sentencing and Punishment of Offenders Act in 2012 removed many categories of law from eligibility for funding. In 2013 and 2014, the number of civil cases granted funding for representation and/or legal advice dropped by 62 per cent. The 2012 legislation reversed the position whereby legal aid was accessible for all civil cases other than those excluded by the Access to Justice Act 1999. The categories removed from the scope of legal aid were: family cases where there was no proof of domestic violence; forced marriage or child abduction; immigration cases that did not involve asylum or detention; housing and debt matters, unless they constituted an immediate threat to a person's home; welfare benefit cases (except appeals to the high court); employment cases that did not involve human trafficking or a contravention of the Equality Act of 2010; and most clinical negligence cases.[47]

What historian – what History – could love this law? It was managed by lawyers; it affected a relatively small number of people; it was not

---

44 'ORDERS OF THE DAY LEGAL AID AND ADVICE BILL Order for Second Reading read', Commons Sitting of Wednesday 15 December 1948, *Hansard* Fifth Series, Volume 459, 1177–352.

45 Commons Sitting of Friday 26 October 1945, *Hansard* Fifth Series, Volume 414, 2349–472.

46 Hudson, *Towards a Just Society*, p. 21.

47 Howard, 'Legal Aid Cuts'; Legal Aid, Sentencing and Punishment of Offenders Act 2012 (49 Eliz. II, c. 10). www.legislation.gov.uk/ukpga/2012/10/contents/enacted, accessed on 27 January 2019; 'Legal aid statistics: April 2013 to March 2014', www.gov.uk/government/statistics/legal-aid-statistics-april-2013-to-march-2014, accessed on 27 January 2019. This account from Emma Howard's *Guardian* datablog: www.theguardian.com/law/datablog/2014/sep/09/legal-aid-in-england-and-wales-what-is-changing, accessed on 27 January 2019. Also, *Justice Denied: Impacts of the Government's Reforms to Legal Aid and Court Services on Access to Justice*, TUC, London, 2016.

universally accessed, as were the health and education services[48]...;
it was not 'owned' by the people, as the National Health Service is
believed to be owned.[49] It is as difficult to write about *historically* as
William Godwin found the legal aspects of the Commonwealth and
Protectorate difficult to write about: because *they didn't happen*. And
anyway, narratology demands of legal and historical narratives (of all
narratives) that something happens in the world: some ball bouncing,
somewhere. Anything you do write about the history of legal aid provision will have History's ziggy shape, for it is about how people got and
get hurt. But legal aid provision did not contain within it its own demise
except in the most strict fiscal sense, *not* because it wasn't possible to
tell it as a Marxist story of proclamation/revocation, revolution/counter-
revolution, but because...it never really happened, or it happened par-
tially, or its provisions were eroded.

And there are severer constraints than this on historians telling stories out of legal records. The narratives they purport to be are often not
true, in the everyday and historical sense of 'true' ('this thing, spoken
here, happened'). Sir John Baker has told us that we – historians – may
not be very interested in the legal abstractions that shape, for instance,
the medieval and early modern plea rolls (plea rolls were the pieces of
parchment recording details of legal actions in the English high courts).
Historians are interested in 'what happened to people in real life', he says;
not in the legal fact (or fiction) that if 'a plaintiff alleged a trespass to the
person on 1 December 1498 at Chesterton in the county of Cambridge
and the defendant pleaded not guilty, the jury would have to find for
the defendant even if the evidence at the trial showed a battery on 2
November 1497 at Combermere or even Oxford. The details of the time
and place were as immaterial as the details of the force and arms'. The
names of the people involved, place, circumstance, date were sometimes
irrelevant to the narrative deposited in the court records. He reminds
us that, as late as the nineteenth century, law students were still told by
an authority on pleading that a pleader might assign '"any time that he
places to a given fact; provided that it was not inherently impossible".'[50]

[48] Hudson, *Towards a Just Society*; Tom Smith and Ed Cape, 'The Rise and Decline of
    Criminal Legal Aid in England and Wales', Asher Flynn and Jacqueline Hodgson
    (eds.), *Access to Justice and Legal Aid: Comparative Perspectives on Unmet Legal Need*,
    Hart, Oxford and London, 2017, pp. 63–86.
[49] https://weownit.org.uk/public-ownership/nhs, accessed 3 February 2019; John Henley,
    'A Portrait of the National Health Service: "It's almost like a religion"', *Guardian*, 17
    January 2016.
[50] John Baker, '"Authentic Testimony"? Fact and Law in Legal Records', *Collected
    Papers on English Legal History*, Cambridge University Press, Cambridge, 2013,
    Volume 3, pp. 1513–27.

Such records are 'a dangerous minefield…strewn with concealed traps for the historian who saunters into them without an understanding of the conventions of the system which produced them'.[51] What such legal documents do tell truth about is not an anterior social reality but the state of the law: they *do* tell law's story (or fiction).[52] We really shouldn't complain: did not Sir Edward Coke tell us nigh on three hundred years ago that we should not 'meddle…with the Laws of this Realm, before… [we] confer with some Learned in that Profession'?[53] And we must evidently abandon the belief, held by many historians of the European eighteenth century, that 'judicial records…created a space of captured speech' – that *the actual words* of young women seeking their settlement or complaining of assault are preserved therein. And maybe we should stop crying at the sad and desperate stories the records appear to preserve, maybe even lay off the tears provoked by Arlette Farge's *Goût de l'archive* and *Le Bracelet de parchemin* – provoked by her description of the Archives Nationales and the Bibliothèque de l'Arsenal, Paris, where she opened the police bundles that are records of suicide, carrying still the smell of the Seine water in which a young woman drowned herself long ago.[54] And there is always the practical solution proposed by Andrew Prescott: that *as historians*, we pay attention to legal records *as text*, and text as produced in society (in his argument, medieval English society); ask questions, for example, about the clerks who transcribed the records of law administration. 'Their concern' he says, 'was to ensure conformity with the correct legal form, and they would take short cuts and even invent details where necessary'. Administrative documents preserved in archives tell stories which are shaped by their institutional and governmental context and are 'as deceptive and full of invention as more self-consciously literary works'. We should know, as critics and historians, about this textual world where practices and assumptions were very different from our own.[55]

William Godwin explained to the readers of his *Commonwealth* that English law was 'technical'. All the law considered in his book was to be thought of as pertaining to a particular field of knowledge, bound by

---

[51] Baker, '"Authentic Testimony"?', p. 1515.

[52] Ibid., p. 1517.

[53] See above, p. 27.

[54] Arlette Farge, *Le goût de l'archive*, Editions du Seuil, Paris, 1989; *The Allure of the Archive*, trans Thomas Scott-Railton, Foreword by Natalie Zemon Davis, Yale University Press, New Haven, CT, and London, 2013; *Le Bracelet de parchemin. L'Ecrit sur soi, XVIII siècle*, Fayard, Paris, 2003.

[55] Andrew Prescott, 'Tall Tales from the Archive', *Cambridge Companion to British Historical Literature*, forthcoming. I am extremely grateful to Andrew Prescott for discussion of these questions.

its own specialist language; those wishing to understand it must abide by the language terms of the art or science of the law. The law required specialist terms to be understood and, though he did not say this to his readers, he had done his best to interpret those terms, and how they had been understood, in the period from 1640 to 1660 in England. Had he read Blackstone in preparing *Commonwealth*, as he had read the *Commentaries* for his *Cursory Strictures* thirty years before? Did he read the twenty-fourth chapter of Book II, 'Of Things Personal'? He had much to do in these years with the disposal of his own moveable property, and the attorneys who led him through the labyrinthine law of things personal. He was involved in regularising his widowed daughter's – Mary Shelley's – financial situation, but his main legal problem was the encroaching bankruptcy of his business, The Juvenile Library, which involved lawyers from at least 1817 through to the final declaration in 1825.[56] Blackstone's view from 1766 was cheerful, describing how different modern times (and modern law) were from that remote feudal period when the courts had 'a very low and contemptuous opinion of all personal estate, which they regarded as only a transient commodity'. There had been 'frequent forfeitures inflicted by the common law, of all a man's goods and chattels, for misbehaviours and inadvertencies that at present hardly seem to deserve so severe a punishment'. Now, with the rise of commerce – commerce being 'entirely occupied in this species of property' – and the greatly increased opulence of life, the law conceived a different idea of *things* because there were more of them; they were more valuable and valued than they had been in remote times. From reason and convenience and to meet the needs of a commercial society, the courts had adopted 'a more enlarged and less technical mode' of considering a person and his property. You might read the words 'less technical' in a spirit of irony if you were embroiled with the law, personally, intellectually, and historically, as Godwin was in the 1820s, particularly in the *persona* of historian, for all your efforts were to understand those technicalities and explain them to others.

You can, as a historian, make a narrative out of the law you find, as Godwin did, in *Commonwealth*. But you are faced with the technical barrier of the story that is already there and already told. Law's already told story comes from the English courtroom where the 'adversarial

---

[56] Charlotte Gordon, *Romantic Outlaws: The Extraordinary Lives of Mary Wollstonecraft and Mary Shelley*, Penguin Random House, London, 2015, pp. 471–2; Peter Marshall, *William Godwin: Philosopher, Novelist, Revolutionary* (1984), PM Press, Oakland, CA, 2017, pp. 336–61. I am grateful to Mark Philp for pointing out how much Godwin was in the grip of the law during these years.

regime of trial' holds sway (as opposed to 'the inquisitorial "quest for truth" of Continental law'). What determines the 'truth' of an English trial at common law is, in legal terms, 'the verdict given at the end, which retrospectively reinterprets hitherto ambivalent or conflicting evidence into a singular meaning which is inscribed as history' – a true story.[57] The history is already *there*, before the historian arrives to tell it, or, to put it as Rose Vassilou, protagonist of Drabble's *Jerusalem the Golden* did (as in one of the epigraphs to 'An Ending'), it 'just go[es] on and on, with the same basic data, no matter what happens after the case is set in motion'. Or as Laurence Sterne had it, the historian stands there watching 'a coalition of the gown, from all the bars of it, driving a damned dirty, vexatious cause before them, with all their might and main, the wrong way' – or any which way – to its end, which is that 'singular meaning ... inscribed as history' – before you get there.[58] In 1862, Anthony Trollope wrote a novel to explore all these questions, framed by the categories adversarial/inquisitorial, common law/codification, story-telling/truth seeking. He has one of his cast of legal characters say that 'If I, having committed a crime, were to confess my criminality to the gentleman engaged to defend me, might he not be called on to say: "Then, O my friend, confess it also to the judge; and so let justice be done ..." But who would pay a lawyer for counsel such as that?'[59] His attorneys and barristers all attend a conference at Birmingham at which the peculiarities of the English are gratifyingly demonstrated in a presentation from an eminent German legal theorist. His audience does not have high hopes of it: on the train to Birmingham one attorney thinks 'to practical Englishmen most of these international congresses seem to arrive at nothing ... [but words]. Men will not be talked out of the convictions of their lives ... no amount of eloquence will make an English lawyer think that loyalty to truth should come before loyalty to his client'.[60]

The what-might-have-been of the laws of England dissolves in a night-time scene in the hotel bedroom of the great Von Bauhr, who knows full well that the English lawyers who heard his lecture 'had regarded him as an impersonation of dullness'. Yet as he sits in his hotel room cosied-up in his old dressing gown 'there ran thoughts which

---

[57] Martin A. Kayman, 'Trials of Law and Language: *Caleb Williams* and John Horne Tooke', Monika Fludernik and Greta Olson (eds.), *In the Grip of the Law: Trials, Prisons and the Space Between*, Peter Lang, Frankfurt, 2004, pp. 83–104.
[58] For Sterne, see above, p. 17; for the 'singular meaning', Kayman, 'Trials', p. 104.
[59] Anthony Trollope, *Orley Farm* (1862), Oxford University Press, Oxford, 1985, p. 118.
[60] Trollope, *Orley Farm*, p. 165.

seemed to lift him lightly from the earth into an elysium of justice and mercy. And at the end of this elysium, which was not wild in its beauty, but trim and orderly in its gracefulness, – as might be a beer-garden at Munich, – there stood among flowers and vases a pedestal, grand above all other pedestals in that garden; and on this there was a bust with an inscription: – "To Von Bauhr, who reformed the laws of nations."' He loves everyone! – 'all Germans, all Englishmen, even all Frenchmen, in his very heart of hearts, and especially those who had travelled wearily to this English town that they might listen to the results of his wisdom'. He dreams of codifying all law, every nation's law – neatly, comprehensively – of something like a pocket book to which all had access – 'he loved the world, and that he would willingly spend himself in these great endeavours for the amelioration of its laws and the perfection of its judicial proceedings'.[61] He then departs the text, though not the imagination of his readers, who will remember his benevolent dream of *How Things Might Be* as they listen to the cast of English lawyers, first on the train back to London cogitating on how they might *get their clients off*, and then fretting and agitating and arguing and offering up willing blindness to the inequities of the English laws of property, probate, and evidence, through 500 pages.

You have to go on hoping for that one person (that one historian) to cross the moat, scale the walls, and say: *It was like this*. And would that be so difficult to do? The place is obviously fortified (high walls, moat) but it's not as impregnable to the imagination (to the thought of *doing something about it all*) as the castle at the top of the hill built in the legal reveries of Franz Kafka, Walter Benjamin and George Agamben. By use of Kafka's meditations on the law and by way of Benjamin's meditation on Kafka, Agamben flashes before us a picture of the time After Law. In '"the village at the foot of the hill on which the castle is built"' a newly arrived attorney leafs through the pages of old law books. Outside

---

[61] Ibid., p. 173. Trollope based these early scenes on the congresses of the National Association for the Promotion of Social Science, founded in 1857. Its inaugural meeting was held at Birmingham. It incorporated the Society for Promoting the Amendment of the Law, and there was much discussion of law reform at Congress (in the 1860s, some of it comparative), but Von Bauer is a fiction. 'Birmingham' is the very site of hard-headed empiricism: Louise Miskell, *Meeting Places: Scientific Congresses and Urban Identity in Victorian Britain*, Ashgate, Farnham, 2013; *Transactions of the National Association for the Promotion of Social Science, 1857*, John W. Parker, London, 1858; Christine L. Krueger, *Reading for the Law: British Literary History and Gender Advocacy*, University of Virginia Press, Charlottesville, VA, and London, pp. 201, 244; Coral Lansbury, *The Reasonable Man–Trollope's Legal Fiction*, Princeton University Press, Princeton, NJ, 1981; Glynn-Ellen Fisichelli, 'The Language of Law and Love: Anthony Trollope's *Orley Farm*', *ELH*, 61:3 (1994), pp. 635–53, for Trollope and the law.

in the street the children play with Law's discarded objects – bundles of parchment, old writs and depositions, perhaps – as they might with a cardboard box put out for recycling or an abandoned car tyre.[62] In Agamben's image, the lawyer and the children in the street are both playing with disused objects: studying old books is just as much play as kicking a cardboard box around the village square; indeed 'liberation is the task of play, or study'. The discarded law records and car tyre are 'found after the law'. And what is done – played – after the law 'is not a more proper and original use value that precludes the law, but a new use that is born only after it'. This is a place and state and activity After the Law.[63]

Agamben's foretelling of *After the Law* employs (or allows to be employed) a composite image that was never there in the first place, in Kafka. In Benjamin's essay on Franz Kafka, he asks us to consider 'the village at the foot of Castle Hill'; then, pages and pages away from this brief mention of The Castle, under a quiet lamp, the new attorney Bucephalus leafs over the pages of old law books.[64] If the reader imagines the new attorney doing this in the bar of The Bridge Inn or Castle Inn in Kafka's *The Castle*, it is because of the translation history of Kafka's earlier fable, 'The New Advocate'. In this fable, a new advocate arrives to work at a large law firm (a bureau, says Kafka's original German text).[65] In English-English the closest term for 'advocate' is 'barrister'; in any case, the new advocate is not an attorney. Things are further confused by translating 'law firm' or 'bureau' as 'the bar', as in 'The American Bar Association' or in the US and British meaning of 'the bar' as the legal profession as an institution (hence in English-English a 'barrister' as member of 'the bar').[66] Through these multiple translations and slippages (the latter term used in the spirit of 1980s narratology, with which this chapter opened!) between Continental, English

---

[62] The genealogy of this image is: Franz Kafka, 'The New Attorney', *The Country Doctor* (1919); Walter Benjamin, 'Franz Kafka: On the Tenth Anniversary of His Death' (1934, 1966), *Illuminations* (1970), Random House, London, 1999, pp. 108–35; George Agamben, *State of Exception* (2003), University of Chicago Press, Chicago, IL, 2005, p. 64. Also Kafka's parable 'Before the Law' (1915, 1919) in *The Country Doctor*, which finally appeared in *The Trial* in 1925, after Kafka's death.

[63] Agamben, *State of Exception*, p. 65; Catherine Mills, 'Playing with Law: Agamben and Derrida on Postjuridical Justice', *South Atlantic Quarterly*, 107:1 (2008), pp. 15–36.

[64] Walter Benjamin, 'Franz Kafka', *Illuminations*, pp. 108–35, 122, 135.

[65] 'The New Advocate' ('Der neue Advokat') is included in Franz Kafka, *Metamorphosis, and Other Stories* (2007), trans. Michael Hofmann, Penguin Random House, London, 2007, p. 159; 171–2 for 'Before the Law'.

[66] Alex Murray and Jessica Wyte (eds.), *The Agamben Dictionary*, Edinburgh University Press, Edinburgh, 2011, 'Study', p. 187.

and US legal systems and legal terms, the way is free for Agamben's readers to see the new attorney sitting in a quiet corner of The Castle Inn, pondering the old law books.

But there's no room in this inn to tell the joke that begins 'A horse walks into a bar'. It's actually the other members of the law firm (advocates, barristers) not drinkers, who – in Kafka's original story – don't mind too much the new advocate being there, despite his bearing a strong resemblance to a horse.[67] He *is* a horse; he is Bucephalas, the Great Alexander's horse, retired from the hurly-burly of the battlefield; retired from aiding rapine, pillage and conquest by *force majeure*. 'With remarkable insight, people tell one another that with society ordered as it is, Bucephalus is in a difficult situation, and for that reason, and for his historical role, he deserves compassion. Today – to state the obvious – there is no Alexander the Great'.[68] Having gone back – from his former life – going backwards in the old books – the new advocate is at the beginning of transforming 'existence into writing'. 'Reversal', Benjamin had said, 'is the direction of learning'. 'Under a quiet lamp, far from the din of Alexander's battles, he read and turns the pages of our old books'.[69] As a legal scholar, continues Benjamin, Bucephalus remains true to his trade, 'except that he does not seem to be *practising* [my italics] law'. That's something new in Kafka's work, says Benjamin, for 'the law which is studied and not practised any longer is the gate to justice'.[70]

[67] You can find fifty 'horse-walks-into-a-bar' jokes by typing the sentence into Google. The most common is Joke #6000 from https://unijokes.com/, accessed on 5 February 2019 . Michael Hofmann appears to suggest that you should actively find the joke: 'it is related ... that when some of ... [Kafka's] stories were read aloud, people – including Kafka – fell about laughing. He is often ... very funny'. *Metamorphosis* (2007), p. xiii.

[68] This is Michael Hofmann's translation for the Penguin edition of *Metamorphosis* (2007), p. 159. The translation of Benjamin's essay has the members of the bar telling themselves, 'with amazing insight, that Bucephalus' position under our present social system is a difficult one and that he therefore – and also because of his world-historical significance – deserves to be met halfway. Today, as no one can deny, there is no Alexander the Great'.

[69] In the newer Hofmann translation, the New Advocate 'turns the pages of our old folios'.

[70] Benjamin, 'Franz Kafka', p. 134. Benjamin makes comparisons here between the Kafka parables 'Before the Law' and 'The New Attorney'. In the former, a man from the country wants to gain entry to the law through an open doorway, but the doorkeeper tells him that he can't go through *at this moment*. The man asks if he can ever go through, and the doorkeeper says that it is possible but not right now. The man waits by the door for years; he bribes the doorkeeper with everything he has. The doorkeeper accepts the bribes so that the man doesn't think he hasn't tried. The man waits at the door until the hour of his death. With his last breath he asks the doorkeeper why, though everyone seeks the law, no one else has approached the door in all these long years. The doorkeeper answers *No one else could ever be admitted here, since this gate was made only for you. I am now going to shut it.*

Members of the law firm have no objection to the new attorney; they can see a use for him. The time of Alexander may be long gone, but people still know how to murder each other; 'nor is there any lack of skill at stabbing your friend over the banquet table with a lance'.[71] But the arrival of a new lawyer/advocate/attorney (what you will; it's a fable) in the village at the foot of Castle Hill, would provoke as much antagonism and confusion as the arrival of K. the Land Surveyor in Kafka's *The Castle*. In this text, people can see no use for a land surveyor. And in a tiny village polity which is governed through and by a Castle bureaucracy, there is no law. Or rather, Law is there, but does not figure; it's an inoperative Law. At one point K. the Land Surveyor remarks that 'I and perhaps the law too have been shockingly abused', a complaint which goes absolutely nowhere.[72] In the tales told to K. by various women whose families have mysteriously lost employment, property, honour and reputation through The Castle Administration, 'attorneys' are mentioned. 'We have some very clever lawyers here', says Olga to K. 'What kind of lawyers?', K. pertinently asks.[73] Not the kind of lawyer that appears in court, where witnesses have been summoned, and a magistrate or judge operates. There is no law apparatus *at all* in this village. Punished a family may be in Olga's account, but by the dream-like, menacing movements of a vast bureaucracy, not by 'the law'. This not a place After the Law; it is pre-law, or Before the Law; or the 'prehistoric world' that Benjamin points out to us, where 'laws and definite norms remain unwritten'.[74]

Not so with any of the villages in *History and the Law*, any village inn, or the alehouse that *may be* in the village of Stephen Dunn's 'History'. We are allowed to imagine an attorney walking into a bar in one of these places because of the translation history of Kafka's essay, which has just been recounted. In some of them, there *may have been* the same educated, juridico-political discussion of the new attorney's life and career as there is in 'The New Advocate'; there *may be* among the (imagined) drinkers men with parcels of lands to transfer, testamentary and probate

[71] Benjamin, 'Franz Kafka', p. 134.
[72] Franz Kafka, *The Castle* (1926), Oxford University Press, Oxford, 2009, p. 64.
[73] Kafka, *The Castle*, pp. 171, 186–7.
[74] Bejamin, 'Franz Kafka', p. 111; Gunther Teubner, 'The Law before It's Law: Franz Kafka on the (Im)possibility of Law's Self-reflection', *German Law Journal*, 14:2 (2013), pp. 405–22. For Kafka's own legal experience in pre-war Prague, Richard A. Posner, 'Kafka: The Writer as Lawyer' [review of *Franz Kafka: The Office Writings*, Stanley Corngold, Jack Greenberg, Benno Wagner (eds.), Princeton University Press, Princeton, NJ, 2009], *Columbia Law Review*, 110:1 (2010), pp. 207–15.

business to transact, a daughter or two to settle in marriage, and some new knitting frames to invest in. You believe that they are farmers, merchants, master hosiers...all with some property, all busy weaving together the threads of agrarian capitalism. They're not in a state *after* law; they're in the usual old state of exception, that condition of living seemingly devoid of law but 'so essential to the juridical order'; for some reason Law appears to be essential to that order, says Agamben; it seeks 'in every way to assure a relation with it', in order to preserve itself.[75] Down in *this* village, *After Law* may be in a process of becoming, but for the moment, there are wills to witness, land deeds to have drawn up, marriage settlements to dictate – to an attorney.

In the villages of Stephen Dunn's 'History' there is no need for attorneys, new or old. The people have no property to hold or dispose of. The law is the king, with maybe a lord chamberlain to expedite proceedings should you, on commission of some offence against his will, be brought before him. And yet you *know* the King's Law: it is in you; it makes you, defines what paltry personhood you may possess. When things become worse than they were before, you can conceive of conspiring to change them. Because Law *is*, and it is in you and you in it, you can imagine, out of a sense of legal wrong, crossing the moat, scaling the walls of The Castle. So too – much more so – with the poor and paupers, servants and textile workers of *History and the Law*, who knew enough about attorneys to consider paying one to get what they wanted if they could not find it in a magistrate's parlour. They may not have had the means to go to law, but they were interpellated by it; it defined and made them. It is 'everywhere'; if they can find the money and a lawyer 'they will fight for their rights by means of law'. If that's not possible, they will still feel a sense of *legal* wrong.[76]

Thompson wrote shortly before the time scholars started to frame the legal consciousness of the poor and dispossessed, past and present, as controlled by the binaries of power and resistance, hegemony and counter-hegemony.[77] *History and the Law* has detailed what some of the

---

[75] Agamben, *State of Exception*, p. 51.

[76] E. P. Thompson, *Whigs and Hunters: The Origins of the Black Act* (1975), Penguin, Harmondsworth, 1977, p. 261.

[77] Jean Comaroff, *Body of Power, Spirit of Resistance: The Culture and History of a South African People*, University of Chicago Press, Chicago, 1985; Sally Engle Murray, *Getting Justice and Getting Even: Legal Consciousness among Working-Class Americans*, University of Chicago Press, Chicago and London, 1990; I. Kostiner, 'Taking Legal Consciousness Seriously: Beyond Power and Resistance', Paper Presented at the Annual Meeting of the Law and Society Association, Chicago, May 2004, www.allacademic.com/meta/p116866_index.html, accessed 25 January 2016.

poor *did* by way of everyday resistance: make a joke, write a threatening letter or purchase a different kind of letter from a drunken copy clerk in a pub. They do not love this law, but they have its number; they know what it is *about*, and that it is the same for many of them. Out of their own experience of the Law, they hold up under it; they are holding on.[78]

---

[78] Mervyn Jones's novel *Holding On*, Quartet, London, 1973, proposes endurance – not giving in – 'don't let the bastards grind you down' – as a form of resistance in working-class communities, *c.* 1880–1960.

Bibliography

Archival Documents

Bodleian Library

MS. Abinger c. 15, 22 Apr. n.y., Joseph Johnson to William Godwin, Fol(s).: 20r & 21v.; William Godwin to? Joseph Johnson, 2 January 1797 [for 1798], Fol(s).: 86–7.

Birmingham, Library of

Archives and Collections, MS 3069/11/11, Birmingham Attorney's Day Book 1785–1790.

British Library

BL Add. MS 2446, 'Collectanea Hunteriana, Vol: XII Being Memoirs connected with the literary history of Great Britain', ff. 26–7.

Derbyshire County Record Office

M77 vol. 2, Parish Records, Ashover Parish Register.
Q/SO 1/9, Quarter Sessions Records, Translation Sessions, 1776.

East Sussex County Record Office

AMA 6192/1, notebook of Richard Stileman of Winchelsea, JP, 1819–1827.

London Metropolitan Archives

P74/LUK/111, St. Luke's Chelsea, Workhouse and Discharge Register, January 1782–December 1800.

Lincoln's Inn Library,

A.P.B., 19, Dampier Manuscripts, Easter Term, 1778.

B.P.B., 377, Dampier Manuscripts, 'Surrey. The King agt the Inhabitants of Thames Ditton'.

L.P.B., 104, Dampier Manuscripts, 'King agst. Inhabitants of Hulcot'.

Misc. Ms.592. Manuscript Diary of Philip Ward of Stoke Doyle, Northamptonshire, 1748–1751.

The National Archives (TNA)

ADM 1/1906, Captains' Letters 1780–1781.

ADM 25/101, Half-Pay Registers July–December 1781.

ADM 36/10121, Navy Transports.

ADM 51/982, Captains' Logs, pt 10.

ADM L/T84, Lieutenants' Logs, HMS Thames.

ASSI 21/38, Summer 1819, Crown Minute Book, Somerset.

ASSI 23/10, Western Circuit Goal Book, Somerset Summer Circuit 1819.

ASSI 24/18/3, Special Commissions 1830, Recognizance Book. County of Southampton. Callendar of the Prisoners, in the County Goal at Winchester, for Trial at the Special Session...December 18, 1830.

ASSI 25/15/16, Somerset. Felonies & Assgs Sumr: 1819, 59th Geo 3rd.

C 193/44, Chancery and Lord Chancellor's Office: Crown Office: Miscellaneous Books, 1738–1746.

C 193/45, Chancery and Lord Chancellor's Office: Crown Office: Miscellaneous Books, 1746–1783.

C 202/142/2, 3, C 202/149/2, C202/152/1, Chancery: Petty Bag Office: Writ Files, return of writs.

C 231/10, Chancery and Lord Chancellor's Office: Crown Office: Docket Books, 1721–1746.

C 231/11, Chancery and Lord Chancellor's Office: Crown Office: Docket Books, 1746–1763.

C 234/43, Chancery and Lord Chancellor's Office: Crown Office: Fiats for Justices of the Peace. Yorkshire (North Riding), 1706–1923.

HO 42/19/48, Folio 233.

HO 42/19/50, Folios 238–9.

HO 42/46/27, Folios 68–71.

HO 42/47/11, Folios 26–31.

HO 42/47/137, Folios 311–312B.

HO 42/47/142, Folios 323–323A.

HO 42/49/134, Folios 292A–292B.

HO 42/51/55, Folios 126–128B.

HO 42/52/108, Folios 265–268.

HO 42/52/121, Folios 292A.

HO 42/55/55, Folios 125–127.

HO 130/1. Hants. Report of Convictions &c under the Special Commission.

KB 16/18/1, Records of Orders Files, 17 Geo. III, 1776–1777.

KB 16/19/5, Records of Orders Files, 25 Geo. III, 1784–1785.
PROB 11/1106.
PROB 11/1142.

North Yorkshire County Record Office

QDO(S) Justices Sacrament certificates and oaths (1740–1741).
QJO Justices Qualification oaths (1745–1779).
QSB Quarter Sessions Bundles (1741, 1742, 1743, 1744, 1745, 1749, 1762).
QSM 2/22 North Riding Quarter Sessions Minute and Order Books 1740–
    1741, 1745–1749, 1750–1763.

Nottinghamshire Archives

DD 311/1–6, Diaries of Joseph Woolley, framework knitter, for 1801, 1803,
    1804, 1809, 1813, 1815 [photocopies]; DD 1704/1–5 [originals].
DDME 3/1–10, Attorneys Day Book… the predecessor of Messrs Mee & Co [of
    East Retford?], 1824–1884.
M8050 (1772–1812) M8051 (1805–1810) Notebooks of Sir Gervase
    Clifton JP.

Scone Palace Archives, Murray Family Papers, Earls of Mansfield

NRA(S) 0776, box 68, King's Bench Papers, 1782–1785.
RH4/151/1 'Miscellaneous papers relating to actions heard before Mansfield,
    c. 1742–1785'.

Shropshire Archives

1060/168–71, Justicing Notebooks of Thos. N. Parker, 1805–1840.
QS/3/1,1708–1800, Quarter Sessions Records, Minutes.

Somerset Heritage Centre

D\PC\hard.m/6/3/5, Overseers' Accounts and Rates, 1813–1822, parish of
    Hardington Mandeville.
D\PC\hard.m/6/3/27, Hardington Mandeville Bastardy Orders.
D\P\hard.m/2/1/2;   D\P\hard.m/2/1/4;   D\P\hard.m/2/1/5,   Hardington
    Mandeville marriages and baptism.

Stationers Company Archive

TSC/1/E/06/133, Register of entries of copies, 1795–1799.

Surrey History Centre

QS2/6 Surrey Quarter Sessions Order Books.
5568 Thames Ditton Parish Records, Baptisms, 1763–1887.
2568/7/4 Thames Ditton Parish Records, Poor Rate Assessment and Vestry Minutes, 1778–1796.
2568/8/4 Thames Ditton Parish Records, Overseers' Accounts, 1773–1805.

University of Nottingham, Manuscripts and Special Collections

Cl A 572/1–3; 572/2/1, Clifton of Clifton 'Solicitor's Accounts 1810–1812'.

Warwickshire County Record Office

CR3036/1, Wratislaw, W. F., Solicitors Rugby, firm's letter book 1825–1827.
CR3074/1, Bretherton's Solicitors Rugby, Daybook 1814–1818.

Warwick University Modern Record Centre

MSS. 369/1/1–152, MSS. 369/2/1–103, E. E. Dodd/E. P. Thompson research correspondence.

West Yorkshire Archives, Bradford District Record Office

16D86/1150, Sharp Bridges Accounts.

West Yorkshire Archives, Wakefield District Record Office

QS10/25 West Riding of Yorkshire Quarter Sessions, Quarter Sessions Order Books, 1767–1769.
QS1/107/3–7 West Riding of Yorkshire Quarter Sessions, Quarter Sessions Rolls.

York City Archives

Y/ORD/5/2/1/17 Quarter Sessions Minute Books, 1740–1749.
Y/ORD/5/2/1/18 Quarter Sessions Minute Books, 1750–1759.
Y/ORD/5/2/1/19 Quarter Sessions Minute Books, 1760–1769.

Parliamentary Papers and Other Government Publications

The Gazette www.thegazette.co.uk/.
Great Britain, House of Commons. Courts of Request. Abstract Return of the Courts of Requests... 1840 (619) XLI. 555.

Hansard Fifth Series, Volume 123.
Hansard Fifth Series, Volume 139.
Hansard Fifth Series, Volume 163.
Hansard Fifth Series, Volume 367.
Hansard Fifth Series, Volume 371.
Hansard Fifth Series, Volume 372.
Hansard Fifth Series, Volume 377.
Hansard Fifth Series, Volume 379.
Hansard Fifth Series, Volume 380.
Hansard Fifth Series, Volume 381.
Hansard Fifth Series, Volume 392.
Hansard Fifth Series, Volume 414.
Hansard Fifth Series, Volume 430.
Hansard Fifth Series, Volume 459.
Hansard Fifth Series, Volume 480.
Hansard Fifth Series, Volume 494.
Historical Manuscript Commission, *Report on the Manuscripts of Lord Polwarth Preserved At Mertoun House, Berwickshire... Presented to Parliament by Command of His Majesty*, Volume 5, HMSO, London, 1961.
Parliamentary History of England, from the Earliest Period to the Year 1803, XIX, 1777 to... 1778, London, 1814.
Parliamentary History of England... XXV, 1785 to... 1786, London, 1814.
Report of the Committee on Legal Aid and Legal Advice in England and Wales [under the Chairmanship of Lord Rushcliffe], Cmd. 6641, His Majesty's Stationery Office, London, 1945.

Seventeenth-, Eighteenth- and Nineteenth-Century Law, Literature and History

Account of the Execution of Mary of Shrewsbury for the Murder of Her Bastard Child; God's Judgement Upon False Witnesses, Alston, London, 1775.
Alinda; Or, the Child of Mystery. A Novel, 3 vols., B. & R. Crosby, London, 1812.
Answer to a Letter Addressed to the Dean of York, in the Name of Dr Topham, for the author, York, 1758.
Assigns of Richard and Edward Atkyns, *Baron and Feme; A Treatise of the Common Law Concerning Husbands and Wives*, John Walthoe, London, 1700.
Attorney, *An Attorney's Practice Epitomized; or, The Method, Times and Expenses of Proceeding in the Courts of King's Bench and Common Pleas*, 8th ed., Henry Lintot, London, 1757.
Ayres, William Thomas, *A Comparative View of the Differences between the English and Irish Statute and Common Law. In a Series of Analogous Notes on the Commentaries of William Blackstone*, for the author, Dublin, 1780.
Barrister at Law, *Legal Recreations, Or Popular Amusements in the Laws of England*, 2 vols., J. Bew and 11 others, London, 1792.

Barry, Edward, *The Present Practice of a Justice of the Peace; and a Complete Library of Parish Law. Containing the Substance of All the Statutes and Adjudged Cases*, 4 vols., G. G. and J. Robinson, Oxford and Cambridge, 1790.

Beattie, James, 'On Poetry', *Essays. On Poetry and Music, As They Affect the Mind. On Laughter, and Ludicrous Composition. On the Utility of Classical Learning*, William Creech, Edinburgh and E. & C. Dilly, London, 1776.

Beattie, James, *The Theory of Language. In Two Parts*, Strahan, Cadell & Creech, Edinburgh, 1788.

Beauties of English Prose: Being A Select Collection of Moral, Critical, and Entertaining Passages, Disposed in the Manner of Essays, Vol. 2, Hawes Clarke and Collins and 3 others, London, 1772.

Becher, John Thomas, *Observations on the Punishment of Offenders, and the Preservation of the Peace, Occasioned by the Trespasses, Riots, and Felonies Now Prevalent in the County of Nottingham*, S. & J. Ridge, Newark, 1812.

Being An Abstract, of the Several Titles and Partitions of the Law of England, Digested into Method. Written by a Learned Hand, John Walthor, London, 1713.

Bicheno, James Ebenezer, *Observations on the Philosophy of Criminal Jurisprudence*, R. Taylor, London, 1819.

Bird, John Barry, *Laws Respecting Masters and Servants, Articled Clerks, Apprentices, Manufacturers, Labourers and Journeymen*, 3rd ed., W. Clarke, London, 1799.

Blackstone, William, *An Analysis of the Laws of England*, Clarendon Press, Oxford, 1756.

'The Lawyer's Farewell to His Muse', Robert Dodsley (ed.), *A Collection of Poems in Six Volumes. By Several Hands*, R. and J. Dodsley, London, 1758, Vol. 4, pp. 224–8.

Commentaries on the Laws of England. Book I: Of the Rights of Persons (1765), Oxford University Press, Oxford, 2016.

Commentaries on the Laws of England. Book II: Of the Rights of Things (1766), Oxford University Press, Oxford, 2016.

Commentaries on the Laws of England: Book III of Private Wrongs (1768), Intro. Thomas P. Gallanis, Oxford University Press, Oxford, 2016.

Commentaries on the Laws of England: Book IV of Public Wrongs (1769), Intro. Ruth Paley, Oxford University Press, Oxford, 2016, pp. 49–61.

Commentaries on the Laws of England in Four Books. By Sir William Blackstone... the Twelfth Edition, with the Last Corrections of the Author; and with Notes and Additions by Edward Christian, A. Strahan and W. Woodfall for T. Cadell, London, 1793–1795.

Reports of Cases Determined in the Several Courts of Westminster-Hall, from 1746 to 1779: by the Honourable Sir William Blackstone, Knt, One of the Justices of the Court of Common Pleas: With Memoirs of His Life, 2nd edn, Revised and Corrected with Copious Notes and References, Including Some from the mss of the Late Mr Sergt. Hill, by Charles Heaneage Elsley, Esq, in Two Volumes, S. Sweeney, R. Pheney and A. Maxwell, London, 1828.

Bodichon, Barbara Leigh Smith, *A Brief Summary, in Plain Language, of the Most Important Laws Concerning Women, Together with a Few Observations Thereon*, Chapman, London, 1854.

Bond, John James, *Handy-book of Rules and Tables for Verifying Dates with the Christian Era*, Bell and Daldy, London, 1869.

Boswell, James, *The Life of Samuel Johnson, LL.D*, Vol. 1 (1791), J. Davis, London, 1820.

Bott, Edmund, *Digest of the Laws Relating to the Poor, by Francis Const*, 3 vols., Strahan, London, 1800.

Bronte, Emily, *Wuthering Heights* (1847), Penguin, Harmondsworth, 1965.

Brown, George, *The New English Letter-writer ... Agreeable to the Forms ... Executed by the Most Eminent Attorneys*, Hogg, London, 1780.

Brown, Joasiah, *Reports of Cases, upon Appeals and Writs of Error, in the High Court of Parliament; from the Year 1701, to the Year 1779*, 7 vols. (1779–1783), P. Uriel, London, 1783.

Bryant, Barrett, *The Code Napoléon. Verbally Translated from the French*, 2 vols., W. Reed, London, 1811.

Buckland, Alfred Cecil, *Letters to an Attorney's Clerk, Directions for His Studies and General Conduct*, for the author, London, 1824.

Burchell, Joseph, *Arrangement and Digest of the Law in Cases, Adjudged in the King's Bench and Common Pleas from the Year 1756 to 1794, Inclusive*, T. Jones, London, 1796.

Buret, Eugène, *De la misère des classes laborieuses en Angleterre et en France*, 2 vols., Paulin, Paris, 1840.

Burke, Edmund, 'Fragment: An Essay towards an History of the Laws of England c. 1757' (1757), T. O. McLoughlin, James T. Boulton, and William B. Todd (eds.), *The Writings and Speeches of Edmund Burke, Vol. 1: The Early Writings*, Oxford University Press, Oxford, 1997.

Reflections on the Revolution in France, and on the Proceedings in Certain Societies in London Relative to That Event. In a Letter Intended to Have Been Sent to a Gentleman in Paris, J. Dodsley, London, 1790.

Burn, Richard, *The Justice of the Peace, and Parish Officer*, 3 vols., A. Millar, London, 1762.

Ecclesiastical Law ... in Two Volumes, H. Woodfall and W. Strahan, London, 1763.

A History of the Poor Laws: With Observations (1764), Augustus M. Kelly, Clifton, NJ, 1973.

The Justice of the Peace and Parish Officer. The Tenth Edition, in Four Volumes, Woodfall and Strahan, London, 1766.

The Justice of the Peace, and Parish Officer ... The Twelfth Edition. In Four Volumes, T. Cadell, London, 1772.

The Justice of the Peace, and Parish Officer. By Richard Burn, LL.D. Chancellor of the Diocese of Carlisle, and One of His Majesty's Justices of the Peace for the Counties of Westmorland and Cumberland. The Fourteenth Edition: To Which Is Added an Appendix, Including the Statutes of the Last Session of Parliament (20 G. 3.) and Some Adjudged Cases. In Four Volumes, T. Cadell, London, 1780.

The Justice of the Peace and Parish Officer. The Fifteenth Edition, in Four Volumes, Strahan and Woodfall, London, 1785.

A New Law Dictionary: Intended for General Use, As Well as for Gentlemen of the Profession. By Richard Burn, Ll. D. Late Chancellor of the Diocese of Carlisle. And Continued to the Present Time by John Burn, Esq. His Son, One of His Majesty's Justices of the Peace for the Counties of Westmorland and Cumberland. In Two Volumes, T. Cadell, London, 1792.

The Justice of the Peace, and Parish Officer. By Richard Burn, LL.D. Late Chancellor of the Diocese of Carlisle. Continued to the Present Time by John Burn, Esq. His Son, The Eighteenth Edition; Revised and Corrected. In Four Volumes, Strahan and Woodfall, London, 1793.

Burrow, James, *Decisions of the Court of King's Bench upon Settlement Cases; from the Death of Lord Raymond in March 1732, to June 1776, inclusive... Second Edition*, His Majesty's Law-Printers for E. Brooke, London, 1786.

Byron, George Lord, *The Works of Lord Byron: Letters and Journals*, Rowland E. Prothero (ed.), John Murray, London, 1898.

Caldecott, Thomas, *Reports of Cases Relative to the Duty and Office of a Justice of the Peace, from Michaelmas Term 1776, Inclusive, to Trinity Term 1785, Inclusive*, 3 vols., P. Uriel, London, 1786.

The Caledonian Bee; Or, A Select Collection of Interesting Extracts from Modern Publications. With elegant copperplates, R. Morison, Perth; Vernor and Hood, London, 1795.

Chapman, Thomas, *The New Universal Letter Writer*, T. Sabine, London, 1790.

'Character and Conduct of an Attorney: To the Editor of the Legal Observer', *The Legal Observer, or Journal of Jurisprudence*, 8:203 (1833), pp. 72–3.

Chitty, Joseph, *A Practical Treatise on the Criminal Law*, 4 vols., A. J. Valpy, London, 1816.

Chute, Chaloner William, *Equity under the Judicature Act; or, The Relation of Equity to Common Law*, Butterworth's, London, 1874.

Clapham, Samuel, *A Collection of the Several Points of Sessions' Law, Alphabetically arranged; contained in Burn and Williams on the Office of a Justice, Blackstone's Commentaries, East and Hawkins on Crown Law, Addington's Penal Statutes, and Const and Nolan on the Poor Laws, in two volumes*, Butterworth, Clarke, London, 1818.

'Codification Controversy: Mis-Statements and Mistakes of Mr. Humphreys', *Law Magazine; or, Quarterly Review of Jurisprudence*, 1:3 (1828–1829), pp. 613–37.

Coke, Edward, *An Abridgement of the Lord Coke's Commentary on Littleton Collected by an Unknown Author; Yet by a Late Edition Pretended to Be Sir Humphrey Davenport, Kt. and in This Second Impression Purged from Very Many Gross Errors Committed in the Said Former Edition. With a Table of the Most Remarkable Things Therein*, W. Lee, D. Pakeman, and G. Bedell, London, 1651.

The Reports of Sir Edward Coke Kt. in English, in thirteen parts compleat; (with references to all the ancient and modern books of the law.) Exactly translated and compared with the first and last edition in French...To which are now added the respective pleadings in English. The whole newly revised, R. Gosling, London, 1738.

Coleridge, Henry Nelson, *The Genuine Life of Mr. Francis Swing*, W. Joy, London, 1831.

Colman, George, and David Garrick, *The Clandestine Marriage: As It Is Acted at the Theatre-Royal in Drury-Lane*, A. Leathley and 8 others, Dublin, 1766.

Const, Francis, *Decisions of the Court of the King's Bench, upon the Laws Relating to the Poor. Originally Published by Edmund Bott Esq. of the Inner Temple, Barrister at Law; Revised... by Francis Const Esq. of the Middle Temple*, 3rd ed., 2 vols., Whieldon and Butterworth, London, 1793.

Cooper, Miss, '–(now Mrs. MADAN) [written] in her Brother's Coke upon Littleton', Dodsley (ed.), *Collection*, pp. 228–9.

County Magistrate [Samuel Glasse], *The Magistrate's Assistant; or, A Summary of Those Laws Which Immediately Respect the Conduct of a Justice of the Peace*, R. Raikes, Gloucester and London, 1788.

County Magistrate, *A Letter Addressed to the Agriculturalists in General, and to the Magistrates and Clergy in Particular throughout the Kingdom, on the Subjects of Hiring, Service and Character*, Longman and Whittaker, London, 1821.

'Court of King's Bench. Attorney's Letter.–Probable Cause', *Legal Observer, or Journal of Jurisprudence*, 2:29 (1831), pp. 29–30.

Cowell, John, *The Interpreter, Or, Book Containing the Signification of Words Wherein Is Set Forth the True Meaning of All ... Words and Terms as Are Mentioned in the Law-writers or Statutes... Requiring Any Exposition or Interpretation; A Work Not Only Profitable but Necessary for Such as Desire Thoroughly to Be Instructed in the Knowledge of Our Laws, Statutes, or Other Antiquities*, F. Leach, London, 1658.

Cries of London, As They Are Daily Exhibited in the Streets; with an Epigram in Verse, Adapted to Each. Embellished with sixty-two elegant cuts. To which is added, a description of the metropolis in verse, E. Newbery, London, 1796.

Dalton, Michael, *The Country Justice: Containing the Practice, Duty and Power of the Justices of the Peace, as well as in as out of their Sessions*, Henry Lintot, London, 1742.

Day, Joseph, *Thoughts on the Necessity and Utility of the Examination Directed by Several Acts of Parliament, Previous to the Admission of Attorneys at Law and Solicitors; Together with Some Observations on the Constitution and Regulations of the Society of Clerks to His Majesty's Signet in Scotland, and on Several Rules of the Courts of King's Bench and Common Pleas Relating to Attorneys; The Whole applying to a bill proposed to be brought into Parliament for the incorporating and better regulation of attorneys at law and solicitors*, for the author, London, 1795.

Dialogue on Rick-burning, Rioting, &c. between Squire Wilson, Hughes, his Steward, Thomas, the Bailiff, and Harry Brown, a Labourer, C. J. G. & F. Rivington, London, 1830.

Dibdin, Thomas, *The Will for the Deed: A Comedy in Three Acts, As Performed at the Theatre-royal Covent Garden*, Longman, London, 1805.

Domestic Management; or The Art of Conducting a Family with Instructions to... Servants in General, Addressed to Young Housekeepers, H. D. Symonds at the Literary Press, London, 1800.

Douglas, Sylvester, *Reports of Cases Argued and Determined in the Court of the King's Bench in the Nineteenth, Twentieth, and Twenty-first Years of the Reign of George III, The Third Edition*, Strahan and Woodfall, London, 1790.

Reports of Cases Argued and Determined in the Court of the King's Bench, 4 vols., Sweet & Stevens, Milliken, London and Dublin, 1813–1831.

Durnford, Charles, and Edward Hyde East, *Term Reports in the Court of the King's Bench*, 7 vols., Butterworth and Cooke, London and Dublin, 1817.

Echard, Laurence, *The History of England: From the Beginning of the Reign of King Charles the First, to the Restoration of King Charles the Second. Containing the Space of Above 35 Years. Volume the Second*, Jacob Tonson, London, 1718.

Edgeworth, Richard Lovell, *Essays on Professional Education*, J. Johnson, London, 1809.

Enfield, William, *Observations on Literary Property (1774)*, The Literary Property Debate: Eight Tracts, 1774–1775, Stephen Parks (ed.), Garland, New York, 1974.

Excise [By Permission of the Honourable Commissioners of Excise], *Cases of Appellants Relating to the Tax on Servants, with the Opinion of the Judges thereon*, Office for Taxes, London, 1781.

Exposition of the Hair Powder Act, Setting Forth Its Legal Operation; with a Full Abstract of the Act; by A Barrister, G. G. and J. Robinson, London, 1795.

Familiar Summary of the Laws Respecting Masters and Servants, Henry Washbourne, London, 1831.

Fielding, Henry, *Tom Jones* (1749), ed. and intro. R. P. C. Mutter, Penguin, London, 1966.

Amelia. In four volumes, A. Millar, London, 1751–1752.

The History of Tom Jones, a Foundling... In three volumes, T. Longman, B. Law & Son and 14 others, London, 1792.

Fiennes, Celia, *Through England on a Side Saddle in the Time of William and Mary, Being the Diary of Celia Fiennes... (1662–1741) with an introduction by Emily Wingfield Griffiths*, Field and Tuer, London, 1888.

Figaro, *The Novelties of a Year and a Day, in a Series of Picturesque Letters on the Characters, Manners, and Customs of the Spanish, French, and English Nations... by Figaro*, for the author, London, 1785.

Fitzgerald, Percy, *The Life of Laurence Sterne, in Two Volumes*, Chapman and Hall, London, 1864.

Freemasons' Magazine; or, General and Complete Library, Vol. 5, J.W. Bunney, London, 1793.

Gentleman of the Inner Temple, *The Cases of the Appellants and Respondents in the Cause of Literary Property, Before the House of Lords: Wherein the Decree of Lord Chancellor Apsley Was Reversed, 26 Feb. 1774... with Notes, Observations, and References*, J. Bew and 3 others, London, 1774.

The Grounds and Rudiments of Law and Equity; Alphabetically Digested; Containing a Collection of Rules or Maxims,... with Three Tables... The second edition, T. Osborne, London, 1751.

Gisborne, Thomas, *An Inquiry into the Duties of Men in the Higher and Middle Classes of Society in Great Britain, Resulting from their Respective Stations, Professions and Employments*, 2nd ed., 2 vols., B. & J. White, London, 1795.

Glasse, Samuel, *The Magistrate's Assistant; Or, A Summary of Those Laws, Which Immediately Respect the Conduct of a Justice of the Peace*, R. Raikes, Gloucester, 1788.

Godwin, William, *An Enquiry Concerning Political Justice* (1793) ed. with an Introduction and Notes by Mark Philp, Oxford University Press, Oxford, 2013.

Cursory Strictures on the Charge Delivered by Lord Chief Justice Eyre to the Grand Jury, October 2, 1794. First Published in the Morning Chronicle, October 21, C. and G. Kearsley, London, 1794, pp. 20–1.

Answer to Cursory Strictures ... First published in The Times, 25 Oct, 1794, D. L. Eaton, London, 1794.

A Reply to An Answer to Cursory Strictures, Supposed to Be Wrote by Judge Buller, by the Author of Cursory Strictures, D. L. Eaton, London, 1794.

Things As They Are; or The Adventures of Caleb Williams (1794, 1831), Penguin, London, 1987, p. 196.

Caleb Williams; or, Things As They Are, 2nd ed., G. G. & J Robinson, London, 1796.

'Of Servants', *The Enquirer. Reflections on Education, Manners and Literature. In a Series of Essays,* G. G. And J. Robinson, London, 1797, pp. 201–11.

History of the Commonwealth of England, From Its Commencement, to the Restoration of Charles the Second, Volume the First. Containing the Civil War, Henry Colborn, London, 1824.

History of the Commonwealth of England, From Its Commencement, to the Restoration of Charles the Second, Volume the Second, Henry Colborn, London, 1826.

History of the Commonwealth of England, From the Death of Charles the First to the Protectorate, Volume the Third, Henry Colborn, London, 1827.

History of the Commonwealth of England, From Its Commencement, to the Restoration of Charles the Second, Volume the Fourth, Oliver, Lord Protector, Henry Colborn, London, 1828.

Collected Novels and Memoirs of William Godwin ... Volume 3 ... Caleb Williams, Pamela Clemit (ed.), William Pickering, London, 1992.

Grant, Alexander, *The Progress and Practice of a Modern Attorney; Exhibiting the Conduct of Thousands towards Millions! To which are added, the different Stages of a LawSuit, and attendant Costs ... Instructions to both Creditors and Debtors ... Cases of Individuals who have suffered from the Chicane of pettyfogging attornies . . .,* for the author, London, 1795.

Hale, Matthew, *An Analysis of the Law. Being a Scheme or Abstract, of the Several Titles and Partitions of the Law of England, Digested into Method. By Sir Matthew Hale, Kt., late Lord Chief Justice of the Court of King's Bench. The 2nd edition corrected. With the Addition of an Alphabetical Table,* Strahan, Tonson and four others, London, 1713.

Hands, Williams, *The Solicitor's Practice on the Crown Side of the Court of the King's Bench, with an Appendix Containing the Forms of the Proceeding,* J. Butterworth, London, 1803.

Hanway, Jonas, *Virtue in Humble Life: Containing Reflections on the Reciprocal Duties of the Wealthy and the Indigent, the Master and the Servant . . .,* 2 vols., J. Dodley, Brotherton & Sewell, London, 1774.

'Hardships of Lawyers' Clerks', *Legal Observer, or Journal of Jurisprudence,* 8:225 (1834), pp. 412–13.

Hargrave, Francis, *An Argument in Defence of Literary Property: By Francis Hargrave, Esq.*, for the author, London, 1774.

Harriet; Or, the Innocent Adultress. In two volumes, R. Baldwin, and J. Bew, London, 1779.

Harrison, Joseph, *The Accomplish'd Practiser in the High Court of Chancery. Shewing the Whole Method of Proceedings,... Together with a List of the Officers and Their Fees... the Seventh Edition... with Additional Notes and References... by John Griffith Williams,... in Two Volumes...*, T. Whieldon; and R. Pheney, London, 1790.

Hawkins, Sir John, *Charge to the Grand Jury of Middlesex*, Edward Brooke, London, 1780.

Haynes, Freeman Oliver, *Outlines of Equity*, Macmillan, London, 1858.

Hazlitt, William, *Political Essays: With Sketches of Public Characters*, William Hone, London, 1819.

Hill, Samuel, *Clarke's New Law List; Being a List of the Judges and Officers of the Different Courts of Justice... and a Complete and Accurate List of Certified Attornies, Notaries &c in England and Wales with the London Agents to the Country Attornies*, J. & W. T. Clarke, London, 1816.

'History of England, from the First Invasion to the Twenty Seventh Year of Charles II' [review], *The Monthly Review from January to April Inclusive*, 10:43 (1829), pp. 389–95.

History of Little Goody Two-Shoes; Otherwise called Mrs. MARGERY TWO-SHOES: With the Means by which she acquired her Learning and Wisdom, and in consequence thereof her Estate..., John Newbery, London, 1766.

Hobler, Francis, *Familiar Exercises Between an Attorney and His Articled Clerk*, J. F. Dove, London, 1831.

Huntingford, John, *The Laws of Masters and Servants Considered*, for the author, London, 1792.

Hurlstone, Thomas, *Just in Time; A Comic Opera, in Three Acts. As Performed at the Theatre-royal, Covent-garden*, Debrett, London, 1792.

Hutton, William, *Courts of Request; Their Nature, Utility, and Powers Described, with a Variety of Cases, Determined in that of Birmingham*, Pearson and Rollason, Birmingham and R. Baldwin, London, 1787.

Impey, John, *The New Instructor Clericalis: Stating the Authority, Jurisdiction and Modern Practice of the Court of the King's Bench: With Directions for Commencing and Defending Actions, Entring up Judgements, Suing out Executors and Proceeding in Error*, W. Strahan and W. Woodfall, London, 1782.

Inchbald, Elizabeth, *A Simple Story* (1791), Oxford University Press, Oxford, 2009.

J. B., *An English Expositor Teaching the Interpretation of the Hardest Words Used in Our Language; with Sundry Explications, Descriptions and Discourses*, John Leggatt, London, 1641.

Jennings, H. C., *A Free Inquiry into the Enormous Increase of Attornies, with Some Reflections on the Abuse of Our Laws. By an Unfeigned Admirer of Genuine British Jurisprudence*, Debrett, London, 1785.

Juvenile Miscellany of Facts and Fiction, with Stray Leaves from Fairy Land, Volume I, Houlston and Stoneman, London, 1844.

Keble, Joseph, *An Assistance to Justices of the Peace, for the Easier Performance of Their Duty*, for the author, London, 1683.

Kenrick, William, *An Address to the Artists and Manufacturers of Great Britain; Respecting an Application to Parliament for the Farther Encouragement of New Discoveries and Inventions in the Useful Arts*, Domville and five others, London, 1774.

Kilner, Dorothy, *Life and Perambulations of a Mouse*, John Marshall, London, 1784.

Knox, Vicesimus, *Essays Moral and Literary*, 13th ed., Vol. 1, Charles Dilly, London, 1793.

   Elegant Extracts; Or, Useful and Entertaining Pieces of Poetry, Selected for the Improvement of Young Persons, Johnson, Baldwin and 12 others, London, 1803.

Latitat, C., 'A Lawyer's Love-letter to his Mistress', *The Weekly Magazine, or, Edinburgh Amusement*, VI (1769), p. 402.

'Law of Attorneys. Attorney's Letter.–Tender', *Legal Observer, or Journal of Jurisprudence*, 4:95 (1832), p. 240.

'Law of Attorneys. Attorney's Letter.–Tender', *Legal Observer, or Journal of Jurisprudence*, 4:96 (1832), p. 255.

Law, Edmund, *Observations Occasioned by the Contest about Literary Property*, for the author, Cambridge, 1770.

Law Grammar; Or, An Introduction to the Theory and Practice of English Jurisprudence, Containing Rudiments and Illustrations, G. G. and J. Robinson and 4 others, London, 1791.

Laws Relating to Masters and Servants. With Brief Notes and Explanations to Render Them Easy and Intelligible to the Meanest Capacity. Necessary to Be Had in All Families, Henry Lintot, London, 1755.

Laws Respecting Women, as They Regard Their Natural Rights, or Their Connections and Conduct; in Which Their Interests and Duties as Daughters, Wives, Wards, Widows, Heiresses, Mothers, Spinsters, Legatees, Sisters, Executrixes, &c. are ascertained and enumerated, J. Johnson, London, 1777.

Leach, Thomas, *Cases in Crown Law, Determined by the Twelve Judges; by the Court of King's Bench and by Commissioners of Oyer and Terminer, and General Goal delivery from the Fourth Year of George the Second [1730] to the Fortieth Year of George the Third, the Third Edition with Corrections and Additions, in Two Volumes*, Butterworth, Cadell and Davies, London, 1800.

London Tradesman: A Familiar Treatise on the Rationale of Trade and Commerce, as Carried on in the Metropolis of the British Empire. By Several Tradesmen, Simpkin & Marshall, London, 1819.

Macaulay, Baron Thomas Babbington, *Critical, Historical, and Miscellaneous Essays and Poems*, Vol. I, Carey, Philadelphia, 1841.

Macaulay, Catharine, *A Modest Plea for the Property of Copy Right*, Edward and Charles Dilly, London, 1774.

Maguire, John MacArthur, 'Poverty and Civil Litigation', *Harvard Law Review*, 36:4 (1923), pp. 361–404.

Maitland, F. W., with Sir Frederick Pollock, *History of English Law before the Time of Edward I*, Cambridge University Press, Cambridge, 1895.

Marriott, William, *The Country Gentleman's Lawyer; and the Farmer's Complete Law Library … 4th ed. To which is added the … acts of Parliament … passed since the publication of the 3rd edn., viz. from 1801 to 1803*, F. C & J. Rivington, London, 1803.

Minchin, William, *An Essay to Illustrate the Rights of the Poor, by Law: Being a Commentary on the Statute of King Henry the VII. Chapter 12. With Observations on the Practice of Suing and Defending In forma Pauperis and Suggestions for Extending the Benefits of Such Practice*, Edward Dunn, London, 1815.

Mitford, Mary Russell, *Our Village: Sketches of Rural Character and Scenery*, Vol. 5, Whittaker, London, 1824.

Morgan, Lady, *Woman and Her Master*, 2 vols., Henry Colburn, London, 1840.

N. H. *The Ladies Dictionary, Being a General Entertainment of the Fair-sex; A Work Never Attempted Before in English*, John Dunton, London, 1694.

Noble, Mark, *Memoirs of the Protectorate-house of Cromwell; Deduced from an Early Period, and Continued down to the Present Time:… Together with an Appendix: and Embellished with Elegant Engravings*, for the author, Birmingham, 1784.

Nolan, Michael, *A Treatise of the Laws for the Settlement of the Poor*, 2 vols., J. Butterworth, London, 1805.

Norton, Caroline, *A Plain Letter to the Lord Chancellor on the Infant Custody Bill*, James Ridgway, London, 1839.

'Notes and News', *The Academy*, 101 (1874), pp. 395–8.

'Novels. ART. 20. Things As They Are; or, the Adventures of Caleb Williams. By William Godwin. In 3 vols., 12mo. 9s. Crosby. 1794', *The British Critic*, 4 (1794), pp. 70–1.

Pashley, Robert, *Pauperism and the Poor Laws*, Longman, Brown, Green & Longmans, London, 1852.

Phillipps, W., *The Principles of Law Reduced to Practice*. Hen. Twyford, Thomas Dring, John Place, London, 1660.

Phillips, Jacob, *A Letter from a Grandfather to His Grandson, an Articled Clerk: Pointing Out the Right Course of His Studies and Conduct*, George Wilson, London, 1818.

Piozzi, Hester Lynch, *Anecdotes of the Late Samuel Johnson, LL.D. during the Last Twenty Years of His Life*, T. Cadell, London, 1786.

Points in Law and Equity, Selected for the Information, Caution, and Direction, of All Persons Concerned in Trade and Commerce; with References to the Statutes, Reports, and Other Authorities, Upon Which They Are Founded, T. Cadell, London, 1792.

Present for Servants, from Their Ministers, Masters, or Other Friends, 10th ed., John Rivington for the SPCK, London, 1787.

Pye, Henry James, *A Commentary Illustrating the Poetic of Aristotle, by Examples Taken Chiefly from the Modern Poets. To which is prefixed, a new and corrected edition of the translation of the Poetics*, John Stockdale, London, 1792.

Reflections or Hints founded upon Experience and Facts, touching the Law, Lawyers, Officers, Attorneys, and others concerned in the Administration of Justice…, for the author, London, 1759.

Reflections on the Relative Situations of Master and Servant, Historically Considered, W. Miller, London, 1800.

Reithra, 'The Lawyer's Dream', *The Metropolitan Magazine*, 13:51 (1835), pp. 330–6.

Ruggles, Thomas, *The History of the Poor: Their Rights, Duties and the Laws Respecting Them*, 2 vols., J. Deighton, London, 1793.

Scott, John, *Observations on the Present State of the Parochial and Vagrant Poor*, Edward & Charles Dilly, London, 1773.

Sharp, Granville, *A Representation of the Injustice and Dangerous Tendency of Tolerating Slavery; or of Admitting the Least Claim of Private Property in the Persons of Men, in England. In Four Parts*, Benjamin White & Robert, London, 1769.

Shaw, Joseph, *The Practical Justice of Peace: or, a Treatise Shewing the Present Power and Authority of That Officer,...Compiled from the Common and Statute Law, the fifth edition...in two volumes*, Thomas Osborne and Edward Wicksteed, London, 1751.

    The Practical Justice of Peace, and Parish and Ward-officer: or, a Treatise Shewing the Present Power and Authority of These Officers,...The sixth edition, corrected and very much enlarged, James Hodges and Edward Wicksteed, London, 1756.

Speech of the Right Honourable John, Earl of Clare, Lord High Chancellor of Ireland, in the House of Lords of Ireland, on a Motion Made by Him, on Monday, February 10, 1800, J. Milliken, London, 1800.

Spence, George, *The Code Napoleon, Or, The French Civil Code*, William Benning, London, 1827.

Spence, Thomas, 'THE DERBY ADDRESS...', *Pigs' Meat; Or, Lessons for the Swinish Multitude. Published in Weekly Penny Numbers, Collected by the Poor Man's Advocate (An Old Veteran in the Cause of Freedom) in the Course of His Reading for More Than Twenty Years. Intended to Promote among the Labouring Part of Mankind Proper Ideas of Their Situation, of Their Importance, and of Their Rights. And to Convince Them That Their Forlorn Condition Has Not Been Entirely Overlooked and Forgotten, Nor Their Just Cause Unpleaded, Neither by Their Maker Nor by the Best and Most Enlightened of Men in All Ages... The Third Edition*, for the author, Hive of Liberty, London, 1795, pp. 230–5.

Sterne, Laurence, *The Life and Opinions of Tristram Shandy, Gentleman* (1759–1767), Penguin, Harmondsworth, 1967.

Stephen, George, *Adventures of an Attorney in Search of Practice*, Saunders and Otley, London, 1839.

Stewart, James, *Plocacosmos; Or, the Whole Art of Hair Dressing; Wherein Is Contained, Ample Rules for the Young Artizan, More Particularly for Ladies Women*, for the author, London, 1782.

Strange, Sir John, *Reports of Adjudged Cases in the Courts of Chancery, King's Bench, Common Pleas and Exchequer, from Trinity term in the second year of King George I, to trinity term in the twenty-first year of King George II... In two volumes*, for the author, Dublin, 1756.

Taylor, John, *Autobiography of a Lancashire Lawyer, Being the Life and Recollections of John Taylor, Attorney-at-Law... edited by James Clegg*, The Daily Chronicle Office, Bolton, 1888.

'*Things As They Are; or, the Adventures of Caleb Williams. By William Godwin.* 3 Vols. 12mo. 10s 6d sewed. Crosby. 1794', *The Critical Review, or The Annals of Literature*, 11 (1794), pp. 290–6.

Thompson, William, *Appeal on Behalf of One Half of the Human Race, against the Pretensions of the Other Half, Men, To Retain them in Political, and Thence In Civil and Domestic Slavery; in Reply to A Paragraph of Mr. Mill's Celebrated 'Article on Government'*, Longman and eight others, London, 1825.

Transactions of the National Association for the Promotion of Social Science, 1857, John W. Parker, London, 1858.

Treatise of Feme Coverts: Or, the Lady's Law. Containing All the Laws and Statutes Relating to Women, B. Lintot, London, 1732.

Trollope, Anthony, *Orley Farm* (1862), Oxford University Press, Oxford, 1985.

View of Real Grievances: With the Remedies Proposed for Redressing Them, for the author, London, 1772.

Wakeman, Sir Ofsey, and R. Lloyd Kenyon (eds.), *Orders of Shropshire Quarter Sessions*, 5 vols., for the authors, Shrewsbury, n.d.

Wallace, James and Charles Townshend, *Every Man His Own Letter-Writer*, J. Cooke, London, 1782.

Warren, Samuel, *The Moral, Social and Professional Duties of Attornies and Solicitors*, Blackwood, Edinburgh and London, 1848.

Wight, John, *More Mornings at Bow Street: A New Collection of Humorous and Entertaining Reports*, for the author, London, 1827.

Williams, Sydney Edward, *Outlines of Equity: A Concise View of the Principles of Modern Equity*, Stevens, London, 1900.

Williams, T., *Everyman His Own Lawyer, or, A Complete Law Library. Containing the Laws Affecting in Every Possible Circumstance and Situation in which Persons Can Be Placed in the Ordinary Occurrences of Life, with an explanation of the most frequent Terms of Law... Second Edition*, Shirley, Neeham and Jones, London, 1818.

Williams, Thomas Waller, *The Whole Law Relative to the Duty and Office of a Justice of the Peace*, 4 vols., John Stockdale, London, 1812.

Willis, James, *On the Poor Laws of England: The Opinions of Blackstone, Addison, Wimpey, Winchelsea, Young, Rumford, Estcourt, Gilbert, Stewart, Eden, Pitt, Nasmith, Townsend, Pew, Davies, Colquhoun, Weyland, Bate, Rose, Monck, Malthus, Whitbread, and the Society for Bettering the Condition of the Poor*, John Lambert, London, 1808.

Wilson, Thomas, *An Accurate Description of Bromley, in Kent, Ornamented with Views of the Church and College*, J. Hamilton and T. Wilson, Bromley, 1797.

Wit's Museum. Or an elegant Collection of Bon Mots, Repartees, &c. rational and entertaining. Many of which are original..., William Lane, London, 1789.

Wollstonecraft, Mary, *Thoughts on the Education of Daughters: With Reflections on Female Conduct, in the More Important Duties of Life*, J. Johnson, London, 1787.

An Historical and Moral View of the Origin and Progress of the French Revolution; and the Effect It Has Produced in Europe, 2 vols., J. Johnson, London, 1790.

Original Stories from Real Life; with Conversations, Calculated to Regulate the Affections, and Form the Mind to Truth and Goodness, J. Johnson, London, 1791.

A Vindication of the Rights of Woman: With Strictures on Political and Moral Subjects, J. Johnson, London, 1792.

A Vindication of the Rights of Woman (1792), Penguin, London, 1992.

The Wrongs of Woman; or Maria. A Fragment in Two Volumes, Posthumous Works of the Author of a Vindication of the Rights of Woman, in Four Volumes, Joseph Johnson, London, 1798.

Wollstonecraft Godwin, Mary, *Maria: Or, the Wrongs of Woman. A Posthumous Fragment. By Mary Wollstonecraft Godwin. Author of A Vindication of the Rights of Woman*, Printed by James Carey, Philadelphia, 1799.

Woman Turn'd Bully: A Comedy, Acted at the Duke's Theatre, T. Dring, London, 1675.

Zouch, Henry, *Hints Respecting the Public Police: Published at the Request of the Court of Quarter Sessions Held at Pontefract, April 24, 1786*, John Stockdale, London, 1786.

Secondary Sources and Other Modern Material

Abidor, Mitchell (ed. and trans.), *The Permanent Guillotine: Writings of the Sans-Culottes*, PM Press, Oakland, CA, 2018.

Adlington, Hugh, 'Restoration, Religion, and Law: Assize Sermons 1660–1685', Peter McCullough, Hugh Adlington, and Emma Rhatigan (eds.), *The Oxford Handbook of the Early Modern Sermon*, Oxford University Press, Oxford, 2011, pp. 423–41.

Agamben, George, *State of Exception* (2003), University of Chicago Press, Chicago, IL, 2005.

Aitken, Jo, '"The Horrors of Matrimony among the Masses": Feminist Representations of Wife Beating in England and Australia, 1870–1914', *Journal of Women's History*, 19 (2007), pp. 107–31.

Alberti, Fay Bound, '"An Angry and Malicious Mind"? Narratives of Slander at the Courts of York, *c.* 1660–c.1760', *History Workshop Journal*, 56 (2003), pp. 59–77.

Alpert, Herbert, and Gerald Thomas, 'Two Patterns of an International Tale: The Lawyer's Letter Opened', *Fabula: Zeitschrift für Erzählforschung/Journal of Folktale Studies/Revue d'Etudes sur le Conte Populaire*, 42: 1–2 (2001), pp. 32–63.

Amsterdam, Anthony G., and Jerome Bruner (eds.), *Minding the Law*, Harvard University Press, Harvard, MA, 2002.

Aurell, Jaume, *Theoretical Perspectives on Historians' Autobiographies: From Documentation to Intervention*, Routledge, London, 2016.

Austin, Frances, 'Letter Writing in a Cornish Community in the 1790s', David Barton and Nigel Hall (eds.), *Letter Writing as a Social Practice*, John Benjamins, Amsterdam and Philadelphia, 1999.

Aylett, Philip, 'A Profession in the Market Place: The Distribution of Attorneys in England and Wales, 1730–1800', *Law and History Review*, 5:1 (1987), pp. 1–30.

Bailey, Joanne, '"I Dye by Inches": Locating Wife Beating in the Concept of a Privatization of Marriage and Violence in Eighteenth-century England', *Social History*, 31:3 (2006), pp. 273–94.

'All He Wanted Was to Kill Her That He Might Marry the Girl: Broken Marriages and Cohabitation in the Long Eighteenth Century', Rebecca Probert (ed.), *Cohabitation and Non-marital Births in England and Wales, 1600–2012*, Palgrave Macmillan, Basingstoke, 2014, pp. 51–64.

Baker, John, '"Authentic Testimony"? Fact and Law in Legal Records', *Collected Papers on English Legal History*, Cambridge University Press, Cambridge, 2013, Vol. 3, pp. 1513–27.

Baldick, Chris, *The Social Mission of English Criticism, 1848–1932*, Oxford University Press, Oxford, 1983.

Balmford, Peter, 'Stephen, Sir George (1794–1879)', *Oxford Dictionary of National Biography*, Oxford University Press, Oxford, 2004.

Barber, Sarah, 'The Engagement for the Council of State and the Establishment of the Commonwealth Government', *Historical Research*, 63:150 (1990) pp. 44–57.

Barfoot, C. C., and Theo D'haen (eds.), *Tropes of Revolution: Writers Reactions to Real and Imagined Revolutions, 1789–1999*, Rodopi, Amsterdam and Atlanta, GA, 1991.

Barker, G. F. R., 'Best, William Draper, first Baron Wynford (1767–1845)', rev. Hugh Mooney, *Oxford Dictionary of National Biography*, Oxford University Press, Oxford, 2004.

Baron, Jane B., and Julia Epstein, 'Is Law Narrative?' *Buffalo Law Review*, 45 (1997), pp. 142–87.

Barrell, John, *Imagining the King's Death: Figurative Treason, Fantasies of Regicide, 1793–1796*, Oxford University Press, Oxford, 2000.

Barrell, John, and John Mee (eds.), *Trials for Treason and Sedition, 1792–1794*, 8 vols., Pickering and Chatto, London, 2006–2007.

Bartlett, Kenneth, *The Experience of History*, Wiley, Malden, MA, 2016.

Barty-King, Hugh, *Her Majesty's Stationery Office: The Story of the first 200 Years 1786–1986*, Her Majesty's Stationery Office, London, 1986.

Batho, Gordon, 'The History of the Teaching of Civics and Citizenship in English Schools', *The Curriculum Journal*, 1:1 (1990), pp. 91–100.

Beard, Mary Ritter, *Woman as Force in History: A Study in Traditions and Realities*, Macmillan, New York, 1946.

Beattie, Cordelia, and Matthew Frank Stevens (eds.), *Married Women and the Law in Premodern Northwest Europe*, Boydell & Brewer, Woodbridge, 2013.

Beattie, John, *Crime and the Courts in England, 1660–1800*, Oxford University Press, Oxford, 1986.

Beier, A. L., 'Poor Relief in Warwickshire 1630–1660', *Past & Present*, 35 (1966), pp. 77–100.

Belle, dir. Amma Asante, DJ Films, Isle of Man Film, Pinewood Pictures, BFI, 2013.

Benjamin, Walter, 'Franz Kafka: On the Tenth Anniversary of His Death' (1934, 1966), *Illuminations* (1970), Random House, London, 1999, pp. 108–35.

Bentley, Michael, *Modern Historiography: An Introduction* (1999), Routledge, London, 2005.

Bertelsen, Lance, *Henry Fielding at Work: Magistrate, Businessman, Writer*, Palgrave, New York, 2000.

Binfield, Kevin, *Writings of the Luddites*, Johns Hopkins University Press, Baltimore and London, 2011.

Bingham, Tom, *Dr Johnson and the Law*, Inner Temple London and Dr Johnson's House Trust, London, 2010.

Boyer, Allen D., 'Coke, Sir Edward (1552–1634), lawyer, legal writer, and politician', *Oxford Dictionary of National Biography*, Oxford University Press, 2004.

Brant, Clare, 'The Tribunal of the Public: Eighteenth-Century Letters and the Politics of Vindication', Caroline Bland and Máire Cross (eds.), *Gender and Politics in the Age of Letter Writing, 1750–2000*, Ashgate, Aldershot, 2003, pp. 15–28.

Brooks, Christopher W., *Lawyers, Litigation and English Society since 1450*, Hambledon, London, 1998.

Brooks, Christopher W., and Michael Lobban, 'Apprenticeship or Academy? The Idea of a Law University, 1830–1860', Jonathan A. Bush and Alain Wijffels (eds.), *Learning the Law: Teaching and the Transmission of English Law, 1150–1900*, Bloomsbury, London, 1999, pp. 353–82.

Brooks, Christopher, 'Litigation, Participation and Agency', *The British and Their Laws*, David Lemmings (ed.), Boydell Press, Woodbridge, 2005, pp. 155–81.

Brooks, Peter, and Paul Gewirtz (eds.), *Law's Stories: Narrative and Rhetoric in the Law*, Yale University Press, New Haven and London, 1996.

Brooks, Peter, 'Narrativity of the Law', *Law and Literature*, 14:1 (2002), pp. 1–10.

'Narrative in and of the Law', James Phelan and Peter J. Rabinowitz (eds.), *A Companion to Narrative Theory*, Wiley, Maldon, MA, and Oxford, 2005, pp. 415–27.

Brown, Robert C., 'The Law of England During the Period Commonwealth', *Indiana Law Journal*, 6:6 (1931), pp. 359–82.

Brown, Roger L., 'John Hughes, Attorney', *Montgomeryshire Collections*, 92 (2004), pp. 79–85.

Bruner, Jerome, *Making Stories: Law, Literature, Life*, Harvard University Press, Cambridge, MA, and London, 2002.

Bugg, John, *The Joseph Johnson Letterbook*, Oxford University Press, Oxford, 2016.

Byrne, Paula, *Belle: The True Story of Dido Belle*, William Collins, London, 2014.

Campbell, Elaine, 'Exploring Autoethnography as a Method and Methodology in Legal Education Research', *Asian Journal of Legal Education*, 3:1 (2015), pp. 95–105.

Cannon, John, 'Lyttelton, Thomas, second Baron Lyttelton (1744–1779)', H. C. G. Matthew and Brian Harrison (eds.), *Oxford Dictionary of National Biography*, Oxford University Press, Oxford, 2004.

Carlile, Diane, '"A comon and sottish drunkard you have been": Prosecutions for Drunkenness in the York Courts c. 1660–1725', *York Historian*, 16 (1999), pp. 32–44.

Carrard, Philippe, 'History as a Kind of Writing: Michael De Certeau and the Poetics of Historiography', *South Atlantic Quarterly*, 100:2 (2001), pp. 465–83.

Carroll, Berenice A., 'Mary Beard's *Women as a Force in History*: A Critique', Berenice A. Carroll (ed.), *Liberating Women's History: Theoretical and Critical Essays*, University of Illinois Press, Urbana, 1976, pp. 26–41.

Cash, Arthur H., *Laurence Sterne: The Early and Middle Years*, Routledge, London, 1992.

Catalogue of the Pamphlets, Books, Newspapers, and Manuscripts Relating to the Civil War, Commonwealth, and Restoration, collected by George Thomason, 1640–1661, Trustees of the British Museum, London, 1908; repr, Ann Arbor, 1977.

Champion, W. A., 'Recourse to the Law and the Meaning of the Great Litigation Decline, 1650–1750: Some Clues from the Shrewsbury Local Courts', Christopher Brooks and Michael Lobban (eds.), *Communities and Courts in Britain, 1150–1900*, Hambledon, London, 1997, pp. 179–98.

Chaplin, Sue, 'Before the Law – Godwin's Caleb Williams', Sue Chaplin (ed.), *The Gothic and the Rule of Law*, Palgrave Macmillan, New York, 2007, pp. 125–42.

Chase, Malcolm, Gregory Claeys, Rachel Hammersley, Alastair Bonnett, and Keith Armstrong, *Thomas Spence: The Poor Man's Revolutionary*, Breviary Stuff, London, 2014.

Chernock, Arianne, *Men and the Making of Modern British Feminism*, Stanford University Press, Stanford, CA, 2010.

Clark, Alex, 'Drawn from Life: Why Have Novelists Stopped Making Things Up?' *Guardian*, 23 June 2018.

Clark, Elizabeth A., *History, Theory, Text: Historians and the Linguistic Turn*, Harvard University Press, Cambridge, MA, and London, 2004.

Clark, Polly, *Larchfield*, Quercus, London, 2017.

Cockburn, James, 'The North Riding Justices, 1690–1750: A Study in Local Administration', *Yorkshire Archeological Journal*, 41:3 (1965), pp. 481–515.

Cole, Daniel H., '"An Unqualified Human Good": E. P. Thompson and the Rule of Law', *Journal of Law and Society*, 28:2 (2001), pp. 177–203.

Colley, Linda, *Britons: Forging the Nation, 1707–1837*, Yale University Press, New Haven, CT, 1992.

Colls, Robert, *Identity of England*, Oxford University Press, Oxford, 2002.

Comaroff, Jean, *Body of Power, Spirit of Resistance: The Culture and History of a South African People*, University of Chicago Press, Chicago, IL, 1985.

Conley, John A., 'Doing It by the Book: Justice of the Peace Manuals and English Law in Eighteenth-Century America', *Journal of Legal History*, 6:3 (1985), pp. 257–98.

Corfield, Penelope J., 'Eighteenth-Century Lawyers and the Advent of the Professional Ethos', Philippe Chassaigne and Jean-Philippe Genet (eds.), *Droit et société en France et Grande Bretagne: Law and Society in France and England*, Publ. de la Sorbonne, Paris, 2003, pp. 103–26.

Time and the Shape of History, Yale University Press, New Haven, CT, and London, 2007.

Cotterell, Mary, 'Interregnum Law Reform: The Hale Commission of 1652', *English Historical Review*, 83 (1968), pp. 518–22.

Craven, Matthew, 'Theorising the Turn to History in International Law', Anne Orford and Florian Hoffmann (eds.), *The Oxford Handbook of the Theory of International Law*, Oxford University Press, Oxford, 2016, pp. 21–37.

Craven, Paul, and Douglas Hay (eds.), *Masters, Servants and Magistrates in Britain and the Empire, 1562–1955*, University of North Carolina Press, Chapel Hill, NC, 2004.

Crawford, Patricia, 'Charles Stuart, that man of blood' (1977), *Parergon*, 32:3 (2015), pp. 43–63.

Croft, Andy, 'Walthamstow, Little Gidding and Middlesborough: Edward Thompson the Literature Tutor', Richard Taylor (ed.), *Beyond the Walls: 50 Years of Adult and Continuing Education at the University of Leeds, 1946–1996*, University of Leeds, Leeds, 1996, pp. 144–56.

Cromartie, Alan, 'The Rule of Law', John Morrill (ed.), *Revolution and Restoration: England in the 1650s*, Collins and Brown, London, 1992, pp. 53–69.

'Hale, Sir Mathew (1609–1676), judge and writer', *Oxford Dictionary of National Biography*, Oxford University Press, Oxford, 2004.

Cross, Wilbur L., *The Life and Times of Laurence Sterne*, Macmillan, New York, 1909.

Cuttica, Cesare, 'What Type of Historian? Conceptual History and the History of Concepts: A Complex Legacy and a Recent Contribution', *History and Theory*, 51:3 (2012), pp. 411–22.

Deakin, Simon, and Frank Wilkinson, *The Law of the Labour Market: Industrialization, Employment and Legal Evolution*, Oxford University Press, Oxford, 2005.

Dean, Dennis R., 'Morgan, Sydney, Lady Morgan (bap. 1783, d. 1859)', *Oxford Dictionary of National Biography*, Oxford University Press, Oxford, 2004.

Derrida, Jacques, *The Post Card: From Socrates to Freud and Beyond*, trans. Alan Bass, University of Chicago Press, Chicago, IL, 1987.

Devereux, Simon, 'The Promulgation of the Statutes in Late Hanoverian Britain', David Lemmings (ed.), *British and Their Laws*, Boydell Press, Woodbridge, 2005, pp. 80–101.

Ditz, Toby L., 'Formative Ventures: Eighteenth-Century Commercial Letters and the Articulation of Experience', Rebecca Earle (ed.), *Epistolary Selves: Letters and Letter-Writers, 1600–1945*, Ashgate, Aldershot, 1998, pp. 60–78.

Dodd, Edward Ernest, '"A Useless Hearing": To the Editor of the Manchester Guardian', *Manchester Guardian*, 26 July 1922.

'Latin Teaching', *The Times*, 44471, 5 January 1927.

A History of the Bingley Grammar School, 1529–1929, Percy Lund, Bradford, 1930.

'Reconstruction in Burma and Malaya', *Four Colonial Questions: How Should Britain Act? Papers Prepared for the Fabian Colonial Bureau by Col. S. Gore-Browne, Rita Hinden, C. W Greenridge and E. E. Dodd*, Fabian Publications, London, 1944.

The New Malaya, Research Series No. 115, Fabian Publications, London, 1946.

'Bingley Enclosures', *Bradford Antiquary*, 7:35 (1950), pp. 293–302.

'Priestthorpe and the Rectory of Bingley', *Bradford Antiquary*, 8:36 (1952), pp. 1–20.

Bingley Parish and Township Records, Harrison, Bingley, 1953.

'Bingley Chantry Endowments', *Bradford Antiquary*, 8:37 (1954), pp. 91–9.

'Two Bingley Postscripts', *Bradford Antiquary*, 8:39 (1958), pp. 194–6.

'Bingley Volunteers in the Napoleonic War', *Bradford Antiquary*, 8:39 (1958), pp. 209–12.

Bingley: A Yorkshire Town through Nine Centuries, Harrison, Bingley, 1958.

'Alarm at Elland', *Bradford Antiquary*, 12 (1964), pp. 124–30.

Donnelley, F. K., 'The Levellers and Early Nineteenth Century Radicalism', *Labour History Review*, 49 (1984), pp. 24–8.

Downes, Stephanie, Sally Holloway, and Sarah Randles (eds.), *Feeling Things: Objects and Emotions through History*, Oxford University Press, Oxford, 2018.

Drabble, Margaret, *The Needle's Eye* (1972), Penguin, Harmondsworth, 1973.

Drescher, Seymour, 'Manumission in a Society without Slave Law', *Slavery and Abolition*, 10 (1989), pp. 85–101.

Dunn, Stephen, 'History', *The New Yorker*, 10 March 2008.

What Goes On, W. W. Norton, New York, 2013.

Durston, Gregory J., *Fields, Fens and Felonies: Crime and Justice in Eighteenth-Century East Anglia*, Waterside Press, Hook, 2016.

Dyer, Christopher, 'Beresford, Maurice Warwick (1920–2005)', *Oxford Dictionary of National Biography*, Oxford University Press, Oxford, 2009.

Dyer, Gary, 'The Arrest of Caleb Williams: Unnatural Crime, Constructive Violence, and Overwhelming Terror in Late Eighteenth-Century England', *Eighteenth-Century Life*, 36:3 (2012), pp. 31–56.

Eastwood, David, *Governing Rural England: Tradition and Transformation in Local Government, 1780–1840*, Oxford University Press, Oxford, 1994.

Egerton, Robert, 'Historical Aspects of Legal Aid', *Law Quarterly Review*, 61 (1945), pp. 87–94.

Ellis, Carolyn, Tony E. Adams, Arthur P. Bochner, 'Autoethnography: An Overview', *Forum Qualitative Sozialforschung/Forum: Qualitative Social Research*, 12:1 (2011) [np. online].

Ellis, Samantha, *Take Courage: Anne Bronte and the Art of Life*, Chatto and Windus, London, 2017.

Erikson, Amy Louise, 'Coverture and Capitalism', *History Workshop Journal*, 59 (2005), pp. 1–16.

Farge, Arlette, *Le goût de l'archive*, Editions du Seuil, Paris, 1989.

Le Bracelet de parchemin: L'Ecrit sur soi, XVIII siècle, Fayard, Paris, 2003.

The Allure of the Archive, trans. Thomas Scott-Railton, foreword by Natalie Zemon Davis, Yale University Press, New Haven and London, 2013.

Feather, John, 'The Book Trade in Politics: The Making of the Copyright Act of 1710', *Publishing History*, 19:8 (1980), pp. 19–44.

Feldman, David, 'Settlement and the Law in the Seventeenth Century', Steven King and Ann Winters (eds.), *Settlement and Belonging in Europe, 1500–1930s*, Berghahn, New York and Oxford, 2013, pp. 29–53.

Fermanis, Porscha, 'William Godwin's "History of the Commonwealth" and the Psychology of Individual History', *The Review of English Studies*, 61:252 (2010), pp. 773–800.

Fifoot, Cecil, *Lord Mansfield*, Clarendon Press, Oxford, 1936.

Finn, Margot, *The Character of Credit: Personal Debt in English Culture, 1740–1914*, Cambridge University Press, Cambridge, 2003.

Fisichelli, Glynn-Ellen, 'The Language of Law and Love: Anthony Trollope's Orley Farm', *ELH*, 61:3 (1994), pp. 635–53.

Florida Edition of the Works of Laurence Sterne, Vol. VII: The Letters, Part I: 1739–1764, Melvyn New and Peter de Voogd (eds.), University Press of Florida, Gainesville, FL, 2009.

Fludernik, Monika, 'A Narratology of the Law? Narratives in Legal Discourse', *Critical Analysis of Law*, 1:1 (2014), pp. 87–109.

Fowler, Roger, *Language in the News: Discourse and Ideology in the Press*, Routledge, Abingdon, 1991.

Frey, Sylvia R., *Water from the Rock: Black Resistance in a Revolutionary Age*, Princeton University Press, Princeton, NJ, 1991.

Friedman, Lawrence M., 'High Law and Low Law', *FIU Law Review*, 10:1 (2014), pp. 53–67.

Fyfe, Thomas Alexander, *Charles Dickens and the Law*, Chapman and Hall, London, William Hodge, Edinburgh, 1910.

Gaisman, Jonathan, 'Will the Genius of the Common Law Survive', *Standpoint*, February 2018 [np; online].

Gallagher, Noelle, 'Don Quixote and the Sentimental Reader of History in the Works of William Godwin', *Historical Writing in Britain, 1688–1830: Visions of History*, Palgrave Macmillan, Basingstoke, 2014, pp. 162–81.

Galloway, Alexander R., 'History Is What Hurts: On Old Materialism', *Social Text*, 34:2 (2016), pp. 125–41.

Gattrell, Vic, *City of Laughter: Sex and Satire in Eighteenth-Century London*, Atlantic, London, 2006.

Gerrard, Christine, 'Lyttelton, George, first Baron Lyttelton (1709–1773)', *Oxford Dictionary of National Biography*, Oxford University Press, Oxford, 2004.

Gibbons, Stephen Randolph, *Captain Rock, Night Errant: The Threatening Letters of Pre-famine Ireland, 1801–1845*, Four Courts, Dublin, 2004.

Gibson, William, 'Sermons', Jeremy Gregory (ed.), *The Oxford History of Anglicanism, Volume II: Establishment and Empire, 1662–1829*, Oxford University Press, Oxford, 2017, pp. 270–88.

Ginsburg, Jane C., 'Exceptional Authorship: The Role of Copyright Exceptions in Promoting Creativity', Susy Frankel and Daniel Gervais (eds.), *The Evolution and Equilibrium of Copyright in the Digital Age*, Cambridge University Press, Cambridge, 2014.

Glaisyer, Natasha, *The Culture of Commerce in England, 1660–1720*, Boydell Press, Woodbridge, 2006.

Glassey, L. K. J., and Norma Landau, 'The Commission of the Peace in the Eighteenth Century: A New Source', *Bulletin of the Institute of Historical Research*, 45 (1972), pp. 247–65.

Goodway, David, 'E. P. Thompson and the Making of The Making of the English Working Class', Croft (ed.), *Beyond the Walls*, pp. 133–43.

Goodwin, Gordon, 'Lemon, Robert (1779–1835), archivist', *Oxford Dictionary of National Biography*, Oxford University Press, Oxford, 2004.

Gordon, Charlotte, *Romantic Outlaws: The Extraordinary Lives of Mary Wollstonecraft and Mary Shelley*, Penguin Random House, London, 2015.

Gordon, Lyndall, *Vindication: A Life of Mary Wollstonecraft*, Virago, London, 2006.

Goreily, Tamara, 'Gratuitous assistance to the "ill-dressed": Debating civil legal aid in England and Wales from 1914 to 1939', *International Journal of the Legal Profession*, 13:1 (2006), pp. 41–67.

Grande, James, 'The Roots of Godwinian Radicalism: Norfolk Dissent in the Diary', *Bodleian Library Record*, 24:1 (2011), pp. 35–43.

Gray, Drew D., 'The People's Courts? Summary Justice and Social Relations in the City of London, c. 1760–1800', *Family & Community History*, 11:1 (2008), pp. 7–15.

Griffin, Carl J., *The Rural War: Captain Swing and the Politics of Protest*, Manchester University Press, Manchester, 2012.

Gunn, A. W., 'Eighteenth-Century Britain: In Search of the State and Finding the Quarter Sessions', John Brewer and Eckhart Hellmuth (eds.), *Rethinking Leviathan: The Eighteenth-Century State in Britain and Germany*, Oxford University Press, Oxford, 1999, pp. 99–126.

Halliday, Paul D., *Habeas Corpus: From England to Empire*, Belknap Press of Harvard University Press, Cambridge, MA, and London, 2010.

'Authority in the Archives', *Critical Analysis of the Law*, 1:1 (2014), pp. 110–42.

Hannam, June, 'Women's history, feminist history', www.history.ac.uk/makinghistory.

Hartog, Henrik, 'Abigail Bailey's Coverture: Law in a Married Woman's Consciousness', Austin Sarat and Thomas R. Kearns (eds.), *Law in Everyday Life*, University of Michigan Press, Ann Arbor, MI, 1993.

Hassard-Short, A. H., 'Legal Aid for the Poor', *Journal of Comparative Legislation and International Law*, 23:1 (1941), pp. 27–37.

Hay, Doug, et al., *Albion's Fatal Tree: Crime and Society in Eighteenth-Century England*, Penguin, Harmondsworth, 1975.

Hay, Doug, 'Legislation, Magistrates and Justices: High Law and Low Law in England and the Empire', David Lemmings (ed.), *British and their Laws*, Boydell Press, Woodbridge, 2005, pp. 59–79.

Hay, Douglas, 'Patronage, Paternalism, and Welfare: Masters, Workers and Magistrates in Eighteenth-Century England', *International Labour and Working-Class History*, 27 (1998), pp. 27–47.

Helfield, Randa, 'Constructive Treason and Godwin's Treasonous Constructions', *Mosaic*, 28:2 (1995), pp. 43–62.

Helmling, Steven, 'Failure and the Sublime: Frederic Jameson's Writing in the '80s', *Postmodern Culture*, 10:3 (2000), pp. 6–35.

Henley, John, 'A Portrait of the National Health Service: "It's almost like a religion"', *Guardian*, 17 January 2016.

Heward, Edmund, 'Lord Mansfield's Notebooks', *Law Quarterly Review*, 92 (1976), pp. 438–55.

Hicks, Peter, 'Late 18th-Century and Very Early 19th-Century British Writings on Napoleon: Myth and History', *La Fondation Napoléon/Napoleonica. La Revue*, 9:3 (2010), pp. 105–117.

Hill, Bridget, 'The Links between Mary Wollstonecraft and Catharine Macaulay: New Evidence', *Women's History Review*, 4:2 (1995), pp. 177–92.

'Macaulay, Catharine (1731–1791)', *Oxford Dictionary of National Biography*, Oxford University Press, Oxford, 2004; online ed., May 2012.

Hill, Christopher, *The Experience of Defeat: Milton and Some Contemporaries*, Faber and Faber, London, 1984.

Hindle, Steve, *The State and Social Change in Early Modern England*, Macmillan, Basingstoke, 2000.

Hobsbawm, Eric, and George Rudé, *Captain Swing*, Lawrence and Wishart, London, 1969.

Hoeckley, Cheri Larsen, 'Anomalous Ownership: Copyright, Coverture, and Aurora Leigh', *Victorian Poetry*, 36:2 (1998), pp. 135–61.

Horne, Thomas A., *Property Rights and Poverty: Political Rights in Britain, 1605–1834*, University of North Carolina Press, Chapel Hill, NC, 1990.

Houston, R. A., *Peasant Petitions: Social Relations and Economic Life on Landed Estates, 1600–1850*, Palgrave Macmillan, Basingstoke, 2014.

Howard, Emma, 'Legal Aid Cuts: "The forgotten pillar of the welfare state" – A Special Report', *Guardian*, 25 September 2014.

Hudson, Alastair, 'Regeneration, Legal Aid and the Welfare State (1998)', www.alastairhudson.com/legalsystem/legalaid&welfarestate.pdf.

Towards a Just Society: Law, Labour and Legal Aid, Pinter, London, 1999.

Hudson, John, *F. W. Maitland and the Englishness of English Law: Selden Society Lecture Delivered in the Old Hall of Lincoln's Inn July 5th, 2006, Selden Society Lecture; 2006*, Selden Society, London, 2007.

Hudson, Pat, *The Genesis of Industrial Capital: A Study of the West Riding Wool Textile Industry c. 1750–1850*, Cambridge University Press, Cambridge, 1986.

Hunt, Peter (ed.), *International Companion Encyclopedia of Children's Literature*, 2nd ed., 2 vols., Routledge, Abingdon, 2001.

Icke, Peter, *Frank Ankersmit's Lost Historical Cause: A Journey from Language to Experience*, Routledge, London, 2011.

Innes, Joanna, 'Parliament and the Shaping of Eighteenth-Century Social Policy', *Transactions of the Royal Historical Society*, 5th Series, 40 (1990), pp. 63–92.

'The State and the Poor: Eighteenth-Century England in European Perspective', John Brewer and Eckhart Hellmuth (eds.), *Rethinking Leviathan: The Eighteenth-Century State in Britain and Germany*, Oxford University Press, Oxford, 1999, pp. 225–80.

Jackson, Bernard S., 'Narrative Theories and Legal Discourse', Cristopher Nash (ed.), *Narrative in Culture: The Uses of Storytelling in the Sciences, Philosophy and Literature*, Routledge, London, 2005.

Jackson, Mark, *New-Born Child Murder: Women, Illegitimacy and the Courts in Eighteenth-Century England*, Manchester University Press, Manchester, 1996.

Jameson, Frederic, *The Political Unconscious: Narrative as a Socially Symbolic Act* (1981), Methuen, London, 1983.

Jolly, Margaretta, and Liz Stanley, 'Letters as/not a genre', *Life Writing*, 2:2 (2005), pp. 91–118.

Kader, David, and Michael Stanford (eds.), *Poetry of the Law: From Chaucer to the Present*, University of Iowa Press, Iowa City, IA, 2010.

Kafka, Franz, *The Castle* (1926), Oxford University Press, Oxford, 2009. *Metamorphosis, and Other Stories*, Penguin Random House, London, 2015.

Kalsem, Kristin (Brandser), 'Looking for Law in All the Wrong Places: Outlaw Texts and Early Women's Advocacy', *Review of Law and Women's Studies*, 13:2 (2004), pp. 273; also *Faculty Articles and Other Publications*, Paper 12 (2003). http://scholarship.law.uc.edu/fac_pubs/12.

Karsen, Peter, *Between Law and Custom: High and Low Legal Cultures in the Lands of the British Diaspora – the United States, Canada, Australia, and New Zealand, 1600–1900*, Cambridge University Press, Cambridge, 2002.

Kavanaugh, Ann, 'FitzGibbon, John, first earl of Clare (1748–1802), lord chancellor of Ireland', *Oxford Dictionary of National Biography*, Oxford University Press, Oxford, 2008.

Kayman, Martin A., 'Trials of Law and Language: Caleb Williams and John Horne Tooke', Monika Fludernik and Greta Olson (eds.), *In the Grip of the Law: Trials, Prisons and the Space Between*, Peter Lang, Frankfurt, 2004, pp. 83–104.

Kelsey, Sean, 'Constructing the Council of State', *Parliamentary History*, 22:3 (2003), pp. 217–41.

Kennedy, David, 'Autumn Weekends: An Essay on Law and Everyday Life', Austin Sarat and Thomas R. Kearns (eds.), *Law In Everyday Life*, University of Michigan Press, Ann Arbor, MI, 1995, pp. 191–236.

King, Peter, 'The Summary Courts and Social Relations in Eighteenth-Century England', *Past and Present*, 83 (1984), pp. 125–83. *Crime and the Law in England 1780–1840: Remaking Justice from the Margins*, Cambridge University Press, Cambridge, 2006.

Kippen, Kim, 'Poor Law, Coverture, and Maintaining Relations in King's Bench, 1601–1834', Tim Stretton and Krista J. Kesselring (eds.), *Married Women and the Law*, McGill-Queen's University Press, Ithaca, 2013, pp. 64–89.

Kirton, J., 'The Eighteenth Century Country Attorney, Professionalism and Patronage: The Hodgkinsons of Southwell', *Transactions of the Thoroton Society of Nottinghamshire*, 115 (2011), pp. 119–37.

Kitson, Peter J., '"Not a reforming patriot, but an ambitious tyrant": Representations of Cromwell and the English Republic in the late Eighteenth and Early Nineteenth Centuries', Timothy Morton and Nigel Smith (eds.), *Radicalism in British Literary Culture, 1650–1830: From Revolution to Revolution*, Cambridge University Press, Cambridge, 2002, pp. 183–200.

Koselleck, Reinhart, *The Practice of Conceptual History: Timing History, Spacing Concepts*, Stanford University Press, Stanford, CA, 2002. *Futures Past: On the Semantics of Historical Time*, Columbia University Press, New York, NY, 2005.

Kostiner, I., 'Taking Legal Consciousness Seriously: Beyond Power and Resistance', *Paper Presented at the Annual Meeting of the Law and Society Association*, Chicago, IL, 27 May 2004, www.allacademic.com/meta/p116866_index.html.

Krueger, Christine L., *Reading for the Law: British Literary History and Gender Advocacy*, University of Virginia Press, Charlottesville, VA, 2010.

Kuist, James M., 'New Light on Sterne: An Old Man's Recollections of the Young Vicar', *PMLA*, 80:5 (1965), pp. 549–53.

Landau, Norma, 'Going Local: The Social History of Stuart and Hanoverian England', *Journal of British Studies*, 24:2 (1985), pp. 273–81.

'Laws of Settlement and the Surveillance of Immigration in Eighteenth-Century Kent', *Continuity and Change*, 3 (1988), pp. 391–420.

'The Eighteenth-Century Context of the Laws of Settlement', *Continuity and Change*, 6:3 (1991), pp. 417–39.

Langbein, John H., *The Origins of Adversary Criminal Trial*, Oxford University Press, Oxford, 2003.

Langford, Sarah, *In Your Defence: Stories of Life and Law*, Doubleday, London, 2018.

Lansbury, Coral, *The Reasonable Man – Trollope's Legal Fiction*, Princeton University Press, Princeton, NJ, 1981.

Larkin, Philip, *The Whitsun Weddings*, Faber and Faber, London, 1964.

Lee, Robert, *Rural Society and the Anglican Clergy, 1815–1914: Encountering and Managing the Poor*, Boydell Press, Woodbridge, 2006.

Lees, Lynn Hollen, *The Solidarities of Strangers: The English Poor Laws and the People, 1700–1948*, Cambridge University Press, Cambridge, 1998.

Lemmings, David, *Professors of Law: Barristers and English Legal Culture in the Eighteenth Century*, Oxford University Press, Oxford, 2000.

(ed.), *The British and Their Laws in the Eighteenth Century*, Boydell Press, Woodbridge, 2005.

(ed.), *Crime, Courtrooms and the Public Sphere in Britain, 1700–1850*, Ashgate, Farnham, 2012.

Law and Government in England during the Long Eighteenth Century: From Consent to Command, Palgrave Macmillan, Basingstoke, 2015.

Lieberman, David, *The Province of Legislation Determined: Legal Theory in Eighteenth-Century Britain*, Cambridge University Press, Cambridge, 1989.

Linebaugh, Peter, *The London Hanged: Crime and Civil Society in the Eighteenth Century*, Penguin, London, 1991.

Lobingier, Charles Sumner, 'Napoleon and His Code', *Harvard Law Review*, 32:2 (1918), pp. 114–34.

Locker, Kitty, '"Sir, This Will Never Do": Model Dunning Letters, 1592–1873', *International Journal of Business Communication*, 22:2 (1985), pp. 39–45.

Lorimer, Douglas, 'Black Slaves and English Liberty: A. Re-Examination of Racial Slavery in England', *Immigrants and Minorities Review*, 3 (1984), pp. 121–50.

Lupton, Christina, *Reading and the Making of Time in the Eighteenth Century*, Johns Hopkins University Press, Baltimore, MD, 2018.

Lyes, John, *"A Strong Smell of Brimstone": The Solicitors and Attorneys of Bristol, 1740 to 1840*, Bristol Branch of the Historical Association, Bristol, 1999.

Maloutis, Nick, 'History's Zig-Zag Shape Runs Through Us', *Business*, 21 November 2016.

Major, Emma, 'Trusler, John (1735–1820)', *Oxford Dictionary of National Biography*, Oxford University Press, Oxford, 2004.

Madam Britannia: Women, Church and Nation, 1712–1812, Oxford University Press, New York, 2012.

Malcolm, Janet, *The Silent Woman: Sylvia Plath and Ted Hughes* (1993), Picador, London, 1994.

Mar, Maksymilian Del, and Michael Lobban, *Law in Theory and History: New Essays on a Neglected Dialogue*, Hart, London, 2016.

Marshall, Peter, *William Godwin: Philosopher, Novelist, Revolutionary* (1984), PM Press, Oakland, CA, 2017.

McEwan, Ian, *The Children Act*, Faber, London, 2014.

'The Law versus Religious Belief', *Guardian*, 5 September 2014.

McKeown, Michael, *The Origins of the English Novel, 1600–1740*, Johns Hopkins University Press, Baltimore, MD, 1987.

McLynn, Frank, *Crime and Punishment in Eighteenth-Century England*, Routledge, London, 1989.

Mead, Rebecca, *My Life in Middlemarch*, Penguin Random House, London, 2015.

Medieval Settlement Research Group, *Annual Report I*, 1986. https://medieval-settlement.com/publications/journal/. Accessed 16 August 2019.

Mee, John, 'William Cobbett, John Clare and the Agrarian Politics of the English Revolution', Timothy Morton and Nigel Smith (eds.), *Radicalism in British Literary Culture, 1650–1830: From Revolution to Revolution*, Cambridge University Press, Cambridge, 2002, pp. 167–82.

Meiring, Jean, 'Conversations in the Law: Sir William Jones's Singular Dialogue', *The Concept and Practice of Conversation in the Long Eighteenth Century, 1688–1848*, Cambridge Scholars Publishing, Newcastle, 2008, pp. 128–50.

Meyer, Philip, *Storytelling for Lawyers*, Oxford University Press, Oxford, 2014.

Milne, Esther, *Letters, Postcards, Email: Technologies of Presence*, Routledge, New York, 2010.

Miskell, Louise, *Meeting Places: Scientific Congresses and Urban Identity in Victorian Britain*, Ashgate, Farnham, 2013.

Molekamp, Femke, '"Of the Incomparable Treasure of the Holy Scriptures": The Geneva Bible in the Early Modern Household', Matthew Dimmock and Andrew Hadfield (eds.), *Literature and Popular Culture in Early Modern England*, Ashgate, Farnham, 2009.

Morgan, Gwenda, and Peter Rushton, 'The Magistrate, the Community and the Maintenance of an Orderly Society in Eighteenth-Century England', *Historical Research*, 76:191 (2003), pp. 75–6.

Morgan, Richard I., 'The Introduction of Civil Legal Aid in England and Wales, 1914–1949', *Twentieth Century British History*, 5:1 (1994), pp. 38–76.

Morrill, John, 'The Impact on Society', John Morrill (ed.), *Revolution and Restoration: England in the 1650s*, Collins and Brown, London, 1992, pp. 91–111.

Morrow, John, 'Republicanism and Public Virtue: William Godwin's History of the Commonwealth of England', *The Historical Journal*, 34:3 (1991), pp. 645–64.

Munslow, Alun, *Narrative and History*, Palgrave Macmillan, Basingstoke, 2007.

Murphy, W. T., *The Oldest Social Science? Configurations of Law and Modernity*, Clarendon Press, Oxford, 1997.

Murray, Alex, and Jessica Wyte (eds.), *The Agamben Dictionary*, Edinburgh University Press, Edinburgh, 2011.

Murray, Sally Engle, *Getting Justice and Getting Even: Legal Consciousness among Working-Class Americans*, University of Chicago Press, Chicago, IL, and London, 1990.

Myers, John E. B., *Myers on Evidence in Child, Domestic, and Elder Abuse Cases*, 2 vols., Aspen, New York, 2005.

Myers, Norma, 'Servant, Sailor, Soldier, Beggarman: Black Survival in White Society, 1780–1830', *Immigrants and Minorities*, 12:1 (1993), pp. 47–74.

Newey, Vincent, 'Robinson, Henry Crabb (1775–1867)', *Oxford Dictionary of National Biography*, Oxford University Press, Oxford, 2004.

Oakeshott, Michael, *Experience and Its Modes*, Cambridge University Press, Cambridge, 1986.

Oldham, James, 'Buller, Sir Francis, first baronet (1746–1800)', *Oxford Dictionary of National Biography*, Oxford University Press, Oxford, 2004.

Outhwaite, R. B., *The Rise and Fall of the English Ecclesiastical Courts, 1500–1860*, Cambridge University Press, Cambridge, 2006.

Paley, Ruth, 'After Somerset: Mansfield, Slavery and the Law in England, 1772–1830', Norma Landau (ed.), *Law, Crime and English Society, 1660–1830*, Cambridge University Press, Cambridge, 2002.

Pateman, Carol, *The Sexual Contract*, Polity Press, Cambridge, 1988.

Pauley, Benjamin, '"Far from a Consummate Lawyer": William Godwin and the Treason Trials of the 1790s', Ulrich Broiche et al. (eds.), *Reactions to Revolutions: The 1790s and Their Aftermath* (Kulturgeschichtliche Perspektiven, 2), Lit, Münster, 2007, pp. 203–30.

Pham, Julie, 'J. S. Furnivall and Fabianism: Reinterpreting the "Plural Society" in Burma', *Modern Asian Studies*, 39:2 (2005), pp. 321–48.

Phillips, Mark Salber, '"If Mrs Mure Be Not Sorry for Poor King Charles": History, the Novel, and the Sentimental Reader', *History Workshop Journal*, 43 (1997), pp. 110–31.

Society and Sentiment: Genres of Historical Writing in Britain, 1740–1820, Princeton University Press, Princeton, NJ, 2000.

Phillips, Nicola, *Women in Business, 1700–1850*, Boydell Press, Woodbridge, 2006.

Philp, Mark, *Godwin's Political Justice*, Duckworth, London, 1986.

'William Godwin's Diary', *The Last Stand: Napoleon's 100 Days in 100 Objects*, www.100days.eu/items/show/100.

Pike, Judith E., '"My name was Isabella Linton": Coverture, Domestic Violence, and Mrs Heathcliff's Narrative in Wuthering Heights', *Nineteenth-Century Literature*, 64 (2009), pp. 347–83.

Plamper, Jan, *The History of Emotions: An Introduction*, Oxford University Press, Oxford, 2015.

Polin, Raymond, and Colin Polin, *Foundations of American Political Thought*, Peter Lang, Pieterlen, 2009.

Polloczek, Dieter Paul, 'Trappings of a Transnational Gaze: Legal and Sentimental Confinement in Sterne's Novels', in Dieter Paul Polloczek (ed.), *Literature and Legal Discourse: Equity and Ethics from Sterne to Conrad*, Cambridge University Press, Cambridge, 1999, pp. 20–71.

Popkins, Jeremy D., *History, Historians, and Autobiography*, University of Chicago Press, Chicago, IL, 2005.

Posner, Richard A., 'Reviews: Legal Narratology', *University of Chicago Law Review*, 64:2 (1997), pp. 737–47.

'Kafka: The Writer as Lawyer', *Columbia Law Review*, 110:1 (2010), pp. 207–15.

Poustie, Sarah, 'Re-Theorising Letters and "Letterness"', *Olive Schreiner Letters Project Working Papers on Letters, Letterness & Epistolary Networks*, Number 1, Edinburgh, 2010.

Prest, Wilfrid, 'Blackstone as Architect: Constructing the Commentaries', *Yale Journal of Law & the Humanities*, 15:1 (2003), pp. 103–31.

'The Experience of Litigation in Eighteenth-Century England', David Lemmings (ed.), *British and Their Laws*, Boydell Press, Woodbridge, 2005, pp. 133–54.

William Blackstone: Law and Letters in the Eighteenth Century, Oxford University Press, Oxford, 2008.

'Blackstone as Historian', *Parergon*, 32:3 (2015), pp. 183–203.

Purvis, June, 'From "Women Worthies" to Post-structuralism? Debate and Controversy in Women's History in Britain', in June Purvis (ed.), *Women's History: Britain, 1850–1945 – An Introduction*, Routledge, London, 1995, pp. 1–19.

Raban, Dana, '"In a Country of Liberty?" Slavery, Villeinage and the Making of Whiteness in the Somerset Case (1772)', *History Workshop Journal*, 72 (2011), pp. 5–29.

Rajan, Tilottama, 'Framing the Corpus: Godwin's "Editing" of Wollstonecraft in 1798', *Studies in Romanticism*, 39:4 (2000), pp. 511–31.

Ramsay, James, *An Essay on the Treatment and Conversion of African Slaves in the British Sugar Colonies*, T. Walker and five others, Dublin, 1784.

Rawley, James A., *The Transatlantic Slave Trade: A History*, Norton, New York, 1981.

Rawson, Claude (ed.), *Henry Fielding (1707–1754): Novelist, Playwright, Journalist, Magistrate – A Double Anniversary Tribute*, Associated Universities Press, Cranbery, NJ, 2008.

Reed-Danahay, Deborah (ed.), *Auto/Ethnography: Rewriting the Self and the Social*, Berg, Oxford and New York, 1997.

Rees, Lowri Ann, '"The Wail of Miss Jane": The Rebecca Riots and Jane Walters of Glanmedeni, 1843–4', *Ceredigion*, 15:3 (2007), pp. 37–68.

Reid, Alastair J., 'Hill, John (1863–1945)', *Oxford Dictionary of National Biography*, Oxford University Press, Oxford, 2004.

Renwick, Chris, *Bread for All: The Origins of the Welfare State*, Allen Lane, London, 2018.

Ridley, R. T., 'Echard, Laurence (bap. 1672, d. 1730), historian', *Oxford Dictionary of National Biography*, Oxford University Press, Oxford, 2004.

Rigney, Anne, 'History as Text: Narrative Theory and History', Nancy Partner and Sarah Foot (eds.), *The SAGE Handbook of Historical Theory*, Sage, London, 2012, pp. 183–201.

Rogers, Nicholas, 'Vagrancy, Impressment and the Regulation of Labor in Eighteenth-Century Britain', *Slavery and Abolition*, 15 (1994), pp. 102–13.

Rosaldo, Renato, 'Elaborating Thompson's Heroes: Social Analysis in History and Anthropology', Harvey J. Kaye and Keith McClelland (eds.), *E.P. Thompson: Critical Perspectives*, Polity, Cambridge, 1992, pp. 103–24.

Rose, Mark, *Authors and Owners: The Invention of Copyright*, Harvard University Press, Cambridge, MA, 1993.

Ross, Ian Campbell, *Laurence Sterne: A Life*, Oxford University Press, Oxford, 2001.

Roth, Paul A., 'Narrative Explanations: The Case of History', *History and Theory*, 27:1 (1988), pp. 1–13.

Rothschild, Emma, *The Inner Life of Empires: An Eighteenth-Century History*, Princeton University Press, Princeton, NJ, 2011.

Rowe, John Townsend, *Trade and Plumb-cake for Ever, Huzza! The Life and Work of John Newbery, 1713–1767: Author, Bookseller, Entrepreneur and Pioneer of Publishing for Children*, Colt, Cambridge, 1994.

Rule, John, 'Edward Palmer Thompson (1924–1993)', *Oxford Dictionary of National Biography*, Oxford University Press, Oxford, 2004.

Rumbold, Valerie, 'Madan, Judith (1702–1781)', *Oxford Dictionary of National Biography*, Oxford University Press, Oxford, 2004.

Sanger, Charles Percy, *The Structure of Wuthering Heights*, Hogarth Essays XIX, Hogarth Press, London, 1926.

Schmidt, Albert J., 'Lawyer Professionalism in Rural England: Changes in Routine and Rewards in the Early Nineteenth Century', *Lincolnshire History and Archaeology*, 32 (1997), pp. 25–39.

Schneider, Gary, *The Culture of Epistolarity: Vernacular Letters and Letter Writing in Early Modern England, 1500–1700*, University of Delaware Press, Cranbery, NJ, 2005.

Scott, Joan W., 'The Evidence of Experience', *Critical Inquiry*, 17:4 (1991), pp. 773–97.

Searby, Peter, and the Editors, 'Edward Thompson as Teacher: Yorkshire and Warwick', John Rule and Robert Malcolmson (eds.), *Protest and Survival: The Historical Experience*, Merlin, London, 1993, pp. 1–23.

Seaward, Paul, 'Hyde, Edward, first earl of Clarendon (1609–1674), politician and historian', *Oxford Dictionary of National Biography*, Oxford University Press, Oxford, 2004.

Semmel, Stuart, *Napoleon and the British*, Yale University Press, New Haven, CT, and London, 2004.

'British Uses for Napoleon', *MLN*, 120:4 (2005), pp. 733–46.

Seymour, Miranda, *Mary Shelley*, John Murray, London, 2000.

Sharpe, Andrew, 'Lilburne, John (1615?–1657), Leveller', *Oxford Dictionary of National Biography*, Oxford University Press, Oxford, 2006.

Sharpe, J. A., '"Such Disagreement betwyxt Neighbours": Litigation and Human Relations in Early Modern England', J. A. Bossy (ed.), *Disputes and Settlements: Law and Human Relations in the West*, Cambridge University Press, Cambridge, 1983, pp. 167–87.

Sharpe, James, 'The People and the Law', Barry Reay (ed.), *Popular Culture in Seventeenth-Century England*, Routledge, London, 1988, pp. 224–70.

Sharpe, Pamela, *Adapting to Capitalism: Working Women in the English Economy, 1700–1850*, Macmillan, Basingstoke, 1996.

'"The Bowels of Compation": A Labouring Family and the Law, *c.* 1790–1834', Tim Hitchcock, Peter King, and Pamela Sharpe (eds.), *Chronicling Poverty: The Voices and Strategies of the English Poor, 1640–1840*, Palgrave Macmillan, London, 1997.

Shave, Samantha A., 'The Welfare of the Vulnerable in the Late 18th and Early 19th Centuries: Gilbert's Act of 1782', *History in Focus*, 14 (2008); www.history.ac.uk/ihr/Focus/welfare/articles/shaves.html.

Pauper Policies: Poor Law Practice in England, 1780–1850, Manchester University Press, Manchester, 2018.

Shaw, Margaret R. B., *Laurence Sterne: The Making of a Humorist, 1713–1762*, The Richards Press, London, 1957.

Siegel, Reva B., '"The Rule of Love": Wife Beating as Prerogative and Privacy', *Yale Law Journal*, 106 (1996), pp. 2117–207.

Sigal, Clancy, *Weekend in Dinlock*, Secker and Warburg, London, 1961.

Simpson, Anthony E., 'The "Blackmail Myth" and the Prosecution of Rape and Its Attempt in 18th Century London: The Creation of a Legal Tradition', *Journal of Criminal Law and Criminology*, 77 (1986), pp. 101–50.

Simpson, K. G., *Henry Fielding: Justice Observed*, Vision, London, 1985.

Slack, Paul, *The English Poor Law, 1531–1782*, Cambridge University Press, Cambridge, 1996.

Slights, William W. E., *Managing Readers: Printed Marginalia in English Renaissance Books*, University of Michigan Press, Ann Arbor, MI, 2001.

Smith, Reginald Heber, 'Legal Aid and Advice: The Rushcliffe Report as a Land-Mark', *American Bar Association Journal*, 33 (1947), pp. 445–7.

'The British Legal Aid and Advice Bill', *The Yale Law Journal*, 59:2 (1950), pp. 320–44.

Smith, Tom, and Ed Cape, 'The Rise and Decline of Criminal Legal Aid in England and Wales', Asher Flynn and Jacqueline Hodgson (eds.), *Access to Justice and Legal Aid: Comparative Perspectives on Unmet Legal Need*, Hart, Oxford and London, 2017, pp. 63–86.

Snell, Keith, *Annals of the Labouring Poor: Social Change and Agrarian England, 1660–1900*, Cambridge University Press, Cambridge, 1985.

'Pauper Settlements and the Right to Relief in England and Wales', *Continuity and Change*, 6:3 (1991), pp. 375–439.

The Parish and Belonging: Community, Identity and Welfare in England and Wales, 1700–1950, Cambridge University Press, Cambridge, 2006.

Snyder, L., 'The Circulation of Newspapers in the Reign of Queen Anne', *The Library*, 23 (1969), pp. 206–35.

Sokol, Mary, *Bentham, Law and Marriage, A Utilitarian Code of Law in Historical Contexts*, Continuum, London and New York, 2011.

Song, Byung Khun, 'Landed Interest, Local Government, and the Labour Market in England, 1750–1850', *Economic History Review*, 2nd ser. 51 (1998), pp. 465–88.

Soper, Kate, 'Introduction', John Stuart Mill, *The Subjection of Women*, Harriet Taylor Mill, *The Enfranchisement of Women*, Virago, London, 1983.

Spellman, W. M., *John Locke*, Macmillan, Basingstoke, 1997.

Spring, Eileen, *Law, Land, and Family: Aristocratic Inheritance in England, 1300 to 1800*, University of North Carolina Press, Chapel Hill, NC, 1993.

St Clair, William, *The Reading Nation in the Romantic Period*, Cambridge University Press, Cambridge, 2004.

Stanley, Liz, 'The Epistolarium: On Theorizing Letters and Correspondences', *Auto/Biography*, 12 (2004), pp. 201–35.

'The Epistolary Gift, the Editorial Third-Part, Counter-Epistolary: Rethinking the Epistolarium', *Life Writing*, 8:2 (2011), pp. 135–52.

Staves, Susan, *Married Women's Separate Property in England, 1660–1833*, Harvard University Press, Cambridge, MA, and London, 1990.

Steedman, Carolyn, 'Battlegrounds: History and Primary Schools', *History Workshop Journal*, 17 (1984), pp. 102–12.

Landscape for a Good Woman, Virago, London, 1986.

'A Weekend with Elektra', *Literature and History*, 6:1 (1997), pp. 17–42.

'Enforced Narratives: Stories of Another Self', Tess Cosslett, Celia Lury, and Penny Summerfield (eds.), *Feminism and Autobiography: Texts, Theories, Methods*, Routledge, London, 2000, pp. 25–39.

'The Servant's Labour: The Business of Life, England 1760–1820', *Social History*, 29:1 (2004), pp. 1–29.

Master and Servant: Love and Labour in the English Industrial Age, Cambridge University Press, Cambridge, 2007.

Labours Lost: Domestic Service and the Making of Modern England, Cambridge University Press, Cambridge, 2009.

'At Every Bloody Level: A Magistrate, a Framework Knitter, and the Law', *Law and History Review*, 30:2 (2012), pp. 387–422.

'Sights Unseen, Cries Unheard: Writing the Eighteenth-Century Metropolis', *Representations*, 118 (2012), pp. 28–71.

An Everyday Life of the English Working Class: Work, Self and Sociability in Early Nineteenth-Century England, Cambridge University Press, Cambridge, 2013.

'Living with the Dead', Carol Smart and Jennifer Hockley (eds.), *The Craft of Knowledge: Experiences of Living with Data*, Palgrave, Basingstoke, 2014, pp. 162–75.

'Lord Mansfield's Voices: In the Archive, Hearing Things', Stephanie Downes, Sally Holloway, and Sarah Randles (eds.), *Feeling Things: Objects and Emotions through History*, Oxford University Press, Oxford, 2018, pp. 209–25.

Poetry for Historians; or, W. H. Auden and History, Manchester University Press, Manchester, 2018.

'Where Have You Been? Creating the City', Pal Brunnstrom and Ragnhild Claesson (eds.), *Creating the City: Identity, Memory and Participation*, Conference proceedings, Institute for Studies in Malmo's History, University of Malmo, 2019, pp. 18–34.

'Social History Comes to Warwick', Miles Taylor (ed.), *The Utopian Universities*, Bloomsbury, London, forthcoming.

Stone, Lawrence, *Road to Divorce: England 1530–1987*, Oxford University Press, Oxford, 1990.

Strachey, Ray, *The Cause: A Short History of the Women's Movement in Great Britain*, Bell, London, 1928.

Stretton, Tim, and Krista J. Kesselring (eds.), *Married Women and the Law: Coverture in England and the Common Law World*, McGill-Queen's University Press, Montreal, 2013.

Sugarman, David, 'Legal History, the Common Law and "Englishness"', Karl Modeer (ed.), *Legal History in Comparative Perspective*, Institute for Legal History, Stockholm, 2002, pp. 213–27.

Sutter, Laurent de, 'Legal Shandeism: The Law in Laurence Sterne's Tristram Shandy', *Law and Literature*, 23:2 (2011), pp. 224–40.

Taylor, James Stephen, *Poverty, Migration and Settlement in the Industrial Revolution: Sojourners' Narratives*, Society for the Promotion of Science and Scholarship, Palo Alto, CA, 1989.

Taylor, Richard (ed.), *Beyond the Walls: 50 Years of Adult and Continuing Education at the University of Leeds, 1946–1996*, University of Leeds, Leeds, 1996.

Tedlock, Barbara, 'From Participant Observation to the Observation of Participation: The Emergence of Narrative Ethnography', *Journal of Anthropological Research*, 47 (1991), pp. 69–94.

Teubner, Gunther, 'The Law before It's Law: Franz Kafka on the (Im)possibility of Law's Self-Reflection', *German Law Journal*, 14:2 (2013), pp. 405–22.

Thomas, Malcolm, 'Malcolm Thomas (1945–2010)', *Library of the Society of Friends Newsletter*, 7 (2011).

Thompson, Dorothy (ed.), *The Essential E. P. Thompson*, New Press, New York, 2001.

Thompson, E. P., *The Making of the English Working Class* (1963), Penguin, Harmondsworth, 1968.

'The Crime of Anonymity', Douglas Hay, Peter Linebaugh, John G. Rule, E. P. Thompson, and Cal Winslow (eds.), *Albion's Fatal Tree: Crime and Society in Eighteenth-Century England* (1975), Verso, London, 2011, pp. 255–344.

Whigs and Hunters: The Origins of the Black Act (1975), Penguin, Harmondsworth, 1977.

The Poverty of Theory and Other Essays, Merlin Press, London, 1978, pp. 35–91, 193–399.

Timmins, Nicholas, *The Five Giants: A Biography of the Welfare State* (1995), Harper Collins, London, 2001.

Todd, Barbara J., '"To Be Some Body": Married Women and the Hardships of the English Laws', Hilda Smith (ed.), *Women Writers and the Early Modern British Political Tradition*, Cambridge University Press, Cambridge, 2010, pp. 343–62.

'Written in Her Heart: Married Women's Separate Allegiance in English Law', Tim Stretton and Krista J. Kesselring (eds.), *Married Women and the Law*, McGill-Queen's University Press, Montréal, 2013, pp. 163–91.

Todd, Janet, *Mary Wollstonecraft: A Revolutionary Life*, Weidenfeld & Nicholson, London, 2000.

(ed.), *The Collected Letters of Mary Wollstonecraft*, Allen Lane, London, 2003.

Tomkins, Alannah, "'I mak Bould to Wrigt": First Person Narratives in the History of Poverty in England, c. 1750–1900', *History Compass*, 9:5 (2011), pp. 365–73.

Tosh, John (ed.), *Historians on History*, 3rd ed., Routledge, Abingdon, 2018.

Trades Union Congress, *Justice Denied: Impacts of the Government's Reforms to Legal Aid and Court Services on Access to Justice*, TUC, London, 2016.

Turner, Cheryl, *Living by the Pen: Women Writers in the Eighteenth Century* (1992), Routledge, London, 1994.

Veall, Donald, *The Popular Movement for Law Reform 1640–1660*, Clarendon Press, Oxford, 1970.

Visser, Nicholas, 'Tristram Shandy and the Straight Line of History', *Textual Practice*, 12:3 (1998), pp. 489–502.

Vogenauer, Stefan, 'Law Journals in Nineteenth-Century England', *Edinburgh Law Review*, 12 (2008), pp. 26–50.

Waddams, Stephen, 'Equity in English Contract Law: The Impact of the Judicature Acts (1873–75)', *Journal of Legal History*, 33:2 (2012), pp. 185–208.

Wales, Tim, 'The Parish and the Poor in the English Revolution', Stephen Taylor and Grant Tapsell (eds.), *The Nature of the English Revolution Revisited*, Boydell Press, Woodbridge, 2013, pp. 53–80.

Ward, Ian, 'A Love of Justice: The Legal and Political Thought of William Godwin', *The Journal of Legal History*, 25:1 (2004), pp. 1–30.

Wardle, Ralph M., *Godwin and Mary: Letters of William Godwin and Mary Wollstonecraft*, University of Kansas Press, Lawrence, KS, Constable, London, 1967.

Weston, Rowland, 'William Godwin's Religious Sense', *Journal for Eighteenth-Century Studies*, 32:3 (2009), pp. 407–23.

Wheeler, Sally, 'Going Shopping', Linda Mulachy and Sally Wheeler (eds.), *Feminist Perspectives on Contract Law*, Glasshouse, London, 2005, pp. 22–49.

Whyman, Susan E., *The Pen and the People: English Letter Writers 1660–1800*, Oxford University Press, Oxford, 2009.

Wood, Andy, *The Politics of Social Conflict: The Peak Country, 1520–1770*, Cambridge University Press, Cambridge, 1999.

Internet and Other Online Sources

www.allacademic.com/meta/p116866_index.html

http://allthingsliberty.com/2014/02/london-gazette/

http://archaeologydataservice.ac.uk/archive

www.bl.uk/books/thomason/thomasoncivilwar.html

www.oxforddnb.com/

www.theguardian.com/law/datablog/2014/sep/09/legal-aid-in-england-and-wales-what-is-changing

www.legislation.gov.uk/aep/Edw1cc1929/25/9/
http://ejournals.library.ualberta.ca/index.php/IJQM/article/viewFile/4205/5401
http://godwindiary.bodleian.ox.ac.uk
http://harryenfield.wikia.com/wiki/Kevin_the_Teenager
www.judiciary.gov.uk/about-the-judiciary/the-judiciary-the-government-and-the-constitution/
judiciary@public.govdelivery.com ('Courts and Tribunals Judiciary All Judgments')
www.100days.eu/items/show/100
www.legislation.gov.uk/ukpga/2012/10/contents/enacted;
www.literaryprintculture.amdigital.co.uk/ (Stationers Company Archive)
www.penelopejcorfield.co.uk/time.htm ('History and Time')
http://founders.archives.gov/
www.history.ac.uk/ihr/Focus/welfare/articles/
www.history.ac.uk/makinghistory.
http://ecssba.rutgers.edu/index.html (Papers of Elizabeth Cady Stanton and Susan B. Anthony Project)
http://scholarship.law.uc.edu/fac_pubs/12
www.standpointmag.co.uk/features-february-2018-jonathan-gaisman-will-the-genius-of-the-common-law-survive
www.law.virginia.edu/html/alumni/uvalawyer/f05/humanities.htm
https://weownit.org.uk/public-ownership/nhs
www.wuthering-heights.co.uk/

Unpublished Work

Hutton, Alexander, '"Culture and Society" in Conceptions of the Industrial Revolution in Britain, 1930–1965', PhD thesis, University of Cambridge, 2014.
Roberts, Michael, 'Wages and Wage-Earners in England: The Evidence of the Wage Assessments, 1563–1725', DPhil thesis, University of Oxford, 1982.

Index